Where Is the Good in the World?

WYSE Series in Social Anthropology

Editors:
James Laidlaw, William Wyse Professor of Social Anthropology, University of Cambridge, and Fellow of King's College, Cambridge
Joel Robbins, Sigrid Rausing Professor of Social Anthropology, University of Cambridge, and Fellow of Trinity College, Cambridge

Social Anthropology is a vibrant discipline of relevance to many areas – economics, politics, business, humanities, health and public policy. This series, published in association with the Cambridge William Wyse Chair in Social Anthropology, focuses on key interventions in Social Anthropology, based on innovative theory and research of relevance to contemporary social issues and debates. Former holders of the William Wyse Chair have included Meyer Fortes, Jack Goody, Ernest Gellner and Marilyn Strathern, all of whom have advanced the frontiers of the discipline. This series intends to develop and foster that tradition.

Recent volumes:

Volume 12
Where Is the Good in the World? Ethical Life between Social Theory and Philosophy
Edited by David Henig, Anna Strhan and Joel Robbins

Volume 11
Making Better Lives: Hope, Freedom and Home-Making among People Sleeping Rough in Paris
Johannes Lenhard

Volume 10
Selfishness and Selflessness: New Approaches to Understanding Morality
Edited by Linda L. Layne

Volume 9
Becoming Vaishnava in an Ideal Vedic City
John Fahy

Volume 8
It Happens Among People: Resonances and Extensions of the Work of Fredrik Barth
Edited by Keping Wu and Robert P. Weller

Volume 7
Indeterminacy: Waste, Value, and the Imagination
Edited by Catherine Alexander and Andrew Sanchez

Volume 6
After Difference: Queer Activism in Italy and Anthropological Theory
Paolo Heywood

Volume 5
Moral Engines: Exploring the Ethical Drives in Human Life
Edited by Cheryl Mattingly, Rasmus Dyring, Maria Louw and Thomas Schwarz Wentzer

Volume 4
The Patient Multiple: An Ethnography of Healthcare and Decision-Making in Bhutan
Jonathan Taee

Volume 3
The State We're In: Reflecting on Democracy's Troubles
Edited by Joanna Cook, Nicholas J. Long and Henrietta L. Moore

For a full volume listing, please see the series page on our website: https://www.berghahnbooks.com/series/wyse

WHERE IS THE GOOD IN THE WORLD?

Ethical Life between Social Theory and Philosophy

Edited by
David Henig, Anna Strhan and Joel Robbins

berghahn
NEW YORK · OXFORD
www.berghahnbooks.com

First published in 2022 by
Berghahn Books
www.berghahnbooks.com

© 2022, 2025 David Henig, Anna Strhan and Joel Robbins
First paperback edition published in 2025

All rights reserved. Except for the quotation of short passages
for the purposes of criticism and review, no part of this book
may be reproduced in any form or by any means, electronic or
mechanical, including photocopying, recording, or any information
storage and retrieval system now known or to be invented,
without written permission of the publisher.

Library of Congress Cataloging-in-Publication Data

Names: Henig, David, editor. | Strhan, Anna, editor. | Robbins, Joel, editor.
Title: Where is the good in the world? : ethical life between social theory and philosophy / edited by David Henig, Anna Strhan and Joel Robbins.
Description: New York : Berghahn Books, 2022. | Series: WYSE series in social anthropology ; volume 12 | Includes bibliographical references and index.
Identifiers: LCCN 2022004641 (print) | LCCN 2022004642 (ebook) | ISBN 9781800735514 (hardback) | ISBN 9781800735521 (ebook)
Subjects: LCSH: Social ethics. | Social values. | Good and evil--Social aspects. | Humanity.
Classification: LCC HM665 .W48 2022 (print) | LCC HM665 (ebook) | DDC 303.3/72--dc23/eng/20220518
LC record available at https://lccn.loc.gov/2022004641
LC ebook record available at https://lccn.loc.gov/2022004642

British Library Cataloguing in Publication Data

A catalogue record for this book is available from the British Library

ISBN 978-1-80073-551-4 hardback
ISBN 978-1-80539-735-9 paperback
ISBN 978-1-80539-913-1 epub
ISBN 978-1-80073-552-1 web pdf

https://doi.org/10.3167/9781800735514

Contents

Acknowledgements	vii
Introduction. The Good between Social Theory and Philosophy DAVID HENIG AND ANNA STRHAN	1

Part I. Theoretical Perspectives

1. Where Is the Good in the World? JOEL ROBBINS	35
2. Nowhere and Everywhere MICHAEL LAMBEK	46
3. Between Durkheim and Bauman: A Relational Sociology of Morality in Practice OWEN ABBOTT	60
4. For the Agony of 'the Good' and of the Moral Courage to Do It IAIN WILKINSON	77
5. Thinking Time, Ethics and Generations: An Auto-ethnographic Essay on the Good between Philosophy and Social Theory VICTOR JELENIEWSKI SEIDLER	91
Part I Commentary STEVEN LUKES	110

Part II. Approaching the Good in Everyday Life

6. 'To See a Sinner Repent Is a Joyful Thing': Moral Cultures and the Sexual Abuse of Children in the Christian Church GORDON LYNCH	123

7. Making the Good Corporate Citizen: Corporate Social
   Responsibility and the Ethical Projects of Management
   Consultancy in Contemporary China   141
   KIMBERLY CHONG

8. 'God Isn't a Communist': Conservative Evangelicals,
   Money and Morality in London   161
   ANNA STRHAN

9. Doing Good: Cultivating Children's Ethical Sensibilities
   in School Assemblies   180
   RACHAEL SHILLITOE

10. Locating an Elusive Ethics: Surface and Depth in a Jewish
    Ethnography   200
    RUTH SHELDON

11. Radical Hope as a Practice of Possibilities: On the Fragility
    of Goodness and Struggles for Justice in Postwar Bosnia
    and Herzegovina   216
    DAVID HENIG

    Part II Commentary   234
    MAEVE COOKE

Index   244

Acknowledgements

Several of the chapters in this volume arose from exchanges and discussions that were generously supported by the School of Anthropology and Conservation and the Department of Religious Studies at the University of Kent. Our discussions also benefitted from the comments and participation of Matthew Engelke, Elaine Graham, James Laidlaw, Lois Lee, Jonathan Mair and Yvonne Sherwood, as well as some of the authors. We would also like to thank Tom Bonnington and Marion Berghahn at Berghahn for their support, and the anonymous reviewers for their suggestions on the volume as a whole. Finally, thanks to Caroline Kuhtz at Berghahn for their help within the final stages of preparing the manuscript, and to Sarah Sibley for her help with copy-editing.

Introduction
The Good between Social Theory and Philosophy

David Henig and Anna Strhan

In one of the early chapters of his 2017 novel *The Golden House*, Salman Rushdie asks: *What is a good life? What is its opposite?* Rushdie identifies that ours is the time when 'the grandeur of the Universal' that the former question entails became increasingly difficult to ask. As he lays out his diagnosis:

> We are so divided, so hostile to one another, so driven by sanctimony and scorn, so lost in cynicism, that we call our pomposity idealism, so disenchanted with our rulers, so willing to jeer at the institutions of our state, that the very word *goodness* has been emptied of meaning and needs, perhaps, to be set aside for a time, like all the other poisoned words, *spirituality*, for example, *final solution*, for example, and (at least when applied to skyscrapers and fried potatoes) *freedom*. (Rushdie 2017: 7)

The rest of the novel then reads more like a series of answers to the latter question about the opposite of the good life. Taking the zeitgeist of American culture and politics as his canvas, Rushdie paints our era in dark colours. There isn't much room on the canvas for goodness.

Rushdie is not alone in such a diagnosis. Over the past two decades, similar dark tones have come to dominate many areas of social and cultural theory. This is hardly surprising. Social science modes of inquiry are profoundly intertwined with the ever-shifting realities of social life they aim to study. This kind of 'double hermeneutics', as Giddens describes the nature of the relationship between the production of social-science knowledge and its subject matter, is an ongoing process, constantly spiralling 'in and out of the universe of social life, reconstructing both itself and that universe as an integral part of that process' (1990: 15–16). This was the case for W.E.B. Du Bois, Émile Durkheim, Harriet Martineau, Karl Marx, Marcel Mauss and Max Weber as it is for contemporary social scientists. And our circumstances are indeed dire.

With the past decade of escalating planetary environmental crisis, protracted economic turmoil, the rise of exclusionary nationalisms and populism, and the global COVID-19 pandemic, set against a longer-term background of the global expansion of destructive neoliberalism, it is easy to understand the growth of a large body of work in the social sciences sounding pessimistic and often apocalyptic notes (Latour et al. 2018). These responses, as Dipesh Chakrabarty puts it, 'saturate our sense of the now' (2021: 22); and ours is a moment of an uncanny realization of how profoundly '[t]he geological time of the Anthropocene and the time of our everyday lives in the shadow of global capital are intertwined' (2021: 10). If there is any glimmer of hope, it is often situated in the tactics of resistance against such hegemonic and oppressive structures of domination, exploitation and destruction (Malm 2021; Ortner 2016; Urry 2016). Attention to such concerns undoubtedly plays a vital role in addressing the ecological, social, political and cultural problems of our age, both at the level of diagnosis and of critique (Fassin 2017; Keane 2020). This body of work resonates with Salman Rushdie's observation about putting aside the question about goodness while instead focusing on its opposites. Does this mean that the workings of aspirational and imaginative endeavours are no longer concerns in people's lives, and can thus be dismissed by social and cultural analysis? This volume contends that this is not the case and that understanding social life calls not only for focus on the darkness of our current times but also for bringing the question of the good to the centre of social science inquiry.

Recent years have witnessed a rapidly growing interest in morality, ethics and values within and beyond the social sciences (Hitlin and Vaisey 2010; Keane 2016; Tomasello 2016). This move has opened up exploration of how people create forms of the good in their actions and social relationships, how they construct and become orientated towards particular moral aspirations and imaginings of the world they want, and the tensions this can create.[1]

The move towards these questions can in part be seen as a reaction against the hopeless register of much social scientific writing, which has been shaped by a dominant focus on suffering (Robbins 2013a), the corrosive effects of neoliberalism and enduring precarity (Eriksen et al. 2015; Han 2018) and the 'dark' dimensions of social life (Ortner 2016). As Ken Plummer argues in relation to sociology, dark as the world

> indeed is, this is not the full story. We also need … sociology to take seriously the idea of hope and the future. Part of our work should routinely be the emancipatory project of imagining better human social worlds for all; and to engage in discussions about the values and practices which need to be developed to nudge us towards this potentially better world. (Plummer 2013)

Similarly in anthropology, a growing number of anthropologists have turned their attention to the study of care, values, ethics, morality, well-being, empathy and hope as a new endeavour to explore 'the different ways people organize their personal and collective lives in order to foster what they think of as good, and to study what it is like to live at least some of the time in light of such a project' (Robbins 2013a: 457).

However, despite the increasing interest in how ideas and practices of the good are intrinsic to social life, there has been almost no sustained dialogue across the social science disciplines. Our volume attempts to foster such an *interdisciplinary* conversation in contemporary social theory and research Bringing together contributions from anthropology, sociology, religious studies and philosophy, with ethnographic case studies of the good from diverse disciplinary debates and settings, past and present, this volume presents the first interdisciplinary engagement with what it means to study the good as a fundamental aspect of social and cultural life. Before we introduce the essays in this collection, we sketch out a map with some of the key coordinates for locating the debates on the good in anthropology and sociology, as two social science disciplines that have been particularly marked by growing interest in the good in recent years, and, in turn, we outline how these debates are situated between philosophy and social theory.[2]

Anthropologies of the Good

Anthropologists have had a long, albeit not always explicitly articulated, interest in the study of the good. The rich anthropological archive consists of numerous accounts of culturally different ways people, individually and collectively, past and present, conceive and enact what is ultimately desirable and meaningful in their lives. Yet these accounts have not always been explicitly conceptualized and theorized in the language of the good. One of the rare early exceptions was Marcel Mauss. In his *Manual of Ethnography* Mauss outlines the importance of studying moral phenomena and morality Unlike Émile Durkheim's view on morality, Mauss understood morality as 'a matter of which people are clearly and organically aware' (2007: 156), and yet as something that cannot be fully encompassed by rules and norms. Morality, Mauss argues, 'is the art of living together, and it can be recognised by the presence of the notion of good' (ibid.).[3] What Mauss gestures at when he speaks of 'the notion of good' around which human action is coordinated and pursued is the sphere of values that is diffused across all domains of social life and that, in turn, sets human action and social worlds in motion (Graeber 2013). Therefore, to situate anthropologists' engagement with the questions about the good, and where and how the good can be located in people's sociocultural worlds, we locate debates on an anthropology of the good in a wider context of anthropological theorizations of values (Robbins, this volume), and increasingly in the study of morality and ethics (Lambek, this volume). By *values*, we refer to 'those things defined as good within a society or social group' (Robbins 2013b:

100). Similarly, in his *Towards an Anthropology of Value*, the late David Graeber identified the study of the good – that is, culturally constructed conceptions of what is ultimately 'desirable in human life' – among the three broad streams of social theory on value (Graeber 2001: 1). In what follows, we distinguish between the anthropological study of *values*, which is concerned with 'what is considered as desirable and/or good within a society' and which focuses on the *realization* of diverse values and on value conflict, and the study of *value*, which is grounded in Marxian foci on production and capital, and which often treats value as a single thing or even substance of which there can be more or less (Elder-Vass 2016; Robbins 2013b: 100; 2019).[4]

Although the focus on values was one of the central themes of anthropological inquiry for a large part of the twentieth century, this never crystallized into a systematic theory (Graeber 2001: 1; Otto and Willerslev 2013). Since the 1980s, anthropologists have reoriented their interest away from the study of values. It is therefore noteworthy that when in 1980 Louis Dumont, one of the most important social scientific value theorists, delivered his Radcliffe-Brown Lecture, he decided to speak about the problem of value(s), as if bidding farewell to the debates that shaped the modern discipline in such a profound way. In just three dozen pages, Dumont (1982) covers a broad and complex conceptual genealogy of the major epistemological and cultural shifts in (European) modern thinking about values, tracing them from Plato to Clyde Kluckhohn, from Thomas Aquinas to Marcel Mauss, with detours to such thinkers as Marx, Polanyi and Voltaire along the way. But the lecture is also significant for a genealogy of an anthropology of the good, as it explicitly engages with the problem of the good and values in social life.

On a broad level, Dumont argues (1982: 209–10, 216) that the emergence of the modern episteme separated epistemology, aesthetics and morals into distinct domains of thought and action, as well as inquiry. As a contrast to modern thinking, Dumont reflects on Plato, for whom the Good was associated with the supreme Being. In this conception of social order, there was no separation between the Good, the True and the Beautiful, though these spheres were hierarchically ordered. For Plato, the Good was supreme yet active value; as Dumont writes, 'perhaps because it is impossible to conceive the highest perfection as inactive and heartless, because the Good adds the dimension of action to that of contemplation' (1982: 209). Here, Dumont does not suggest anthropologists should become Platonists but uses this contrast to point out the epistemic break the modern era brought about. The increasing primacy of scientific rationality and knowledge also created an unbridgeable distinction in modern epistemological positions between *what is* and *what ought to be*, a significant point to which we shall return shortly. The former, associated with scientific truths, became supreme, while the latter, associated with emotions and volition that cannot be measured, became encompassed by the former (ibid.).

Put differently, scientific facts, truths and material things gained primacy as more 'real' and valued, and thus as superior to the ideational and aesthetic domains of human thought and action. Furthermore, the modern era was also the age of discoveries of 'other worlds', which became disastrous for indigenous populations, and which led to the emergence of new world-system hierarchies (Sahlins 2005; Todorov 1992; Wolf 1982). As Dumont argues, the discoveries of other ways of life, cultures and religions relativized the old conceptions of the good (1982: 210). New experiences of cultural difference made talking about the universal Good more difficult for modern thinkers to accept. This was, then, the historical context in which ideas about values emerged. If talking about the good became difficult, Dumont writes, 'we can speak of the value or values that people acknowledge' across cultural difference (ibid.). The concept of value thus became from its inception, in Dumont's view, inherently anthropological for five main reasons: i) values are *social*; ii) configurations of values are *relative* for they vary within/between social and cultural contexts; iii) values *mediate* and intertwine the diverse domains of action, thought, experience and morals; iv) values are *comparative*; v) since we can find values everywhere, they could be considered as an anthropological *universal*. Dumont's key point is that in the concept of value anthropologists have at their disposal 'a word that allows [them] to consider all sorts of cultures and the most diverse estimations of the good without imposing on them our own: we can speak of our values and their values while we could not speak of our good and their good' (1982: 210). While Dumont's lecture draws more on the language of values than of the good, like Marcel Mauss, Dumont clearly saw the good as an inextricable part of thinking about social and cultural values and how these shape people's moral horizons of thought and action. As we shall see below, with the development of anthropological approaches to the study of morality and ethics, contemporary anthropologists have an adequate theoretical toolkit for addressing not only values but also the good. Yet in the genealogy of an anthropology of the good, Dumont's lecture *On Value*, often today considered obsolete, is an important piece.[5]

In the 1980s and 1990s, it was mainly Marxist-inspired anthropologists who continued writing on value. This body of work interrogated the actually existing workings of ever-expanding capitalism in various socio-political settings and ideological legitmations worldwide (e.g. Eiss and Pedersen 2002).[6] In response to the post-Cold War transformations and upheavals, and accelerated processes of globalization, the discipline was also changing in fundamental ways (Trouillot 2003). From the early 1990s onwards, anthropologists largely reoriented their focus away from the critical study of cultural difference and otherness (as approached, for example, through the study of values). The new dominant foci became the study of suffering, trauma and other ills accelerated by the global transformations. In particular, anthropologists documented the devastating effects of neoliberal modernity worldwide (e.g. Han 2012; Muehlebach 2012; also Eriksen et al. 2015; Ortner 2016) and increasingly the environmental devastation of the planet (Haraway et al. 2016; Latour et al. 2018; Tsing 2015). What brings these threads together, broadly speaking, are two interrelated sets of concerns.

First, it is the emergence of a shared focus on what Joel Robbins (2013a) described as 'suffering subject'. Modern anthropology was founded as a study of 'the Other', an imagery that Michelle-Rolph Trouillot (2003) aptly characterized as the savage slot, in a world epistemologically divided between the West and the Rest. The end of the Cold War era was the final straw for such an image of the world, and the discipline's epistemology. The world radically changed, and so did the practice of anthropology. According to Robbins, in response to these transformations, anthropologists started to engage with those people, communities and places who suffered, whether as a result of violence or deprivation. Put differently, the 'savage slot' was replaced with the 'suffering slot'. A key motivation for this shift was the rise of universal models of suffering and trauma that did not reinstantiate the self/other divide, even as it tended to put difference out of play. Sherry Ortner (2016) offered a similar account of the developments of anthropological theories and debates since the 1990s. In Ortner's perceptive reading, the last three decades gave rise to a 'dark anthropology' that responded to the widespread suffering brought about by neoliberalism. For Ortner, the practice of dark anthropology is an ethico-political position that 'emphasizes the harsh and brutal dimensions of human experience, and the structural and historical conditions that produce them' (2016: 49). Nowadays, anthropologists pursue dark anthropology as a response to 'the increasingly problematic conditions of the *real world* under neoliberalism' (Ortner 2016: 50; emphasis added).

Ortner's reference to 'the real world' epitomizes the second set of concerns that have foregrounded the shifts in the discipline in the past three decades. As unproblematic as her statement might seem, it bundles together a number of problems. Let us consider a prime example of studying 'the real world' today, that of a dark anthropology of migration. In her critical essay on the anthropological scholarship and practice of the so-called European 'refugee crisis' of 2015–2016, Heath Cabot persuasively captured these sentiments and predicaments of conducting fieldwork 'at the front lines of suffering' (2019: 266). Cabot has a long and impressive track record of studying migration and the politics of asylum practices of the EU's border regimes. As Cabot writes, the practice of dark anthropology, here in the context of 'real' displacement, often 'takes place in the form of crisis chasing, or the propensity to take crisis as a driver of scholarship,' and continues, '[t]hese trends reinforce particular notions of public interest, usefulness, and social relevance (Greenhouse 2011: 10) that make anthropologists complicit in perpetuating the increasingly neoliberal business aspects of our discipline' (2019: 262). Put differently, Cabot identifies how through the vigorous pursuit of studying 'the increasingly problematic conditions of the *real world* under neoliberalism' anthropologists often reproduce the ills of neoliberalism that they wish to tackle. But this example also clearly illustrates, as Robbins (this volume) writes, how the practice of dark anthropology with its focus on the suffering subject became 'overly attached to attending to phenomena that [anthropologists] thought of as "real"? What became thought of as 'real' is the study of politics, power, practice, suffering and resistance (ibid.). On the other hand, what became considered as unreal, or as not real enough, was not only the study of values but also 'culture, structure, meanings, representations, and shared ideals' (ibid.). Yet 'imagination and reality are reverse sides of the same process' (Graeber 2007: 314). If we return to Dumont's point about the divide in modern epistemological positions between *what is* and *what ought to be*, we can see that with the pursuit of dark anthropology the pendulum swung towards the former position rather than ethnographically exploring specific configurations and articulations of the intertwinements between the two. Anthropologies of the good that have emerged in the past decade need to be understood against this backdrop (Knauft 2019). And here we use the plural noun advisedly to highlight not only commonalities but also some significant distinctions in attending to the good. We identify three major directions of addressing the good that have emerged in anthropology in recent years. Let us address them in turn.

The phrase 'the anthropology of the good' was first introduced in Robbins' article, one we have already discussed, entitled 'Beyond the Suffering Subject: Toward an Anthropology of the Good' (2013a). In his essay, as discussed above, Robbins outlined how the study of the suffering subject came to dominate the discipline. Although the focus on suffering and the dark aspects of human existence gave rise to a very important and formidable body of scholarship that aims to address the burning issues of our era in order to change them, as Robbins commends, the main thrust of his argument is concerned with something else. Namely, how by doing so anthropologists abandoned 'their longstanding tradition of studying cultural difference and putting their findings to crucial use in upending settled Western understandings' (Robbins, this volume). Anthropologists pivoted away from pursuing critical comparison focused on cultural difference, towards 'empathic connection and moral witnessing based on human unity' (2013a: 453). Suffering and trauma have a universal quality. They confront us in their humanity, no matter in what context and circumstances (2013a: 455). This shift in the practice of ethnography is not concerned with how 'people construct their lives *differently* elsewhere' (ibid.: 455, italics added), a point to which we return shortly, but it now focuses on how anthropologists 'offer accounts of trauma that make us and our readers feel in our bones the vulnerability we as human beings all share' (ibid.).[7]

The main thrust of Robbins' argument is not a critique of studying these topics *tout court* but rather to consider a *parallel* perspective and offer a practice of doing anthropology of the good that might enhance these important interventions. Indeed, Robbins shares with this kind of anthropology of the suffering subject the premise that all human beings have the equal right to free themselves of the dark effects of dispossession, trauma or neoliberalism. But the universalizing perspective of the suffering framework often flattens the *diverse possibilities* of human striving, imagining and enacting a better or other life than a person has in the present (also Carrithers 2005). Anthropology of the good is, then, an attempt to 'explore the different ways people organize their personal and collective lives in order to foster what they think of as good, and to study what it is like to live at least some of the time in light of such a project' (2013a: 457). People's diverse ideas and imaginings of the possibilities shouldn't be dismissed as naive, or as a kind of bad-faith alibi. On the contrary, as Graeber (2001: xiii) tirelessly pointed out, comparative ethnography is 'the only discipline capable of addressing the full range of human possibilities', including envisioning possible alternatives to the actually existing oppressive structures. Similarly, Robbins argues, 'if we assume that ideals always and only get either ignored or deployed in nefarious ways, then the anthropology of the good can never get off the ground' (ibid.). The main challenge for the discipline is to challenge 'our own version of the real' and give these 'aspirational and idealizing aspects of the lives of the others a place in our accounts' (ibid.: 458). In other words, it is 'a commitment to the idea that the world could possibly look very differently than it does' (Graeber 2007: 2). Pursuing this commitment requires integrating into our perspective not only *what is* but also the diverse articulations of how people imagine *what ought to* and *could be*.

Ortner (2016) sketches a second approach to the anthropology of the good in her influential article, which we have already mentioned, entitled 'Dark Anthropology and Its Others: Theory since the Eighties', in which she links the emergence of 'dark anthropology' primarily with the pervasive influence of neoliberalism, which is transforming lives on the planet (2016: 51). In turn, contemporary anthropological practice is primarily focused on the dark effects of neoliberalism and the forms of suffering, inequalities and struggles it creates. Ortner traces the emergence of various 'anthropologies of the good' as a direct response to these dark trends within the discipline. On the surface, the two texts by Robbins and Ortner might look similar, and indeed these two texts are increasingly lumped together as programmatic texts in discussions of the anthropologies of the good. However, Ortner's text differs significantly from Robbins' original argument, and it omits several crucial points, including Robbins' emphasis on the role of cultural difference and relativism in anthropological practice (Robbins, n.d.). Furthermore, while Robbins conceived of an anthropology of the good as an attempt to develop a complementary perspective to those focused on suffering, Ortner interprets the emergence of anthropologies of the good *dialectically* as a countermovement, and thus in tension with 'dark anthropology'. From all the emerging and disparate anthropological foci on the good, which include care, empathy, hope, morality, temporality, values and well-being, Ortner selectively highlights only well-being and adds recent anthropological work on happiness[8] to express her uneasiness with the '"happiness turn" in the middle of all the darkness' (2016: 59). As a second important area, she adds the recent 'ethical turn' in anthropology (Laidlaw 2014; Lambek 2010). Here, however, Ortner is critical of the anthropology of morality and ethics for drawing a sharp line between the ethical and the workings of power, inequality and violence in social life. Against this backdrop, Ortner proposes 'a different kind of anthropology of the good: the anthropology of critique, resistance, and activism' (2016: 60) in an attempt to integrate these divergent streams.

Ortner's vision of such an anthropology of the good builds on her previous work on resistance (1995) and identifies three areas: i) the practice of cultural critique, 'which includes writing about conditions of inequality, power, and violence in various parts of the world'; ii) 'a range of mostly theoretical work addressed to rethinking capitalism as a system'; iii) social movements that have taken shape in the neoliberal period' (2016: 61). The underlying thread running through these areas is the role of 'activist anthropologist' as someone directly involved in addressing the neoliberal order. Although Ortner offers a succinct diagnosis of our times, her dark vision of the neoliberal order as determining the conditions under which all humans on the planet live today, and hence experience more or less similar predicaments, has similar homogenizing tendencies as 'the suffering subject' argument. It is a perspective grounded in the epistemic position of the 'real', which through its dialectical position leaves little room for the aspirational and imaginative aspects of the human condition.

In an insightful response to Robbins and Ortner, Bruce Knauft* (2019) observes that anthropologists have engaged the question of the good more in general conceptual debates, while there has been less attempt to apply and substantiate these debates ethnographically (2019: 11). Knauft agrees that people often do meaningfully orient their lives towards some kind of positive value in spite of their actually living circumstances that might be dire and dark and structured by the conditions of inequality and domination (2019: 4). But to substantiate this relationship ethnographically in its socio-historical specificity, Knauft suggests, 'it seems particularly important to combine a critical understanding of local and larger political economy *with* a culturally nuanced understanding of locally constructed positive meaning, resilience, and optimism or happiness' (2019: 4; original emphasis). Our volume shares this nuancing perspective and offers different ethnographically grounded case studies.

The third direction that needs to be mentioned in the genealogy of anthropologists' engagement with the good is in many regards akin to Robbins', but it is nonetheless distinct. It has developed from anthropologists' recent engagement with moral philosophy, Aristotelian virtue ethics, ordinary language philosophy, and in particular Foucault's project on ethics and the hermeneutics of the subject in his later work (Das 2012; Laidlaw 2014; Lambek 2010, 2015; Mattingly and Throop 2018). We explore anthropologists' engagement with philosophy later in the introduction. However, in the context of the debates outlined here so far, it is important to situate the ethical turn in anthropology over the past two decades as a response to the inadequacy of the existing approaches – focused on political and economic structures – to engage with the ethical dimension of human life and existence (Mattingly and Throop 2018: 477). As with anthropological theorizations of values, anthropologists' turn towards the study of morality and ethics is an attempt to study ethnographically how people address in their day-to-day lives 'what it means to live in a world with ideals, rules, or criteria that cannot be met completely or consistently' (Lambek 2015: xi). This body of work showed that people even in the most trying circumstances imagine and aspire to live a life worth living – that is, to obtain some version of a good life (Mattingly 2010, 2014; also Henig, this volume). It also shows how people are evaluative (Keane 2016; Laidlaw 2014; Lambek 2010) and act with ethical criteria of what is right or good and what is wrong in mind, even if 'goodness is not always the outcome' (Lambek 2015: xvii). Such moral thriving and striving, and exercising of ethical judgement, is not just a domain of people's aspirations and imagination but rather an assemblage of imaginings, practices and actions (Mattingly 2014: 8). The anthropology of morality and ethics thus doesn't foreclose the question of the good itself but approaches it from the position of addressing what people consider worth pursuing, and what makes life worth living, through the focus on people's (evaluative) actions.

The Sociology of Moral Life: 'Old' and 'New'

Within the history of sociology, there has been less explicit focus than in anthropology on 'the good'. However, questions about how people evaluate what is good and bad, right and wrong, and the social contexts shaping particular moral ideals and values are central themes within the sociology of morality and can be traced back to the founding thinkers of the discipline. Durkheim is often treated as the founder of sociological approaches to morality in his aim to develop a distinctive 'science of morality', while Weber presented social life as fundamentally value-laden, painting a vivid portrait of how social conditions subject us to the experience of value conflicts and tensions (Wilkinson and Kleinman 2016: 113). Yet the gendered and racialized dynamics of canon formation have meant that the contributions of a number of other theorists in developing sociological approaches to morality and the good have been underplayed. As early as 1838, Harriet Martineau (1802–1876), one of the early pioneers of sociology, was proposing a science of morality in her methodological treatise, *How to Observe Morals and Manners*, as discussed by Abend (2010). Emphasizing the wide variations in how morality is lived in practice, Martineau argued:

> no doctrines yet invented have accounted for some total revolutions in the ideas of right and wrong, which have occurred in the course of ages. A person who takes for granted that there is an universal Moral Sense among men ... cannot reasonably

explain how it was that those men were once esteemed the most virtuous who killed the most enemies in battle, while now it is considered far more noble to save life than destroy it. They cannot but wonder how it was once thought a great shame to live in misery, and an honour to commit suicide; while now the wisest and best men think exactly the reverse. And, with regard to the present age, it must puzzle men who suppose that all ought to think alike on moral subjects, that there are parts of the world where mothers believe it a duty to drown their children, and that eastern potentates openly deride the king of England for having only one wife instead of one hundred. (1838: 22)

Each individual's 'feelings of rights and wrong', she argues, are not innate but rather 'grow up in him from the influences to which he is subjected' (ibid.: 23), and 'every prevalent virtue or vice is the result of the particular circumstances amidst which the society exists' (ibid.: 27). Martineau explored what these circumstances and influences might consist of, examining 'the Feudal System' and US Society, and identifying such features as 'extent of the commerce', life expectancy, population density, ethnicity and race, class, gender, occupation, the nature of people's dwellings, and others, and how these shape morals (discussed in Abend 2010: 571). However, despite this emphasis on social and cultural moral variation, Martineau acknowledges the idea that there are certain shared universal ethical principles, arguing that '[f]or instance, to torment another without any reason, real or imaginary, is considered wrong all over the world. In the same manner to make others happy is universally considered right' (1838: 23; discussed in Abend 2010: 569).

Writing at the same time as Durkheim was developing his science of morality, Jane Addams (1860–1935) also emphasized morality as an intrinsic aspect of social life. Writing before the compartmentalization of social inquiry into distinct fields of sociology, social policy and anthropology, Addams has often been presented as a 'social reformer'. It is only in the last three decades that her contributions to sociological theory have been acknowledged (Deegan 1988; Romero 2020; Wilkinson and Kleinman 2016). Influenced by and in turn influencing pragmatist philosophy (Seigfried 1999), Addams emphasized – echoing anthropologists' sensibilities – that understanding social and moral realities requires immersion in the experiences we are studying. As Wilkinson (this volume) describes, Addams emphasized that for sociologists to develop reflexivity about their own values and how these are shaped by factors such as institutional privilege, class and ethnicity, they need to be 'personally affected by' the conditions they seek to understand, an argument also later developed by Bourdieu (1999a, 1999b). Like Martineau and Durkheim, Addams recognized that our sense of the good is shaped by learnt, embodied social habits, but she placed greater emphasis than either on the significance of care – rather than obligation – and on the interplay between the individual and the social collective in pursuing the good. For her, this construction takes place in our everyday interactions: as social beings, she writes, 'we determine ideals by our daily actions and decisions not only for ourselves, but largely for each other' (Addams 2002: 112).

W.E.B. Du Bois's work has also been neglected in accounts of the sociology of morality, reflecting the broader marginalization of the contribution that the Atlanta School and other historically black colleges and universities made in the development of sociology in the dominant white 'founding-father' narrative (Romero 2020: 4). Du Bois's *The Negro Church* (1903) offered an empirical study of the moral status of the African American community, exploring the perceptions of both black and white Americans. This formed the basis for his subsequent *Morals and Manners among Negro Americans* (1914), which developed an empirical study based on a survey of 'morals and manners', exploring how racism shaped moral status and moral judgements. Questions of moral judgement, striving and ideals are also interwoven throughout *The Souls of Black Folk* (1903). In this, Du Bois's famous concept of double-consciousness illuminates how racialized prejudice leads to particular forms of moral experience as an interplay within the individual subject of competing 'thoughts', 'strivings' and 'ideals', shaped by the drawing of specific moral boundaries. In this sense, Du Bois's work pioneers attending to how particular moral ideals and strivings are created through experiences of suffering and the operations of power and domination, while at the same time powerfully expressing his own vision of the good in terms of a just society, in which those currently 'prisoned shall go free' (2018: 199).

Despite this early concern with morality in the development of sociological theory in the nineteenth and early twentieth centuries, this focus waned. Steven Lukes in 1973 argued that 'the sociology of morality' was 'the great void in contemporary social science' (Lukes 1973: 432), while nearly twenty years later Craig Calhoun noted that 'sociologists have not carried forward Durkheim's tasks of creating a sociology of morality' (Calhoun 1991: 232) and echoing Weber stated that the discipline had become 'unmusical' in its engagement with morality. Calling for a renewed sociological engagement with values and morality, Andrew Sayer in 2011 argued in his *Why Things Matter to People: Social Science, Values and Ethical Life*:

> We are ethical beings, not in the sense that we necessarily always behave ethically, but that as we grow up we come to evaluate behaviour according to some ideas of what is good or acceptable. We compare and admire or deplore particular actions, personal traits, social practices and institutions. How people behave and should behave with respect to one another is undeniably important to us, indeed it is hard to imagine anything more important, yet social science tells us little about our sense of what is good or bad in these matters and why it is so important to us. (Sayer 2011: 143)

Within North American sociology, the turn away from morality and questions of the good in the twentieth century has been attributed to Talcott Parsons's functionalist assimilation of 'the moral domain' within the sphere of norms and 'moral consensus' (Parsons and Shils 1951). As Hitlin and Vaisey put it, 'morality became nearly synonymous with conformity' (2013: 53). Although moral norms and values were significant in the functionalism that dominated North American sociology from the 1940s to the mid-1960s, they were understood normatively – that is, as the basis of social order – and 'were never critically examined' (Stivers 1996: 4).

From the 1960s onwards, this focus on complying with norms and values became increasingly incompatible with the discipline's broader shift 'away from supposedly soft, subjective features of social life towards hard, objective concerns such as resources and power' (Hitlin and Vaisey 2013: 53). Mirroring debates in anthropology, the influence of neo-Marxist approaches across Europe and North America explained social phenomena in terms of power, domination and conflict (Robbins, this volume). Morality was seen as 'at best an ideological reflection of power relations' (Stivers 1996: 12), which hid 'real' interests and therefore not an avenue worth pursuing (Lamont and Thévenot 2000: 6). The cultural and practice approaches that developed in the 1970s – pushing further against focusing on moral norms and morality – likewise contributed to the eventual demise of functionalism. Critics of functionalism, as Owen Abbott notes, highlighted its failure to examine moral variation and value conflict within particular societies, its inability to account for moral change, and overall, perhaps most damagingly, the normative problems of 'equating the moral with the affirmation of deeply problematic institutional norms' (Abbott 2019: 85; also Abbott, this volume). In the end, because morality 'was identified so strongly with Parsonian theory, it went down with the functionalist ship' (Hitlin and Vaisey 2013: 53). Sociological reluctance to engage with morality during this period can also, as Abbott suggests, be linked with the associations between the study of morality and the traditions of Western moral philosophy, which has in broad terms been concerned with the nature of morality, questions of moral judgement, and establishing rational foundations for universalizable principles (2019: 85). Sociologists, he argues, have rightly been 'averse to the modernist philosophic pursuit of moral abstractions via conceptions of universalism, decontextualisation, and the pristine reason of the disembedded, rationally construing subject' (ibid.).

During the 1990s, there was some revival of interest in morality. In their grand theoretical diagnoses of the (post)modern conditions of society, Zygmunt Bauman (1993, 1997) and Anthony Giddens (1991) offered divergent views of the nature of morality and values, but the writings of both of them can be seen as spurred by a sense of the 'disappearance of morality' (Shilling and Mellor 1998: 207). As Stivers put it, the sociological interest in morality that began to appear in the 1990s 'becomes a way of remembering what has been lost as a prelude to resisting the amoral present' (1996: 12). Certainly, as Abbott puts it, the pessimistic lamenting

> of a new era of anomic moral decline and pervasive uncertainty (Bauman 1997), as well as the insistence of the necessity ... for the perpetual re-negotiation of the moral

parameters of our social world ... did little to enhance a research agenda around the recapitulation of morality as a social phenomenon, and contributed only opaquely to questions of how people draw upon and encounter moral perspectives in their daily lives. (Abbott 2019: 86)

The US also saw growing – although somewhat differently inflected – sociological interest in values from the late 1980s and beyond. In a Durkheimian vein, Robert Bellah and colleagues' *Habits of the Heart* (1996), first published in 1985, proposed four different moral cultures in the United States: expressive individualist, utilitarian individualist, civic republican, and biblical, aiming overall to paint a portrait of the moral character and values of the United States. Building on the Durkheimian spirit of Bellah and also drawing on Clifford Geertz's interpretive approach in anthropology, Jeffrey Alexander's distinctive work in cultural sociology developed a structural hermeneutic approach that emphasized the importance of attending to moral meanings and their textures within social life (e.g. Alexander 1988, 2003, 2006). Ronald Inglehart's influential work on value change from the 1970s onwards (e.g. Inglehart and Baker 2000), drawing on data from the World Values Survey, also explored values in relation to broader society, tracing an overall shift from materialist values such as economic security to 'postmaterialist values' such as self-expression. Alongside – although often not in conversation with – this broader macrolevel approach to morality, questions about moral meaning and the cultural constructions of morality emerged in relation to distinct social contexts, perhaps most notably economic sociology, with its distinctive focus on questions of moral values and how these relate to the nature of value (e.g. Lamont 1992; Zelizer 1994; see also Heinich 2020; Skeggs 2014). Also focusing on the question of values, Hans Joas's work in social theory (2000) explored the genesis of values, arguing that values arise in experiences of self-formation and self-transcendence, and offering a differentiation between values, norms and desires.

It has only been since the turn of the twenty-first century, however, that the sociology of morality has (re)emerged as a distinctive area within the discipline, with the establishment in 2012 of a section of the American Sociological Association on *Altruism, Morality, and Social Solidarity* and new handbooks of the sociology of morality (Hitlin and Vaisey 2010) and altruism, morality, and social solidarity (Jeffries 2014). While not often explicitly foregrounded, a focus on the good is intrinsic to this burgeoning sociological literature on morality. Gabriel Abend (2008: 87), for example, defines the sociology of morality as 'the sociological investigation of the nature, causes, and consequences of people's ideas about *the good and the right*' and argues that for sociology to improve its understanding of morality, 'better conceptual, epistemological, and methodological foundations are needed' (ibid.: 118, emphasis added). There is now increasing willingness amongst sociologists to explore morality and the good as intrinsic elements of social life. This growing body of work is often dubbed 'the new sociology of morality' (e.g. Abbott 2019; Hitlin and Vaisey 2010, 2013), although several scholars have pointed out that it has much in common with the 'old' sociology of morality. In his insightful chapter in the *Handbook of the Sociology of Morality*, Abend, for example, notes that the logic of Martineau's 1838 sociology of morality 'is exactly the logic' of much contemporary sociology of morality, as scholars today seek 'to find out what factors account for moral rules, ideas, beliefs, institutions, practices, etc (Abend 2010: 571). They might ask, he notes, 'why people in a particular society or social group have a particular institution (say, slavery, or corporate social responsibility indexes),[10] or a prevalent conviction/value/feeling (say, that slavery is an unjust institution, or that business has moral obligations to society) rather than another' (ibid.).

What *is* new in the 'new' sociology of morality, however, at least in comparison with older Durkheimian, Weberian and Parsonian approaches, is the desire to study morality through empirical studies of contemporary societies and historical sociology (Bargheer and Wilson 2018: 3; Lynch, this volume). Given the fragmentation of the discipline that occurred over the twentieth century, there is also a desire to move counter to centripetal institutional forces by drawing together sociologists from different subfields who are engaged with exploring questions of morality in order to establish the distinctive features of a sociology of morality (Hitlin and Vaisey 2010). Hitlin and Vaisey (2013) propose that the sociology of morality can make distinctive contributions in three main areas.[11] First, it helps define and understand what morality is through exploring 'social and historical variations in what gets classified as moral' (Hitlin and Vaisey 2010: 54). This approach works with a broadly formal understanding of morality, referring 'to understandings of good and bad, right and wrong, worthy and unworthy that vary between persons and between social groups', and encompassing how individuals or groups decide which behaviours or goals are 'the most worthy, and what people *should* believe, feel, and do' (Hitlin and Vaisey 2013: 55). The good, here, is thus whatever a person or group takes it to be, and the important questions following from this are empirical – exploring and accounting for moral variation, for instance. Second, it aims to explore how morality affects action (Hitlin and Vaisey 2013: 60). This includes, for instance, forms of moral motivation, with a growing body of sociological work drawing on approaches in social psychology, cognitive anthropology and neuroscience to explore how moral orientations and senses of moral identity might shape strategies of action over time (e.g. Frye 2012; Vaisey 2009). Third, it aims to explore where morality comes from and, in particular, how social processes 'create and sustain particular forms of morality' (Hitlin and Vaisey 2010: 54) and how and why moralities vary. This might, for instance, involve focus on the role of institutions and organizations across different fields – from medical to humanitarian to economic – or exploring the role that social inequalities or the intersections of class, ethnicity and gender play in shaping values (e.g. Hitlin and Harkness 2018). In this latter emphasis on moral variation, Hitlin and Vaisey argue that the 'new' sociology of morality is more Weberian than Durkheimian in its emphasis that morality 'belongs more to cross-cutting groups and less to society as a whole' (Hitlin and Vaisey 2013: 53). We could also, however, see this emphasis as bringing us again back to Martineau.

In reflecting on why sociology – like anthropology – has turned (again) to questions of the good, we would suggest, as outlined above, that the 'darkness' of the current times is significant. Articulating the importance of a sociology of hope, Les Back notes, writing in the context of the UK, that '[f]rom the national self-mutilations of Brexit to our heating Earth and the polluted landscapes that thicken our oceans and the tragedy of the Covid-19 pandemic, worldly troubles loom large' (2021: 3). In this context, Back argues for the need for 'a different kind of attentiveness to the world... in the service of hope' (ibid.: 4). This kind of attentiveness to hope, as a form of the good, can be seen as one of the distinctive contributions of the sociological focus on morality. Just as the early sociologists – writing in conditions of unprecedented societal upheavals and new forms of division and inequality – sought to place questions about what it might mean to live a good life within such times at the front and centre of the discipline, so also this 'new' concern with morality is animated by the same impulse to understand what really matters to people and why, and the social consequences of this, and to foreground the imaginative possibilities of how things might be otherwise (Sayer 2011; Wilkinson, this volume).

Between Philosophy and Social Theory

While morality, ethics and values wavered as topics of inquiry within sociology and anthropology throughout much of the twentieth century, these themes remained central within moral philosophy. It is not surprising, therefore, that the resurgent anthropological and sociological approaches to questions of morality, ethics and values have drawn from debates in moral philosophy. This conversation between anthropology and philosophy could be seen as initially prompted by James Laidlaw's influential 2001 Malinowski Memorial Lecture (Laidlaw 2002). Laidlaw argued that the reason the anthropology of ethics did not exist at that point was because 'Durkheim's conception of the social so completely identified the collective with the good that an independent understanding of ethics appears neither necessary nor possible' (ibid.: 312. For a critical response, see Lukes, this volume). Jarrett Zigon likewise (2007, 2008) argued that through the influence of Durkheim a Kantian deontological approach became the anthropological norm. This equated morality and the good with rules, duties and obligations, but replacing Kant's moral law with society, following Durkheim's critique of Kant (for a slightly different view, see Robbins 2007). In the years since Laidlaw's article, anthropologists studying morality and ethics have turned to a range of philosophical interlocutors. As outlined in the earlier section, three main philosophical approaches have been especially prominent, as Cheryl Mattingly and Jason Throop (2018) identify in an insightful review of the anthropology of ethics and morality: Foucauldian and neo-Aristotelian traditions of virtue ethics, ordinary language philosophy and phenomenology.

In moving away from Durkheim, anthropologists have been especially drawn to Foucault's later work on the ethics and the care of the self, to the extent that Foucault has now 'dethroned' Durkheim in shaping anthropology's understanding of the moral (Mattingly 2014: 35).[12] Foucault's work has been especially influential in part, as Laidlaw argued (2002), because his approach to ethics allows a concept of 'freedom' in the ethical act while at the same time still acknowledging how modes of socially and culturally habituated embodied practice shape ethical subjects.[13] Foucault's attention to practices of self-cultivation has also inspired widespread attention to Aristotelian virtue ethics and its revival in twentieth-century moral philosophy in the work of Alasdair MacIntyre (1981), Martha Nussbaum (1986) and others. One of the distinctive attractions of Aristotle and neo-Aristotelian philosophies here is their location of ethics as intrinsic to human action and the attention given to the complexities of different dimensions of human activity (Lambek 2010, 2015). As Mattingly and Throop describe, Aristotle presented human action as directed 'to the human cultivation of a good life. This particular view of the good life is thus one that is necessarily enacted ... As such, it is full of frailty and uncertainty because no amount of rules, norms, or even wisdom can preclude the challenge of judging the good in the particular circumstances in which action must be taken' (2018: 481). The good, following MacIntyre, is located within specific practices and internal to them, as opposed to instrumental goals, which are external to specific practices (such as a goal of mastery over others, or a desire for honour). As Lambek puts it, 'a practice is ethical insofar as the goal is not instrumental but reaching for excellence within the particular practice – and for human good or happiness overall in the practice of practices' (2010: 21). Non-Western ethical traditions have also been drawn into this conversation, developing comparative theoretical approaches for exploring forms of virtue and what it is to be a good person or live a good life (e.g. Pandian 2009; Weeratunge 2010).

Alongside Aristotelian approaches, ordinary language philosophy has been a dominant influence in anthropological work on 'ordinary ethics'. Advocates of this approach have located the ethical within the realm of 'ordinary' practice and action, 'as specific acts (performance) and ongoing judgment (practice)' (Lambek 2015: 242). In this body of work, ordinary language philosophy – especially Ludwig Wittgenstein, J.L. Austin and Stanley Cavell – has been drawn on in exploring the formation of criteria for ethical judgement and modes of performativity and acknowledgement. Advocates of ordinary ethics have often situated their understanding of ethics in contrast with notions of the transcendent or the religious (Das 2012; Lambek 2010). This is also the reason why some of its proponents suggested that there is no such thing as the good. Veena Das, for example, claims that ordinary ethics is opposed to any notion of 'the good' that stands 'in alienated majesty separated from all suffering and pain' (in Venkatesan 2015: 438), and she argues that ethical work 'is done not by orienting oneself to transcendental agreed-upon values but rather through the cultivation of sensibilities *within* the everyday' (Das 2012: 149). This understanding of morality is, she argues, premised on 'making dispositions and habits' the 'very substance of a moral way of living' (2015: 65). While religious vocabularies may play a part in this, Das states, drawing on Deleuze's (1998) contrast between the 'morality of living' and 'the European morality of salvation and charity', that these vocabularies do not 'function as the kind of transcendental super-concepts that Wittgenstein warned against' (Das 2015: 65).

In response, Robbins has argued that rejecting the transcendent or the religious as dimensions of the ethical or the good means excluding aspects of life that for many play an important part in constructing forms of value and moral life, such as consciously articulated moral laws or forms of religious ritual (Robbins 2016, on rules see also Clarke 2015). Stanley Cavell – an influential figure in ordinary ethics approaches – likewise argues that visions of and arguments about the good city – what he calls 'an imagination of justice' – are important in the moral life and that utopian moments and transcendental elements may in the end be 'indispensable in the motivation for a moral existence' (Cavell 2004: 18; see Strhan, this volume). This question of the role of utopian and transcendent elements within the realm of the moral and how these are imagined and constructed across space and time is perhaps, however, ultimately an *empirical* question, as is the location of the good within the everyday and the ways in which forms of the good are related to particular forms of suffering and injustice (see Henig, this volume; Wilkinson, this volume). As Michael Jackson puts it, '[t]hese gestures towards everyday ethics, and the ways questions of what is right and good figure in almost every human interaction, conversation, and rationalization, effectively reinscribe the role of ethnography as a method for exploring a variety of actual social situations' (2013: 11).

A third rich seam of anthropological work on moral experience has drawn on phenomenological philosophy – especially hermeneutic phenomenology – to explore questions of responsivity and intersubjectivity (Mattingly and Throop 2018: 482). This approach focuses on the struggle for a good life, the way things address us, matter to us and make claims on us and 'the way that the world and our response to it are inextricably entangled' (Mattingly 2014: 13). Drawing on a range of philosophers, including Emmanuel Levinas, Martin Heidegger and Paul Ricoeur, this approach to morality emphasizes human fragility, finitude, embodiment, moral emotion and 'the limits of life as lived' (Mattingly and Throop 2018: 483). Mattingly (2014) emphasizes that these phenomenological approaches place the focus on the first-person stance[14] of the experiencing subject (who is always-already at the same time a relational being), on the condition of being-with or being-for another, and on the spaces between subjects 'and between those subjects and the world itself' (Mattingly and Throop 2018: 483; see for example Jackson 2012). Countering the critique that phenomenological approaches assert an individualist, Western-centred philosophical hegemony (e.g. Kapferer and Gold 2018), Mattingly and Throop argue that these approaches 'shift attention away from readily made boundaries between individual and world, self and other, thought and thing, ego and alter' and instead invite 'an interrogation of the fluctuating processes by which and through which such distinctions are intersubjectively and intercorporeally constituted and made meaningful' (2018: 483). Drawing on Spinoza as well as Levinas, Heidegger and Ricoeur, Jackson argues that 'ethics concerns the ways species life or individual lives are struggled for and sustained, especially under conditions of insecurity, scarcity, danger, and loss, *as well as* the ways in which life itself flows through all things, connecting all forms of life in a common web' (2013: 6).

While conversations with philosophy have figured prominently in shaping the terms of anthropological approaches to the moral and ethical, it would be fair to say that they have been less developed thus far in sociology. This is in part because the re-emergence of morality as a core theme has been more recent in sociology than anthropology. It can also be attributed to the fact that social theories – including those of Durkheim – have continued to be a resource in sociological approaches to studying morality and the good, and there has therefore been less sense of a need to look beyond the discipline. The ongoing influence of Weber has meant that there has been attention to the significance of Nietzsche in shaping Weber's understanding of moral values and purpose (and their fragmentation) under the cultural conditions of modernity (Wilkinson and Kleinman 2016), as well as wider attention to the significance of Nietzsche's genealogy of morality[15] in developing criteria to map different moralities across space and time (Abend 2014; Bargheer and Wilson 2018).

As in anthropology, virtue ethics is something of a counter-example, as it has figured as one notable philosophical thread in the 'new' sociology of morality. Sayer's analysis of values (2011) critiques notions of detached rationality that have been dominant in Western modernist philosophy and draws on virtue ethics to explore how moral emotions and sentiments, virtues and vices are related to social context. Also drawing virtue theory into conversation with sociology, Owen Abbott likewise notes that much moral philosophy has pursued the formation of moral rules and principles, whereas the 'sociological view is that action and judgement, moral or otherwise, cannot realistically be unravelled from the relational context in which they are constituted' (Abbott 2019: 76). As Seyla Benhabib puts it:

> Modern moral philosophy, and particularly universalist moralities of justice, have emphasized our dignity and worth as subjects at the cost of forgetting and repressing our vulnerability and dependency as bodily selves. Such networks of dependence

and the web of human affairs in which we are immersed are not simply like clothes which we outgrow or like shoes which we leave behind. They are ties that bind; ties that shape our moral identities, our needs, *and our visions of the good life*. The autonomous subject is not the disembodied self; universalist moral theory must acknowledge the deep experiences in the formation of the human being to which care and justice correspond. (Benhabib 1992: 189, cited in Abbott 2019: 75–76, emphasis added)

The emphasis on forms of care and the relational nature of our moral identities and visions of the good emerging in moral philosophy from the 1980s onwards (e.g. Gilligan 1982) have also been drawn into sociological conversation (Abbott 2019; Hegtvedt and Scheuerman 2010). This focus on care in sociological approaches to morality, arising in conversation with feminist philosophy and approaches to the study of families and personal life, has also indexed the relation between morality and power. As Sayer puts it, relations of care are crucial for ethical formation and are typically asymmetric and strongly gendered; they are always also 'relations of power, whether benign or malign' (2011: 178).

Likewise emphasizing the relational constitution of morality and the good, pragmatist philosophy has been another philosophical resource for sociologists. In developing a relational view of moral phenomena as located 'in the intersubjective flow of life'[16] (Abbott 2019: 181), Abbott draws especially on Mead's pragmatism. Mead's understanding of the self as shaped through both socialization and individuation helps to develop a framework for exploring forms of moral subjectivity and reflexive deliberation as always entangled with relations, and how morality involves 'mundane considerations of how to respond to a situation at hand, and deeper dialogic assessment of our own perspectives that can be in some way efficacious for future action and transformative of our viewpoints' (Abbott 2019: 183). Stefan Bargheer (2018) draws on Dewey's pragmatism to develop an approach to morality based on pragmatist theories of valuation. Bargheer argues that forms of moral valuation are embedded in practices and institutions, and he explores how this shaped organized bird conservation in Britain and Germany, as the moral value of birds was shaped through their relational position within particular institutions and practices.

Alongside pragmatism, a number of other philosophical voices have also featured in sociological approaches to morality, perhaps most notably Hannah Arendt, Charles Taylor and Jurgen Habermas (see, e.g., Abbott 2019; Calhoun 1991; Sayer 2011; Wilkinson and Kleinman 2016). As *critical* social theorists, these particular voices engage in 'social criticism guided by an idea of the good society in which the salient obstacles to human flourishing would once and for all have been removed, or who reflect on what it means to engage in such criticism' (Cooke 2006: 7; see also Cooke, this volume). Those sociologists who have drawn on these perspectives have thus often emphasized the normative implications of focusing on forms of morality and the good. Iain Wilkinson notes that forms of morality and politics are interwoven within the work of social scientists and that social science research should be directed towards better understanding 'how "the good" may be known and realised in social life' (this volume; see also Seidler, this volume).[17] Arguing for a 'critical social science', Sayer likewise emphasizes that sociology should be about contributing to human flourishing, and that involves identifying 'what things "are not right as they are"', and why' (Sayer 2011: 244). Sayer traces social scientific reluctance to evaluate how particular social practices contribute (or not) to human flourishing to the wider social construction of morality and knowledge in modernist thought:

> In pressing the question of why anything is good or bad we enter a territory where the ways of thinking we learn as social scientists seem to fail us. The reasons for [this] ... are not only consequences of worries about essentialism and ethnocentrism but go much deeper to the fact-value, science-ethics, positive-normative dualisms of modernist thought, and the subjectivization of values associated with the rise of a liberal society. Critical social science needs to acknowledge its often hidden or repressed premise – that its evaluation of practices imply a conception of human flourishing. (Sayer 2011: 245)

While this range of philosophical voices has played an important role – especially in anthropology – in stimulating important questions and crystallizing terms of debates in the study of morality and the good, our hope is to return to a focus on questions of the good and morality as central topics in social theory.[18] Despite the 'astonishing efflorescence' (Mattingly and Throop 2018: 476) of studies of the moral dimensions of existence within anthropology (and to a lesser extent sociology), it is nevertheless fair to say that questions of the good and morality do not in themselves feature prominently within contemporary social theory, at least as this is currently taught within sociology and anthropology programmes. An influential, recent edited volume on social theory (Benzecry et al. 2017), for example, does not include a chapter on morality or the good,[19] even though these dimensions are inextricably interwoven into what the editors situate as the core concerns of social theory: How is social order possible? What is the role of materiality in the world? What is the role of meaning in the world? And what is the role of practice in the world? (Benzecry et al. 2017: 8–10).

To bring the good (back) into social theory, we also need to bring social theory back more centrally into the study of the good. While sociologists and some anthropologists have engaged with social theories in developing recent approaches to morality and the good (and values, for example),[20] they have been somewhat less prominent in anthropological debates, which have turned instead to philosophy (Mattingly and Throop 2018: 478).[21] Recovering the place of the good within social theory does not mean turning away from philosophy. Indeed, many of the contributions in this volume engage with both philosophy and social theory. However, we hope that future work in this field might productively draw from the rich and diverse resources offered by social theory. If we rethought forms of the good through Jane Addams' approach, seeing it as a form of care, for example, rather than in terms of obligation, debates about 'freedom' or 'unfreedom' appear largely irrelevant to our understanding of moral life as it is lived. Similarly, turning back to Du Bois's consideration of how conditions of suffering, violence and injustice contribute to forms of moral experience and aspiration helps move us beyond the dichotomy that is sometimes articulated between the study of 'the good' and the study of the 'harsh dimensions of social life (power, domination, inequality, and oppression)' (Ortner 2016: 47). As ethics is intrinsic to social life and matters deeply to people, questions of the good and values, and how these are shaped, maintained and contested in everyday life, should, we argue, be seen (once again) as core topics within social theory. By seeking to understand and represent the diversity that exists in understandings of the good and forms of values around the world, the social sciences might thus play an important role in contributing to wider public debates about how people understand, imagine and realize the best ways to pursue lives worth living.

Engagements with the Good

This volume is the first interdisciplinary engagement with the question of how people realize the good in social life. The contributors – working in the fields of sociology, anthropology, religious studies and social philosophy – were invited to reflect on the following questions: What does it mean to study the good as an aspect of social and cultural life? How does focusing on the good enhance and refocus social theory? How do different disciplinary perspectives on the good challenge and enrich each other? To what extent is the concept of the good analytically and conceptually productive, and how should we situate this in relation to debates surrounding the study of ethics and values? What are the interrelations between power and inequality and a 'politics of hope' (Appadurai 2013), between suffering and moral aspiration, and between the ethical and the political (Zigon 2017)? To sustain such an interdisciplinary conversation that is theoretically as well as ethnographically and historically grounded, the volume is divided into two parts. Each part is followed by commentaries, by Steven Lukes and Maeve Cooke respectively, contextualizing the volume in a wider landscape where philosophy and social theory meet, and opening up this conversation to future directions of study.

Bringing anthropology, sociology, social theory and philosophy together, Part I offers a range of perspectives on the good in the emerging social theoretical field of morality and ethics. The volume starts with Joel Robbins' essay, which directly addresses the volume's question: 'Where is the good in the world?' In his answer, Robbins suggests that we should define the good as the study of cultural values. The focus on values offers a productive perspective as the study of values is one of the areas in which philosophy and social theory have converged over a long time. By making this case, Robbins focuses particularly on the work of the classics of social theory, Max Weber and Émile Durkheim, and offers an account of how we can construe values as being sufficiently real in the world to be worthy of study. In response to Robbins' argument, Michael Lambek offers in his chapter a counter-perspective, suggesting that the good is located 'nowhere and everywhere'. Drawing on a range of philosophical inspirations, Lambek suggests that we ought to resist collapsing the ethical and the good. As he argues, 'the good' is first and foremost a criterion of judgment immanent to our human condition. Thus, questions about the good and suffering, as well as about ethics and morality, are inseparable from each other, and, as Lambek suggests, we should simply begin with 'the ordinary' and be satisfied with what we can understand of the complexity and simplicity of life as it is lived.

Owen Abbott's contribution echoes some of the productive tensions emerging from Robbins' and Lambek's conversation. His chapter outlines how in the light of renewed interest in sociology of morality, the notions of the good and morality are an integral facet of all social interactions and therefore need to be attended to in terms of everyday social practice. Abbott's chapter thus provides a dynamic theoretical framework for understanding the good and morality more broadly in the flow of social life that bridges the long-lasting tension in social theory between holistic and individualistic positions. Drawing on the tradition of reflexive sociology (Bourdieu and Wacquant 1992) and the study of social suffering, Iain Wilkinson interrogates the very practice of social science and its motivations (or lack thereof) towards studying how the good may be known and realized in social life. Wilkinson's chapter asks whether the social sciences' practitioners are prepared to endure the antinomies of their practice and hold the moral courage to pursue the good in thought and action whilst facing up to the fact that, more often than not, whatever can be done in our 'dark era' is set to remain woefully inadequate. Yet this does not mean that we ought to give up. In arguing so, Wilkinson makes a powerful case for a humanitarian social science with a focus on human values at its core. Part I concludes with Victor Jeleniewski Seidler's auto-ethnographic essay, which interweaves philosophy and social theory, the personal and the theoretical as mutually constitutive, echoing Wilkinson's call for a reflexive and morally courageous stance from social sciences' practitioners. Reflecting on major shifts in social theory over the last half a century, Seidler traces how the good and ethics have been located and explored across generations within and across social theory, sociology, anthropology, feminism and philosophy, and he shows what it means to think across generations in approaching morality, ethics and the good. Seidler's chapter argues for the importance of approaches that allow for the dignity and integrity of difference.

While the chapters in Part I theorize the concept of the good in relation to debates surrounding the study of ethics, values and morality, Part II brings together six case studies that engage with the question of how people realize the good in social life *empirically*. By examining how people articulate, imagine, construct and contest different forms of the good in different situations and contexts, past and present, the chapters in Part II pluralize, historicize and politicize as much as theorize the questions raised in Part I. In so doing, the case studies directly address Bruce Knauft's observation that there have been only limited attempts to ethnographically elucidate the conceptual and theoretical debates about the good (2019: 11). Yet, as Gordon Lynch demonstrates in his chapter, the interplay between the conceptual debates and empirical material engaging people's notions of the good is as relevant for an ethnographic inquiry as it is for historical research. Lynch's chapter deals with the limits of morality, addressing historical cases of child sexual abuse within Christian churches. Lynch's chapter seeks to bridge the gap between 'dark anthropology' and the anthropology of morality by encouraging discussion of the ways in which the pursuit of the 'good' in social life does not simply encourage a constructive sense of purpose or place but can also be bound up with causing, or failing to attend to, harm. Similarly, Kimberly Chong's chapter shows the importance of thinking through both the anthropology of the good and the 'darker themes' of power, politics and inequality *together*. Situated inside the China arm of a global management consultancy, Chong explores how global corporations seek to socialize their employees into a particular vision of the good through their corporate social responsibility initiatives. Her chapter persuasively shows how studying the projects of corporate citizenship through which employees are encouraged to embody a moral ethos through the notions of the good can help us understand how power is produced, co-opted and retained within global capitalism.

Since Adam Smith, and via Max Weber, the theme of capitalism and ethics has a well-established genealogy in social theory. In her chapter, Anna Strhan explores evangelical Christians' engagement with money in a large conservative evangelical church in London. This might not be an obvious location for the good. Yet as Strhan shows, following different moral threads interwoven in the thoughts and actions of the conservative evangelicals in relation to the place of money in their lives, the good is imagined not only in relation to the value of a capitalist calculative ethic but also to a transcendent grace that exceeds capitalist regimes. Focusing on the good ethnographically allows Strhan to tease out the contradictions and eruptions that evade the logic of capital even amongst those who appear well rewarded by the current economic order. Taking collective worship in English primary schools as her focus of analysis, Rachael Shillitoe's chapter explores how schools perform, mediate and teach different ideas of the good. It documents how schools attempt to cultivate children's ethical subjectivities in both religious and nonreligious frameworks and subsequently how children respond to such strategies. Through her finely-grained ethnography, Shillitoe shows how focusing on the question of 'the good' in relation to childhood contributes to our understanding of the good by exploring how parents teachers, children and policymakers construct and enact particular moral ideas and values in everyday life.

The question of how to locate and study the ethical and moral as an empirical object of research is discussed by Ruth Sheldon. She takes the debates between scholars of 'the good' and proponents of 'ordinary ethics' as a case in point. Drawing on long-term ethnographic research into Jewish life in Hackney, London, Sheldon considers the tensions and consequences of her naming 'the good' and 'ethics' as research objects and asks how these terms resonate within orthodox Jewish contexts that are also gendered in distinctive ways. Sheldon's chapter shows how Jewish ethnography as one under-acknowledged 'other' within the social sciences can speak back to some implicitly Christian, colonial and masculine grammars structuring this field. And, finally, David Henig's chapter takes a similar critical route to show how inadequate the now rather incommensurable theoretical positions focusing either on the good or on the dark conditions that produce inequalities, suffering and despair in the contemporary world have become. Situated in postwar Bosnia and Herzegovina, where people's lives have been drastically constrained by debt and foreshortened aspirational horizons, Henig explores how developing and cultivating practices of hope can become generative for our understanding of how people imagine a good and act on it in situations of suffering and dramatic ruptures. His ethnography shows how individual as well as collective striving for the good, and for a life worth living, is a fragile endeavour, always entangled in suffering, despair and doubt, and in which the outcomes of one's striving are uncertain.

David Henig is Associate Professor of Cultural Anthropology at Utrecht University. He is the author of *Remaking Muslim Lives: Everyday Islam in Postwar Bosnia and Herzegovina* (2020) and the co-editor of *Economies of Favour After Socialism* (2017).

Anna Strhan is Senior Lecturer in Sociology at the University of York. She is the author of *The Figure of the Child in Contemporary Evangelicalism* (2019), *Aliens and Strangers? The Struggle for Coherence in the Everyday Lives of Evangelicals* (2015), *Levinas, Subjectivity, Education: Towards an Ethics of Radical Responsibility* (2012) and the co-editor of *Religion and the Global City* (2017) and *The Bloomsbury Reader in Religion and Childhood* (2017).

Notes

1. In what follows, we use the terms 'morality' and 'ethics' largely interchangeably. We note, however, that the use of the terms is contested, and some anthropologists have emphasized a distinction in the use of these terms (most influentially, perhaps, Zigon 2007, and more recently, and following Bernard Williams (1986), Keane 2016; see also discussions in Laidlaw 2014; Mattingly and Throop 2018).

2. It is worth noting that the study of morality, values and the good is, in different ways, also a theme across the wider social sciences – with longstanding debates in psychology (which, as discussed below, are drawn on within new sociological approaches to morality), as well as political science, social policy, economics, media studies, law and international relations, and work on morality is a growing area within cultural geography. While it is beyond the scope of the present volume to speak to each of these disciplines, we hope and expect the positions that we advance here to be refined and challenged through further interdisciplinary conversation over the coming years.
3. On the importance of Durkheim for the debates on the good, see Lukes – this volume.
4. David Graeber objected to such a division between *values* and *value* in his attempt to develop a more unified approach (2013: 236–37; 2001). Although we pivot towards a more unified approach later in our argument, we still find this distinction analytically productive for understanding the debates of the past three decades (see also Gregory 2014).
5. This is of course only a fragmented account of Dumont's history of value theory, and of its history more broadly understood (see Robbins 2013a).
6. It is important to mention that two seminal anthropological books on value theory were published in the 1980s (Appadurai 1986; Munn 1986). While Munn's book presents rather a culmination and synthesis of her thinking and writing on values, Appadurai's edited volume marks a shift away from the social theory of values towards the study of value (see also Graeber 2001: 30–33). As Chris Gregory pointed out, Appadurai's volume and subsequent work marks a shift towards a radically new theory of value that is 'deliberately and provocatively "posthumanist" in that it allows for the agency of things alongside the agency of people' (2014: 46). And further, Gregory adds, 'Appadurai develops his new theory of value by deliberately and consciously turning Marx upside down. He converts Marx's famous theory of the fetishism of commodities into a methodological principle and argues that it is not labor that gives value to things but things that give value to people' (2014: 48).
7. These trends were anticipated by Webb Keane (2003) already a decade earlier, when he pointed out how the loss of focus on 'cultural relativism' and difference is a loss of a productive tension that has driven the production of ethnographic knowledge since the times of the discipline's founders, namely the tension between 'epistemologies of estrangement and of intimacy'. And as Webb Keane observed, 'the latter has increasingly claimed the epistemological and moral high ground in much cultural anthropology' (2003: 223; see also Robbins n.d.).
8. Happiness was not discussed by Robbins in the original text, though he did take it up later (2015).
9. Knauft continues with his thinking about the good also on his blog: https://scholarblogs.emory.edu/bknauft/good-anthropology-in-dark-times/ [last accessed 29 March 2021].
10. See Kimberly Chong's chapter in this volume.
11. Abend (2010) also notes a fourth area of concern – the 'moral brain' (and engagement with neuroscience and cognitive approaches to morality) – as a distinctive feature of the 'new' sociology of morality.
12. It is important to note that Sherry Ortner grounds her 'dark' diagnosis of the oppressive structures of domination and exploitation, and the way out from these structures, in Foucault's work as well, along with Marx. Yet, as James Laidlaw pointed out in his response to Ortner's argument, Foucault explicitly claimed 'that it was simply a misreading to attribute to him the idea of "a system of domination that controls everything and leaves no room for freedom" (1997: 293)' (Laidlaw 2016: 21; see also Mattingly 2014).
13. A number of anthropologists have questioned this emphasis on 'freedom' in ethical life because of its Western associations (e.g. Das et al. 2014; Keane 2016).

14. See also Sayer's critique (2011) of the third-person perspective in sociological accounts of morality.
15. Nietzsche has also been a significant influence within the anthropology of ethics (e.g Laidlaw 2002, 2014).
16. Zygmunt Bauman (1993) also draws attention to the relational dimensions of ethics, drawing on Emmanuel Levinas's conception of ethics. However, as Abbott discusses (2019, this volume), Bauman's presentation of morality as pre-social draws us away from exploring ethics and morality within everyday life and practice. Strhan (2019) draws on Levinas in a somewhat different vein in developing a sociological approach to ethics, drawing together Levinas and Arendt to trace differing moral impulses within contemporary British society and exploring how these are located within evangelical Christianity.
17. This also resonates with the recent emphasis on social justice approaches within sociology, as powerfully articulated by Mary Romero in her American Sociological Association Presidential Address (Romero 2020).
18. We use the term 'social theory' rather than 'sociological theory' or 'anthropological theory' out of the desire to *re*establish 'an intellectual trading zone' in these debates (Galison 1997). The demarcation of social theory into 'sociological' and 'anthropological' theory emerges out of the strong professionalization of these disciplines, especially in the United States. Benzecry et al. (2017), for example, note that the term 'sociological theory' is 'primarily drawn, and used, by sociologists ... who want to separate what is relevant to their research concerns from other scholarly work that they should not feel obliged to read' (ibid.: 6).
19. The volume does, however, include a chapter on norms (Gross and Hyde 2017) but does not explore these in relation to morality.
20. Fassin (2008, 2012) and Robbins (2007, 2012) have continued to draw on Durkheim (and also Weber in Robbins' case), for example.
21. Since we relate the good to the debates on values/value, let us return once more to David Graeber. In his reflections on writing *Toward an Anthropological Theory of Value*, Graeber echoed this sentiment when he wrote, 'the book seems to have appeared at precisely the moment when the discipline was collectively dismissing all such great debates as somehow passé, in fact, anthropological theory itself (that is, theory that emerged from within anthropology as opposed to theory borrowed from Continental philosophers)' (2013: 221).

References

Abbott, O. 2019. *The Self, Relational Sociology, and Morality in Practice*. London: Palgrave Macmillan.

Abend, G. 2008. 'Two Main Problems in the Sociology of Morality', *Theory & Society* 37(2): 87–125.

———. 2010. 'What's New and What's Old about the New Sociology of Morality', in S. Hitlin and S. Vaisey (eds), *Handbook of the Sociology of Morality*. New York: Springer, pp. 561–84.

———. 2014. *The Moral Background: An Inquiry into the History of Business Ethics*. Princeton, NJ: Princeton University Press.

Addams, J. 2002. *Democracy and Social Ethics*. Urbana: University of Illinois Press.

Appadurai, A. 1986. (ed.). *The Social Life of Things: Commodities in Cultural Perspective*. Cambridge: Cambridge University Press.

———. 2013. *The Future as Cultural Fact: Essays on the Global Condition*. London: Verso.
Alexander, J.C. 1988. (ed.). *Durkheimian Sociology: Cultural Studies*. New York: Cambridge University Press.
———. 2003. (ed.). *The Meanings of Social Life: A Cultural Sociology*. Oxford: Oxford University Press.
———. 2006. *The Civil Sphere*. Oxford: Oxford University Press.
Back, L. 2021. 'Hope's Work', *Antipode* 53(1): 3–21.
Bargheer, S. 2018. *Moral Entanglements: Conserving Birds in Britain and Germany*. Chicago: University of Chicago Press.
Bargheer, S., and N.H. Wilson. 2018. 'On the Historical Sociology of Morality', *European Journal of Sociology* 59(1): 1–12.
Bauman, Z. 1993. *Postmodern Ethics*. Cambridge: Polity.
———. 1997. *Postmodernity and Its Discontents*. Cambridge: Polity.
Bellah, R.N. et al. 1996. *Habits of the Heart: Individualism and Commitment in American Life*. Berkeley: University of California Press.
Benhabib, S. 1992. *Situating the Self: Gender, Community and Postmodernism in Contemporary Ethics*. Cambridge: Polity Press.
Benzecry, C.E., M. Krause and I.A. Reed. 2017. 'Introduction: Social Theory Now', in C.E. Benzecry, M. Krause and I.A. Reed (eds), *Social Theory Now*. Chicago: University of Chicago Press, pp. 1–17.
Bourdieu, P. 1999a. 'Preface', in P. Bourdieu et al., *The Weight of the World: Social Suffering in Contemporary Society*. Cambridge: Polity Press.
———. 1999b. 'Understanding', in P. Bourdieu et al., *The Weight of the World: Social Suffering in Contemporary Society*. Cambridge: Polity Press.
Bourdieu, P., and L. Wacquant. 1992. *An Invitation to Reflexive Sociology*. Chicago: Chicago University Press.
Cabot, H. 2019. 'The Business of Anthropology and the European Refugee Regime', *American Ethnologist* 46(3): 261–75.
Calhoun, C. 1991. 'Morality, Identity, and Historical Explanation: Charles Taylor on the Sources of the Self', *Sociological Theory* 9(3): 232–63.
Carrithers, M. 2005. 'Anthropology as a Moral Science of Possibilities', *Current Anthropology* 46(3): 433–56.
Cavell, S. 2004. *Cities of Words: Pedagogical Letters on a Register of the Moral Life*. Cambridge, MA: Harvard University Press.
Chakrabarty, D. 2021. *The Climate of History in a Planetary Age*. Chicago: The University of Chicago Press.
Clarke, M. 2015. 'Legalism and the Care of the Self: Shariʻah Discourse in Contemporary Lebanon', in P. Dresch and J. Scheele (eds), *Legalism: Rules and Categories*. Oxford: Oxford University Press, pp. 231–57.
Cooke, M. 2006. *Re-Presenting the Good Society*. Cambridge, MA: MIT Press.
Das, V. 2012. 'Ordinary Ethics', in D. Fassin (ed.), *A Companion to Moral Anthropology*. Malden, MA: Wiley-Blackwell, pp. 133–49.
———. 2015. 'What Does Ordinary Ethics Look Like?', in M. Lambek, V. Das, D. Fassin and W. Keane (eds), *Four Lectures on Ethics: Anthropological Perspectives*. Chicago: HAU Books, pp. 53–125.
Das, V. et al. (eds). 2014. *The Ground Between: Anthropologists Engage Philosophy*. Durham, NC: Duke University Press.
Deegan, M.J. 1988. *Jane Addams and the Men of the Chicago School, 1892–1918*. New Brunswick, NJ: Transaction Books.

Deleuze, G. 1998. *Essays Critical & Clinical*. London: Verso.
Du Bois, W.E.B. 2018. *The Souls of Black Folk*. Gorham, ME: Myers Education Press.
Dumont, L. 1982. 'On Value', *Proceedings of the British Academy* 66: 207–41.
Eiss, P.K., and D. Pedersen. 2002. 'Introduction: Values of Value', *Cultural Anthropology* 17(3): 283–90.
Elder-Vass, D. 2016. *Profit and Gift in the Digital Economy*. Cambridge: Cambridge University Press.
Eriksen, T.H. et al. 2015. '"The Concept of Neoliberalism Has Become an Obstacle to the Anthropological Understanding of the Twenty-First Century"', *Journal of the Royal Anthropological Institute* 21(4): 911–23.
Fassin, D. 2008. 'Beyond Good and Evil? Questioning the Anthropological Discomfort with Morals', *Anthropological Theory* 8(4): 333–44.
_____. 2012. 'Introduction: Toward a Critical Moral Anthropology', in D. Fassin (ed.), *A Companion to Moral Anthropology*. Malden, MA: Wiley-Blackwell, pp. 1–17.
_____. 2017. 'The Endurance of Critique', *Anthropological Theory* 17(1): 4–29.
Frye, M. 2012. 'Bright Futures in Malawi's New Dawn: Educational Aspirations as Assertions of Identity', *American Journal of Sociology* 117(6): 1565–624.
Galison, P. 1997. *Image and Logic: A Material Culture of Microphysics*. Chicago: University of Chicago Press.
Giddens, A. 1990. *Runaway World: How Globalisation is Reshaping our Lives*. London: Routledge.
_____. 1991. *Modernity and Self-Identity: Self and Society in the Late Modern Age*. Cambridge: Polity.
Gilligan, C. 1982. *In a Different Voice: Psychological Theory and Women's Development*. Cambridge MA: Harvard University Press.
Graeber, D. 2001. *Toward An Anthropological Theory of Value: The False Coin of Our Own Dreams*. New York: Palgrave.
_____. 2007. *Possibilities: Essays on Hierarchy, Rebellion, and Desire*. Oakland, CA: AK Press.
_____. 2013. 'It Is Value That Brings Universes into Being', *HAU: Journal of Ethnographic Theory* 3(1): 219–43.
Greenhouse, C.J. 2011. *The Paradox of Relevance: Ethnography and Citizenship in the United States*. Philadelphia: University of Pennsylvania Press.
Gregory, C. 2014. 'On Religiosity and Commercial Life: Toward a Critique of Cultural Economy and Posthumanist Value Theory', *HAU: Journal of Ethnographic Theory* 4(3): 45–68.
Gross, N., and Z. Hyde. 2017. 'Norms and Mental Imagery', in C.E. Benzecry, M. Krause, and I. A. Reed (eds), *Social Theory Now*. Chicago: University of Chicago Press, pp. 361–91.
Han, C. 2012. *Life in Debt: Times of Care and Violence in Neoliberal Chile*. Berkeley: University of California Press.
_____. 2018. 'Precarity, Precariousness, and Vulnerability', *Annual Review of Anthropology* 47: 331–43.
Haraway, D. et al. 2016. 'Anthropologists Are Talking – About the Anthropocene', *Ethnos* 81(3): 535–64.
Hegtvedt, K.A., and H.L. Scheuerman. 2010. 'The Justice/Morality Link: Implied, then Ignored, yet Inevitable', in S. Hitlin and S. Vaisey (eds), *Handbook of the Sociology of Morality*. New York: Springer, pp. 331–60.
Heinich, N. 2020. 'Ten Proposals on Values', *Cultural Sociology* 14(3): 213–32.

Hitlin, S., and S.K. Harkness. 2018. *Unequal Foundations: Inequality, Morality and Emotions Across Cultures*. New York: Oxford University Press.

Hitlin, S., and S. Vaisey. 2010. *Handbook of the Sociology of Morality*. New York: Springer.

———. 2013. 'The New Sociology of Morality', *Annual Review of Sociology* 39: 51–68.

Inglehart, R., and W.E. Baker. 2000. 'Modernization, Cultural Change, and the Persistence of Traditional Values', *American Sociological Review* 65(1): 19–51.

Jackson, M. 2012. *Between One and One Another*. Berkeley: University of California Press.

———. 2013. *The Wherewithal of Life: Ethnics, Migration, and the Question of Well-Being*. Berkeley: University of California Press.

Jeffries, V. 2014. *The Palgrave Handbook of Altruism, Morality, and Social Solidarity: Formulating a Field of Study*. London: Palgrave Macmillan.

Joas, H. 2000. *The Genesis of Values*, trans. G. Moore. Cambridge: Polity Press.

Kapferer, B., and M. Gold. 2018. *Moral Anthropology: A Critique*. New York: Berghahn.

Keane, W. 2003. 'Self-Interpretation, Agency, and the Objects of Anthropology: Reflections on a Genealogy', *Comparative Studies in Society and History* 45(2): 222–48.

———. 2016. *Ethical Life: Its Natural and Social Histories*. Princeton, NJ: Princeton University Press.

———. 2020. 'For the Slow Work of Critique in Critical Times', *Public Books* (September 9).

Knauft, B. 2019. 'Good Anthropology in Dark Times: Critical Appraisal and Ethnographic Application', *The Australian Journal of Anthropology* 30(1): 3–17.

Laidlaw, J. 2002. 'For An Anthropology of Ethics and Freedom', *Journal of the Royal Anthropological Institute* 8(2): 311–32.

———. 2014. *The Subject of Virtue: An Anthropology of Ethics and Freedom*. Cambridge: Cambridge University Press.

———. 2016. 'Through a Glass, Darkly', *HAU: Journal of Ethnographic Theory* 6(2): 17–24.

Lambek, M. (ed.). 2010. *Ordinary Ethics: Anthropology, Language, and Action*. New York: Fordham University Press.

———. 2015. *The Ethical Condition: Essays on Action, Person and Value*. Chicago: The University of Chicago Press.

Lamont, M. 1992. *Money, Morals, and Manners: The Culture of the French and the American Upper-Middle Class*. Chicago: University of Chicago Press.

Lamont, M., and L. Thévenot. 2000. *Rethinking Comparative Cultural Sociology: Repertoires of Evaluation in France and the Unites States*. New York: Cambridge University Press.

Latour, B., I. Stengers, A.L. Tsing and N. Bubandt. 2018. 'Anthropologists Are Talking – About Capitalism, Ecology, and Apocalypse', *Ethnos* 83(3): 587–606.

Lukes, S. 1973. *Individualism*. London: Harper & Row.

———. 2010. 'The Social Construction of Morality?', in S. Hitlin and S. Vaisey (eds), *Handbook of the Sociology of Morality*. New York: Springer, pp. 549–60.

MacIntyre, A. 1981. *After Virtue: A Study in Moral Theory*. London: Bloomsbury Academic.

Malm, A. 2021. *How to Blow Up a Pipeline: Learning to Fight a World on Fire*. London: Verso.

Martineau, H. 1838. *How to Observe Morals and Manners*. London: Charles Knight and Co.

Mattingly, C. 2010. *The Paradox of Hope: Journeys through a Clinical Borderland.* Berkeley: University of California Press.

———. 2014. *Moral Laboratories: Family Peril and the Struggle for a Good Life.* Oakland: University of California Press.

Mattingly, C., and J. Throop. 2018. 'The Anthropology of Ethics and Morality', *Annual Review of Anthropology* 47: 475–92.

Mauss, M. 2007. *The Manual of Ethnography.* Oxford: Berghahn.

Muehlebach, A. 2012. *The Moral Neoliberal: Welfare and Citizenship in Italy.* Chicago: The University of Chicago Press.

Munn, N. 1986. *The Fame of Gawa: A Symbolic Study of Value Transformation in a Massim (Papua New Guinea) Society.* Cambridge: Cambridge University Press.

Nussbaum, M. 1986. *The Fragility of Goodness: Luck and Ethics in Greek Tragedy and Philosophy.* Cambridge: Cambridge University Press.

Ortner, S. 1995. 'Resistance and the Problem of Ethnographic Refusal', *Comparative Studies in Society and History* 37(1): 173–93.

———. 2016. 'Dark Anthropology and Its Others: Theory Since the Eighties', *HAU: Journal of Ethnographic Theory* 6(1): 47–73.

Otto, T., and R. Willerslev. 2013. 'Introduction: "Value as Theory": Comparison, Cultural Critique, and Guerilla Ethnographic Theory', *HAU: Journal of Ethnographic Theory* 3(1): 1–20.

Pandian, A. 2009. *Crooked Stalks: Cultivating Virtue in South India.* Durham, NC: Duke University Press.

Parsons, T., and E.A. Shils. 1951. *Toward a General Theory of Action: Theoretical Foundations for the Social Sciences.* Cambridge, MA: Harvard University Press.

Plummer, K. 2013. 'Epilogue: A Manifesto for Critical Humanism in Sociology: On Questioning the Human Social World', in D. Nehring (ed.), *Sociology: An Introductory Textbook and Reader.* Harlow: Pearson, pp. 489–517.

Robbins, J. 2007. 'Between Reproduction and Freedom: Morality, Value, and Radical Cultural Change', *Ethnos* 72(3): 293–314.

———. 2012. 'On Becoming Ethical Subjects: Freedom, Constraint, and the Anthropology of Morality', *Anthropology of This Century* 12. http://aotcpress.com/articles/ethical-subjects-freedom-constraint-anthropology-morality/.

———. 2013a. 'Beyond the Suffering Subject: Toward an Anthropology of the Good', *Journal of the Royal Anthropological Institute* 19(3): 447–62.

———. 2013b. 'Monism, Pluralism, and the Structure of Value Relations: A Dumontian Contribution to the Contemporary Study of Value', *HAU: Journal of Ethnographic Theory* 3(1): 99–115.

———. 2015. 'On Happiness, Values, and Time: The Long and the Short of It', *Hau: Journal of Ethnographic Theory* 5(13): 215–33.

———. 2016. 'What is the Matter with Transcendence? On the Place of Religion in the New Anthropology of Ethics', *Journal of the Royal Anthropological Institute* 22: 767–808.

———. 2019. 'Values and the Value of Secrecy: Barthian Reflections on Values and the Nature of Mountain Ok Social Process', in K. Wu and R.P. Weller (eds), *It Happens Among People: Resonances and Extensions of the Work of Fredrik Barth.* Oxford: Berghahn, pp. 159–70.

———. N.D. 'On the Prospects for a Comparative Study of the Good: Beyond the Dark in Anthropological Relativism'. https://aias.au.dk/fileadmin/www.aias.au.dk/AIAS_Events/Abstracts_final.pdf

Romero, M. 2020. 'Sociology Engaged in Social Justice', *American Sociological Review* 85(1): 1–30.
Rushdie, S. 2017. *The Golden House*. New York: Random House.
Sahlins, M. 2005. 'Cosmologies of Capitalism: The Trans-Pacific Sector of the "World-System"', in *Culture in Practice*. New York: Zone Books, pp. 415–69.
Sayer, A. 2011. *Why Things Matter to People: Social Science, Values and Ethical Life*. Cambridge: Cambridge University Press.
Seigfried, C.H. 1999. 'Socializing Democracy: Jane Addams and John Dewey', *Philosophy of the Social Sciences* 29(2): 207–30.
Shilling, C., and P. Mellor. 1998. 'Durkheim, Morality and Modernity: Collective Effervescence, *Homo Duplex* and the Sources of Moral Action', *British Journal of Sociology* 49(2): 193–209.
Skeggs, B. 2014. 'Values beyond Value? Is Anything beyond the Logic of Capital?', *British Journal of Sociology* 65(1): 1–20.
Stivers, R. 1996. 'Towards a Sociology of Morality', *International Journal of Sociology and Social Policy* 16(1/2): 1–14.
Strhan, A. 2019. *The Figure of the Child in Contemporary Evangelicalism*. Oxford: Oxford University Press.
Todorov, T. 1992. *The Conquest of America: The Question of the Other*. New York: Harper & Row.
Tomasello, M. 2016. *A Natural History of Human Morality*. Cambridge, MA: Harvard University Press.
Trouillot, M-R. 2003. *Global Transformations: Anthropology and the Modern World*. New York: Palgrave Macmillan.
Tsing, A.L. 2015. *The Mushrooms at the End of the World: On the Possibility of Life in Capitalist Ruins*. Princeton: Princeton University Press.
Urry, J. 2016. *What is the Future?* Cambridge: Polity Press.
Vaisey, S. 2009. 'Motivation and Justification: A Dual-Process Model of Culture in Action', *American Journal of Sociology* 114(6): 1675–715.
Venkatesan, S. (ed.). 2015. 'There is No Such Thing as the Good: The 2013 Meeting of the Group for Debates in Anthropological Theory', *Critique of Anthropology* 35(4): 430–80.
Weeratunge, N. 2010. 'Being *Sadharana*: Talking about the Just Business Person in Sri Lanka', in M. Lambek (ed.), *Ordinary Ethics: Anthropology, Language, and Action*. New York: Fordham University Press, pp. 328–48.
Wilkinson, I., and A. Kleinman. 2016. *A Passion for Society: How We Think about Human Suffering*. Oakland: University of California Press.
Williams, B. 1986. *Ethics and the Limits of Philosophy*. Cambridge: Harvard University Press.
Wolf, E.R. 1982. *Europe and the People without History*. Berkeley: University of California Press.
Zelizer, V. 1994. *Pricing the Priceless Child: The Changing Social Value of Children*. Princeton, NJ: Princeton University Press.
Zigon, J. 2007. 'Moral Breakdown and the Ethical Demand: A Theoretical Framework for an Anthropology of Moralities', *Anthropological Theory* 7(2): 131–50.
_____. 2008. *Morality: An Anthropological Perspective*. Oxford: Berg.
_____. 2017. *Disappointment: Towards a Critical Hermeneutics of Worldbuilding*. New York: Fordham University Press.

Part I
Theoretical Perspectives

1
Where Is the Good in the World?

Joel Robbins

The question that brings us together in this volume – Where is the good in the world? – is an important one for social scientists and humanities scholars to take up. It is important because to the extent that it has been asked before, it has proven hard to answer. Some years ago, I published an article that suggested that anthropologists had in recent decades become so interested in the ways things sometimes go badly in the world that they had often come to neglect the ways people try to create the good (Robbins 2013a). Two lines of thought constituted the background of that argument, but I only laid out one of them explicitly in the article itself. I suggested there that in focusing on the study of suffering, an experience they took to have universal qualities, anthropologists had let go of their long-standing tradition of studying cultural difference and putting their findings to critical use in upending settled Western understandings. In making that argument, I wagered that even if anthropologists had abandoned the impulse to focus on cultural variation in relation to things that they considered universally bad, like suffering, they might still be open to studying differences in the ways people defined and sought to produce the good. So one thing I hoped an anthropology of the good might do was put the study of difference back near the top of the anthropological agenda.

The second line of thought feeding into my call for the development of an anthropology of the good, the one that went unmentioned, was a worry I had that another reason anthropologists were increasingly devoted to studying suffering rather than cultural definitions and social productions of the good was that they had become overly attached to attending to phenomena that they thought of as 'real'. It's a little hard to characterize what I had in mind in saying this – that is one reason I left it out of the original paper – but along with suffering, other things that at least in the recent past anthropologists had tended to treat as real were politics, power, practice, affect, lived experience, the body and the everyday. What got thrown in the box marked unreal were things like culture, structure, meanings, representations and shared ideals. This characterization is very broad – I know – and the moment of hyperattachment to the real may have passed in any case, making it hard for you to test my claims against your current intuitions.[1] But even as this second argument remains a bit vague, I bring it up as a path not taken in my original article because I think the good is precisely one of those things that anthropologists invested in the real are, or until recently were, likely to see as not quite real enough – not quite concretely in the world enough – to deserve their attention.

There are a number of ways anthropologists can raise doubts about the reality of the good. Maybe, for example, the good is just an analytic construction created by experts – scholars, to be sure, but also, say, people like priests and judges – and always after the fact of and as an imposition on ordinary life as lived (Robbins 2016a; Venkatesan 2015). For 'real' people, maybe the good is just not something that figures heavily into how they orient to the world. If that is the case, the argument goes, anthropologists would get a lot closer to the lives they want to study if they set aside the very notion of the good. Or perhaps, another kind of argument has it, the fate of the good is not quite that dire. We might be able to say it does have a sort of quasi-existence in the form of ideals and aspirations some people sometimes hold, but even if this is the case, are not individuals' versions of the good so varied and idiosyncratic and often so malleable and shifting as to be beneath social scientific notice? And even more than this, given how rarely people get to realize their ideals and aspirations – how often realpolitik and other pressing practical considerations conduce to put them out of play – isn't focusing on the good too Pollyannaish for a discipline committed to staying in touch with the real? Doesn't it draw attention away from what truly matters in the situations we study? If, as these arguments suggest, the good may not be real, or not very real, and if its unreal qualities render it something to ignore, then the question of where in the world it is turns out to be a crucial one indeed if one wants to claim, as I do, that it is worth studying.

In sketching an approach to answering the question of where the good is in the world, I should start by confessing that, as it happens, when it comes to the good in particular, I think the champions of the real might in fact be on to something – the good 'really' can be hard to locate, at least in the real social world. In what follows, I want to consider why this is so and also to suggest one theoretical map we might, despite our current difficulties, be able to use to reliably find our way to the good in the worlds we study. In order to get my argument off the ground, I am going to identify the good with the phenomenon of values. By values, I mean not just things and states of affairs that human beings desire, but things and states of affairs that they find desirable. The shift here is one to a second order kind of thinking, whereby people evaluate their desires and decide that only some of them are ones they ought to have. Only some desires, we might put it by way of bringing the social into play, are ones people are comfortable being accountable to others for having. The things that are desired in this second order way are the ones that are desirable, and they thus can be said to be or to realize values. If the good is a matter of values, then the question of where the good is in the world can also be phrased as the question of where in the world values might be.

But this latter question turns out to be controversial in its own right. There is a legitimate contender among metaethical theories – philosophical theories about the nature of the ethical – called error theory (the classic reference is Mackie 1977). Error theory holds that in fact values do not exist in the world as we can know it objectively. People may think they do, but they are wrong about that – they are in error. This is so because as a kind of object, values – which are supposed to be out there in the world but also to make claims of desirability on all subjects, regardless of the particularities of their own interests – are, as John Mackie famously put it, ontologically 'queer' – there are no other real things in the world like them that have this quality of defining desirability regardless of personal interest, and so it is best to say that values do not in objective terms exist. There are some error theorists who further hold to a position called fictionalism, which says it is a good thing people believe that values exist, even if they are wrong about this in empirical terms, because without such belief social life would be impossible, or at least more difficult. But even so, for error theorists, there are in reality no such things as values. If we ask them where values are, they can only answer that they exist in people's imaginations, and nowhere else.

If you look at the history of the idea of values, it is not surprising that error theory ends up being an influential metaethical position. For the very notion of values as a category that includes all kinds of desirable things – the ethically good, the aesthetically beautiful and the epistemologically true, for example – is only as old as the second half of the nineteenth century. It appeared in response to the rise of the scientific materialist worldview. One of the hallmarks of that worldview, as opposed to the various versions of the Aristotelian one that it displaced, is the idea that the material world is devoid of purposes, meanings and values. In the materialist worldview, things just are as they are. From this point of view, you cannot get from fact to value precisely because facts are out there in the world and values are not. The notion of values came together just as this materialist worldview was finally running the table of Western sensibility, and in many respects it was created to justify the continued existence of all those academic fields that were not part of the then as now ascendant natural sciences. In fact, many of the same scholars, mostly German, who launched value theory were also major players in the effort to specify what the humanities and the nascent social sciences could do that the natural sciences could not do better – which was to explore human values and the meaningful cultural formations of which they are assumed to be a key constituent. For our purposes, this story is important because it indicates that as soon as scholars began to talk about values as a kind of phenomena or 'realm' of their own, they also conceded that values were not securely part of the material world of which scientists were the masters and that had recently come to define what would count as meaningfully real. It was this concession that launched the problem of where in the world values might be (for an influential version of this history, see Schnädelbach 1984).

Given this background, it was perhaps predictable that early accounts of values in the social sciences, most famously Max Weber's (1949) methodological pronouncements, assumed that values are first and foremost subjective – they are selective filters that individuals use to construe an in reality purposeless material world in ways that render it meaningful and manageable. But if you look at the record of social scientific approaches to values as it developed after the early neo-Kantian moment in which Weber participated, it becomes clear that scholars – Weber (1946) included, once he developed his analysis of the value spheres of modernity – quickly moved beyond such pure subjectivism and began to argue that values have an objective existence as well. They are inside the person, that is true, but they are also out there in the world, at least in some sense. Here is Karl Mannheim (1943: 16) on this issue from 1943:

> To us values [fn. omitted] express themselves first in terms of choices made by individuals: by preferring this to that I evaluate things. But values do not only exist in the subjective setting as choices made by individuals; they occur also as objective norms, i.e. as advice: do this rather than that. In that case they are mostly set up by society to serve as traffic lights in the regulation of human behaviour and conduct. The main function of these objective norms is to make the members of a society act and behave in a way which somehow fits into the pattern of an existing order. Owing to this dual origin, valuations are partly the expression of subjective strivings, partly the fulfilment of objective social functions.

And here is David Graeber, almost 60 years later, in his 2001 book *Toward an Anthropological Theory of Value*:

> [Value] ... is a term that suggests the possibility of resolving on-going theoretical dilemmas; particularly of overcoming the difference between ... theories that start from a certain notion of social structure, or social order, or some other totalizing notion, and theories that start from individual motivations. (Graeber 2001: 20)

Such efforts to have it both ways – to say values are, as it were, not nowhere but everywhere – look good at first glance. But they beg a lot of questions. Are values the same thing inside of subjects, in the subjective world, as they are outside of subjects, in the objective world? If not, why call both kinds of things values? And how do the subjective and objective link up? Do all subjects in a given social formation orient the same way to the same objective values? Questions like these call for complex social theoretical answers. It is the absence of widely agreed upon versions of such answers, I would suggest, that leads contemporary anthropologists to be inclined to intuit that values are after all probably too ontologically queer to be real, or that they are at least less real than the all too real phenomena we ought to be studying.

If we want to say, despite such arguments, that the good really does exist somewhere – if we want to specify where values are in the world – my argument to this point suggests we will need a theory that faces up to the difficulties of claiming that something is both subjective and objective at the same time. I want to make a brief start in the direction of such a theory here. I am going to do so in two ways. First by looking at how Durkheim solved this very problem, one he construed in pretty much the same way as I have here, and then by stressing that values do not look the same inside subjects as they do in the real world, which helps us to appreciate why we find values queer, without having to take the further step of defining them as unreal.

Here is how Durkheim (1974: 81–82) lays out what he sees as the core problem in defining values:

> One the one hand, all value presupposes appreciation by an individual in relation with a particular sensibility. What has value is in some way good; what is good is desired, and all desire is a psychological state. Nevertheless the values under discussion have the objectivity of things. How can these two characteristics, which at first blush appear contradictory, be reconciled? How, in fact, can a state of feeling be independent of the subject that feels it?

The first thing to note is that Durkheim owns up to the queerness problem right away here by acknowledging that to say that something is objective in the sense of being a real object in the world and that it is also in its very nature a matter of subjective desire is 'contradictory'. He goes about 'reconciling' the problem, as he puts it, by means of a type of argument all of us have seen him make before in relation to religion, though many of us do not realize he also deployed it to deal with the problem of where values are in the world. Indeed, the form of his argument is so familiar that I can summarize it very quickly. Values, Durkheim says, arise when people participate in rituals that lead them to enter the kind of heightened state he calls collective effervescence. The feeling of effervescence, he says, leads people to the experience of being in the presence of something greater, more important and, we might say, more desirable than themselves and the things to which their own individual desires are attached. They come to associate this feeling with the objects, ideas, states of affairs and goals that the ritual promotes, and in this way these things become values for them. Subjects encounter these values out there in the world, in the ritual performances they participate in but, as Roy Rappaport (1999) stresses, they do not imagine that they themselves create. Values are therefore objective. But people also come, through their experience of collective effervescence, to find these values inside themselves, in the form of a subset of their desires that, as I discussed at the outset, they define as desirable and are willing to be held to account for having by others in their social world. This is how, Durkheim argues, values can be at once objective and subjective without contradiction and without, we might add, taking a form so queer as to render their ontological status suspect.

As it happens, one can find lots of evidence in the anthropological literature that there are rituals that turn on the representation of single values, or related clusters of them, and that therefore can serve to link participants to these values in the way Durkheim suggests (Robbins 2015). It is not that such rituals only represent one value or a family of related values throughout their entire course, but that they drive towards the realization of them as their conclusion. Often, in fact, rituals begin by representing disvalues or values that compete with the ones they will ultimately produce. In doing this, they become in effect an argument for the importance of the values they focus upon in relation to other values that they express but ultimately discard or encompass in higher ones. But the teleological quality of rituals – their tendency to aim at producing something or some state of affairs – virtually ensures that they will at least make implicit statements about what is most desirable to bring about.

If one wants a concrete example of how this works, one could do much worse than go back to Victor Turner's (1967) classic article 'Symbols in Ndembu Ritual'. The ritual he analyses – the N'kang'a girls' puberty ritual – has as what the Ndembu call its 'senior symbol', the famous milk tree – a tree that exudes a milky white sap. Turner argues that for the matrilineal Ndembu this tree represents breast milk, breasts more generally, bonds between mothers and children, matriliny, tribal custom and, finally, 'at its highest level of abstraction ... the unity and continuity of Ndembu society' (Turner 1967: 21). The rite leads its participants to understand and value this unity – as Turner puts in terms that self-consciously echo Durkheim's statements on values, it transforms the task of fostering such unity from one people feel is 'obligatory' to one they feel is 'desirable'. This does not mean, as Turner stresses, that the Nkang'a ritual does not also represent in dramatic fashion many of the kinds of conflicts that make the value of unity hard to realize in a society that, like that of the Ndembu, is matrilineal and patrilocal. But as the rite unfolds, it resolves into a clear performance of the possibility of realizing the value of unity despite these obstacles.

From Durkheim, then, we can take the point that values have an objective existence in rituals, and that ritual performance serves to locate these objective values inside the subjects who participate in them. But it is not only in rituals that values find an objective existence. On the basis of arguments I do not have space to make here, I think values also exist in the form of certain kinds of exemplary persons and in some cultural forms – such as myths and other kinds of narratives – that are circulated in social interaction (Robbins 2018). As Randall Collins (2004), drawing on Erving Goffman's (1967) deeply Durkheimian notion of ritual interaction has suggested, all successful sociality tends to be at least lightly ritualized and to produce at least some quanta of collective effervescence, and thus interactions with exemplary people or those in which value-laden cultural forms circulate can also serve to lodge values inside of subjects. These few cases I have mentioned – rituals, exemplary persons, socially circulating cultural forms – surely do not exhaust the objective spaces in which values find a foothold and from which they are instilled in subjects through recognizable kinds of social process – but I hope taken together they serve to indicate some of the ways we might go about finding values really there in the world and, at the same time, existing in forms that render them likely to find their way into people's subjective lives.

But of course not everyone living in a social formation acts in the same way or reports finding the same things desirable, and so it is fair to suspect that saying that they all hold the very same values would be a stretch. Might this be a problem for an attempt like the one I am making here to claim that some values are real in more than a subjective sense? How, one might ask, can this diversity between persons come about if values are really out there in the world and exist in forms that render them likely to get inside of people and shape what people find desirable? The diversity of personal values would seem to argue strongly against their objective existence construed in these terms. Indeed, as I mentioned earlier, this very diversity of values is one reason scholars have often tended to treat them as less than real – as the randomly distributed subjective possessions of individuals with no place in the objective order of things.

This problem of the diversity of values across individuals who live in the same social formation brings us to the second issue I want to tackle here – that of the extent to which values take different forms inside and outside of people. For if values are different outside and inside of subjects, then maybe individual diversity is not a threat to the objective existence of values.

During the 1970s and 1980s, many social theorists tackled problems akin to the ones I am raising here, but they formulated them not as a matter of values but as a more general one of how the 'objective' world of society relates to the 'subjective' one of persons. Most often, they defined these theories as attempts to resolve the structure and agency problem. One thing many of them shared was a tendency to claim that the inner world of individuals tended to match in key respects that of society or culture itself, such that people 'spontaneously' acted in ways that reproduced the structures in which they participated. Consider, in this regard, the accepted understandings of Bourdieu's (1977) notion of habitus, which is perhaps the version of this family of theories that remains most influential today. Habitus has come to mean little more than a carefully calibrated internal version of the objective structures that actors confront. As the anthropologist Claudia Strauss (1992) once put it, understandings of the relationship of structure and agency that are like Bourdieu's in this respect rely on a 'fax' model of socialization. On such understandings, what is outside of subjects gets reproduced perfectly inside of them. In the view of models like these, if people turn out not to hold all the same values, or not to rank the ones they hold in the same way, then one would have to assume these values are not part of the structures these people encounter – not part, that is, of the objective, real world that gets transmitted into those people with the same level of reliability as a fax machine transmits a copy of an original document.

Thus, when faced with the empirical observation that even within the same social formation people hold diverse values, or rank them in different ways, one option is to rely on theories that suggest that the subjective world mirrors the objective one in this fax-like fashion and then to declare values less than real because they are not perfectly mirrored in this way. But another option is to argue that something is wrong with such fax models of the relations of structure and subjectivity. I want to take the second option here and argue that the problem is not that values do not exist in the real world that people confront as objective but is rather with the theoretical assumption that at least in relation to values the inside of people has to look a lot like the outside world.

I have already suggested that people encounter values objectively existing in the world in rituals, exemplary persons and socially circulating narratives that lay out single values or clusters of related ones very clearly and in some detail. Although I will amend this picture in a moment, for now let's take this to be the way values objectively exist in the world – as well-formed representations that exist only in particular kinds of social phenomena. From each ritual's or exemplary person's or value-laden narrative's point of view, only one value is a crucial one, and it is this tightness of focus that allows them to present that value so clearly. But, and here is the rub, every social formation I know of houses more than one ritual, more than one exemplary person and more than one value-laden narrative, and some of these highlight different values than others (Robbins 2016b). This is so because all social formations feature more than one value. I have argued elsewhere, drawing on the work of Louis Dumont (e.g. 1980), that this must be the case, and it is in any event empirically well attested (Robbins 2013b). But here what is crucial is that the situations and social forms in which people encounter values as 'objective' in the way I have suggested simplify this situation of value pluralism by presenting values, as it were, one at a time. This is why they can serve as places in which values have the kind of secure, stable identity our folk and not so folk models ascribe to things that are 'real'.

For persons engaged in social life, then, when they encounter values in what I am calling objective form, they tend to do so one value at a time. That is how the outside world of values comes to them. But inside themselves, where subjects have to formulate or otherwise arrive at ideals, aspirations and plans of action, they often experience the various values they have encountered and internalized as in conflict with each other, demanding compromise and partial realization to fit themselves into the shapes of the lives these subjects lead. We are back to Weber here, for he was finely attuned to what Raymond Aron called the phenomenology of value experience as one of conflict and compromise (see Colen 2011). The neat, objective clarity of values found in rituals, stories and encounters with exemplary persons is muddied inside of persons. Or, to be more precise, even inside of subjects each value may be clear in what it defines as desirable, but for each person there is too much desirability to go around, so choices have to be made, the cultivation of a consistent character becomes an arduous task for those who want to have one, and observers encounter the kind of individual-level value diversity that makes them wonder if values are really real after all. My contention is that precisely because in the theoretical terms I have laid out here we can comprehend the complexity of values as subjective phenomena on the basis of an understanding of how people come to hold a surplus of them through encounters with values in objective form in the world, we can be faithful to this complexity without having to consign values to the status of objects that are too queer to be real.

Let me make two points very briefly in conclusion. The first returns to a promise I made in passing earlier that I would complicate the picture I previously presented of where values are in the real, objective world. I have focused on some of the places where they appear in relatively stable, full form – in rituals, exemplary persons and some kinds of narratives. But of course values are also out there, albeit sometimes in more fragmented, partial forms, everywhere in social life. We can find values in how social formations organize and apportion space, in how they organize and apportion time, in the material and immaterial things they produce, and in the kinds of social relations they construct institutions to foster and reproduce (on institutions and values, see Cooke 2020). And beyond this, in ways I have not touched on here at all, all of these social phenomena not only evidence aspects of the values that organize them, but they also express the hierarchical arrangements that hold between these values. A full-fledged anthropology of the good would have to take all this into account. But this is where things get complex, where partial and compromised value realizations in the objective world that people experience lead scholars to imagine that values may exist as analytic abstractions but simply cannot be real things. I have not focused on this aspect of the objective existence of values here, not because I do not think it is crucial, but because I wanted to make as simple a case as I could for the real existence of values.

And this brings me to my second and final concluding point, which we might take as one of method. I think subjects first encounter values as real and come to find them desirable in those places where they appear in clear form and where, as Durkheim taught us, their encounter with them is invested with uplifting social energy and marked off as special. As researchers, we might want to start there too. Like the people we study, once we encounter values as real, we can go on to complicate how we understand both their objective and subjective existence with less risk of recoiling from this complexity by falling back into the easy assumption that values and the good they define simply are not real features of the world. And if we do that, we may be better able to study meaningful differences in that world by focusing on how people living in different social formations construe and live for the good, regaining our focus on the ways those we study struggle to define and realize their own core concerns.

Joel Robbins is the Sigrid Rausing Professor of Social Anthropology at the University of Cambridge. He has a broad interest in the anthropology of Papua New Guinea, anthropological theory, the anthropology of Christianity, religious change, the anthropology of ethics and morals and the anthropology of values. He is the author of numerous publications, including the books *Becoming Sinners: Christianity and Moral Torment in a Papua New Guinea Society* (2004) and *Theology and the Anthropology of Christian Life* (2020).

Note

1. It is, however, telling in regard to what I am claiming that the most successful recent attempt to rehabilitate difference within anthropology – the ontological turn – has had to do so precisely by claiming that differences are part of the really real.

References

Bourdieu, P. 1977. *Outline of a Theory of Practice*, trans. R. Nice. Cambridge: Cambridge University Press.
Colen, J. 2011. *Facts and Values – A Conversation Between Raymond Aron, Isaiah Berlin and Others*. London: Plusprint.
Collins, R. 2004. *Interaction Ritual Chains*. Princeton: Princeton University Press.
Cooke, M. 2020. 'A Pluralist Model of Democracy', in V. Kaul and I. Salvatore (eds), *What is Pluralism?* London: Routledge, pp. 139–54.
Dumont, L. 1980. *Homo Hierarchicus: The Caste System and its Implications*, trans. M. Sainsbury, L. Dumont and B. Gulati. Chicago: University of Chicago Press.
Durkheim, E. 1974. *Sociology and Philosophy*, trans. D.F. Pocock. New York: Free Press.
Goffman, E. 1967. *Interaction Ritual: Essays on Face-to-Face Behavior*. Garden City: Anchor Books.
Graeber, D. 2001. *Toward an Anthropological Theory of Value: The False Coin of Our Own Dreams*. New York: Palgrave.
Mackie, J.L. 1977. *Ethics: Inventing Right and Wrong*. London: Penguin.
Mannheim, K. 1943. *Diagnosis of Our Times: Wartime Essays of a Sociologist*. London: Routledge & Kegan Paul.
Rappaport, R.A. 1999. *Ritual and Religion in the Making of Humanity*. Cambridge: Cambridge University Press.
Robbins, J. 2013a. 'Beyond the Suffering Subject: Toward an Anthropology of the Good', *Journal of the Royal Anthropological Institute* 19: 447–62.
———. 2013b. 'Monism, Pluralism and the Structure of Value Relations: A Dumontian Contribution to the Contemporary Study of Value', *Hau: Journal of Ethnographic Theory* 3(1): 99–115.

———. 2015. 'Ritual, Value, and Example: On the Perfection of Cultural Representations', *Journal of the Royal Anthropological Institute* 21: S18–S29.

———. 2016a. 'What is the Matter with Transcendence? On the Place of Religion in the New Anthropology of Ethics', *Journal of the Royal Anthropological Society* 22(4): 767–808.

———. 2016b. 'Ritual Pluralism and Value Pluralism: Why One Ritual is Never Enough', *Suomen Antropologi* 41(4): 6–13.

———. 2018. 'Where in the World are Values? Exemplarity, Morality and Social Process', in J. Laidlaw, B. Bodenhorn and M. Holbraad (eds), *Recovering the Human Subject: Freedom, Creativity and Decision*. Cambridge: Cambridge University Press, pp. 174–92.

Schnädelbach, H. 1984. *Philosophy in Germany 1831–1933*. Cambridge: Cambridge University Press.

Strauss, C. 1992. 'Models and Motives', in R.G. D'Andrade and C. Strauss (eds), *Human Motives and Cultural Models*. Cambridge: Cambridge University Press, pp. 1–20.

Turner, V. 1967. *The Forest of Symbols: Aspects of Ndembu Ritual*. Ithaca: Cornell University Press.

Venkatesan, S. (ed.). 2015. 'There is No Such Thing as the Good: The 2013 Meeting of the Group for Debates in Anthropological Theory', *Critique of Anthropology* 35(4): 430–80.

Weber, M. 1946. *From Max Weber: Essays in Sociology*, trans. H.H. Gerth and C.W. Mills. New York: Oxford University Press.

———. 1949. *The Methodology of the Social Sciences*, trans. E.A. Shils and H.A. Finch. New York: The Free Press.

2

Nowhere and Everywhere

Michael Lambek

The world imagined is the ultimate good.

— Wallace Stevens

The title of this chapter is a response to the question posed by the title of the book, and a summary of the argument developed in it. The question itself is far from straightforward, and I am somewhat embarrassed with respect to my ability to clarify exactly what I think – or even what I think I think – about the good as a first step towards answering it. There are the questions (I pose to myself) whether what I think is consistent, either at any given moment or over time, and then whether to be more worried about consistency or inconsistency. There is also the considerable matter of whether I can rise above banality in addressing a topic so worked over, so presumptuous and so romanticized as the good.[1] At the same time, I am grateful for the challenge to clarify and elaborate a position. I am also honoured to be included alongside Joel Robbins. Joel's article 'Beyond the Suffering Subject: Toward an Anthropology of the Good' (2013), which has provoked this volume, has the merits of both clarity and breadth of vision that are his trademarks. Nevertheless, whereas much of the debate around Joel's article has centred on the opposition he ostensibly draws between studying suffering and studying the good, I want to insist that they must be studied *together* and not as two separate fields or projects. (In general, I try to avoid slot machines or gambling on exclusive options.)

I did anticipate one of Joel's insights insofar as I began research in Switzerland in 2002 in part because I thought it might balance the contemporary anthropological picture to examine life in a society characterized, to all appearances, by peace and general well-being. Inevitably, though, the good in Swiss life (landscape, democracy, prosperity, cheese, chocolate …) is offset by depictions of complacency, contracting rural livelihoods, tax evasion, xenophobia, suicide and so on. The paper I published on happiness in Switzerland (Lambek 2015a) was difficult to write and even more difficult to get past referees. I thought one could not write about happiness without some irony, but this appeared to run against expectations of evidence-based scholarship. I have not until now written on the good specifically, but I have written on neighbouring subjects like virtue and value, well-being and, more generally, the ethical (Lambek 2015b), and I think, as Joel does, that the good needs to be contextualized in relation to these concepts.

I turned originally to the ethical not in contrast to suffering but because I thought that social theory was focused almost exclusively on power and interest when human action is more complicated than that. I suggested that people often act and exercise their judgment with respect to what they take to be good or true or right (Lambek 2010), but the further I progressed the more complex the questions became, questions of how to live and how to think, as an anthropologist or philosopher, about how people do in fact live and reflect on their actions and lives. As I came to understand and use the concept (Lambek 2015b), ethics is not only about goodness; 'ethical' conveys in the first instance not good, right or justifiable aims or actions but the inevitability of living with distinctions and the necessity of exercising judgment – acting and living with respect to criteria and prior action and judgment.[2]

In truth, I am not very comfortable with the concept of the good as a substantive noun, nor do I wish to consider it as a Platonic form. The same holds for its counterpart, evil.[3] I am happy to leave metaphysics to theology. I prefer to think of the subject as ethical life, an alternative perspective that begins, in the West, as long ago as Aristotle and that, as ethnography shows, is found in the more – and less – objectified relations and reflections of people at all times and places.

Consider Hans-Georg Gadamer's thoughts on this matter. He writes that Aristotle founded ethics 'as a discipline independent of metaphysics. Criticizing the Platonic idea of the good as an empty generality, he asks instead the question of the humanly good, what is good in terms of human action' (Gadamer 1985 [1960]: 278). Gadamer continues,

> The question is whether there can be any such thing as philosophical knowledge of the moral being of man and what role knowledge plays in the moral being of man. If man always encounters the good in the specific form of the particular practical situation in which he finds himself, the task of moral knowledge is to see in the concrete situation what is asked of it or, to put it another way, the person acting must see the concrete situation in the light of what is asked of him in general. But – negatively put – this means that knowledge which cannot be applied to the concrete situation remains meaningless and even risks obscuring the demands that the situation makes. This state of affairs, which represents the nature of moral reflection, not only makes philosophical ethics a methodologically difficult problem, but also gives the problem of method a moral relevance. (1985 [1960]: 279)

It follows that philosophical ethics must not 'usurp the place of moral consciousness [i.e. the actor's responsibility to know and decide] and yet does not seek either a purely theoretical and 'historical' knowledge but, by outlining phenomena, helps moral consciousness to attain clarity concerning itself' (ibid.).

For Aristotle, ethical knowledge concerns practical judgment and the cultivated disposition to judge wisely (*phronesis*). It is thus distinct from theoretical or scientific knowledge (*episteme*) and from technical knowledge (*techne*). It differs from the former insofar as it is not objective; the knower does not stand apart from what she observes, and in contrast, notably, to mathematics, it is not a matter of knowledge of what is unchangeable or that which depends on proof (Gadamer 1985 [1960]: 280). And it differs from the skill of the craftsman insofar as the latter works to produce a stable object while ethics operates with respect to action and to circumstances that are always in motion.[4]

In consequence, then, for Aristotle moral knowledge differs from episteme and techne in that,

> The antithesis to the seeing of what is right is not error or deception, but blindness. A person who is overwhelmed by his passions suddenly no longer sees in the given situation what is right. He has lost his self-mastery and hence lost his own rightness, ie [*sic*] the right orientation within himself, so that, driven by the dialectic of passion, whatever his passion tells him is right seems so. (Gadamer 1985 [1960]: 287)[5]

This is the perspective that, as I understand, also underpins psychoanalytically informed ethical insight and judgment, and it is consonant with a general focus on character. The first sentence here is particularly fine: 'The antithesis to the seeing of what is right is not error or deception, but blindness.' One could add that this is how Oedipus comes – quite literally – to diagnose himself. However, unlike Oedipus, the blindness in question is temporary and subject to the situation; moreover, it can be partial, a matter of degree rather than absolute. It is part of one's character that in the face of any given circumstance one acts more or less virtuously. Likewise, reflections on character – one's own and those of other people – may themselves be more or less insightful.[6]

All of this suggests that how we discuss the good here and now, in abstract theoretical terms, in a debate or an essay, is something quite different from how virtue manifests practically and in character – and that the former is inadequate to the latter.

* * *

In contrast to the practical or hermeneutic standpoint, some philosophers do approach the subject epistemologically and some conceive of natural good – or address conceiving the good naturalistically. This too can be drawn from Aristotle, as in his concern with the humanly good. Thinking about the value of other animals in relation to humans – a currently fashionable topic – philosopher Christine Korsgaard has elucidated the argument that 'everything that is good is good *for* some creature' (n.d), and hence that value is 'tethered in the sense that the good cannot be cut loose from the creature for whom it is good and still be good'. One might think here of the lion and the lamb. However, Korsgaard leaves room for the fact that while values are tethered and hence relative, it is still possible that some could be absolute, 'good for everyone or from everyone's point of view'. She also distinguishes between a functional and a final sense of good. The first is evaluative, as when we speak of a good argument or a good knife, and the second is the sense in which ends and lives are good. She links these concepts to Aristotle's notion that the function of an organic substance is to maintain its own form – that is, that 'its function is to maintain its own way of functioning'. Animals thus take functional goods as final goods – that is, as ends.[7]

This naturalist argument is intriguing, and I have myself distinguished values from meta-values (Lambek 2015b) somewhat along the lines of Korsgaard's separation between evaluative and final good. Nevertheless, I think the identification of evaluative with functional good takes us only so far.[8] I prefer to think of good in terms of the discernment, discrimination or judgment of particular acts, persons and circumstances according to relevant criteria, without tethering it specifically to biological or social function, hence I take it exclusively in an adjectival rather than nominal form. I sacrifice grounding evaluative, adjectival good in an absolute nominal good, whether naturalistically, metaphysically or theologically derived.[9] 'Ethical value', as Faubion observes, 'is an irreducibly semiotic phenomenon' (2011: 91). Philosophically, I am in this respect a sceptic, recognizing, as Sandra Laugier has put it, that ordinary language is 'founded on nothing but itself'. This, she says, is 'a truth about ourselves ... which [Stanley] Cavell defines as "the absence of foundation or of guarantee for our finitude, for creatures endowed with language and subject to their powers and their weaknesses, subject to their mortal condition"' (Laugier 2005: 87).[10] The adequacy of language is to be found in 'the entanglement, the reciprocal involvement of language and life' (ibid : 87) rather than from some transcendental position.

This takes us to the ordinary. For Cavell, after Wittgenstein, the ordinary is not taken for granted but precariously poised between scepticism and transcendence. He writes:

> One struggle is between criteria (i.e., the ordinary) and skepticism (the desire for the empty, freedom from myself); another is between the ordinary and the aphoristic (the desire for the transcendental, for a satisfaction out of the ordinary that is not provided by the provision of language games, that indeed will eventually be disappointed by the correction in language games). (Cavell 2005: 170)

The ordinary is precarious insofar as criteria don't establish the existence of things with certainty but merely tell us what kind of things they are, 'thus leaving open what kind of issue is posed by the sense of needing some further proof of existence – so that criteria do not "fall short" in the specification of the real' (ibid.: 166).

* * *

So much for a philosophical position. However, anthropologically, it is evident that particular values and criteria for discernment *are* most often grounded in human societies and by means of human institutions (that is to say, human societies attempt to ground or authorize them). They are grounded in the first instance by the process of sanctification, which Roy Rappaport demonstrates is a product of liturgical order – that is, the hierarchy of ritual performative enactments. Sanctity is characterized by 'the quality of unquestionableness imputed by congregations to postulates in their nature objectively unverifiable and absolutely unfalsifiable' (1999: 281). Such postulates are enunciated and accepted in the performance of ritual. It is critical in Rappaport's argument that sacred postulates can only be, in a functional sense, good – that is, effective – when they are, in his terms, informationless, and hence neither verifiable nor falsifiable. This means that they provide no direct specific semantic content to the good or the true. Instead, they are deployed to sanctify diverse specific acts, rendering them as right, true or just, as the case requires. Note that this concerns the grounding of criteria for discernment rather than the actual specification of the good in discrete instances. It is what makes ethical evaluation possible rather than providing the substance of such evaluation itself.

Whereas Cavell's is a kind of post-religious appreciation of the world, for Rappaport liturgical order contains (in the sense that it holds back or limits) the threat of scepticism and provides at least moments of certainty, or a glimpse of what certainty might be or where it might be found. Ritual partakes of and contributes to (sanctifies) the ordinary in the sense just mentioned, and there is no sharp or definitive break between the ordinary and the extraordinary; religion is immanent as much as it is transcendent (Lambek 2013) insofar as the liturgical order lies within and articulates life. The utterance of sacred postulates projects sanctification into ordinary existence, operating in the first instance practically rather than abstractly, grounding action before knowledge.[11]

Interestingly, Rappaport, like Korsgaard, ultimately grounds value and the good in nature, arguing that sanctification is adaptive and emerged alongside the evolution of language. However, 'nature' here applies not to the inner quality or functioning of individual species (whether viewed nominally or collectively), and certainly not to genes or to some kind of essence, but rather at the level of populations and the ecosystem, ultimately to the world as an interconnected whole.[12] The final good for Rappaport is adaptiveness – that is, the property of cybernetic systems (ecosystems) to remain flexible. Flexibility, in turn, is understood as 'a product of [both] versatility and orderliness' (1999: 418). What is bad, because inflexible and hence maladaptive, is when the sacred is semantically over-specified – that is, when sacred postulates are rendered too concrete, when, under certain political (e.g. West Bank settlers) or economic regimes (e.g. capitalism), there is a process of 'over-sanctification' to meet particular interests (1999: 440–44). In other words, to raise content-specific propositions to the level of ultimate sacred postulates is to disorder the liturgical hierarchy. Rappaport refers to this as 'apotheosizing the specific and material' and labels it idolatry. Put another way, to over-specify the nature (contents) of the sacred (and hence of the true and the good) is not only to validate some interests at the expense of others; it is to rigidify and threaten the adaptiveness (continued existence) of the system as a whole. Rappaport's model becomes ever more salient as the global ecological crisis unfolds.

Rappaport further addresses the opposition between good and evil as one of truth and falsity. Pernicious lies include states of affairs that violate the truths established performatively in liturgical orders. Even worse are acts that undercut the very basis on which truth is established (as seen, for example, in Donald Trump's continual adverting to 'false news', eroding the division of powers and taking sanctification in vain). Idolatry itself is 'adaptively false' as opposed to 'adaptively true' (1999: 443–44). Thus, while the virtues of Rappaport's holism can also be turned against him to suggest he ignores or underestimates agency, conflict and contingency – in short, history – the criticism is not fully accurate [13] Ultimately, Rappaport's naturalism rests on what he calls a 'fundamental contradiction' of humanity, namely that we are 'a species that lives and can only live, in terms of meanings it itself must fabricate in a world devoid of intrinsic meaning but subject to physical law' (1999: 451). That is a profound observation.[14]

* * *

I began by distinguishing intellectualist and metaphysical concerns with the good from an account of ethical life. I want to be clear that many of the concerns I have raised with respect to the good qua abstract object or foundational value apply equally to the concept of ethics writ large. Just as we might be suspect of singular, insistent, absolute, overly specified and overly consistent articulations of the good, and turn instead to practical invocations and discrimination, drawing contextually, dynamically and ecologically from multiple criteria and incommensurable values, so we might be suspect of arguments that posit ethics as a discrete phenomenon or domain, as a clear and ordered set of rules and principles that everyone should agree on, or as a bounded system of thought or practice that could be objectively abstracted from the flow of life and that could be evaluated for consistency or completeness.[15]

To invoke the ethical and to apply it adjectivally or adverbially in my sense is precisely *not* to claim that there is a specific domain in human life called ethics or that in order for people to act and think ethically they must identify their actions as such, distinguish them specifically from other kinds of action, or justify them in specifically ethical terms. We can distinguish judicious from injudicious ideas and acts, and we do describe and reflect on them in terms of their wisdom, tact, justice, piety, gracefulness and, yes, goodness. In other words, I suggest that we readily make ethical discriminations without having to objectify the idea of ethics (or morality or the good) itself. The ethical is immanent within life before it becomes objectified (metaphysically, socially, historically) over it (Lambek 2015b). Many writers on ethics seem to assume that is not, or should not be, the case – and worry that we risk acting unethically or amorally if we do not acknowledge explicitly that what is at issue is something called ethics. It is as if this opens the abyss of relativism or egoism. For such writers, one could say that the good is founded on or guaranteed by ethics.

I take support here from Bernard Williams, when he argues, in the magnificent *Shame and Necessity* (1993), against singling out the moral as something specific or special and against the idea that cultures that do not do so are somehow lacking by comparison to 'us'. Williams writes,

> It is said that we make a lot of the distinction between the moral and the nonmoral and emphasize the importance of the moral. But how far, and in what ways, is this really true of our life, as opposed to what moralists say about our life? Do we even understand what the distinction is, or how deep it really goes?'

Williams continues, 'There is perhaps no single question on which an understanding of the Greeks can join more helpfully with reflection on our own experience. We paralyse both that understanding and that reflection if we simply take it for granted that the distinction is at once deep, important, and self-explanatory' (1993: 92).

Cora Diamond (2000: 153) makes a similar point when she says, as recently cited by Veena Das (2015: 116), that

> Just as logic is not, for Wittgenstein, a particular subject with its own body of truth, but penetrates all thought, so ethics has no particular subject matter. Rather, an ethical spirit, an attitude to the world and life, can penetrate any world and thought. So the contrast I want is between ethics conceived as a sphere of discourse among others in contrast with ethics tied to everything there is or can be, the world as a whole, life.

Williams turns to the ancient Greeks in a manner explicitly analogous to the way many anthropologists turn to other cultures and for much the same reasons. Contrast and comparison offer a means to contextualize our thoughts and the claims we make about them. And this contextualization in turn circles back to how we can understand those other cultures now freed of our preconceptions about ethics or the good. Anthropology proceeds by means of this hermeneutic spiral. Importantly, this means we neither simplistically embrace cultural relativism nor simplistically reject it; the effect of hermeneutics is rather to relativize relativism. That is the only way to understand the anthropological stance, especially with respect to such matters as locating the good.

What then is ethnographic realism? How do we identify the ethical in Williams' or Diamond's sense? One axis (among several) along which to think about this is whether a better portrait of the ethical dimension of human life is one that appears to be unselfconscious (as in many classic ethnographies) or one that draws attention to itself, whether that is the actors drawing attention to themselves, in front of the ethnographer, as it were, or whether it is the anthropologists drawing attention to themselves, in front of the reader (by means of objectivism, elaborate or obscure theory, rhetorical flourishes, agonized reflexivity, sanctimoniousness, etc.)?[16] It is often remarked that the truly ethical person or ethical act is one that does not draw attention to itself. As the Sakalava saying has it, 'full containers don't rattle *(feno tsy mikobaña)*'. However, these are not generally mutually exclusive alternatives; presentation entails careful judgment. Here aesthetic judgment is closely connected to the balancing among alternative or incommensurable criteria and values intrinsic to, and manifest in, practical judgment (Lambek 2015b). Indeed, aesthetic and ethical judgment are not fully distinguishable from one another. Hence, a possible response to the question of where is the good in the world or, perhaps, where in the world is the good would be to say that one place it manifests is in (or as) beauty.[17] Similarly, in our life with concepts we exercise judgment in how to deploy them (for example, use of concepts like ethics); hence another place where the good may be observed is in the sensitive and sensible deployment of concepts – that is, in thinking itself (Diamond 1988; Lambek 2021).

* * *

One way to summarize this far too rapid tour of thinkers and these fragments of argument is to say that rather than look for the good, for ethics, or, for that matter, for evil, as reified abstractions, idealized metaphysical categories, or natural objects – or even as socially produced objects – perhaps we should simply begin with the ordinary and be satisfied with what we can understand of the complexity and simplicity of life as it is lived. The aim, as Wittgenstein says, lies in 'seeing life itself'.

Of course, this is mediated, and ever more so, by 'the colonization of life worlds' as Habermas (1987 [1981]) compellingly put it. One instrument of such colonization is the regime of ethics, constituted through authoritative rule-books and protocols, ostensible experts, and multiple objectifications. One effect of this colonization of our life world is to teach us that we act either out of instrumental reason or out of ideal goodness, from either selfishness or selflessness (see Parry 1986 on the gift), or perhaps either carelessly or carefully, according to mutually exclusive either/or logics. In a Christian version, we are either sinners or saints; in a legal version, either guilty or innocent. To attend to ordinary ethical life is in part to challenge these binary oppositions and their effects.

We can explore what in practice are the relations between narrating, reflecting on, philosophizing, or turning into art or theory what is done, what has been done, and what is to be done. To art and theory, ethnographers add talk, as expressed in local genres of speech and as acts are put under description (Lambek 2021). We attend as well to the verbally inexpressible or relatively unobjectified forms of response manifest in embodied practices, infinitesimal shifts in tone or posture, or stronger ones of feeling (joy, remorse, disgust, etc.). There is also the public arena with its dynamic interplay, the confluence or clash of the ethical and the political (Arendt 1998 [1958]; Fassin 2015).

We can also explore what in given cultural and historical circumstances and between particular social positions have been considered good, right or appropriate relations between action and response, speech and silence. We can do so with respect to individual lives and character and with respect to communities and traditions – comparing Athens and Sparta, Athens and Jerusalem, Baghdad and Rome, Lhasa and Kyoto, Cambridge and Königsberg. We can compare Pueblo with Plains and West Coast Amerindian societies, drawing on the language that a nineteenth-century German philosopher transformed from a pair of ancient Greek gods (Benedict 2005 [1934]).[18] Or we can dive deeply into how the concepts and feelings articulated in a particular society give rise to practices we might otherwise find ethically incomprehensible, as in Michelle Rosaldo's exposition of Ilongot headhunting (1980). Each of these articulations, juxtapositions and lines of comparison opens horizons along which particular criteria, concepts, values, language games and experiences are set off, complemented, compromised, balanced and challenged by others.

As subjects and as scholars, we orchestrate and reflect on such articulations more or less finely, with more or less perspicuity. We can glimpse insight and blindness in human lives, adaptiveness or destructiveness in ways of life. But we need to keep in mind, as Veena Das (2015) puts it, the fundamental opacity of our experience and of the world and that (following Cavell) having a life together in language draws on trust in others rather than in an external correspondence between language and world. This is one way in which to see that ethics (as engagement, as practical judgment, as attention, as care) is immanent to life. As Das also suggests, we are haunted by a sense of complicity in a world in which bad things happen. Goodness here could be simply a matter of non-cruelty in our relations with others in the face of what she and James Laidlaw 'agree ... in both Jainism and Hinduism ... [to be] a response to the intolerable realization that one cannot live without committing some violence on the world' (2015: 109). Claims concerning the good could also be ways to evade this recognition.

* * *

A concept central to my argument against substantializing or over-specifying the good is that of the incommensurability of terms and values. Without directly addressing incommensurability (a concept too often confused with contradiction or incompatibility), I would like to close with a salutary remark from John Austin, who is wise and witty even in his footnotes. Offering 'a general warning in philosophy', he says:

> It seems to be too readily assumed that if we can only discover the true meanings of each of a cluster of key terms, usually historic terms that we use in some particular field (as, for example, 'right', 'good' and the rest in morals), then it must without question transpire that each will fit into place in some single, interlocking, consistent, conceptual scheme. Not only is there no reason to assume this, but all historical probability is against it, especially in the case of a language derived from various civilizations as ours is. We may cheerfully use, and with weight, terms which are not so much head-on incompatible as simply disparate, which just do not fit in or even on. Just as we cheerfully subscribe to, or have the grace to be torn between, simply disparate ideals – why *must* there be a conceivable amalgam, the Good Life for Man? (1970: 203, n. 1)

Austin is, first of all, indicating, after Wittgenstein, that the meaning of a term like 'good' can only be found in its use (there is no final or 'true' meaning) and that it is likely to have distinct and incommensurable ('simply disparate') uses in a variety of fields or language games. One could, then, perhaps think of 'the good' as a polythetic class. But more strongly than this, Austin is making the astute observation that ethical life is in general not constituted by living to a single ultimate end or meta-value and that ethical reflection and practice do not proceed systematically. We have 'the grace to be torn between ... disparate ideals', and there is no reason – empirical, logical, practical, foundational – or indeed 'ethical' – for positing or anticipating otherwise. Ethical life is neither consistent nor complete. Alasdair MacIntyre (1984) may give us brilliant depictions of past ethical systems, ostensibly far more coherent than our own, but these are historical idealizations. Derived from the texts of philosophers and poets rather than from practice, they can only be abstractions from the hurly-burly of life. Attempts to impose fully coherent systems clearly expose the risks entailed by Rappaport's over-sanctification, namely inflexibility, not to mention various forms of prejudice, interest and cruelty.

In sum, in response to the question David Henig and Anna Strhan have posed in the title of this book, I would say it is a mistake to conceive of the good as an object whose specific location we may discover or a concept whose essence or composition we can come to know better than we have in the past or do now. Instead, as I have tried to show, I conceive of the good as *both* an abstract and semantically empty value, or perhaps a meta-value, whose specific attributes are unfixed ('nowhere'), *and* as a practical judgment whose application is ubiquitous but circumstantial ('everywhere'). From a naturalist perspective at its broadest, the good lies in adaptive ecosystemic flexibility, which means again that it is no one thing to which one can point. The good is not something we find out there in the world, in a specific location, as it were. On occasion, we realize goodness in practice, but as a concept it is something we can only debate.[19] The fact that the debate is borderless and endless does not invalidate it. Sometimes it is good to be complacent, and sometimes it is good to be idealistic, but sometimes it is good (better?) – perhaps even necessary – to acknowledge blindness, complexity, incommensurability, inconsistency, incompleteness, relativity and the final undecidability of life.

Michael Lambek has held a Canada Research Chair in the Anthropology of Ethical Life at the University of Toronto Scarborough. He has conducted long-term ethnographic fieldwork in the Indian Ocean islands of Mayotte and Madagascar. He is currently interested in the intersection of anthropology with philosophy and especially in articulating ethical dimensions of action. He is the author of numerous books, including most recently *The Ethical Condition: Essays on Action, Person, and Value* (2015), *Island in the Stream: An Ethnographic History of Mayotte* (2018) and *Concepts and Persons* (2021).

Notes

1. This is a revised draft of a talk first delivered at the conference on 'Where is the good in the world?' held at the University of Kent, Canterbury, May 18–19, 2016. Thanks to David Henig and Anna Strhan for the invitation and to David for much conversation, to the Canada Research Chairs for providing time to write, to participants at the event, and to a perspicacious referee of an earlier draft. I maintain some of the informality of address and polemical tone that the original occasion of 'debate' encouraged. This chapter is somewhat idiosyncratic and is definitely not meant as a review of the anthropological literature on ethical life.
2. By judgment I do not mean either legal or moralistic pronouncements but the way we must make our way through incommensurable and sometimes incompatible alternatives, jumping in or holding back, attempting to live virtuously as the balance between opposing vices, tuning our attention, and doing so both in each circumstance and with respect to longer trajectories.
3. See now Olsen and Csordas 2019, whose otherwise useful overview mixes instances of actual evil, attributions of evil and symbols of evil, a confusion that seems almost intrinsic to the subject yet somewhat less characteristic of discussions of the good. There is also the open question of how one moves from judgments of what is bad or wrong to the absolute finality that evil ('pure evil') connotes.

4. Gadamer's is but one reading of Aristotle and mine but one reading of Gadamer. One referee has argued that I fail to 'acknowledge that Aristotle himself does not ever propose that ethics involves the work of the self on itself. Aristotle's rigid distinction between technē and praxis blocks such a possibility ...'. In fact, I am not arguing that Aristotle does so, or that work on the self is necessarily the sole or exemplary way to understand ethics; I stand to one side from the Foucauldian-inspired positions so admirably developed by James Faubion (2011) and James Laidlaw (2014). On the difference between our respective but not antithetical positions, see the insightful essay by Cheryl Mattingly (2012).
5. There is much here about passion that begs discussion, but this is not the place. From within a Freudian tradition, Stephen Mitchell (1988) has well criticized the 'metaphor of the beast within'. Note the issue for Aristotle is one of 'self-mastery' and its lapses, not of innate goodness or badness. For a different kind of approach to the relation of passion and ethics, see Lambek (2010).
6. Among such reflections are whether certain people are not merely momentarily blind but dispositionally vicious.
7. As Faubion notes, 'Aristotle is often classified as an ethical "naturalist" for regarding ethical development and the achievement of the good life as the development and consummation of human nature. He is, however, very much [also?] a nurturist in regarding the realization of the virtues as the result entirely of pedagogy and practice' (2011: 55). It is striking how different this is from most other animals – of whom one can hardly speak either of moral cultivation or of acting in ways that would be counter to their functional good or the consummation of their nature.
8. There is also the matter of whether 'functional good' for any given species, and notably our own, is not without heterogeneity and that the virtues are not as harmonious and consistent with one another as Aristotle saw them.
9. To quote Faubion again, 'Aristotle himself points out the inescapable plurality of "the good." Once again, the anthropologist of ethics is indebted to his wisdom' (2011: 100).
10. Laugier does not give a source for this quotation.
11. Rappaport is not always explicit on this point.
12. Rappaport (and Gregory Bateson) were post-humanist well *avant la lettre* and more rigorously (and less sentimentally) so than many who have come after.
13. For ethics from the perspective of a more historicizing version of systems theory, see Faubion's (2011) revision of Luhmann.
14. Like Aristotle's nature and nurture, it could be said to both acknowledge and transcend the opposition between nature and culture, to go precisely *'par-delà'* (see Descola 2005).
15. Of course, we live with attempts to do precisely that. See, for example, Bernard Williams' (1985) distinction between morality and ethics. On the objectification of ethics, see Keane (2016). My argument has parallels with that of Talal Asad (1993) with respect to 'religion'. Didier Fassin (2015) likewise is disinclined to objectify the ethical; in his case because, as he shows, it is continuous with the political.
16. Compare Michael Fried's reflections (2008) on absorption and theatricality as alternate modes of representation in painting and photography.
17. In Malagasy, the word *tsara* covers both 'good' and 'beautiful'. Of course, we have to take into account the way discernment of beauty (taste) expresses and reinforces forms of social distinction (Bourdieu 2010 [1979]) – but this applies to the discernment of virtue as well.
18. The reference is to Nietzsche's distinction in *The Birth of Tragedy* between Apollonian and Dionysian tendencies.
19. In Gallie's (1956) famous phrase, it is an 'essentially contested concept'.

References

Arendt, H. 1998 [1958]. *The Human Condition*. Chicago: University of Chicago Press.
Asad, T. 1993. *Genealogies of Religion*. Baltimore: Johns Hopkins University Press.
Austin, J.L. 1970. *Philosophical Papers*. J.O. Urmson and G.J. Warnock (eds). New York: Oxford University Press.
Benedict, R. 2005 [1934]. *Patterns Of Culture*. New York: Mariner Books.
Bourdieu, P. 2010 [1979]. *Distinction: A Social Critique of the Judgment of Taste*. London: Routledge.
Cavell, S. 2005. 'Performative and Passionate Utterance', in S. Cavell, *Philosophy the Day After Tomorrow*. Cambridge, MA: Harvard University Press, pp. 155–91.
Das, V. 2015. 'What Does Ordinary Ethics Look Like?', in M. Lambek, V. Das, D. Fassin and W. Keane (eds), *Four Lectures on Ethics: Anthropological Perspectives*. Chicago: HAU Books, pp. 53–125.
Descola, P. 2005. *Par-delà nature et culture*. Paris: Gallimard.
Diamond, C. 1988. 'Losing Your Concepts', *Ethics* 98(2): 255–77.
_____. 2000. 'Ethics, Imagination, and the Method of Wittgenstein's *Tractatus*', in A. Crary and R. Read (eds), *The New Wittgenstein*. London: Routledge, pp. 149–73.
Fassin, D. 2015. 'Troubled Waters: At the Confluence of Ethics and Politics', in M. Lambek, V. Das, D. Fassin and W. Keane (eds), *Four Lectures on Ethics: Anthropological Perspectives*. Chicago: HAU Books, pp. 175–210.
Faubion, J. 2011. *An Anthropology of Ethics*. Cambridge: Cambridge University Press.
Fried, M. 2008. *Why Photography Matters as Art as Never Before*. New Haven: Yale University Press.
Gadamer, H-G. 1985 [1960]. *Truth and Method (Wahrheit und Method)*. New York: Crossroad.
Gallie, W.B. 1956. 'Essentially Contested Concepts', *Proceedings of the Aristotelian Society*, New Series 56: 167–98.
Habermas, J. 1987 [1981]. *Theory of Communicative Action, Volume Two: Lifeworld and System: A Critique of Functionalist Reason*, trans. Thomas A. McCarthy. Boston, MA: Beacon Press.
Keane, W. 2016. *Ethical Life: Its Natural and Social Histories*. Princeton: Princeton University Press.
Korsgaard, C. N.D. 'Animal Selves and the Good', Handout for talk at Centre for Ethics. University of Toronto. March 14, 2016.
Laidlaw, J. 2014. *The Subject of Virtue*. Cambridge: Cambridge University Press.
Lambek, M. 2010. 'How To Make Up One's Mind: Reason, Passion, and Ethics in Spirit Possession', in M. Goldman and J. Matus (eds), Special issue on Models of Mind, *University of Toronto Quarterly* 79(2): 720–41.
_____. 2013. 'Introduction: What is "Religion" for Anthropology?', in J. Boddy and M. Lambek (eds), *A Companion to the Anthropology of Religion*. Boston: Wiley-Blackwell, pp. 1–32.
_____. 2015a. 'Le Bonheur Suisse, Again', in H. Walker and I. Kavedzija (eds), Special issue The Values of Happiness: Ethnographic Perspectives on Living Well, *Hau* 5(3): 111–34.
_____. 2015b. *The Ethical Condition*. Chicago: University of Chicago Press
_____. 2021. *Concepts and Persons*. The Tanner Lecture 2019. Toronto: University of Toronto Press.
Laugier, S. 2005. 'Rethinking the Ordinary: Austin *after* Cavell', in R. Goodman (ed.), *Contending with Stanley Cavell*. Oxford: Oxford University Press, pp. 82–99.

MacIntyre, A. 1984. *After Virtue*. 2nd ed. Notre Dame, IN: University of Notre Dame Press.
Martin, P. 2015. 'Review: *The Whole Harmonium: The Life of Wallace Stevens*', *The Economist*, 9 April, 83.
Mattingly, C. 2012. 'Two Virtue Ethics and the Anthropology of Morality', *Anthropological Theory* 12(2): 161–84.
Mitchell, S. 1988. *Relational Concepts in Psychoanalysis*. Cambridge, MA: Harvard University Press.
Olsen, W.C., and T.J. Csordas. 2019. 'Introduction', in W.C. Olson and T.J. Csordas (eds), *Engaging Evil: A Moral Anthropology*. New York: Berghahn, pp. 1–31.
Parry, J. 1986. 'The Gift, the Indian Gift and the "Indian Gift"', *Man* (N. S.) 21: 453–73.
Rappaport, R. 1999. *Ritual and Religion in the Making of Humanity*. Cambridge: Cambridge University Press.
Robbins, J. 2013. 'Beyond the Suffering Subject: Toward an Anthropology of the Good', *Journal of the Royal Anthropological Institute* 19(3): 447–62.
Rosaldo, M. 1980. *Knowledge and Passion: Ilongot Notions of Self and Social Life*. Cambridge: Cambridge University Press.
Williams, B. 1985. *Ethics and the Limits of Philosophy*. Cambridge MA: Harvard University Press.
_____. 1993. *Shame and Necessity*. Berkeley: University of California Press.

3

Between Durkheim and Bauman
A Relational Sociology of Morality in Practice

Owen Abbott

As the chapters in this book attest, there has been a recent resurgence of interest in morality as an object of study in various disciplines in the social sciences, notably anthropology, sociology and also social geography (see for example Hitlin and Vaisey 2013; Lambek 2010; Smith 1997). In sociology, after being out of favour for several decades, there have been renewed attempts to provide properly sociological theories of morality (Abbott 2020; Joas 2000), while empirical sociological research is increasingly willing to address topics of family relationships, social movements, political participation and contestation, inequalities, and even social practices themselves, in moral terms (Abend 2013). Such sociological approaches take morality to refer to 'understandings of good and bad, right and wrong, worthy and unworthy that vary between persons and between social groups' (Hitlin and Vaisey 2013: 55). This resurgence has coincided with 'relational' approaches to sociology becoming the dominant paradigm for understanding social life and social phenomena (Prandini 2015). The ascendency of relational sociology has much to do with its capacity to undermine both holist and individualist modes of thinking simultaneously. It is able to cut between these traditional dualistic stances of social theorizing by conceptualizing social phenomena not as substances external to interaction, but as being relationally produced and dynamically unfolding in the interdependent practice of relationally-moulded individuals. Likewise, relational sociology does not reduce social phenomena to the actions of detached subjects, but rather sees individuals and their agency as being the product of the relations in which they are embedded. However, the value of relational sociology to sociological approaches to morality is so far underexplored. In this chapter, I argue that relational sociological approaches are of specific value to social scientific studies of the good for two main reasons.

Firstly, such approaches allow us to conceptualize morality in terms that avoid the dualistic tendencies towards holism and individualism that have often seeped into sociological conceptualizations of morality. As will be discussed through critiques of Emile Durkheim's (holist) and Zygmunt Bauman's (individualist) attempts to formulate sociological approaches to morality, such bifurcating accounts become problematic for understanding moral action in a way that coheres with how morality is engaged with in practice. This brings us to the second contribution relational approaches can make to understanding morality sociologically. Namely, an interactionist relational sociology allows us to understand morality as a social phenomenon that is enacted, sustained and transformed in interactional practice. By conceptualizing social phenomena as being produced and dynamically unfolding in the interdependent interaction of relationally-entangled individuals, relational sociology provides a theoretical framework that avoids the dualistic separation of the individual and social context in how morality is conceptualized, and it provides a basis for viewing morality as being principally engaged with in the relationally-entangled doing of social life.

Relational Sociology

Relational sociology argues that the 'most appropriate analytic unit for the scientific study of social life is the network of social relations and interactions between actors' (Crossley 2011: 1). The language of relations is used to explain social phenomena on both a micro and a macro scale in a way that subverts the necessity of reverting to outmoded sociological dualisms (holism-individualism, structure-agency), which have inhibited the capacity of social theories to explain social phenomena in a way that coheres with how social practice is actually lived in the interactional realities of everyday life.

The success of relational sociology lies in its capacity to undermine both sides of dualistic assumptions in social theorizing simultaneously. Against theories oriented towards individualism or subjectivism, or which designate agency in terms of individualistic agentive capacities, it is argued that individuals, their agency, and their action, are necessarily constituted in social relations (Burkitt 2016). Against perhaps stronger 'holist' conventions in sociology of referring to 'society' in terms of substantive social structures, relational sociology postulates that 'society' and 'social structures' should be understood as continually emergent relations that exist between interdependent interactors (Dépelteau 2008). That is, the relational view conceptualizes 'both individuals and larger formations in which they participate (like collectivities, institutions, and social systems) as belonging to the same order of reality, a relational order' (Powell and Dépelteau 2013: 3). This manoeuvre posits the individual as inextricably constituted by social relations, while concurrently seeing 'social structures' as being comprised of the relations that exist between interacting individuals, and thus argues that social phenomena, at all levels of analysis, are constituted by nothing more than interdependent social relations (Powell 2013).

Broadly construed social phenomena, including moral phenomena, are reconceptualized as being constituted and maintained across vast, historically-emergent networks of interaction, which manifest features of our social environments such as languages, institutions, cultural practices and so forth (Crossley 2011). Such phenomena are conceptualized in processual terms, as being produced through ongoing interaction, and thus as being ever in the making (Schatzki 2016). Yet this is not to imply that social phenomena are thus the result of individual action, because it is within these networks that individuals and their actions are themselves constituted. Relational approaches deliver this argument on several grounds. Firstly, individuals, their subjectivities, dispositions and also their 'higher' faculties for social and moral evaluation and judgement are fundamentally moulded within the relational interactions that comprise their socialization, which also embeds the individual within the practices and networks that make up their social world (Mead 1934). Secondly, individual action is given form and course by the orders of practice and institutional arrangements within which it is enacted (Elias 1991). Significantly, relational approaches also emphasize how actions emerge intersubjectively in interaction between actors who 'profoundly affect each other as they interact' (Barnes 2000: 64). The malleability of conceptualizing phenomena in terms of relations, rather than static 'structures', allows relational approaches to facilitate explanations that recognize that the subjectivities and actions of reflexively-capable individuals are formed, moulded and enacted across a multitude of emergent, variable and indeterminate interactional settings, which are engaged with by actors from very different social positions.

In addressing the question 'where is the good in the world?', I argue that the processual picture offered by relational approaches enables us to see how moral phenomena – including values, obligations and understandings of the good – are shared and sustained, but also remoulded, as they are variably engaged with and enacted by individuals in practice. Such a view thus allows plural and intersecting understandings of the good to be depicted as fundamentally socially constituted, but also as being variably engaged with by differentiated individuals in relation to the specific and intersubjectively emergent situations in which they are acting. This perspective thus coheres with increasingly common arguments for conceptualizing morality in terms of practice. Such arguments emphasize morality as a phenomenon that is constituted and enacted within intersubjective practice by individuals whose moral understandings, values and actions are likewise conceptualized as being moulded and engaged with in relationally-entangled interaction. This then extends the argument already engrained in revived sociological (e.g. Sayer 2005), anthropological (e.g. Lambek 2015) and some philosophic (e.g. Herman 2000) stances on morality that suggests that 'everyday moralities' are an ordinary and integral aspect of participation in social life, and that it is at the level of ordinary practice that the majority of moral action occurs.

Dualistic Moral Theorizing

The dualistic separation of society and the individual that relational approaches criticize in social theory in general has also played out in dominant sociological accounts of morality, with the sociologies of morality developed by Durkheim and Bauman exemplifying holist and individualist accounts respectively (Shilling and Mellor 1998). The shortcomings of these accounts for providing a picture of morality that coheres with how it is engaged with in practice not only point to the need for a relational approach to moral theorizing, but also demonstrate why ordinary practice should guide how sociology conceptualizes of morality.

We begin with Durkheim, whose work established many of the arguments for studying morality as a social phenomenon. For Durkheim, morality expressly exists as a 'social fact', and it should be studied as such. He contended that morality exists as binding 'rules that in effect determine behaviour' (Durkheim 1982: 69), and sociology should thus analyse the concrete forms that 'moral reality' takes at a societal level (Durkheim 1979a: 92). This reflects Durkheim's broader ontological and epistemological arguments regarding what social phenomena are and how they should be considered, which 'rests wholly on the basic principle that social facts must be studied as things, that is, as realities external to the individual' (Durkheim 1979b: 37–38). 'Moral facts' are accordingly conceptualized by Durkheim as consisting of definite 'rules for action' (1984: xxv) that constitute 'the totality of ties which bind each of us to society' (1984: 398). Societies are comprised of the binding force of moral rules, and individual consciousness is formed as a product of the social and moral facts that encompass the society of which the individual is part (Durkheim 1984). Consequently, for Durkheim, moral rules have authority over individuals and command their action not necessarily because of positive or adverse consequences, but because individuals are compelled to adhere to them as a result of their existence in a society in which these rules take an institutionalized form (Hookway 2015).

Durkheim's recognition that morality cannot be understood in abstraction from the societal context from which it takes its force was comparatively radical for its time, and this recognition provides the basis for sociological approaches to morality still (Junge 2001). Yet, the position he assumes is archetypical of a holist position on morality: it depicts morality as existing as binding rules of conduct that are set over and above the consciousness and interaction of individuals, and which individuals are obliged to follow as a result of their social existence. This basis has several problematic implications. Firstly, Durkheim's objectivist picture of society, coupled with the functionalist conceptualization of morality in terms of binding rules that are imperative to social cohesion, falters on 'assumptions about universal internalization and unproblematic consensus' (Hitlin and Vaisey 2013: 53). His depiction of morality as the obligatory and binding rules of conduct of a society looks past the diverse, contested and shifting nature of moral beliefs, values and understandings of the good within a social context, in which quite profound differences and deep-seated contestations of what a society is and what it should be coexist (Sayer 2005).

Further, because Durkheim's (1982: 70) position sees the moral realities of a society as existing 'independent of their individual manifestations', moral difference and contestations to the prevailing order must necessarily be seen as a product of structural social change, and this obscures the role individual moral consciousness and action play in this process. For Durkheim, individual moral consciousness exists as the social assimilation of the individual into the obligatory rules of conduct in their society, meaning that these moral realities determine the consciousness and action of individuals. Durkheim's 'top-down' functional determinism thus annuls individual consciousness as being a potentially efficacious force of differentiated moral action and moral transformation (Hookway 2015: 278).

Durkheim consequently offers an unwieldy perspective on how moral action occurs in practice because the morality of an action is conceptualized as being external to the interactions of individuals. Durkheim for example argues that 'when I perform my duties as a brother, husband or citizen ... I fulfil obligations which are defined ... external to myself and my actions' (Durkheim 1982: 50). It is of course true that general moral expectations of what it is to be a good brother or a good spouse are socially constructed. But Durkheim's externalist position reifies such obligations as having a reality and form that exists in abstraction from the specific interactional realities through which they are enacted and reconstituted. Obligations associated with brotherhood and marriage do not just hang there as objective forms, either to be actuated or not. Not only does the meaning of such obligations differ significantly between individuals and social groups, but also how they are understood and enacted emerges interpersonally between actors (Finch 1989; Smart and Neale 1999). Indeed, Benhabib (1992) exemplifies this point through a situation in which a brother finds himself in financial trouble, and in which there is an obligation on older brothers to help. Benhabib argues that it may transpire that not fulfilling this obligation might prove to be the morally 'correct' decision; while financial aid may in some instances be benevolent, in others it may lead to continued dependency, or be provided in order to maintain an oppressive power imbalance (see also Smart and Neale 1999).

As will be discussed below, obligations and the 'right thing to do' emerge intersubjectively (Finch 1989), and the enactment of values and moral expectations varies considerably in relation to individual dispositions and subjectivities on the one hand and the practical realities of the social situation in which they may be enacted on the other (Smart and Neale 1999). By characterizing morality as external to the interdependent practice of individuals, Durkheim not only presents moral obligations and values as having a life of their own beyond such interaction, but also overlooks how in the dynamics of social life 'vague values must always first be translated by individual effort into concrete orientations, balanced with other considerations, and possibly revised on the basis of the consequences of action' (Joas 2000: 18). It is not clear how such transformation and variance in action would be possible when such obligations are conceptualized as external to actors and their interactions. The relational approach thus argues that it is in the course of intersubjective interaction that moral meanings and obligations are sustained and transformed, and this is possible only insofar as they are brought into the experience of relationally-moulded individuals and enacted in interdependent interaction.

At the other end of the spectrum, Bauman (1989) critiques Durkheim for discounting the individual as a source of morality, and for equating morality with the authoritative dominance of social structures. For Bauman (2005), Durkheim's position undermines the characteristic feature of morality, namely the personal assumption of responsibility for the other, often in the face of prevailing social influences. It also means that society is presumed to be the arbiter that engenders and secures the individual's capacity to act morally. This in itself overlooks how society can be 'morally silencing' and oppressive of individual moral consciousness (Bauman 1989: 174; Hookway 2015). Bauman's (1989) classic *Modernity and the Holocaust* resoundingly argued that the horrors of the holocaust exemplify how obligated deference to the collective can expropriate individual moral responsibility to the demands of authority while repressing alternative moral voices and precipitating intolerance towards moral variation. These are the beginnings of Bauman's complete departure from, and inversion of, Durkheim's arguments regarding the source of moral action (Shilling and Mellor 1998).

Where Durkheim reduces morality to the following of rules and norms, Bauman contends that morality exists as the autonomous assumption of responsibility on the part of the individual, undertaken irrespective of, and often in opposition to, dominant social prescriptions of conduct (Crone 2008). Drawing on the work of Emmanuel Levinas, Bauman presents morality as existing as an 'infinite' responsibility, which the individual must bear in the face of the other (Bauman 1998: 15). It is driven by a spontaneous and unorderable impulsive responsiveness to the other, which provokes within the person the demand of boundless responsibility. The indubitable call towards 'being for the other' that is instigated by the 'face' of the other is based on a moral impulse that Bauman (1993: 35) explicitly argues is 'primal' and prior to social influence: 'well before we are told authoritatively what is "good" and what "evil" (and sometimes what is neither) we face the choice between good and evil; we face it already at the very first, inescapable moment of encounter with the Other' (Bauman 1995: 2). In stark contrast to Durkheim, Bauman

(2008) argues moral impulse and moral concern is prior to social norms and rules; the moral impulse derives from the 'original' encounter with the other 'at the birth of subjectivity' (Bauman 2008: 40), prior to the imposition of the social, and it is in fact rule- and norm-laden sociality that hinders moral impulse. Put simply, the impulse of which Bauman talks is not a consequence of socialization; in fact, he argues that the *'process of socialization consists in the manipulation of moral capacity* – not in its production' (Bauman 1989: 178, emphasis original).

On this basis, Bauman builds a very particular view of what morality entails. Because the individual's subjectivity is constituted through responsibility to the other, our moral impulse 'is triggered off by the mere presence of the Other as a face', which elicits within us the demands of an unbounded responsibility to that other, and action is moral to the extent to which this responsibility is actuated (Bauman 1991: 143). Such is the extent of the demands of this responsibility that moral action is conceptualized by Bauman (1993: 48) as being necessarily non-reciprocal: the 'indispensable, defining trait ... of a moral stance' is 'one-sidedness, not reciprocity; a relation that cannot be reversed'. Quite the opposite of Durkheim, Bauman's perspective contends that 'moral action is connected with the ultimate and indispensable responsibility of the person' (Junge 2001: 109), a responsibility that springs from 'the primal and primary "brute fact" of moral impulse' (Bauman 1993: 35).

Bauman's (1990: 33) express intention was to advance an 'inherently consistent sociological theory of morality'. However, it is hard to see how this is possible on a basis of pre-social impulse (Crone 2008; Junge 2001). Not only are notions of pre-social moral impulse and demands of infinite responsibility sociologically problematic (Morgan 2014; Shilling and Mellor 1998), but Bauman's subsequent argument that action is moral when innate moral impulse is enacted to the extent that our boundless responsibility to the other is fulfilled establishes an unachievable degree of 'moral sainthood' as the basis of properly moral action (Hookway 2017).

Locating the source of moral action upon pre-social impulse also fails to account for the role of complex social relationships in the constitution of what moral action entails and in how it is enacted (Shilling and Mellor 1998). Bauman does argue that moral impulse is intersubjectively triggered, but by conceptualizing morality as the boundless and non-reciprocal response to the stimulation of our primal impulse by the other, acts that suitably satisfy Bauman's conditions of moral action are presented as being in some way beyond the social, beyond the cultural historicities that constitute and define a moral action as such, as well as beyond specific interpersonal relations that orient the course of what moral action entails. This means that normative expectations, socially-moulded values, and acquired wisdom cannot play a constitutive role in guiding moral action or understandings of the good. A sociological perspective must surely rest on the argument that moral understandings and moral action, rather than being dependent upon a pre-social impulse, are shaped within 'histories of networks of interaction that have generated the morals' in question (Crossley 2011: 2), and that our capacity to understand and enact our moral responsibility is 'unavoidably contingent upon our habits, traditions, customs, and the means of justification and resolution accepted in the communities we recognize as our own' (Morgan 2014: 136).

Bauman's individualist conception of the source of moral action is also unable to appreciate how moral actions and the form they take are to a certain extent constituted within the intersubjective situations in which they ensue. We can return to Benhabib's (1992) exemplification of how understanding the 'right' or 'good' course of action in the giving of financial aid to one's brother is contextually tied to the relationships between the relevant parties. Of course, Bauman did not argue that moral impulse decrees what the right course of action should be for all people in all circumstances, and he would not argue that actuating one's moral impulse necessitates providing financial relief to a sibling in need. Yet, by designating morality as being prior to social relationships, social discourse and reflective rumination, Bauman overlooks that our brothers' situation may indeed provoke an overwhelming urge to give alms, but upon deliberation we may decide that doing so is not the right thing to do. Perhaps we have learnt from experience that our brother has a habit of expecting to be bailed out after bad choices, while social discourse surrounding interventions and dependency relationships has taught us that the 'moral' thing may be to let our brother struggle now so that they learn to stand on their own in the future, being 'cruel to be kind', as it were. The point is not just that this course of action is unlikely to adhere to the boundless conditions of responsibility that Bauman asserts but also that what the 'moral' course might be does not sprout from primal impulse, but rather is moulded within a nexus of interpersonal relationships and situational circumstance, which interact with variably held and enacted social discourses.

While Bauman (1993) occasionally exalts the ordinary moral capacity of ordinary people, the severity with which he designates the 'defining traits of a moral stance' as 'one-sidedness, not reciprocity; a relation that cannot be reversed' (Bauman 1993: 48) means that much of ordinary moral practice cannot be conceptualized in moral terms, because such practice tends to be bound up with ordinary expectations of behaviour, such as reciprocity, mutuality and respect (Crone 2008). Such is the purity of Bauman's conceptualization of the moral that most ordinary moral practice is excluded. He describes morality in terms of the unattainably abstract, and thus turns attention away from morality as an ordinary aspect of everyday practice.

Relational Sociology and Morality in Practice

Albeit in opposite ways, the accounts given by Durkheim and Bauman both characterize morality as being constituted in abstraction from social practice, and consequently, neither approach aligns cogently with descriptions of how morality is lived and engaged with in intersubjective life. Conversely, a relational approach to morality would see the good not as either contained in social structure or based on individual consciousness or impulse, but as being constituted, sustained and transformed in relational interaction. Relational perspectives glide between Durkheim's holism and Bauman's individualism by contending that moral phenomena are 'of course held by individuals, but they do not originate with the individual. They are intersubjectively constructed in communicative interaction', and this shapes the consciousness and action of individuals, meaning that moral phenomena are sustained and shared as they are variably enacted within complex networks of interdependent interaction, which produce and uphold social forms and figurations of moral meaning, understandings and conduct (Luckmann 2002: 19).

This approach is beneficial because it is able to conceptualize morality as an essentially social phenomena, as with Durkheim, without defining morality in externalist terms, as something that has a reality beyond the relationally-oriented interactions of individuals. This then discards the static structural determinism of Durkheim's arguments and facilitates a view of morality as something that is variably and intersubjectively done by individuals in the course of interdependent interaction.

In order to make the claim that this relational stance provides the most appropriate frame through which moral phenomena can be understood, it needs to be shown that morality is something that is precipitated in interactional practice. It happens to be the case that sociological interest in morality has resurfaced as 'fixed, substantive definitions of the moral' have been repealed in favour of reconceptualizing morality as being ordinarily and disparately enacted in routine participation in everyday life (Hitlin and Vaisey 2013: 54). Indeed, when duly considered, it is evident that many aspects of everyday practice are entrenched with moral bearing in how they are enacted and understood. People regularly espouse moralized standpoints towards a multitude of social issues – sexism, lying, how children should be disciplined, charitable giving – and they enact their moral understandings through encouraging children to learn and to travel, keeping in regular contact with parents, volunteering for a political party, avoiding certain shops or activities that they consider to be morally dubious, or holding their tongue in order to avoid offending a relative even if they disagree with them (Sanghera 2016; Sie 2015).

In recognizing that morality is an ordinary and integrated facet of routine social life, it becomes apparent that acting morally 'is thus not about duty for its own sake, nor about the ends or purpose of morality', but instead stems from 'the open-ended texture of everyday moral life' (Herman 2000: 30–31). From this viewpoint, attention shifts from conceptualizing moral understanding and behaviour in abstracted terms, and towards a depiction of 'moral competence as it is revealed in practice' (Hermann 2015: 121), which is exhibited, for example, in caring practices of parenting (Bowden 1996), in the well-documented boundary work of grandparents to support their child's parenting without interfering (May and Lahad 2019), in tactful decisions made in the delivering of bad news (Maynard 1996), or as we make time for a friend in need (Hermann 2015).

Emphasizing morality as a phenomenon that is principally engaged with in ordinary living has directed sociological consideration towards the notion that it is in everyday interactional practice that moral orders and understandings are enacted, maintained and remoulded (Emirbayer and Maynard 2010). Goffman's (1959, 1967, 1968) work is instructive here, as it highlights the myriad of nuanced actions that are routinely conducted in order to align performances of self with ordinary moral expectations of behaviour that define an interactional context. For example, Goffman (1959) analysed how orders of conversation are followed to avoid rudeness, how distance is kept between individuals in public to prevent discomfort, how 'tactful blindness' is shown to avoid causing embarrassment to others, and how sanctioning and corrective practices are enacted in response to transgression. These analyses reflect how social interaction flows between ritualized social niceties we enact to maintain face on the one hand, and morally-oriented actions taken in the moment of practice on the other (Jacobsen and Kristiansen 2015). For example, in *Stigma* (1968), Goffman illuminates how ordinary expectations of expressive control are amplified as people set their face and divert their gaze when they encounter a person with a marked physical abnormality to avoid causing offence. Likewise, Donnelly and Wright (2013) apply Goffman's work to show how careful tactful blindness (as opposed to sanctioning glances and cursory challenges) are favoured when disturbances to the interactional order of a church service are caused by a churchgoer with a disability.

A key aspect of Goffman's arguments, and the arguments of practice theories more generally, is that such performances are not conducted in isolation; they are the product of, and only make sense in relation to, a 'more or less stable background of other performances' (Rouse 2007: 505–6), which engenders the 'impression that there are proper ways to go about the business of everyday life' (Warde 2016: 152). Such orders of practice show how moral orders, obligations and expectations are socially held, yet as Goffman and ethnomethodological research has shown, an externalist picture of social structure is unable to account for how such orders are maintained. While Goffman sought to illuminate the ritualized nature of routine patterns of interaction that mean orthodoxies of practice are generally available, he also saw that the intersubjectively emergent and contingent circumstance of interactional performances means that order is 'ever in a process of being achieved' (Emirbayer and Maynard 2010: 239). This includes not just the enactment of appropriate conduct, but also small-scale practices such as the sanctioning of untoward behaviour through expressive challenges and apologies for transgression (Donnelly and Wright 2013). Although interactional orders are 'predicated on a large base of shared cognitive' and 'normative' presumptions

(Goffman 1983: 5), in practice they also need to be coordinated and calibrated through the continual 'correcting, sanctioning, criticizing [and] approving' of others (Frega 2015).

Indeed, Goffman (1959: 141) details the interactional work undertaken in the maintenance of tact and the avoidance of 'destructive information' that is liable to 'discredit' fellow actors in a way that is morally problematic. For example, the tactful 'under-communication' of certain facts often reflects a concerted moral concern for protecting the 'face' and welfare of others (ibid.). This has been exemplified in research into the moral significance of family secrets (Smart 2011). Such secrets are common in nearly every family in some form, and while secrets are often maintained for self-interested reasons, secrets are also kept to allay judgement, stigma and ostracization: 'keeping illegitimacy secret could be a means of defending from outside scrutiny and adverse judgement', but likewise 'the telling or not telling of secrets can defend an individual against other family members ... e.g. keeping secret one's sexual orientation in order to maintain relationships' (Smart 2011: 540; Barnwell 2019). Such secrets often provide a means for maintaining relationships in their current form or for preventing damage to others because unearthing adoption or criminality, for example, can cause the narratives, identities and welfare of a family and its members to be rewritten (Smart 2011).

Maintaining such secrets can thus often reflect concern for the well-being of affected others or the desire to avoid conflict within complexly intertwined relations. We are largely able to comport ourselves appropriately to such situations through embodied moral experience: 'I sense the embarrassment of a person, and turn the conversation aside' (Mandelbaum 1955). Yet, it is not always the case that each person in an interactional setting shares the same knowledge of what is off-bounds, or the same tactful appreciation of the situation, or indeed the same willingness to uphold a secret. As Goffman (1959: 88) argues, 'any member of the [performance] has the power to give the show away or to disrupt it by inappropriate conduct', so the maintenance of the current order will often require some degree of 'teamwork' in the flow of practice; for example, through 'pretending not to hear', diverting conversation, cautionary glances, the challenging of awkward questions, and indeed reprimanding the tactlessness of those who bring up risky subjects.

Such situated responsiveness to interpersonal interactions is part and parcel of the maintenance of personal relationships in situations that confront us in everyday life, and it is illustrative of how morality is often engaged with in practice. Indeed, research into personal lives has provided a catalyst for the emergence of the renewed brand of sociological consideration of morality precisely because this realm of social life regularly necessitates everyday moral concern, often in a way that reflects socially-orientated expectations and obligations on the one hand, and the intersubjective emergence of action on the other (Holdsworth and Morgan 2007). Importantly, evidence from this field challenges both Durkheimian arguments for seeing moral meanings and obligations as contained by social structure while also showing, contra Bauman, that moral decisions, even when taken at an individual level, are not describable in terms of unaccompanied individual consciousness or impulse; instead, such decisions are deeply entangled in relations and are moulded intersubjectively.

Research has illustrated that while family life is 'animated by and linked to wider notions of right and wrong' (Holdsworth and Morgan 2007: 405), which are drawn from 'ideas about moral obligations derived from wider culture' (Finch 1989: 143), interpretations of one's own responsibility and obligations towards one's family vary considerably in reflection of the circumstances and expectations of familial relationships, with subjective interpretations of responsibilities and obligations developing and emerging interpersonally between family members, often in relation to unfolding situational contexts, which mould assessments of what the 'proper thing to do' is in practice (Abbott 2020).

'Even in situations where rights and duties seem more fixed' (Finch 1989: 143), such as obligations of care for elderly parents, how these obligations operate in practice is 'a matter for negotiation' within families, which are weighed up in relation to practical and interpersonal factors such as proximity, gender,[1] quality and history of relationships, other caring responsibilities such as parenting, availability of and willingness to use professional care services, changing needs and wishes of the cared for parent, and the extent to which each party is perceived to be 'pulling their weight' (Finch and Mason 1990: 151). Contrary to Durkheim's assessment, in practice obligations and their enactment are far from clear-cut (Finch 1989). Rather than determining conduct, shared normative obligations provide touchstones that are woven into the emergent moral decisions and negotiations undertaken within personal relationships, which themselves develop intersubjectively as mutually entangled actors mould the directionality of the decisions that are taken (Smart and Neale 1999).

Elsewhere, research into moral decisions associated with moving away from home have challenged Durkheimian notions of the structural determination of moral consciousness by illustrating how such decisions are reflexively negotiated at an individual level, often through very personal consideration of one's own responsibility towards others. However, such research also illustrates how these decisions cannot be properly understood from the stance of isolated individual moral consciousness, let alone pre-social impulse (Holdsworth and Morgan 2007; Jones 1999). Such decisions have been shown to be framed by social realities, such as local youth employment rates, as well as being situated within more nuanced interpersonal relations that mould subjective senses of acceptance and belonging (Jones 1999). And while decisions to move away from hometowns are faced at a personal level, Holdsworth and Morgan (2007) detailed how their participants' processes of reflexive consideration drew on perceived expectations of both specific and generalized others, which were navigated and capitulated against as considerations of responsibility and potential to cause pain to loved ones were weighed up alongside feelings of belonging, practical realities and desires to prosper and give meaning to their lives. The perceived expectations of others were brought into their moral decision-making in order to construct what is 'normal' for their family, friends and community more broadly, to negotiate perceived expectations and sensitivities that friends and family may hold towards their departure, and to weigh these up in relation to personal desires and acutely felt discourses and experiences of opportunity and deprivation, all of which were operationalized and negotiated in the course of arriving at a position on what 'the right thing to do' is (Holdsworth and Morgan 2007: 405). Moral decisions of this kind are indeed taken from an individual perspective, yet in Bauman's interpretation considerations of generalized social expectations, practical realities, and personal wants obscure the extent of our responsibility, rather than being seen as constitutive of the context in which moral action occurs, and of what moral behaviour might be. Moral decisions about what is 'good' or what the 'right' course of action is cannot realistically be unravelled from the relational context in which they are constituted; understanding how moral decisions and actions are taken in practice means taking seriously that moral perspectives are socially situated, and that the enactment of moral judgements occurs and is moulded within the messy entanglements of social life.

Conclusion

Both the immeasurable individual responsibility of Bauman and the reified externalism of Durkheim conceptualize of morality in terms abstracted 'from the practices in which [it] become[s] operative' (Joas 2000: 18). Not only does this mean that their approaches are able to contribute little to the question of how morality – whether conceptualized as the assumption of personal responsibility or the enactment of social values – is applied in interaction (Joas 2000), but it also means that they are unable to accurately conceptualize of the intersubjective constitution and sustainment of moral phenomena. The contention of a properly sociological theory of morality is that moral phenomena are, like all other social phenomena, constituted through the doing of social life within complex networks of interdependent interaction. As exemplified above, our senses of obligations to our family are derived from wider culture, but they are learnt and continue to emerge through interactions and in relation to the particulars and circumstances of our own family relationships. What constitutes a moral action does not derive from the extent to which demands of an infinite responsibility have been attained, but neither do moral expectations and obligations just hang there with a meaning that exists outside of interactional relations. A relational approach allows us to conceptualize how moral action and the 'good' or 'right thing to do' are moulded in unfolding interactional practice between actors, through which broader moral understandings and expectations are drawn on, and thereby are upheld and transformed in interactions.

This perspective, then, argues that it is through relational interaction that different understandings of the good – for example of what considerate conduct involves, of what the expectations of care in a particular relationship entail, of how terms of moral evaluation and judgement are used, and even our broadly construed understandings of what is just – are sustained, moulded and remoulded. Complex social formations produced by vast historical networks of interaction engender broadly shared moral meanings and expectations, normative restrains, and cultural and legal frameworks of permissibility and value that fundamentally mould the consciousness, understanding and action of individuals. All these frame what moral action entails. But it is through interaction that these are brought into the experience of individuals, and they are brought to bear and sustained insofar as they are engaged with in practice.

Acknowledgements

My thanks go to Anna Strhan, David Henig, Joel Robbins and Natalie-Anne Hall for their feedback on earlier drafts of this chapter.

Owen Abbott has worked as a lecturer in sociology at the University of Manchester and the University of York. He is currently undertaking a Leverhulme funded fellowship project into forgiveness in personal relationships at Cardiff University. As well as forgiveness, his research focuses on the sociology of morality, with an emphasis on everyday morality and moral practice. His first book *The Self, Relational Sociology, and Morality in Practice* was awarded the British Sociological Association Philip Abrams Prize 2020 for best first and sole authored book.

Note

1. Gender is significant not only because research has shown that women tend to provide more care for elderly parents overall, but also because gender has been shown to become significant to how responsibilities for caring are divvied up, with it often being assumed between siblings that men will do more of the caring for fathers and women for mothers, especially when it comes to intimate care such as bathing (Grigoryeva 2017).

References

Abbott, O. 2020. *The Self, Relational Sociology, and Morality in Practice*. London: Palgrave Macmillan.
Abend, G. 2013. 'What's New and What's Old about the New Sociology of Morality', in S. Hitlin and S. Vaisey (eds), *Handbook of the Sociology of Morality*. New York: Springer, pp. 561–84.

Barnes, B. 2000. *Understanding Agency: Social Theory and Responsible Action* (1 edition). SAGE Publications Ltd.
Barnwell, A. 2019. 'Family Secrets and the Slow Violence of Social Stigma', *Sociology* 53(6): 1111–26.
Bauman, Z. 1989. *Modernity and the Holocaust*. Polity Press.
———. 1990. 'Effacing the Face: On the Social Management of Moral Proximity', *Theory, Culture & Society* 7(1): 5–38.
———. 1991. 'The Social Manipulation of Morality: Moralizing Actors, Adiaphorizing Action', *Theory, Culture & Society* 8(1): 137–51.
———. 1993. *Postmodern Ethics*. Oxford: Wiley-Blackwell.
———. 1995. *Life in Fragments: Essays in Postmodern Morality*. Oxford: Wiley-Blackwell.
———. 1998. 'What Prospects of Morality in Times of Uncertainty?', *Theory, Culture & Society* 15(1): 11–22.
———. 2005. 'Durkheim's Society Revisited', in J.C. Alexander and P. Smith (eds), *The Cambridge Companion to Durkheim*. Cambridge: Cambridge University Press, pp. 360–82.
———. 2008. *Does Ethics Have a Chance in a World of Consumers?* Harvard University Press.
Benhabib, S. 1992. *Situating the Self: Gender, Community and Postmodernism in Contemporary Ethics*. Cambridge: Polity Press.
Bowden, P. 1996. *Caring: Gender-Sensitive Ethics*. London: Routledge.
Burkitt, I. 2016. 'Relational Agency: Relational Sociology, Agency and Interaction', *European Journal of Social Theory* 19(3): 322–39.
Crone, M. 2008. 'Bauman on Ethics – Intimate Ethics for a Global World?', in M.H. Jacobsen and P. Poder (eds), *The Sociology of Zygmunt Bauman: Challenges and Critique*. London: Routledge, pp. 59–74.
Crossley, N. 2011. *Towards Relational Sociology*. Routledge.
Dépelteau, F. 2008. 'Relational Thinking: A Critique of Co-Deterministic Theories of Structure and Agency', *Sociological Theory* 26(1): 51–73.
Donnelly, C.M., and B.R.E. Wright. 2013. 'Goffman Goes to Church: Face-Saving and the Maintenance of Collective Order in Religious Services', *Sociological Research Online* 18(1): 143–55.
Durkheim, É. 1979a. 'Introduction to Ethics', in W.S.F. Pickering (ed.), *Durkheim: Essays on Morals and Education*. London: Routledge & Kegan Paul, pp. 79–96.
———. 1979b. *Suicide: A Study in Sociology*. Glencoe, IL: Free Press.
———. 1982. *The Rules of Sociological Method*. Glencoe, IL: Free Press.
———. 1984. *The Division of Labor in Society*. Glencoe, IL: Free Press.
Elias, N. 1991. *The Society of Individuals*. London: Continuum.
Emirbayer, M., and D.W. Maynard. 2010. 'Pragmatism and Ethnomethodology', *Qualitative Sociology* 34(1): 221–61.
Finch, J. 1989. *Family Obligations and Social Change*. Cambridge: Polity Press.
Finch, J., and J. Mason. 1990. 'Filial Obligations and Kin Support for Elderly People', *Ageing & Society* 10(2): 151–75.
Frega, R. 2015. 'The Normative Structure of the Ordinary', *European Journal of Pragmatism and American Philosophy*, *VII*(VII-1). DOI: https://doi.org/10.4000/ejpap.370.
Goffman, E. 1959. *The Presentation of Self in Everyday Life*. New York: Doubleday.
———. 1967. *Interaction Ritual: Essays on Face-to-Face Interaction*. Chicago: Aldine.

_____. 1968. *Stigma: Notes on the Management of Spoiled Identity*. New York: Simon & Schuster.
_____. 1983. 'The Interaction Order: American Sociological Association, 1982 Presidential Address', *American Sociological Review* 48(1): 1–17.
Grigoryeva, A. 2017. 'Own Gender, Sibling's Gender, Parent's Gender: The Division of Elderly Parent Care among Adult Children', *American Sociological Review* 82(1): 116–46.
Herman, B. 2000. 'Morality and Everyday Life', *Proceedings and Addresses of the American Philosophical Association* 74(2): 29–45.
Hermann, J. 2015. *On Moral Certainty, Justification and Practice – A Wittgensteinian Perspective*. Houndmills, Basingstoke: Palgrave Macmillan.
Hitlin, S., and S. Vaisey. 2013. 'The New Sociology of Morality', *Annual Review of Sociology* 39: 51–68.
Holdsworth, C., and D. Morgan. 2007. 'Revisiting the Generalized Other: An Exploration', *Sociology* 41(3): 401–17.
Hookway, N. 2015. 'Moral Decline Sociology: Critiquing the Legacy of Durkheim', *Journal of Sociology* 51(2): 271–84.
_____. 2017. 'Zygmunt Bauman's Moral Saint: Reclaiming Self in the Sociology of Morality', *Acta Sociologica* 60(4): 358–67.
Jacobsen, M., and S. Kristiansen. 2015. *The Social Thought of Erving Goffman*. London: Sage.
Joas, H. 2000. *The Genesis of Values*. Cambridge: Polity Press.
Jones, G. 1999. 'The Same People in the Same Places'? Socio-Spatial Identities and Migration in Youth', *Sociology* 33(1): 1–22.
Junge, M. 2001. 'Zygmunt Bauman's Poisoned Gift of Morality*', *The British Journal of Sociology* 52(1): 105–19.
Lambek, M. (2015). *The Ethical Condition: Essays on Action, Person, and Value*. Chicago: University of Chicago Press.
Lambek, M. (ed.). (2010). *Ordinary Ethics: Anthropology, Language and Action*. New York: Fordham University Press.
Luckmann, T. 2002. 'Moral Communication in Modern Societies', *Human Studies* 25(1): 19–32.
Mandelbaum, M.H. 1955. *The Phenomenology of Moral Experience*. Glencoe, IL: Free Press.
May, V., and K. Lahad. 2019. 'The Involved Observer: A Simmelian Analysis of the Boundary Work of Aunthood', *Sociology* 53(1): 3–18.
Maynard, D.W. 1996. 'On "Realization" in Everyday Life: The Forecasting of Bad News as a Social Relation', *American Sociological Review* 61(1): 109–31.
Mead, G.H. 1934. *Mind, Self, and Society: From the Standpoint of a Social Behaviorist: 1* (C. Morris, ed.). Chicago: University of Chicago Press.
Morgan, M. 2014. 'The Poverty of (Moral) Philosophy: Towards an Empirical and Pragmatic Ethics', *European Journal of Social Theory* 17(2): 129–46.
Powell, C. 2013. 'Radical Relationism: A Proposal', in C. Powell and F. Dépelteau (eds), *Conceptualizing Relational Sociology: Ontological and Theoretical Issues*. New York: Palgrave Macmillan, pp. 187–207.
Powell, C., and F. Dépelteau. 2013. 'Introduction', in C. Powell and F. Dépelteau (eds), *Conceptualizing Relational Sociology: Ontological and Theoretical Issues*. New York: Palgrave Macmillan, pp. 1–12.

Prandini, R. 2015. 'Relational Sociology: A Well-defined Sociological Paradigm or a Challenging "Relational Turn" in Sociology?', *International Review of Sociology* 25(1): 1–14.
Rouse, J. 2007. 'Practice Theory', *Division I Faculty Publications*. Paper 43.
Sanghera, B. 2016. 'Charitable Giving and Lay Morality: Understanding Sympathy, Moral Evaluations and Social Positions', *The Sociological Review* 64(2): 294–311.
Sayer, A. 2005. *The Moral Significance of Class*. Cambridge: Cambridge University Press.
Schatzki, T. 2016. 'Practice Theory as Flat Ontology', in G. Spaargaren, D. Weenink & M. Lamers (eds), *Practice Theory and Research: Exploring the Dynamics of Social Life*. London: Routledge, pp. 28–42.
Shilling, C., and P.A. Mellor. 1998. 'Durkheim, Morality and Modernity: Collective Effervescence, Homo Duplex and the Sources of Moral Action', *The British Journal of Sociology* 49(2): 193–209.
Sie, M. 2015. 'Moral Hypocrisy and Acting for Reasons: How Moralizing Can Invite Self-Deception', *Ethical Theory and Moral Practice* 18(2): 223–35.
Smart, C. 2011. 'Families, Secrets and Memories', *Sociology* 45(4): 539–53.
Smart, C., and B. Neale. 1999. *Family Fragments?*. Oxford: Wiley.
Smith, D.M. 1997. 'Geography and Ethics: A Moral Turn?' *Progress in Human Geography* 21(4): 583–90.
Warde, A. 2016. *The Practice of Eating*. Cambridge: Polity Press.

4

For the Agony of 'the Good' and of the Moral Courage to Do It

Iain Wilkinson

In recent years, I have championed a form of social inquiry that sets problems of social suffering as its core concern. This involves a commitment to expose both the social causes of human misery as well as the extent to which embodied pains and sufferings are constituted through the moral experience of social life. A focus is brought to the ways in which human adversities and afflictions are conditioned at the level of cultural meaning and normative expectation. People's social encounters and negotiations with 'the problem of suffering' are studied both as dynamic elements within significant instances of personal change and as part of wider processes of social, cultural and political innovation.

More recently, in collaboration with the medical anthropologist Arthur Kleinman, I have further argued that the study of social suffering must be allied to the practice and pedagogy of caregiving (Wilkinson and Kleinman 2016). Here an emphasis is placed on the fact that social life is inherently moral and that it always involves us in enactments of substantive human values. Social science cannot be withheld from this understanding. Social scientists cannot operate above the fray of morality and politics. Their work matters not only in terms of the quality of knowledge it delivers but also in terms of the moral character and political consequences of the research techniques and writing practices that are committed to its production and distribution. If social scientists are not prepared to take these seriously as issues for critical analysis and debate, then on this view they are not only set to evade their object of study but also operate from a position where they disavow themselves as social beings with an active stake in the world. Here the commitment to participate in acts of caregiving is taken both as a morally appropriate response to human suffering as well as a necessary part of the attempt to better understand how 'the good' may be known and realized in social life. Indeed, here we are encouraged to interrogate social science over the extent to which it is adequately motivated and equipped to operate as a means to do some good in the world.

I recognize, however, that within the wider community of social science there are many who take the view that such interests and commitments are ill-advised and that they should not be endorsed but rather taken up as matters for critique. Some of the most forceful critical objections that are raised in response to the attempt to fashion anthropology and sociology as ameliorative practices that contribute to the realization of humane forms of society are directed towards those working to document, protest against and respond with care for people in conditions of social suffering (Fassin 2012: 21–43; Massé 2007; Mcrobbie 2002; Nguyen and Peschard 2003; Ticktin 2014; Vitellone 2004). In this regard, the social science that is engaged with documenting and responding to problems of social suffering is derided for its inevitable shortcomings and failures. It is also variously portrayed as morally misguided, devoid of political insight or as lacking a sufficiently critical understanding of the workings of power in society. Critics argued that, while attempting to do some good in response to a world of social suffering, social science is all too often to be found colluding with systems of power and privilege that cause many of the harms that are done to people.

In writing this chapter, I do not seek to deny these accusations or evade such criticism. I accept that it is often the case that those engaged in research and writing on social suffering adopt positions and take actions that, with the benefit of critical hindsight, can be cast as morally misguided and politically naïve. I would argue, however, that it is better to fail trying to do some good in the world rather than cling to the high ground of critique. I further contend that critique that leaves the world untouched, and protest that does not engage in active struggle for change, is set to become no more than a convoluted distraction – and all the more so when it is reduced to operating as a stylized academic performance tailored for conference debate and seminar room discussion.

Experiences of social suffering involve people in many deeply perplexed problems of moral meaning and action. In these contexts, individuals are not only set to be agonized by the harms that are done to themselves and others but also by the problem of knowing what to say and how to respond. Those engaged in the attempt to translate such experience into scripts of social science are set to be immersed in many epistemological difficulties, ontological uncertainties and much moral disquiet through their efforts to document people's miseries and pains; and perhaps, even more so through the experience of trying and failing to respond to this with adequate forms of practical care. In this context, 'the good' is readily identified as a social agony, and commitments to do good are known from the outset to be inherently agonized. 'The good' is withheld from vilification and, rather, it is approached as a value that is set to make science question ever more reflexively, alert to its human significance and consequences. Inevitably, however, it is set to leave us with many troubling questions relating to the capacities and capabilities of social science, as well as many doubts over whether it is possible to sustain the moral courage to make it so engaged.

In what follows, I offer a brief review of contemporary debates over 'the good' within contemporary social science. Whilst most of this work has been developed in connection with debates over the moral character and purpose of anthropology, it can also be used to interrogate the value and ambition of any social science that holds itself justified by humanitarian endeavour. In this I aim to make clear that my sympathies lie in the direction of an approach to the social agony of the good as a spur to more 'radicalized' forms of humanitarian commitment and action. I then move to outline a perspective on social suffering where the difficulty of discerning 'the good' and the frustrations of making this applied to care are taken as a necessary part of the acquisition of social understanding and of the process of learning how to make this practically relevant. This takes Pierre Bourdieu's essay on 'Understanding' as a founding methodological statement and as a troubled guide to praxis (Bourdieu 1996, 1999b). It contends that the social science that matters most can only take place on the condition that its practitioners are prepared to endure the antinomies of their practice and, further, hold steadfast with the moral courage to pursue the good in thought and action whilst facing up to the fact that, more often than not, whatever can be done is set to remain woefully inadequate and insufficient.

The Good Debate

As I understand it, there are three main areas of debate over 'the good' in contemporary anthropology. The first of these concerns the idea of anthropology as a field of study and how anthropologists are disposed to account for their academic identity, theoretical frameworks and methods of research. Here Joel Robbins' contends that since the 1990s a major 'turn' has taken place whereby anthropologists have shifted their attention away from documenting the lived experience of 'primitive' societies that are identified as 'other' to their 'own' and instead have made conditions of violence, oppression, extreme material deprivation and mental anguish their core concern (Robbins 2013). On this view, in an age where their discipline is increasingly set to be regarded as a tainted relic of western colonialism, anthropologists have made a bid to survive into the future by relinquishing their identity as an 'enlightened' discipline engaged in studying 'savage' societies and, rather, have aligned themselves with a global humanitarianism committed to exposing and combatting the harms done to people in contexts of human suffering. This new 'anthropology of suffering' not only aims to document how human misery is caused and conditioned by society but also 'to realize the shared humanity that links us to others who suffer' (Robbins 2013: 456). It tends to be involved with a global public health movement and is often committed to combining anthropological study with medical interventions designed to combat diseases of poverty and to secure minimum standards of primary health care. Robbins argues, moreover, that here anthropologists are inevitably made to devote more analytical attention to how people imagine the good in their lives and take actions to create it as a lived reality; and he adds that insofar as they might 'do justice to the different ways people live for the good', anthropologists might also be involved in 'finding ways to let their efforts inform their own' (Robbins 2013: 459). Accordingly, on this account, anthropology is not only set to be more involved in studying manifestations of empathy and care in human relationships but also to serve as a resource for public debate over our ethical ideals and moral practices. It draws a focus to the narratives that are commonly deployed as a means to account for the history of anthropology and its contemporary purpose (Das et al. 2015).

A second area of debate is more heavily involved in critically questioning a particular set of approaches to 'doing good', namely, those associated with the humanitarian practices of transnational nongovernmental organizations such as Oxfam and Médecins Sans Frontières. In this context, there is also a tendency to hold the virtue of medical anthropology up for critical debate. Most studies are committed to exposing how humanitarianism in practice falls short of realizing its aims and objectives, and how in many instances humanitarian aid workers, health professionals and political activists operate as unwitting accomplices to actions that result in delivering harm to vulnerable populations. As Miriam Ticktin observes, a large portion of this work comes from an avowedly critical branch of anthropology that appears to be fixed firmly against the kinds of proposals advanced by Robbins (Ticktin 2014: 277). Insofar as efforts at doing good are made to adhere to bureaucratic procedures, curtailed by market forces and subsumed within militarized interventions, then they are portrayed as serving to extend neoliberal governmental power relations and the politics of exception (Fadlalla 2008; Nguyen 2010; Ticktin 2011). Indeed, drawing heavily on the critical interrogations of 'humanitarian reason' advanced by Michel Foucault and Giorgio Agamben, it seems many are inclined to endorse Didier Fassin's argument that, insofar as humanitarianism in practice inevitably involves an imposition of hierarchies of value on human life that institutes 'radically unequal' orders of social control, it should be morally condemned (Agamben 1998, 2005; Fassin 2012; Foucault 1977, 1978, 1991). Here it appears that the overriding aim of anthropological engagements with the good is to render them as objects of critique; and even while the conditions and purpose of such critique might be approached as a matter for critical debate, this is overwhelmingly committed to its refinement (Fassin 2017). Critique in and of itself is extolled as a supreme value.

Arguably, however, it is now possible to delineate a third approach that, while acknowledging the validity of the critical objections outlined above, seeks to move beyond a position of pure critique so as to involve itself in an attempt to reconfigure humanitarian values and agendas. This involves an emphasis being placed on the potential for the political conflicts and moral controversies generated by humanitarian social actions to yet deliver us into new understandings of our shared humanity and what is involved in doing good to others. In this vein, a number of writers point to the ways in which it is possible to read Michel Foucault as not so much working to advance a wholesale rejection of humanitarianism but rather committing to make it operate on a more radical plain. While acknowledging that Foucault stands fundamentally opposed to any philosophy or politics that operates from the premise that we have an intrinsic 'human nature' or that our humanity resides in an 'essence' that needs to be freed from corruption and constraint, it is argued that, nevertheless, he remains committed to a distinctive politics of humanity. For example, Ben Golder contends that Foucault's involvement in humanitarian campaigns for prison reform and his public support for humanitarian protests on behalf of the plight of the Vietnamese boat people represents 'an ethic of critical engagement with human rights, with-in and against existing human rights, in the name of an unfinished humanity' (Golder 2010: 3). Similarly, David Campbell argues that ultimately Foucault aims to provide the groundwork for a 'radicalised humanitarianism' (Campbell 1998). He contends that at the same time as this is designed to operate with due regard for the potential for humanitarian commitments to cause harm, it also seeks to corral these towards 'an affirmation of life' and 'being human' that operates to affirm our potential for alterity (Campbell 1998: 519). Here the anthropological engagement with 'the good' essentially concerns a movement to refine critically an analytical and ethical standpoint that takes its cues from Foucault's unfinished 'humanitarian' project. In the first instance, this appears to be resolved to clearing the theoretical space for a renewed narrative engagement with how commitments to 'the good' may be incorporated within studies of multiple and disparate 'techniques of the self' (Laidlaw 2002). It is initiated by the view that humanitarian thought and action may be radically revised so that they do not comply with systems of domination but rather operate as components of an exercise in human freedoms. Yet, more often than not, precisely how this should be achieved is left as a matter for future inquiry.

On my reading it appears that, as far as these areas of debate are concerned, social science exists in a deeply agonized state. There are, however, some important differences to be drawn between these areas when it comes to understanding how practitioners are set to experience and relate to their frustrations. Most notably, there is the difference between those left vexed as a result of their attempts to establish morally acceptable principles as compared to those left reeling under the experience of having failed to live by them in practice. While the former is largely committed to devising an analytical framework for carrying out 'the study of morality', the latter is more heavily preoccupied with documenting the conflicts of value and harmful unintended consequences that result from humanitarian efforts at doing good in the world.

Some of the debate over 'the good' is wholly theoretical. For example, Julia Cassaniti and Jacob Hickman portray this as essentially concerned with mapping out the dimensions of an analytical framework that is adequately equipped to provide anthropologists with the conceptual means to render 'the moral domain' in all its diversity and conflicts as an object for study (Cassaniti and Hickman 2014). Along with fellow social theorists such as James Laidlaw (2014) and Jarrett Zigon (2008), moreover, this is understood to require a break with a Durkheimian heritage that is blamed for leaving their discipline theoretically ill-equipped for the proper study of people's moral dispositions and expressions. Moreover, as Zigon puts it, it encourages anthropology to engage 'in a dialogue with 20th-century continental philosophies of sociality and ethics', and more directly with the intellectual legacy of, and political fallout from, Michel Foucault's work (Zigon 2007: 131). It also leaves it wrestling with the deep paradoxes featured in some of Foucault's later essays and interviews, where he appears to be left struggling to break free from a critical position that offers nothing besides denunciation; and even to the point where critique falls prey to its own problematizations and suspicions, and exposes the critical observer as 'part of what she observes' (Folkers 2016: 20).

It is deep worries concerning the value conflicts borne and compromises committed under the effort to set humanitarian ideals in practice that are also preoccupying anthropology. In this respect, it is important to attend to the ways in which anthropologists are set to be greatly discomforted by the conditions and demands of their ethnographic practice. As Arthur Kleinman notes, the very fact that an ethnographer is exposed to the moral worlds of others is likely to make her 'self-reflexively critical of her own positioning and the commitments and problems it leads to' (Kleinman 1999: 414–15); and an emphasis should be brought to the fact that such self-critical reflexivity tends to most intensively form part of the moral experience of those anthropologists who are not only engaged in the attempt to bear witness to gross incidences of human affliction but, further, move to take upon themselves a portion of the burden to care for those 'in' suffering. In this regard, many of those involved in critical debates over what constitutes 'the good' and how to carry it out in practice are not so much animated by problems of intellect but rather by anxieties aroused and distresses borne through the moral discomfort of direct involvement in many frustrated, ill-fated and failed acts of caregiving. In these instances, the critiques of writers such as Didier Fassin and his many followers are a product of deeply destabilizing and highly divisive experiences of *engagement* with the attempt to combat and ameliorate incidences of social suffering

In what follows, I am essentially concerned with how we should relate to such experience; and further with questions relating to what we should do with the epistemological difficulties, ontological uncertainties and moral disquiet provoked through the pain of not just being made to bear witness to human suffering but also, and perhaps more so, from the experience of trying and failing to respond to this with an adequate form of practical care. In this regard, my interest lies in how to manage humanitarian disappointments and the inherent risks and dangers of the attempt to set humanitarian ideals in practice. This offers a perspective on how we should handle the reaction of, and disposition to, critique. It seeks, moreover, to withhold 'the good' from vilification and rather approach it as a human value that is set to always involve us struggling to make it better known and better realized in practice.

From a Perspective on Social Suffering

It might be argued that some studies of social suffering need to be more involved in critically questioning the values enshrined in their methods of social documentation and how these may entail deleterious consequences. It may often appear that a commitment to describe and make known the harms that are done to people is prioritized over a concern to expose how the data gathering and documentary techniques of social science fall woefully short of accomplishing this aim. Researchers can be more preoccupied with issuing a protest against what suffering does to people than with the potential for social science to operate as the unwitting accomplice to forms of political reason and moral practice that place individuals in harm's way. Many of the critical objections to research and writing on social suffering, while inviting readers to engage with some complex issues of political meaning and social ethics, are rooted in a simple complaint; namely, that its practitioners are not sufficiently engaged with critique, and especially that which draws the discriminatory consequences and harmful effects of humanitarianism into focus. Research and writing on problems of social suffering is portrayed as philosophically underdeveloped and politically naïve. It is argued that, either through bad faith or by compliance with established governmental regimes, its practitioners fail to pay adequate heed to the extent to which, in terms of moral virtue, their work is left hollowed-out by its compromises with established structures of power and interest (Calhoun 2008; Fassin 2012; Mcrobbie 2002; Redfield 2005; Vitellone 2004).

A possible response to such criticisms is found in Pierre Bourdieu's attempt to explain the motives guiding the ethnographic practice and writing style of *La Misère du Monde* (1993), later published in English as *The Weight of the World* (Bourdieu et al. 1999). In the 'Preface' and the later essay entitled 'Understanding', he explains that in addition to documenting how individuals give voice to the everyday misery of life in poor housing conditions and of working in poorly paid and deeply alienating conditions, he is also inviting sociologists to reflect critically on how 'the sociological point of view' is made possible and what kind of knowledge is advanced through the translation of people's experience into the conceptually refined language of social science (Bourdieu 1999a, 1999b).

Bourdieu declares that he is particularly worried by the moral position occupied by social commentators, who for the sake of advancing a critically refined point of view are required to operate from an 'objectivising distance that reduces the individual to a specimen in a display case' (Bourdieu 1999a: 2). He identifies his discipline with theories and methods in which 'we do nothing but gloss one another' (Bourdieu 1999b: 607) and goes so far as to label them as types of 'symbolic violence' that not only work to distort the reality of people's lived experience but also perpetrate harm. At one level, Bourdieu is alarmed by the lack of empathy and absence of everyday understanding of those writing about the miseries of the world from 'very privileged' positions where they are set at a safe distance from the suffering they bear witness to. At another level he is worried by the potential for the rationalizing conventions of academic writing to operate as a means to clear-up and cut a neat path through the many hermeneutic confusions and epistemological frustrations borne by people struggling to make adequate moral sense of situations of extreme adversity. Bourdieu argues that many of the methods used to mine empirical data for core material that holds analytical value as 'social science' result in treating much of the moral and semantic agony endured through damaging experiences of social life as no more than an inchoate noise or as an irrelevant waste by-product. He encourages his readers to be morally preoccupied by the knowledge that academic writing works to 'filter out' some of the most essential components of the pain and distress borne by people in real-life contexts of social suffering. Bourdieu recognizes that texts devoted to capturing the 'emotional force' of experiences of human suffering 'can ... generate ambiguity [and] even confusion, in symbolic effects', but he sides with the view that a greater danger lies in the extent to which the 'gloss' of sociology leaves readers unmoved and with no zeal for change (Bourdieu 1999b: 623). Ultimately, he declares that his decision to document unvarnished experiences of social suffering is a bid to 'touch and move the reader, to reach the emotions, without giving in to sensationalism, [so] that they can produce the shifts in thinking and seeing that are often the precondition for comprehension' (ibid.).

Willem Schinkel explains that this decision 'to let the sufferings of the ordinary man speak for themselves' was the result of Bourdieu's long-standing frustration with his own sense of powerlessness when documenting the reproduction of inequality (Schinkel 2003: 79). *The Weight of the World* is Bourdieu's attempt to raise the volume on the contradictions that he inhabits and enacts through his sociological practice (Bourdieu 2000). For Schinkel, such work should be read as a 'daring venture' to expose the *doxa* of the sociological field to critical question so as to channel such critical self-reflexivity towards a debate over the value bounds and condition of what passes for sociological understanding. Accordingly, while on the one hand Bourdieu champions sociology as a form of knowledge that holds value as a means to equip people with a capacity to understand and possibly undo the social causes of their misery, on the other hand he aims to make us sceptically orientated towards this account of sociology and its worth. At the same time Bourdieu uses *The Weight of the World* to issue a political protest against conditions of social suffering, he also seeks to make it operate as a protest against the academic conventions of his discipline and himself as an academic sociologist.

I have argued that this commitment to critical self-reflexivity in social inquiry is taken a step further in the pioneering example of Jane Addams' approach to 'doing sociology' outside the academy (Wilkinson 2014; Wilkinson and Kleinman 2016: 161–73). In a manner akin to Bourdieu, Addams advocates a deliberate courting of value conflicts and life 'perplexities' as a means to gather sociological insight into people's social states (Schneiderhan 2011; Seigfried 2002). She operates with a commitment to the view that emotionally challenging experiences are essential components of social understanding (Addams 1965 [1892]; 1998 [1910]; 2002 [1902]). Like Bourdieu, Addams contends that we 'learn bodily' (Bourdieu 2000: 141). On her account, for sociologists to become reflexively orientated towards the social values they embody and enact, they must endure emotionally distressing experiences of perplexity; and further argues that this is best achieved through them being personally affected by, and politically involved in, the conditions they are seeking to understand. Most notably, Addams' emphasizes that social understanding is acquired through us being involved in care *in practice* – we stand to learn about the social meaning and value of human lives through the experience of *doing* care work. The emotional demands, practical challenges, moral dilemmas and relational difficulties involved in taking care of others are taken as a pedagogy by which it is made possible to understand both how social life is made possible and how its conditions can be transformed for the better and perhaps, on occasion, even fashioned as 'good'.

In a similar vein, Arthur Kleinman argues that through such commitments social research becomes a 'moral epidemiology' that is bound to make us discomforted by the value-conflicts we embody (Kleinman 1999: 389). On this account, the cultivation of social consciousness understanding is set to be personally destabilizing, and all the more so in contexts where researchers record experiences of social violence or where they aim to be particularly attentive to the harms done to people through adverse conditions of everyday life. Increasingly, moreover, Kleinman also contends that it is through involvement in the morally demanding and sometimes difficult acts of care for people that we embody practices that may educate us as to our social meaning and state – that is, that it is made possible for us to grasp how social life takes place though enactments of substantive human values (Kleinman 2019).

Likewise, Paul Farmer holds that experiences of moral disquiet and emotional upset are necessary for galvanizing movements to promote the rights of the poor and for forging ties of solidarity with victims of social injustice.

Farmer argues that in the context of his advocacy of health care as a basic human right 'the road from unstable emotions to genuine entitlements – rights – is one we must travel if we are to transform humane values into meaningful and effective programs that will serve precisely those who need our empathy and solidarity most' (Farmer 2006: 153 and 164). Farmer is resigned to the fact that in his research and writing on diseases of poverty experienced among some of the most socially and economically disadvantaged populations of the world he is always set to be agonized by the dilemma of how to strike an appropriate balance between, on the one hand, the imperative to expose the calamitous effects of disease at the level of human experience and, on the other, a professional commitment to subject these to technically precise terms of analysis and finely elaborated critique. Moreover, a further emphasis in his work is brought to the extent to which contending with the structural conditions that deliver people into conditions of social suffering requires us to marry analytical rigour with the direct *experience* of many uncomfortable 'everyday obligations' of care (Farmer 2013).

All those mentioned above recognize that, through their work, they have been immersed in a social agony. It is not simply the case that this takes place as a condition of their engagement with social suffering but rather that it is an inescapable part of the attempt at understanding what suffering does to people. It is also held to be a necessary component of the acquisition of social consciousness and of knowledge of people in social terms; for this is taken to be founded on experiences where one is challenged to endure, as Max Weber puts it, 'the antinomies of existence' and to have a commitment to see how much we can stand (Wilkinson and Kleinman 2016: 112–13). It approaches the gathering of research data, the act of writing and the attempt to make this matter for people as always liable to court trouble and as always risking failure. The pedagogy of care sets the moral courage of social science on trial, and perhaps inevitably it is set to expose it as inherently deficient and wanting. In contexts of social suffering, the passion by which social understanding is made possible is inordinately difficult, and all the more so if it risks committing itself to actually doing some good.

Conclusion

Merrill Singer provides some of the most sustained reflections on how a 'critical medical anthropology' might develop a praxis that marries a commitment to apply anthropology to projects of practical care with the effort to develop critical theories about the world in which it operates (Singer 1989, 1990; 1995; Singer and Baer 2018). Writing with Barbara Rylko-Bauer and John Van Willigen, he describes this as a search for the means to achieve 'a systematic joining of critical social theory with a pragmatic engagement with contemporary problems' (Rylko-Bauer, Singer and Van Willigen 2006: 178). In practice,

Singer's approach involves a movement to combine an application of anthropology to the gathering of practically useful and policy relevant data about human experiences and relationships with forms of writing that are devised to make readers more politically alert to wider structures of power and inequality in society. The aim is to balance humanitarian practice with critique. Against those who contend that anthropologists must choose either to work as outside critics' or as 'inside ameliorators' of society, Singer argues that it is possible to devise pragmatic strategies of engagement where critiquing the injustices of the world co-exist with work applied to rectify those injustices (Rylko-Bauer, Singer and Van Willigen 2006: 183). He argues that it is possible for anthropology to operate both as a 'system-challenging' movement in health care and as an accomplice to caring interventions that engage with 'life beyond the ivory tower' (Singer 1995: 99).

Singer's articles tend to feature lists of the critical concerns and worries that need to be more fully 'acknowledged' as matters for debate. 'Applied anthropologists' are encouraged to openly confront their 'colonial heritage', to recognize that they operate within social fields that are organized around unequal power relations, and to take all opportunities available to them to expose the ways in which social institutions and systems operate to perpetuation exploitative patterns of human interaction and exchange (Singer 1989, 1990, 1995: 81). In some instances, these also include a plea for recognition to be brought to the fact that, in the contexts of health care, anthropologists are made to operate in arenas of political and moral struggle where they are made to *embody* social relations in contradiction that involve them associating with individuals with 'opposed interests' and with 'marked differences in their capacity to mobilize institutional power' (Singer 1995: 86). It might be argued, however, that Singer tends to tread rather lightly around this point, and especially where this is set to be considered in contexts of social suffering.

I have argued that in the context of engagements with problems of social suffering the embodied experience of such contradictions takes place at a pitch and with an intensity that is extremely difficult to bear, and in some of its most painful aspects this may even be unbearable. This may well result in the undoing of anthropology and sociology so that our research and writing is exposed as devoid of human value and as politically useless. In part, this is due to the brute fact that in contexts of social suffering social science is made to contend with situations and experiences where considerable harm is done to people. These are conditions where the most painful antinomies of human existence are gathered with a magnitude and force that is set to damage and destroy lives. As such they operate to greatly increase the volume of discord between the objectifying and analytical refined languages of social science and the moral substance of human experience of being immersed in anguish and debilitating pain. Here it often appears, as Vieda Skultans puts it, that this is akin to 'the impossibility of the well-fed anthropologist carrying out a participant observation study of famine' (Skultans 1998: 21).

It is widely recognized that towards the end of his life Bourdieu was wrestling with the agony of his praxis. On many accounts, as he moved to fashion his work as a politically engaged 'public sociology', he was left struggling to reconcile his critical theory with his passion for an applied politics of emancipation. It might be argued that ultimately he was left trapped in the anguish of knowing that he could not match the ambition of his analytical practice with a programme of action that was adequate to enable people to escape their social suffering. Accordingly, in the late documentary of his life and work, *La Sociologie est un Sport de Combat* (2001) (distributed in English under the title *Sociology is a Martial Art*), it often appears that his manner of praxis concludes in a contortion of protest against many immovable structures of domination (Swartz 2003).

In this chapter, I have argued that such protest should be accompanied by practices of care. For Addams, 'doing sociology' entailed the activity of taking care of others. It proceeded with a commitment to the understanding that the effort to do good was the only means to discover what good might be practically possible and how it might yet be better realized (Dale and Kalob 2006). It challenges us to find the moral courage to act whilst knowing that this is always set to immerse us in social agony. Yet, it is only by and through this that we might stand to grasp the social and human value of our lives and actions. There is not much to offer by way of comfort here, but it may be the only way by which it is possible to make our work matter and to identify it with some human promise. In this regard, I contend that any movement of 'critique' or 'resistance' should be allied to the pedagogy of caregiving as an essential component of a positively geared 'ethics of possibility' and of any involvement of social science in the task of building more humane forms of society (Appadurai 2013; Ortner 2016).

Iain Wilkinson is Professor of Sociology at the School of Social Policy, Sociology and Social Research at the University of Kent. He is the co-author (with Arthur Kleinman) of *A Passion for Society: How We Think about Human Suffering* (2016), and author of *Risk, Vulnerability and Everyday Life, Suffering: A Sociological Introduction*, and *Anxiety in a Risk Society* (2009).

References

Addams, J. 1965 [1892]. 'The Subjective Necessity for the Social Settlements', in
    C. Lasch (ed.), *The Social Thought of Jane Addams*. Indianapolis: Bobbs-Merrill.
_____. 1998 [1910]. *Twenty Years at Hull House*. New York: Penguin.
_____. 2002 [1902]. *Democracy and Social Ethics*. Urbana: University of Illinois Press.
_____. 1998. *Homo Sacer: Sovereign Power and Bare Life*, Stanford, CA: Stanford
    University Press.
Agamben, G. 2005. *States of Exception*. Chicago: University of Chicago Press.
Appadurai, A. 2013. *The Future as Cultural Fact: Essays on the Global Condition*.
    London and New York: Verso.

Bourdieu, P. 1996. 'Understanding', *Theory, Culture & Society* 13(2): 17–37.
_____. 1999a. 'Preface', in Bourdieu et al., *The Weight of the World: Social Suffering in Contemporary Society*. Cambridge: Polity Press.
_____. 1999b. 'Understanding', in Bourdieu et al., *The Weight of the World: Social Suffering in Contemporary Society*. Cambridge: Polity Press.
_____. 2000. *Pascalian Meditations*. Cambridge: Polity.
Bourdieu, P. et al. (eds). 1999. *The Weight of the World: Social Suffering in Contemporary Society*. Cambridge: Polity Press.
Calhoun, C. 2008. 'The Imperative to Reduce Suffering: Charity, Progress, and Emergencies in the Field of Humanitarian Action', in M. Barnett and T.G. Weiss (eds), *Humanitarianism in Question: Power, Politics, Ethics*. Ithaca: Cornell University Press, pp. 73–97.
Campbell, D. 1998. 'Why Fight: Humanitarianism, Principles, and Post-structuralism', *Millennium – Journal of International Studies* 27: 497–521.
Cassaniti, J.L., and J.R. Hickman. 2014. 'New Directions in the Anthropology of Morality', *Anthropological Theory* 14(3): 251–62.
Dale, C., and D. Kalob. 2005. 'Embracing Social Activism: Sociology in the service of Social Justice and Peace', *Humanity & Society* 30(2): 121–52.
Das, V. et al. 2015. 'There is No Such Thing as the Good: The 2013 Meeting of the Group for Debates in Anthropological Theory', *Critique of Anthropology* 35(4): 430–80.
Fadlalla, A.H. 2008. 'The Neoliberalization of Compassion: Darfur and the Mediation of American Faith, Fear, and Terror', in J.L. Collins, M. di Leonardo and B. Williams (eds), *New Landscapes of Inequality: Neoliberalism and the Erosion of Democracy in America*. Santa Fe: School for Advanced Research Press, pp. 209–28.
Farmer, P. 2006. 'Never Again? Reflections on Human Values and Human Rights', in G.B. Peterson (ed.), *Tanner Lectures on Human Values*, Vol. 26. Salt Lake City: University of Utah Press.
_____. 2013. 'Health, Healing and Social Justice: Insights from Liberation Theology', in M. Griffin and J. Weiss Block (eds), *In the Company of the Poor: Conversations with Dr Paul Farmer and Fr. Gustavo Gutierréz*. New York: Orbis Books.
Fassin, D. 2012. *Humanitarian Reason: A Moral History of the Present*. Berkeley: University of California Press.
_____. 2017. 'The Endurance of Critique', *Anthropological Theory* 17(1): 4–29.
Folkers, A. 2016. 'Daring the Truth: Foucault, Parrhesia and the Genealogy of Critique', *Theory, Culture & Society* 33(1): 3–28.
Foucault, M. 1977. *Discipline and Punish: The Birth of the Prison*. London: Allen Lane.
_____. 1978. *The History of Sexuality: An Introduction*. New York: Vintage.
_____. 1991. 'Governmentality', in C. Burchell, C. Gordon and P. Miller (eds), *The Foucault Effect: Studies in Governmentality. With Two Lectures by and an Interview with Michel Foucault*. Chicago: University of Chicago Press.
Golder, B. 2010. 'Foucault and the Unfinished Human of Rights', *Law, Culture and the Humanities* 20(10): 1–21.
Kleinman, A. 1999. 'Experience and its Moral Modes: Culture, Human Conditions and Disorder', in G.B. Peterson (ed.), *The Tanner Lectures on Human Values*. Salt Lake City: University of Utah Press.
_____. 2019. *The Soul of Care: The Moral Education of a Husband and a Doctor*. New York: Viking Press.
Laidlaw, L. 2002. 'For an Anthropology of Ethics and Freedom', *The Journal of the Royal Anthropological Institute* 8(2): 311–32.

Laidlaw, J. 2014. *The Subject of Virtue: An Anthropology of Ethics and Freedom*. Cambridge: Cambridge University Press.

Massé, R. 2007. 'Between Structural Violence and Idioms of Distress: The Case of Social Suffering in the French Caribbean', *Anthropology in Action* 14(3): 6–17.

McRobbie, A. 2002. 'A Mixed Bag of Misfortunes? Bourdieu's Weight of the World', *Theory, Culture & Society* 19(3): 129–38.

Nguyen, V.K. 2010. *The Republic of Therapy: Triage and Sovereignty in West Africa's Time of AIDS*. Durham: Duke University Press.

Nguyen, V.K., and K. Peschard. 2003. 'Anthropology, Inequality, and Disease: A Review', *Annual review of Anthropology* 32(1): 447–74.

Ortner, S.B. 2016. 'Dark Anthropology and its Others: Theory Since the Eighties', *HAU: Journal of Ethnographic Theory* 6(1): 47–73.

Redfield, P. 2005. 'Doctors, Borders, and Life in Crisis', *Cultural Anthropology* 20(3): 328–61.

Robbins, J. 2013. 'Beyond the Suffering Subject: Toward an Anthropology of the Good', *Journal of the Royal Anthropological Institute* 19(3): 447–62.

Rylko-Bauer, B., M. Singer and J.V. Willigen. 2006. 'Reclaiming Applied Anthropology: Its Past, Present, and Future', *American Anthropologist* 108(1): 178–90.

Schinkel, W. 2003. 'Pierre Bourdieu's Political Turn?', *Theory, Culture & Society* 20(6): 69–93.

Schneiderhan, E. 2011. 'Pragmatism and Empirical Sociology: The Case of Jane Addams and Hull-House 1889–1895', *Theory and Society* 40(6): 589–617.

Seigfried, C.H. 2002. 'Introduction to the Illinois Edition', in J. Addams (ed.), *Democracy and Social Ethics*. Urbana: University of Illinois Press.

Singer, M. 1989. 'The Coming of Age of Critical Medical Anthropology', *Social Science & Medicine* 28(11): 1193–203.

———. 1990. 'Reinventing Medical Anthropology: Toward a Critical Realignment', *Social Science & Medicine* 30(2): 179–87.

———. 1995. 'Beyond the Ivory Tower: Critical Praxis in Medical Anthropology', *Medical Anthropology Quarterly* 9(1): 80–106.

Singer, M., and H. Baer. 2018. *Critical Medical Anthropology*. New York: Routledge.

Skultans, V. 1998. *The Testimony of Lives: Narrative and Memory in Post-Soviet Latvia*. London: Routledge.

Swartz, D.L. 2003. 'From Critical Sociology to Public Intellectual: Pierre Bourdieu and Politics', *Theory and Society* 32(5–6): 791–823.

Ticktin, M. 2011. *Casualties of Care: Immigration and the Politics of Humanitarianism in France*. Berkeley: University of California Press.

———. 2014. 'Transnational Humanitarianism', *Annual Review of Anthropology* 43: 273–89.

Vitellone, N. 2004. 'Habitus and Social Suffering: Culture, Addiction and the Syringe', *The Sociological Review* 52(2): 129–47.

Wilkinson, I. 2014. 'On the Task of Making Social Inquiry Aligned to Caregiving: An Invitation to Debate', *Anthropology & Medicine* 21(1): 87–99.

Wilkinson I., and A. Kleinman. 2016. *A Passion for Society: How We Think About Human Suffering*. Berkeley: University of California Press.

Zigon, J. 2007. 'Moral Breakdown and the Ethical Demand: A Theoretical Framework for an Anthropology of Moralities', *Anthropological Theory* 7(2): 131–50.

———. 2008. *Morality: An Anthropological Perspective*. Oxford: Berg.

5

Thinking Time, Ethics and Generations
An Auto-ethnographic Essay on the Good between Philosophy and Social Theory

Victor Jeleniewski Seidler

I had spent the morning trying to finish reading the paper 'There is no such thing as the good' (Venkatesan et al. 2015). It was introduced by Jonathan Mair and Soumhya Venkatesan talking about 'Wittgenstein's spade', stating

> Speakers invited to debate a motion are expected to emphasise the differences between their own view and that of the opponents, and to play down the similarities. When the imperatives of competition are set aside and arguments are considered with a cool head, it often turns out that the two sides have more in common than they realized or were willing to admit. (Venkatesan et al. 2015: 430–31)

I wondered what this 'cool head' was supposed to be and whether it tacitly referred to a tradition of Western rationalist masculinity that could somehow stand back and assess. While I am not sure about 'cool heads', I welcomed that questions around ethics had become a 'hot topic' in anthropology in a way that could not be said about sociology to the same extent.

I wondered whether there was something about anthropology as a discipline – possibly to do with its size and history – that made certain programmatic moves within the discipline possible. For a long time the relatively small size of anthropology allowed for a certain understanding of its historical development and, as I was discovering, that questions raised about the turn towards ethics were partly inspired by Foucault's later shift in his writings towards ethics and subjectivities (Laidlaw 2014). Foucault is clear about the break he makes with his earlier concerns with power/knowledge even though he acknowledges he cannot easily explain this shift theoretically.[1] This seemed a significant influence in the turn towards ethics in anthropology, even if not the particular formulations that were being made towards the notion of the good that had emerged from different sources (see the Introduction to this volume).

I was not really aware of much of this when I had been invited to act as one of the rapporteurs for a workshop being organized by Anna Strhan and David Henig under the title 'Where is the good in the world? Cross-disciplinary interventions, Future Directions' held at the University of Kent, Canterbury in May 2016. I knew Anna from a Wittgenstein reading group in London, where we had also been thinking about Wittgenstein's practices of philosophical ethnography. We had also engaged, in different ways as researchers, with the work of Veena Das and the work that had been collected by Michael Lambek around the idea of ordinary ethics (Lambek 2010).

This work also carried a certain implicit relationship with ordinary language philosophy and an inspiration from the work of Stanley Cavell and, as I was to learn, set itself against ideas of particular notions of ethical expertise that had been developed in the growing field of medical anthropology. As was to become clearer, there were interesting tensions between 'ordinary ethics' within this intellectual tradition and what we might think of as an earlier existentialist tradition of everyday ethics. This was a tradition with a different but possibly related genealogy that stretched back to the politics of everyday life and transformations of the self of the late '60s. Stimulated by the events of May '68 in Paris and the resistance to the Vietnam War, and later by the women's movement and the diverse movements in sexual politics, it situated ethical relationships between the personal and the political.

In Britain, it was a younger generation of activists who responded to the philosophical challenges of '68 that were largely rejected by the dominant ethical traditions of the time, shaped through a clash between Kantian and Utilitarian tradition and the contemporary moral theories being developed at the time through arguments between Richard Hare and Philippa Foot. Even Iris Murdoch, who sought to show certain resonances between the limits of this tradition and French existentialist traditions, does not engage with '68 or the challenges of the women's movement.[2]

In contrast, Foucault joined Jean Paul Sartre and Simone De Beauvoir in acknowledging the ethics and politics of everyday life that were being imagined. Foucault helped found the Prison Information Group or GIP to provide a way for prisoners to voice their concerns and thus show they had their own counter-narratives that ethically challenged the dominant criminological discourses through which they were spoken. It is through visibility, Foucault writes, that modern societies exercise their controlling systems of power and knowledge. For Foucault, knowledge should transform the self. When asked in a 1982 interview whether he was a philosopher, historian, structuralist or Marxist, he replied 'I don't feel that it is necessary to know exactly what I am. The main interest in life and work is to become someone else than you were not in the beginning' (cited in Martin et al. 1988: 9).

I was reminded of these shifts in time and ways of thinking both personally and theoretically as I wondered whether I had given myself enough time to get to London St. Pancras station to catch the new high-speed train to Canterbury. I recalled memories of travelling to Canterbury when I was a graduate philosophy student, taking a transfer course to do an MA in Sociology in late September 1967. I was joining a department at Kent that contained both anthropologists and sociologists. These related disciplines were then taught together so that we could later chose a disciplinary direction. We spent a good deal of time learning about theories of social stratification, as it was known at the time, before the challenges of renewed engagements with Marx and traditions of structural-functionalism that moved across the disciplinary boundaries of anthropology and sociology.

In what follows, I offer four intersecting auto-ethnographic reflections on how the good and ethics have been located and explored across generations within and across social theory, sociology, anthropology and philosophy. In the first reflection, I explore relationships between 'ordinary language philosophy' and 'everyday ethics' and the resistance to engaging questions of everyday ethics in the turn towards post-structuralism that was so defining for a generation that came into the academy in the 1980s and after.

In the second reflection, I explore and question the disavowal of the 'personal' and 'experience' as sources of knowledge and how this relates to Durkheim's understanding of morality and the good. In the third reflection, I consider what it means to think across generations in approaching ethics, and the significance of gender. In the final reflection, I reflect on the limitations of a Durkheimian approach to the good and argue for the importance of approaches that allow for the dignity and integrity of difference.

Memories and Genealogies

Reflecting back about the interdisciplinary character of the historical moment, we were also close as postgraduate students to certain young academics in the philosophy and politics department. With Tony Skillen, Richard Norman and Sean Sayers, we were part of a founding group of *Radical Philosophy* though we carried different theoretical and political traditions. With Richard Norman, who had done his PhD with Peter Winch, there was a shared interest in Wittgenstein and through the influence of Winch the beginnings of an engagement with Kierkegaard's *Purity of Heart* and Simone Weil's *Oppression and Liberty*. These were texts that Winch was introducing, along with Rush Rhees, at King's College, London. I would sometimes attend their postgraduate philosophy seminars on Wittgenstein, travelling to London to attend. I was trying to navigate tensions between the empiricist sociologies I was being introduced to, and so between philosophy and social theory.[3]

Winch was known for *The Idea of a Social Science* (Winch 1958), but it was clear, even then, that he was not really identified with some of the ways his work was being read and was more engaged with writing about Wittgenstein and later Simone Weil in the book that he finally completed as *Simone Weil: "The Just Balance"* (1989). There was a tension I felt between the empiricism that was dominant in the Kent sociology/anthropology department and the interests that I had developed as an undergraduate in Wittgenstein, when I had attended postgraduate seminars given by Elizabeth Anscombe, herself a student of Wittgenstein.[4] Although she read Wittgenstein with less of an engagement with the social, our interest in the social was nevertheless encouraged by referring back to childhood contexts where we had learnt certain concepts in particular familial and social relationships and practices and so as part of what Wittgenstein names as 'forms of life'.

But despite different emphases in their readings of Wittgenstein, Anscombe and Winch shared a scepticism that he could be helpfully thought about as a 'philosopher of language' or the idea that he was doing 'conceptual analysis' as it was often called. Anscombe said that Wittgenstein's therapeutic method, which stressed the non-existence of definitive form of language discoverable by philosophers, was a tremendous liberation that had freed her from philosophical confusion. Wittgenstein shared with the post-structuralist tradition, which was to become decisive in the social sciences in the 1970s, an uneasy form of 'linguistic determinism' – the term is not really useful – where it was assumed that it was through language that experience came to be articulated. Yet there were also significant differences in relation to language, and they had very different ideas about tensions between 'language' and 'experience'.

Within the post-structuralist tradition as shaped through Foucault's work, there was an abiding notion that 'there was no experience' that existed prior to language. There was an assumption that it was only through discursive practices that subjectivities could be articulated and people could come to know the world. But this ignored the tensions that Wittgenstein was constantly aware of in *Philosophical Investigations* between language and experience (1953). He had learnt that not everything could be said, and often what was most important in life could not be sayable. In diverse ways this could lead you astray to think that Wittgenstein was developing 'a philosophy of language' where language existed as an autonomous structure providing meaning to a disenchanted world or to insist that he was 'an ordinary language' philosopher.[5]

Taking the fast train from St. Pancras, I realized that in the late '60s and early '70s you could only take much slower trains from Charing Cross and Victoria, and I used to enjoy the reflective time it gave me. But for me, it was also evoking memories of my time moving between London and Canterbury and my interdisciplinary journeys between philosophy and sociology whilst also reading anthropological texts. I was reading Evans-Pritchard but also recognizing that there were connections being made between philosophy and anthropology through Wittgenstein's work, partly in relation to his *Remarks on Frazer's The Golden Bough* (Wittgenstein 2018).

There were discussions at the time about understanding other cultures and questions of cultural relativism that touched on questions of ethics and the good. There were also discussions provoked at the time through Winch's writings on Evans-Pritchard, and questions of oracles and truth-telling in his 'Understanding Primitive Societies', as societies in the global South were still called.[6] There were also connections suggested between philosophy and social theory and the shaping of possible interdisciplinary imaginations, though many of these were not to be developed through a dominant structuralist turn that tended to treat ethics and the good as just another discourse. For a brief moment, there were lively discussions about the languages through which you could *make sense* of other cultures and how important it is to understand their practices through their own languages and, I am tempted to say given the focus of this volume, 'conceptions of the good'.

I remember when I first met Lawrence Blum on a visit to Oxford, where I would journey to postgraduate philosophy lectures. We walked around the town and talked about relationships between Wittgenstein, ethics and social theory, particularly resonances that we discovered with Durkheim. The seminars held at Balliol College in the early 1970s exploring the boundaries between philosophy and social theory were organized by Steven Lukes, Alan Montefiore and Charles Taylor. Taylor was at this time having a considerable impact with his work on Hegel on transforming the postgraduate culture and encouraging people at the time to read Heidegger.[7]

People were thinking across the boundaries of philosophy and the social sciences but were at the same time wary of the claims of scientific objectivity and wanting to treat claims to truth and objectivity with some care. Clifford Geertz was often a visitor, and he would contribute to discussions. There was a shared interest in the writings of the later Wittgenstein, who helped shape a generation's turn towards the social in philosophy through his notion of 'forms of life', but this would be channelled in different ways. Reflecting back, there was an interest in making connections between *doing philosophy* and concepts in everyday life and the social relationships and practices within which they were embedded. These connections were influential on a younger generation influenced by the women's movement and sexual politics as well as the events of '68 and the student movement. There was a clear commitment among this generation of scholars towards realizing the good in social life in terms of *living your politics* and the idea of *becoming* the transformation you wanted to see in the wider society.

Before Donald Davidson's influence shifted the terms of ordinary language philosophy, there was a brief time, encouraged by *Radical Philosophy*, when philosophers were seemingly becoming more politically sensitive and aware. Through a resonance with Wittgenstein's later work, there seemed to be an opening to appreciate relationships of class, race, gender and sexualities. There were possibilities of critiquing as 'forms of life' sexist, racist, patriarchal and homophobic assumptions that were reproduced with limited awareness in 'ordinary language' philosophy. Language, ordinary as well as of social theory, was also tacitly shaped through histories and colonial relations of power as anthropologists started discussing at the time (Asad 1973). Wittgenstein's vision of 'forms of life' – even though he was largely interested in creating anthropological thought-experiments (Palmié 2018) – could, it was hoped, also be historically *grounded* and possibly reframed through attention to the workings of diverse relations of power.[8]

Durkheim, Morality and Social Theory

During this period, I came to reflect that there were resonances between Wittgenstein's later writings and Durkheim's explorations of the social nature of ethics. There were ways that Durkheim's recognition of the moral nature of the social could allow you to think that anthropologies and sociologies framed within a Durkheimian tradition were already dealing with the moral when they were engaging the social. If we could think of society as a moral entity, this raised the question of whether morality was a clearly defined realm of social life. There was an awareness that it was the constraining aspect of social rules that would be experienced as forms of external obligation, which Durkheim had learnt from Kant while arguing that the moral law could somehow be identified with the social.[9]

There seemed to be shift in Durkheim's later work that I explored in *Unreasonable Men: Masculinities and Social Theory* (Seidler 1994), as he draws more directly from a Kantian tradition of cognitive categories through which the social is apprehended. I traced the ways Kant had framed a categorical distinction between nature and culture that could foster a disembodied vision of knowledge and how this shared a vision that it was only a dominant European white masculinity that could take its reason for granted. I was exploring how notions of justice and power that operated within the public realm alone set the masculine terms for classical forms of social theory. But Durkheim's functionalist thinking found it difficult to engage histories in other than the dualistic terms of mechanical and organic solidarities. There was an *unease*, I argued, about how individuals came to be socialized as they accepted the higher morality of society in contrast to their individual egoistic and selfish interests.

As Kant's moral law presented individuals with a higher moral vision of themselves where they were prepared to curb their individual egoistic desires in the name of the higher ethical demands of the moral law, so Durkheim framed individuals having to accept the moral law that they had supposedly given to themselves, through accepting the social that was framed through laws within a democratic polity they had supposedly voted for themselves.

Differences were too easily regarded as signs of pathology as the 'normal' was established as a moral regime that people – whatever their class, religious, ethnic backgrounds – could accept within a French republican tradition that still insists that it is *as* individuals that citizens are the bearers of legal and political right. Durkheim was framing a culture of assimilation in which religious and ethnic differences, including his own Jewish difference,[10] could be transcended as people learnt to identify themselves primarily as French citizens who held the cherished republican values of liberty, equality and fraternity.

Durkheim's moral character was at least partly formed through a Kantian modernity. It was as a rational moral self that he existed as an ethical human, and it was through his reason that he could appreciate the moral claims of the social. He had learnt within a liberal moral culture within the terms of an Enlightenment rationalism that he could *transcend* his Jewish differences so as to exist as a rational self in his own right. In this he was tacitly echoing Marx in relation to his Jewishness in 'On the Jewish Question', insisting it was in transcending particular identities or backgrounds, including Jewishness, that you could come to exist as truly human and so as a person in your own right.

As Durkheim had to deal with the realities of anti-Semitism as they emerged in France through the Dreyfus case, he insisted on the importance of upholding French republican values and arguing that Dreyfus was being unjustly charged. His responses to the 'Dreyfus affair' may well have shaped shifts in his own social theory and strengthened a commitment to French republican values. He needed to feel that his thinking was shaped not through traces of Jewish cultural memories and family legacies but as a rational human being whose arguments would be assessed as rational on the basis of their truth and objectivity alone.

This in turn shaped the development of sociology as a way of engaging the social world in an objective, impartial way, framed through the terms of a scientific rationalism that disavows the researcher's personal experience. This was a dominant tradition Wittgenstein had been questioning in a sustained way throughout his philosophical work. Yet despite Durkheim's remaining firmly within the tradition of scientific rationalism, both he and Wittgenstein in different ways questioned liberal individualism and utilitarian visions of society as collections of individuals each living out their own interests and desires. And both were willing to question utilitarian traditions within ethics.

But if there was some acceptance of differences of class, 'race', ethnicities, gender and religions, there was an overall sense for Durkheim that these differences could be given their due while at the same time being integrated within a social whole, in his holistic conception of the social. Durkheim sustains a vision of social order at the same time as he elevates the society as a *higher* moral reality that people have to submit to for their own good, even if it is not immediately evident to them. In this way, the social could also become a form of self-protection, as Durkheim could *disavow* his Jewish difference *as* a private and personal matter with little consequence for the intellectual work he does as a rational self and as a citizen within a French Republican tradition.

Theories of social stratification that we were learning at Kent in the late '60s as a way of introducing us to think sociologically did not deny the existence of class differences – or gender, sexual and racialized differences. Sociologists were beginning to name these differences that had often been tacitly *shamed* according to the values of a liberal moral culture, as they were learning to think across the boundaries of public and private spheres. Partly through the early impact of feminism disturbing social and political theory – including Marxism, which had sustained a distinction between public and private spheres, insisting that injustice, inequalities and oppression were only real within the public sphere – these differences were tacitly marginalized within traditions of structural-functionalism, as they showed *how* they worked in the higher interests of a functioning democratic society.

As radical students were turning to Marx and engaging in the anti-Vietnam war movement, I remember a particular protest in the dining hall of Elliot College at the University of Kent. We took it in turns to stand up and protest against the speech of George Brown, then foreign secretary, and the United States intervention in Vietnam. We made demands for student rights in the university and were concerned with the *relevance* of what we were learning in enabling us to understand the workings of Imperial and Colonial power and the military-industrial complex.

There was also a sense of joy and a focus upon liberation as students took to the streets in Paris in May '68, with workers and students able to support each other – an idea of the politics of everyday life – in reclaiming the streets of Paris and Grosvenor Square in London as sites of resistance and rebellion. Difficult to recall given the histories since, but there was a feeling of hope, an embodied sense that the world could be transformed radically as different groups learnt to identify and name their particular struggle against their oppression.

It's hard for a younger generation brought up in a very different technological world to believe that we learnt to communicate through leaflets produced and then passed quickly and efficiently from hand to hand, though you were often left with ink on your fingers. There was, even then, a sense of a generational conflict and an awareness that we had grown up into a very different post-war world with opportunities for learning that our parents never had.

We felt a sense of ethical responsibility to speak truth to power but also to engage ethnographically with our own lives through practices of consciousness-raising, anticipating how much could be learnt from reflecting upon our lived histories and experiences. There were connections to the civil rights movements in the US and the struggles of Black power and black consciousness movements in different parts of the world, including South Africa and the anti-apartheid movement. There was an awareness that a better world was possible and that disciplinary academic knowledges could be renewed through creating new personal and political imaginations. We underestimated the forces of capital that we were up against and the powers they had to call upon.

Everyday Ethics across Generations and through Gender

When I got to the bed and breakfast where we were staying for the workshop at Kent, I got into talking over tea with Jonathan Mair about how anthropology and ethics were alive as concerns in an earlier generation. He filled me in about more recent discussions around everyday ethics and the ways that Foucault's later writings had been part of the inspiration for James Laidlaw's work and the recent publication of *The Subject of Virtue: An Anthropology of Ethics and Freedom* (2014) and also for the earlier collection edited by Michael Lambek (2010) *Ordinary Ethics: Anthropology Language and Action*.

As we talked, I realized that there was an earlier engagement with everyday ethics in sociology, although it was not necessarily named as such, that had to do with the politics of everyday life and later with the practice of consciousness-raising within the women's movement that men had also re-created for themselves. There was a sense in the men's consciousness-raising groups that we were making connections between our subjective experience as men and the power we might assume in relationships. But there was also the vulnerability when, for example, boys were sent to public school at the age of 8 and learnt to accept that it was somehow 'good' for them to follow in the footsteps of their fathers and that they should feel grateful for the sacrifices their families had made to send them there. If they felt isolated, lonely and abandoned, they only had themselves to blame, and they could be assured that, however painful, the experience *would make a man of them*.

There was, then, an affective politics emerging through different forms of consciousness-raising groups that were explored by women within the women's movement and men who recognized the ease with which they had learnt to intellectualize their experience within a rationalist culture that taught them to live in their heads. Women insisted that men had to learn to do their own affective labour and *take more emotional responsibility for themselves*. This was part of a challenge to traditional patriarchies that allowed men to take their power within intimate relationships for granted, relying upon women to do the *emotional work* in helping to make them emotionally legible to themselves.

In this conversation with Jonathan across generations, I was identifying *how* sexual politics had engaged with ethics and an implicit understanding of the good in terms of gender equality, partly through a critical relationship with its own moralism as I had explored in *Recreating Sexual Politics: Men, Feminism and Politics* (Seidler 2009). We were drawing connections between lived personal experiences and the anxieties, fears and hopes we might be carrying from our pasts.

Tracing wider cultural and historical shifts in relationships, both personal and political, that we were living through, there was *an ethics of everyday life* that for me at least resonated with Wittgenstein's later philosophy. There was a way that consciousness-raising could be a space for ethical and philosophical/political reflection and action though the different forms it takes, with different groups re-imaging the practice for their own purposes. People would often be engaged with what they could *do* in *making changes* in relationships and everyday lives in order to create more equal emotional relationships, at least with intimate spaces, as they sought strength and conviction to challenge wider sexist, patriarchal, homophobic, class and racist relationships of power and domination.

As we learnt to listen to each other across generations, we also discovered *how* difficult it could be to communicate the ethical quality of these practices of consciousness-raising in a very different economic, cultural and political world. For a moment, I felt as if I was the member of a lost tribe talking about practices and relationships that a younger generation had known about intellectually but somehow felt they had absorbed in their pro-feminism as men, without having had to experience it for themselves. These histories and cultural memories could seem to make little sense in the present moment of austerity after a global financial crisis that left little hope that the world can be changed.

After the struggles over Brexit in the UK and the global Covid-19 pandemic, these times can seem even more distant. It was as if I was talking out of the hopes of another time that felt like a foreign country. As I spoke with Jonathan Mair about his fieldwork in Mongolia, I was left wondering about the personal inspirations for particular field work sites. I wondered whether anthropologists are encouraged to explore these personal connections and cultural assumptions or put them aside as they learn to be 'good listeners'.

Often there is a reluctance to explore some of the personal sources of the research we are doing, but as Max Weber acknowledged in his seminal essay 'Science as a Vocation', there are ways that these sources often inform the projects we take on, even if not the methods that we later apply. But I would argue that often people are confronted at different stages in a research project with emotional or intellectual issues that they have not resolved, nor could they have resolved at the outset of their research. In different ways, we can be ethically challenged by our research projects and the issues that emerge, which might go beyond the schedule we had set up and our carefully framed methodology. We can be *questioned* in unexpected ways, and it will often only be by taking *time out* that we can do the personal and theoretical work that allows us to return to the project in a different relationship. Rather, research projects involve a journey, and the interviews you do and the ethnographic encounters you have can question you at different levels of your experience in ways that you could *not* possibly have anticipated.

I learnt this most acutely working with Alice Hohenlohe on her PhD on third-generation German memory after the Holocaust and National Socialism.

There were moments when the ethnography touched her in different ways, asking her to question how she had learnt about these histories at her Catholic school and what conversations she had had with her mother when she got home.

There was a clear gender dynamic, with her mother actively encouraging her in her research and at some level wanting her to use her research to have conversations with her own mother – Alice's grandmother – who had lived through the war and been obliged to migrate from what had been the Eastern borders of Germany. She had wanted Alice to have conversations that she could *not* have possibly had herself, and she was keen to listen in or at least hear about them. These gendered dynamics over generations were also shown with her father being more reluctant to engage with their own family histories – so it took time for her to recognize a photograph of her father in a Wehrmacht uniform that had been sitting in the living room, so much part of the furniture that it was only later as the research developed that she could *see it* at all for what it represented. There were times when she felt she had to withdraw from the research to *take time* to reflect upon the questions the research was making of her and also to recognize that she had to find her own way of doing the research so that she was no longer doing it for her mother but for herself.[11]

Ethnography is a method that is used in different ways across sociology and anthropology, and as the workshop and this volume encouraged us to think about 'Cross-disciplinary interventions', it was helpful to consider how prepared students are for the field and the different geographical and cultural contexts they could find themselves in that might question them in radically different ways. There were times when Alice needed to take *time out* from tracing her family history during Hitler's time and the war so that she could explore emotional and theoretical issues that were coming up for her . There was a sense that she wanted to know but did *not* want to know about atrocities her family might have been involved in organizing. There were hesitations that made it easier for her to engage with her informants, who also shared a sense that they really wanted to know but also did *not* want to know at the same time. Sometimes they also had to deal with conflicts between what they were learning at school and what they were hearing at home, and this could be a conflict that young people chose to resolve in quite different ways.

But had she not been prepared to do this auto-ethnographic work – something that can sometimes involve engaging with emotional work that you might need support with – Alice would have been unlikely to gain the quality of interviews; people might well have been less willing to share their doubts, anxieties and fears had she not been willing herself to go to these places in her own personal and familial histories. As a supervisor, and as trust was slowly established over time, I supported her through this process and hopefully helped her believe in her own capacities to deal with whatever was coming up for her.

There was also another dynamic, harder to put in words but no doubt shaping the ethics of this specific research project, that Alice had chosen to work with me and that I was Jewish and that many people in my family had been murdered in the Shoah. I am not sure whether we dealt with this well or possibly as directly as we could have done, and it also reflected some of the personal issues that came up for me during the years of supervising the project. There was also the realization that Alice felt she could not have done this project in Germany. This partly had to do with university hierarchies and the ways recent German histories are still engaged with the dominance of positivist scientific methodologies. But she also discovered that she found it really hard to write when she was in Germany, and there was something about the emotional distance that she needed, possibly also from her family, in order to move her research forward. She had to come to terms with her own history and experience as third generation, but she also noted that it was in London when she discovered that what she had learnt in school *as history*, and so existing in a neutral and impersonal space of its own, was in fact *forming and shaping* the emotional histories that she carried in the present.

Gender, Difference and 'the Good'

As anthropologists are often working in a foreign language that they have had to learn to do their ethnographic work, it might seem to those outside the discipline as if the distance somehow protects you. Yet talking to Jonathan Mair, who had done his field work in Mongolia, he acknowledged how in reality similar issues emerge, sharing *how* questions of belief had fascinated him since childhood and that this had informed his interest in doing work in the anthropology of religion and so also ethics.

As a student, he had witnessed the turn towards an anthropology of ethics, partly under the influence of Foucault's later writings. But it was also interesting to explore how issues of gender had often *not* been engaged with in his generation of researchers because it was assumed that feminism was an issue that they *already* knew about, and given that they were living in a culture of greater gender equality, it was really the concern of an earlier generation.

Yet issues of gender *are* still present both in the workings of academic hierarchies and also in the research people are doing, even if they may today be sometimes less attuned to it. For my generation of sociologists, consciousness-raising was itself an ethical-political practice that sought to implicitly question a Durkheimian tradition of socialization that assumed that individual psyches were shaped through the social forces and relationships. In acknowledging how the *personal is political*, such practices questioned the dualistic sociological traditions that contrasted 'individual' and 'society' within a liberal framework.

Durkheimian traditions of socialization often assume individuals supposedly take on the values of the wider integrated society as their own. But feminist, queer and anti-racist theories have questioned Durkheimian traditions as, for example, young women recognized *how* within a sexist culture they have often learnt to relate to themselves as sexual objects and see themselves through the eyes of dominant masculinity. Even in cultures of greater gender equality, often it is in the unequal division of labour in childcare that traditional hierarchies can reveal themselves.

The return of a language of everyday sexism shows that fourth-generation feminists are engaging their own visions of the good society as they question the notion that they are living in a culture that is supposedly post-gender, as it was post-racial. A younger generation of activist feminists who were politicized through the global financial crisis of 2008 have questioned post-structuralist feminisms that emerged in the 1980s. They challenged notions of theoretical progress that fixed 'sexism' as a term of '70s' feminism that had long been transcended and somehow allowed themselves to forget earlier interpretations of the feminist idea that the *personal is political*. They felt assured that they had moved on theoretically and distanced themselves from an essentialism that they too easily saw present in earlier feminist writings.

But even if the challenges of postcolonial and women of colour were well taken, there were ways that post-structuralist feminisms too easily forsook the existential impact of experience, which they assumed too readily to be an effect of discursive practices. There was a deconstructive move towards texts that, despite the insights they provided, unwittingly worked to silence women's voices in making the notion of identity problematic. Decolonizing feminists have long argued that if we engage the complexity of postcolonial identities we can avoid fixing people into pre-given categories and so render it possible for people to also create their own subjectivities, often in opposition to prevailing cultural norms.

Wittgenstein's later philosophy acknowledges a tension between language and experience and the difficulties that people can have in giving voice to themselves within the prevailing cultural norms. There was a resonance between his writings and early feminist practices of consciousness-raising that should not be romanticized, but when such practices of consciousness-raising worked well, they worked as affective ethical-political practices. They helped shape a form of everyday ethics that was also embodied, as they encouraged people to *make connections* between their lived experience and the structures of power within families, schools and the wider society that had shaped their subjectivities.

Different generations of feminist scholars and activists have questioned prevailing notions of 'the good' that have traditionally reflected dominant white European masculinities. Feminists have often felt uneasy about notions of 'the good' that have attempted to locate women in positions of subordination within masculine worlds. It was too easy to introduce notions of the good that worked *to silence* women and somehow undermine the diversity of their own notions of ethics, values and their alternative conceptions of the good.

Too often, across different cultures, women have been identified with notions of selflessness and putting the needs of others before their own within dominant Christian traditions as they have also been secularized within European modernities.

In his paper in Canterbury (Robbins, this volume), Joel Robbins allowed space to question a Durkheimian tradition of socialization that somehow assumed that, unless pathological, people would shape their inner psychic lives through the norms and values of the dominant society that they internalized and made their own. But he was implicitly also challenging post-structuralist traditions that were also wary of the tensions that could exist between inner psychic lives and the prevailing discourses through which experience and subjectivities were supposedly articulated.

As I argue in *Unreasonable Men: Masculinity and Social Theory* (Seidler 1994), there are ways that the good, represented as a higher ideal around which society can be integrated, often reproduces the ideals of a dominant masculinity that can alone take its reason and rationality for granted. Often this dominant masculinity has legislated what is 'the good' for others without *listening* to what they have to say for themselves. But feminism challenges such disembodied visions of knowledge and the prevailing distinctions between nature and culture upon which they depend. In this sense, there are lines connecting Durkheim and later post-structuralisms that sustain distinctions between culture and nature that have, as Caroline Merchant insisted, brought about the death of nature, reducing living nature to dead matter and defining progress as the control and domination of nature.

This is a distinction sustained within Kantian ethical traditions that have so fundamentally shaped European modernities when they have distanced themselves from the counter-Enlightenment and romantic critiques as I argued in *Kant, Respect and Injustice: The Limits of Liberal Moral Theory* (Seidler 1986). Though not widely recognized at the time, I was drawing upon feminist ethics as a critique of rationalist modernities through their insistence on the interrelation between our bodies/our selves and insistence upon the embodied nature of human beings, questioning prevailing Cartesian dualisms between mind and body. They were also preparing the ground to acknowledge emotions and feelings as sources of knowledge and so widening conceptions of respect for persons.[12] There were also resonances with the early queer theory of Audre Lorde's *Sister Outsider*, which talked about the difficulties of undoing the master's house through using the master's tools. She writes, 'It is not our differences that divide us. It is our inability to recognise, accept, and celebrate those differences' (everydaypower.com).[13]

In the discussions that emerged in the workshop, there was a sense that there were different visions of good that had to be recognized and appreciated in the world. We needed to remember, for example, those who had acted to rescue Jews during the Second World War, even though they were relatively few. They showed what was possible, even though many risked their own deaths. But we also need to acknowledge, as the Oliners do in the uneasily named *The Altruistic Personality*, that it was often not those who had been brought up with religious or Kantian secular moral principles who did the rescuing but those who had had very individualized moral upbringing in which they were encouraged to do what they felt to be right, which was why so many refused to be labelled moral exemplars; they insisted they were only doing what any human being would do if a suffering stranger came to their door.[14]

In discussion, Robbins acknowledged that for some anthropologists there is a real tension between their own values and emotional experience and what they discover in the field. He worked within a small community in Papua New Guinea that had converted to evangelical Christianity and had moved from collectivist values towards individualist values (Robbins 2004), so echoing what Louis Dumont presents as a cultural shift in values. But his loyalty to Durkheim, as he also acknowledges, is partly because he wants to recognize how ethics is often a matter of constraint – of the obligations that people feel to do what is right, even if this goes against their personal feelings and desires. This is the constraint Durkheim learns to recognize with Kant.

This approach allows for a Protestant vision of a transcendent good that calls for renunciation and a commitment against evil, as defined within an evangelical tradition. However, the universalism of this kind of understanding of the good is for me suspect because of the ease with which Christian universalism has been used to stigmatize Jewish differences that have been identified as Carnal Israel, as Daniel Boyarin has explored. We need, I would argue, approaches that allow for the dignity and integrity of difference, rather than approaches that draw upon a Christian universalism to give difference its place within an integrated functionalist vision of society.[15]

We should be wary of how particular approaches to morality and the good can – as they did for Durkheim and aspects of his own Jewishness – be a form of self-protection in not having to engage with issues of class, 'race', gender, disabilities and sexualities that we have been slow to fully acknowledge within social theory, let alone philosophy, which has tended to hold more rigidly than other disciplines to notions of a rationalist universalism that so often undermine and trivialize the significance of historical and cultural differences.

Victor Jeleniewski Seidler is Professor Emeritus in Social Theory at the Department of Sociology, Goldsmiths University of London. He has published across the boundaries of social theory, including works such as *Making Sense of Brexit: Democracy, Europe and Uncertain Futures* (2018), *Recovering the Self: Morality and Social Theory* (1994), *Unreasonable Men: Masculinity and Social Theory* (1994), *Remembering Diana: Cultural Memory and the Reinvention of Authority* (2013), *Urban Fears and Global Terrors: Citizenship, Multiculture and Belongings after 7/7* (2007), *Remembering 9/11: Terror, Trauma and Social Theory* (2013) and *Ethical Humans: Life, Love, Labour, Learning and Loss* (2021).

Notes

1. For a helpful understanding of shifts in Foucault's work and his turn towards ethics, we might see how his work was actually aimed at refuting the position that Reason (or 'rationality') is the sole means of guaranteeing truth and the validity of ethical traditions. Thus, to criticize Reason is not to reject all notions of truth and ethics as some of his critics claimed. His ideas developed and changed over time. He shows a significant shift in his thinking in *Technologies of the Self* (Foucault 1988).
2. An interesting engagement with contemporary analytical moral philosophy and its striking resonances with some aspects of existentialist tradition in their focus upon moments of choice, see Iris Murdoch's essays in the collection *Existentialists and Mystics: Writings on Philosophy and Literature*, especially 'Metaphysics and Ethics' (Murdoch 1997a) and 'Vision and Choice in Morality' (Murdoch 1997b), and for a sense of her politics at the time, 'A House of Theory' (Murdoch 1997c).
3. This was part of a generational experience of students who had been led from an interest in Wittgenstein's later *Philosophical Investigations* (1953) into considerations of the social and political through his reflections on 'forms of life'. At Kings, with the occasional visit of Rush Rhees, there was an intellectual space created to help us think about relations between philosophy and the social, where this was understood in moral terms. Winch was widely known for his *The Idea of the Social Science and its Relation to Philosophy* (1958), a text he felt uneasy about in his shift towards writing about ethics. For a sense of the development of Winch's work and his later interest in Simone Weil, see, for example, Winch (1972, 1987, 1989).
4. For an introduction to Anscombe's philosophical work, see, for example, her major work *Intention* (1957), and in relation to ethics, *Ethics, Religion and Politics* (1981).
5. There has been considerable discussion about how to evaluate the breaks between Wittgenstein's earlier and later work, with some philosophers insisting that there is much greater continuity than people supposed. But there are also arguments about how this continuity might be imagined and what it means about whether Wittgenstein was responding to shifts in his life and the changed historical world or whether there is an internal conceptual development from earlier to later writings as has been argued for by Cora Diamond and James Conant as a 'resolute' reading. For some helpful reflections, see, for instance, Crary and Read (2000), and for a helpful review that places these different readings in a wider context, see Hertzberg (2003).
6. There were also the responses by Alasdair MacIntyre, Steven Lukes, Martin Hollis, Bryan Wilson and others in a lively discussion provoked around issues of understanding 'other societies'. For a sense of these historical moments and discussions provoked across the boundaries of philosophy and the social sciences, see, for instance, Wilson (1973) and Hollis and Lukes (1982).
7. Charles Taylor had recently published *Hegel* (1975), and there was also a widely read shorter version *Hegel and Modern Society* (1979). He was also to publish an influential collection of his essays under the title *Human Agency and Language* (1985). This was before his influential *Sources of the Self* (1992). More recently, his selected essays have been published in *Dilemmas and Connections* (Taylor 2014).
8. There was a struggle over his legacy, which, for a while, was influential around issues of belief in anthropology (e.g. Needham 1972) but had limited impact with sociology and its turn towards Marx and traditions of Western Marxism in the 1970s and the ensuing conflicts with Althusser's widespread influence in the reshaping of social sciences.
9. Durkheim's explorations of morality in relation to the social are presented in Durkheim (1984, 1961, 1958, 1995). See also the discussions of ethics in relation to postmodernity in Bauman (1995a, 1995b) and Giddens (1991).

10. For some helpful engagement with Durkheim's thinking about Jewishness and assimilation, see Lukes (1973), Hyman (1979) and Strenski (1997).
11. Alice Hohenlohe explains the different stages in her research project in the introduction to her book *In the Presence of the Past: Third Generation Germans and the Cultural Memory of National Socialism and the Holocaust* (2011).
12. My book *Kant, Respect and Injustice: The Limits of Liberal Moral Theory* (Seidler 1986) was part of a trilogy that explored the genealogy of different traditions of respect, inequality and injustice.
13. Audre Lorde's *Sister Outsider* (1984) brings together her essays written between 1976 and 1984, showing the roots of Lorde's intellectual and political development and demonstrating her own form of intersectional feminism. She writes 'I am not free while any woman is unfree, even when her shackles are very different from my own. And I am not free as long as one person of Colour remains chained. Nor is any of you.'
14. Samuel Oliner was ten years old when his entire family was murdered by the Nazis in Poland. He went on, with Pearl Oliner, to write *The Altruistic Personality: Rescuers of Jews in Nazi Europe* (1988). The book explores the experiences and motivation of those uncommon individuals who aided Jews without thought to any compensation of any kind.
15. Daniel Boyarin explores traditions of Christian anti-Semitism and the ways that Jews were identified with their bodies and with a spirituality that was bound to be defective because it could not transcend bodies in *Carnal Israel: Reading Sex in Talmudic Culture* (Boyarin 1993). See also Boyarin (1994).

References

Anscombe, G.E.M. 1957. *Intention*. Oxford: Blackwell.
_____. 1981. *Ethics, Religion and Politics: The Collected Papers of G. E. M. Anscombe*. Oxford: Blackwell.
Asad, T. (ed.). 1973. *Anthropology and The Colonial Encounter*. Amherst: Ithaca Press.
Bauman, Z. 1995a. *Postmodern Ethics*. Cambridge: Polity.
_____. 1995b. *Life in Fragments: Essays in Postmodern Moralities*. Cambridge: Polity.
Boyarin, D. 1993. *Carnal Israel: Reading Sex in Talmudic Culture*. Berkeley: University of California Press.
_____. 1994. *A Radical Jew: Paul and the Politics of Identity*. Berkeley: University of California Press.
Crary, A., and R. Read (eds). 2000. *The New Wittgenstein*. London: Routledge.
Durkheim, E. 1958. *Professional Ethics and Civic Morals*. Glencoe, IL: The Free Press.
_____. 1961. *Moral Education* Glencoe, IL: The Free Press.
_____. 1984. *The Division of Labour in Society*. London: Macmillan.
_____. 1995. *The Elementary Forms of Religious Life*. New York: The Free Press.
Foucault, M. 1988. 'Technologies of the Self', in L. Martin, H. Gutman, and P. Hutton (eds), *Technologies of the Self: A Seminar with Michel Foucault*. Amherst: University of Massachusetts Press, pp. 16–49.
Giddens, A. 1991. *Modernity and Self-Identity*. Cambridge: Polity.
Hertzberg, L. 2003. 'The New Wittgenstein', *Philosophy* 78: 425–30.
Hohenlohe, A. 2011. *In the Presence of the Past: Third Generation Germans and the Cultural Memory of National Socialism and the Holocaust*. London: Goldsmiths College.
Hollis, M., and S. Lukes (eds). 1982. *Rationality and Relativism*. Oxford: Blackwell.

Hyman, P. 1979. *From Dreyfus to Vichy: The Remaking of French Jewry 1906–1939*. New York: Columbia University Press.
Laidlaw, J. 2014. *The Subject of Virtue: An Anthropology of Ethics and Freedom*. Cambridge: Cambridge University Press.
Lambek, M. (ed.). 2010. *Ordinary Ethics: Anthropology, Language, and Action*. New York: Fordham University Press.
Lorde, A. 1984. *Sister Outsider: Essays and Speeches*. Berkeley: Crossing Press.
Lukes, S. 1973. *Emile Durkheim: His Life and Work*. London: Penguin.
Martin, L., H. Gutman and P. Hutton (eds). 1988. *Technologies of the Self: A Seminar with Michel Foucault*. Amherst: University of Massachusetts Press.
Murdoch, I. 1997a. 'Metaphysics and Ethics', in P. Conradi (ed.), *Existentialists and Mystics: Writings on Philosophy and Literature*. London: Chatto and Windus, pp. 59–75.
——. 1997b. 'Vision and Choice in Morality', in P. Conradi (ed.), *Existentialists and Mystics: Writings on Philosophy and Literature*. London: Chatto and Windus, pp. 76–98.
——. 1997c. 'A House of Theory', in P. Conradi (ed.), *Existentialists and Mystics: Writings on Philosophy and Literature*. London: Chatto and Windus, pp. 171–86.
Needham, R. 1972. *Belief, Language and Experience*. Chicago: Chicago University Press.
Oliner, S., and P. Oliner. 1988. *The Altruistic Personality: Rescuers of Jews in Nazi Europe*. New York: Free Press.
Palmié, S. 2018. 'Translation is Not Explication: Remarks on the Intellectual History and Context of Wittgenstein's *Remarks on Frazer*', in L. Wittgenstein, *The Mythology in Our Language: Remarks on Frazer's Golden Bough*, trans. Stephan Palmié. Chicago: Hau Books, pp. 1–27.
Robbins. J. 2004. *Becoming Sinners: Christianity and Moral Torment in a Papua New Guinea Society*. Berkeley: University of California Press.
Seidler, V.J. 1986. *Kant, Respect and Injustice: The Limits of Liberal Moral Theory*. London: Routledge.
——. 1994. *Unreasonable Men: Masculinity and Social Theory*. London: Routledge.
——. 2009. *Recreating Sexual Politics: Men, Feminism and Politics*. London: Routledge.
——. 2022. *Ethical Humans: Life, Love, Labour, Learning and Loss*. London: Routledge.
Strenski, I. 1997. *Durkheim and the Jews of France*. Chicago: University of Chicago Press.
Taylor, C. 1975. *Hegel*. Cambridge: Cambridge University Press.
——. 1979. *Hegel and Modern Society*. Cambridge: Cambridge University Press.
——. 1985. *Human Agency and Language*. Cambridge: Cambridge University Press.
——. 1992. *Sources of the Self*. Cambridge, MA: Harvard University Press.
——. 2014. *Dilemmas and Connections: Selected Essays*. Cambridge, MA: Harvard University Press.
Venkatesan, S. et al. (ed.). 2015. 'There is No Such Thing as the Good: The 2013 Meeting of the Group for Debates in Anthropological Theory', *Critique of Anthropology* 35(4): 430–80.
Wilson, B. (ed.). 1973. *Rationality*. Oxford: Blackwell.
Winch, P. 1958. *The Idea of the Social Science and its Relation to Philosophy*. London: Routledge.
——. 1972. *Ethics and Action*. London: Routledge.

———. 1987. *Trying to Make Sense*. Oxford: Oxford University Press.
———. 1989. *Simone Weil: A Just Balance*. Cambridge: Cambridge University Press.
Wittgenstein, L. 1953. *Philosophical Investigations*, trans. G.E.M. Anscombe. New York: Macmillan.
———. 2018. *The Mythology in Our Language: Remarks on Frazer's Golden Bough*, trans. Stephan Palmié. Chicago: Hau Books.

Part I Commentary

Steven Lukes

At least three distinct issues seem to me to be raised in the foregoing pages. In what follows, I will comment on each and conclude with a question that they jointly raise.

Suffering or Diversity?

The debate that this book continues seems to rest upon an inversion of what has been called the 'Anna Karenina principle' evoked by Tolstoy's unforgettable sentence: 'Happy families are all alike; every unhappy family is unhappy in its own way'. For the two articles that frame the debate – Joel Robbins's 'Beyond the Suffering Subject' (Robbins 2013) and Sherry Ortner's 'Dark Anthropology and its Others' (Ortner 2016) – agree that one can see suffering as universally recognizable as such, whereas what constitutes happiness, in a family or elsewhere, or, more generally, 'the good' takes many different forms, found in different forms of life, on which mainstream anthropology used to focus but does so no longer. Thus Robbins wrote of a 'new way of writing ethnography … in which we do not primarily provide cultural context so as to offer lessons in how lives are lived differently elsewhere, but in which we offer accounts of trauma that make us and our readers feel in our bones the vulnerability we as human beings all share'. Ortner acknowledges the value of contemporary work on well-being and the anthropology of critique, resistance and activism and the alternative visions of the future embedded in social movements challenging the existing neoliberal social order. But this acknowledgement falls short of what Robbins sees the focus on suffering as threatening to eclipse: namely, anthropology's promise to reveal 'differences in the way people defined and sought to produce the good'.

What anthropology promised was of course multiple: among other things, lessons of better ways to live (Mead 1928), astonishment (Shweder 1991), deprovincialization (Geertz 2000), 'self-parochialization' (Mahmood 2005: xiv),[1] horror stories (Turnbull 1972), satire (Geertz 1988), deep unifying structures despite the differences (Lévi-Strauss 1963) and much more. The question raised here is: do accounts of how lives are lived differently, involving different ways of defining and seeking to produce the good, impinge upon our judgments of good and bad, right and wrong – and, if so, how? Is what is at issue here just a switch of attention, focusing on newly pressing questions, with the successive eclipse of the appeal of cultural relativism, cultural self-determination and multiculturalism and the rise of human rights discourse? This seems to be Robbins's position: the 'turn' to suffering has gone too far; we now need an 'ethical turn', since we *also* need to return to the earlier project. Wilkinson, by contrast, seems to view the one as excluding the other: social scientists 'cannot operate above the fray of morality and politics', and anthropology and sociology should be 'ameliorative practices that contribute to the realisation of humane forms of society' (assuming that we all already agree on what counts as 'humane').

Is Lambek right that suffering and the good must be studied together? Can we attend to both suffering and the good simultaneously? Or is there a real issue here? Does adopting the 'ethnographic stance' stand apart from making ethical judgments? The question before us is 'Where is the good?' Does anthropological knowledge contaminate our answer to the prior question 'What is the good?' To sharpen the point in a familiar way (repeated in innumerable discussions with undergraduates): does understanding the ritual functions of what we call female genital mutilation preclude our calling it so? Does it require either what Cook calls 'moral recusal' (Cook 1999) or even endorsement of the practice *in situ*? Similarly, are there ever any grounds for hesitating to speak of child sexual abuse as described in Lynch's chapter?[2] More challengingly, does Ruth Sheldon's subtle ethnographic uncovering of the wisdom and confident self-possession that lies below the surface in orthodox Jewish women's self-understanding put talk of patriarchal domination into question? Answering these questions requires closer attention to what is meant by different ways of defining and seeking to produce the good. My provisional comment on this first issue is that Robbins and Lambek must be right: both suffering and diversity must coexist within the scope of anthropology. (Indeed, both are present in David Henig's chapter below tracing war victims' transition to seeking social justice.) Yet there is something right about Wilkinson's position: we should not hesitate to acknowledge the various harms that many forms of FGM inflict on women, the sexual abuse of children, or indeed the subordination of women (where the 'suffering' may be an external imputation).

Somewhere or Nowhere and Everywhere?

There has indeed been an ethical turn among anthropologists over the last two decades, inaugurated by James Laidlaw's Malinowski lecture of 2001 setting out the case for 'An anthropology of Ethics and Freedom' (Laidlaw 2002). Here one key issue has been what we may call *the demarcation problem*: how to distinguish what is ethical from what is not. Michael Klenk has helpfully distinguished between two broad approaches (Klenk 2019). On the one hand there are anthropologists, influenced by virtue ethics and by Aristotle, Foucault and MacIntyre, who focus on character formation – on what kind of person one ought to be – and the inculcation of dispositions; examples are Saba Mahmood (Mahmood 2005), Charles Hirschkind (2001, 2006) and Laidlaw himself (Laidlaw 1995, 2014). But this can plausibly only cover part of the ethical domain. On the other hand, Klenk mentions the practitioners of 'ordinary ethics', among whom Lambek is a central figure (Lambek 2010, 2015) alongside Veena Das (Das 2012) and others, influenced by J.L. Austin, Paul Grice and Stanley Cavell and focusing on everyday interactions.

Advocates of this latter approach often insist on its being free from any content-based restrictions. This is to respond to the demarcation problem by refusing to engage – to say, in effect, that there is no such problem. It is to assert that ethics, as the quotation from Cora Diamond suggests, is like logic, with 'no particular subject-matter'. It is not 'a sphere of discourse among others': it is an 'attitude to the world and life' that 'can penetrate any world and thought'. So we cannot distinguish ethical evaluations from strategic, tactical and prudential ones, or ethical judgments from epistemic or aesthetic judgments or from those that occur within the spheres of etiquette or the law or particular groups and associations. Ethics is everywhere and nowhere.

But this is to contravene – without explaining why – not only what philosophers argue but what people 'ordinarily' assume: that there is something to be demarcated. Bernard Williams famously argued that our ethical concerns are focused on 'Socrates' question', namely 'how one should live' (Williams 1985), and Webb Keane (Keane 2016), who also focuses on everyday interactions, takes this further, arguing that 'ethical life' picks out 'those aspects of people's actions as well as their sense of themselves and of other people (and sometimes entities such as gods or animals) that are oriented with reference to values and ends that are not in turn defined as the means to some further end' (2016: 4). It involves evaluation of self and others and operates at the 'middle ground of social interaction where people are provoked to cooperate or dispute, to explain themselves to one another, and, above all, to see themselves – through one another's eyes – or refuse to do so' (ibid.: 6). Thus ethics centres on

> the question of how one should live and what kind of person one should be. This encompasses both one's relations to others and decisions about right and wrong acts. The sense of 'should' directs attention to values, meaning things that are taken by the actor to be good in their own right rather than as means to some other ends. This refers to the point where the justifications for actions or ways of living stop, having run up against what seems self-evident – or just inexplicable gut feeling. As such values can also motivate the sense that the rules and obligations of a morality system are binding on one's specific actions. (Keane 2016: 20–21)

Studies within ethics 'focus on virtues, values and ways of life'. Within ethics, morality occupies

> the space within which people find themselves giving accounts, justifying, excusing, accusing, explaining, denying, praising, blaming, and all the other activities in which ethical categories and stances are made explicit. (Ibid.: 233)

Moralities, then, are 'a sub-species within ethics', 'more or less context-free, more or less explicit, systems of obligations', centring on 'obligations that are supposed to be grounded in consistent principles of great generality', which 'draw on features of interaction', and 'the ethics of interaction in turn respond to the precepts made available by morality systems' (Keane 2016: 20 and 134). Furthermore, whereas Williams focused exclusively on the Western philosophical tradition, in particular Kant and Kantianism and utilitarianism, Keane observes that there are 'many morality systems', citing, for instance, various kinship and marriage systems, imperial China and premodern Europe. Keane's suggestion seems to me to be a very promising one, with the further advantage of deploying and developing Williams's account of the 'peculiar institution' of morality and rendering it less peculiar by opening it up for comparative study.

Keane's account of ethical life demarcates it in terms of final or intrinsic 'goods'. It recalls Charles Taylor's 'strong evaluations' and Harry Frankfurt's 'second order volitions'. Robbins's version is 'a second order kind of thinking, whereby people evaluate their desires and decide that only some of them are ones they ought to have. Only some desires, we might put it by way of bringing the social into play, are ones people are comfortable being accountable to others for having'. I agree with Robbins's insistence that we should see these as 'real' – that is, existing independently of our interpretations of them and as available for investigation. Where, then, should we turn to investigate them? A helpful answer is threefold: (1) to what represents and sustains them over time: in rituals, exemplary individuals, myths and countless other external facts, from architectural styles (of, say, banks and churches) and the layout of cities to linguistic usages and modes of dress; (2) to what motivates people to think and act as they do – often, as Keane writes, in a manner that is 'instinctual, habitual, fragmentary and contradictory and does not require anyone's full awareness'; and (3) to the mechanisms or processes that interrelate (1) and (2), rendering the outer inner and the inner outer. That involves attending to all the ways in which symbolic representations more or less imperceptibly shape and are shaped by individuals' attitudes and beliefs but also to the successes and failures of attempts to inculcate the moralities that render those representations explicit. The studies in the second part of this book exemplify some of these possibilities. Thus both (1) and (3) can be seen at work in the managerial project (involving a bicycle ride) to inculcate corporate citizenship in contemporary China and in the role of school assemblies in aiming to forge ethical subjects; and (2) is at work in all the ethnographic chapters – in Anna Strhan's account of conservative Evangelicals' desire for a transcendental 'value beyond value', in Sheldon's 'Jewish ethnography' among Haredi women and in Henig's account of the internal struggles of victims of the Bosnian War.

And Then, of Course, There Is Durkheim

A third issue that traverses these pages is the matter of Durkheim, and in particular his alleged role in blocking the path to an adequate anthropology of ethics and morals. This suggestion was initially made by Laidlaw, when he uttered the remark cited above in his influential Malinowski lecture,[3] and it is taken up by Abbott in this volume. Laidlaw's Durkheim misled us into a narrow view of morality as a set of 'socially enforced external constraints on behavior'. Laidlaw's Durkheim offered us a 'peculiarly narrow conception of ethical life' (Laidlaw 2002: 317) that equates 'the moral with society', which is 'understood … to be based on moral obligations, and indeed defined … as being a system of moral facts', where morals derive 'directly from social collectivities'. The result is a conception of the social that 'so completely identifies the collective with the good that an independent understanding of ethics seems neither necessary nor possible' (2002: 312). Abbott likewise characterizes Durkheim as depicting morality as 'existing as binding rules of conduct that are set over and above the consciousness and interaction of individuals'. He contrasts Durkheim's 'holist position on morality', his 'static structural determinism', his 'top-down functional determinism', his 'externalist position' that 'reifies such obligations as having a reality and form that exists in abstraction from the specific interactional realities through which they are enacted and reconstituted' with the 'the messy entanglements of social life' (Abbott, this volume).

It is, of course, true that Durkheim's sociological vision was not focused on interaction in Abbott's sense – on the 'intersubjective constitution and sustainment of moral phenomena'. Yet it is incorrect, as an interpretative matter of Durkheim scholarship[4] and in relation to this book's topic, to write, as Abbott does, of 'Durkheim's reified externalism' and thereby neglect both the development of his views about morality and his accounts of ritual, myth and symbolism. As for the first, it is already clear in *Suicide* and most explicitly in the lecture course on *Moral Education* that the earlier focus on constraint in the form of 'binding rules of conduct' has developed to acknowledge the inseparability of the 'right' and the 'good' and to embrace the role of 'attachment' to the aspirations and ideals of social groups and, furthermore, to the key role of reflective autonomy (admittedly narrowly conceived) in modern conditions (Durkheim 2002 [1924]). And as for the second, Durkheim's contribution to understanding ritual (foreshadowed in his early foray into crowd psychology and fully set out in *The Elementary Forms*) has indelibly influenced sociological/anthropological thinking about sacredness and solidarity, as widely applied to both religious and secular contexts. Among the most recent examples is Randall Collins's theory of 'interaction ritual chains' (Collins 2004). Collins draws on Durkheim and (like Abbott) on Goffman to describe situations that are viewed as micro-rituals that are 'emotionally intense and cognitively focused', linking social morphology and social symbols. As Philip Smith has observed, this is a reworking of Durkheim's discovery of 'how the sacred emerges from a process in which the group engages in coordinated action with a common focus of attention', often involving 'rhythmic entrainment in activities such as singing and dancing', with 'a barrier against outsiders', a 'shared emotional mood' and 'symbols that are sacred or totemic for the group', leading to 'solidarity and belonging, a sense of morality and a distribution of emotional energy that powers up participants for a while afterwards' (Smith 2020: 194–99). A notable aspect of this application of Durkheim, singularly relevant to the chapters of this book, is its focus on small-scale, low-key activities in everyday life.

Goods or Values?

I conclude with some tentative observations about what I above called 'the prior question' to which this book's title demands an answer, namely 'What is the good'? The Taylor-Frankfurt-Robbins-Keane[5] approach suggests that mutually accountable desirability is the key to what Robbins seeks to identify. How, then, are we to identify 'the good'?

Philosophers typically but not always, assume that their task is to seek, more or less boldly, to arrive at the single best answer. Often, in the anglophone analytical tradition, they appeal, from G.E. Moore to John Rawls, to 'our' intuitions and devise, like Derek Parfit and Frances Kamm, carefully constructed thought-experiments about imagined scenarios to refine the principles from which to draw convincing conclusions. Nietzsche criticized the moral philosophers of his time for having

> only a crude knowledge of moral *facts*, selected arbitrarily and abbreviated at random – for instance, as the morality of their surroundings, their class, their church, their *Zeitgeist*, their climate and region and of being poorly informed (and not particularly eager to learn more) about peoples, ages, and histories. (Nietzsche 2001: 73–74)

And Alasdair MacIntyre has complained that in our time there is

> not even a hint of a suggestion that courses in social and cultural anthropology and in certain areas of sociology and psychology should be a prerequisite for graduate work in moral philosophy. Yet without such courses no adequate sense of the varieties of moral possibility can be acquired. (MacIntyre 2013: 31)

Some philosophers are coming to acknowledge the force of this critique, notably Owen Flanagan, author of *The Geography of Morals* (2017), and Stephen Darwall and others, who write that

> too many moral philosophers and commentators on moral philosophy have been content to invent their psychology or anthropology from scratch and do their history on the strength of selective readings of texts rather than comprehensive research into contexts. (Darwall et al. 1992: 188–89)

What, then, are we to expect from such research? How are sociologists and anthropologists to answer the 'prior question'? Traditionally, at least ever since Boas until the turn to suffering, anthropologists have assumed that their task was to seek, more or less boldly, a diversity of answers: that there are multiple and various ways of conceiving of what is a good life and how to live it, for the individual and communities, and what it is to be a good person, and that therefore the range of the ethical extends way beyond the intuitions and thought-experiments of the philosophers. So I want to conclude by asking whether we can say anything helpful about the plausible *limits* of that diversity. There have of course always been those (e.g. Cook 1999) who hold that there is much less than we think, claiming that apparent disagreements usually turn out on inspection to rest on misinterpretation: that what look like disagreements are really alternative context-relative instantiations of underlying commonalities – of the same underlying values. Some, such as Michele Moody-Adams, even argue that it is 'difficult (at best) to establish that one has indeed *found* a genuine instance of fundamental disagreement' (Moody-Adams 1997).

Plainly, there will be limits to what is going to count as mutually accountable desirability, on the other side of which lie cruel, degrading and oppressive forms of life that appear to have widespread endorsement within some cultural and subcultural contexts in the name of 'the good'. As Victor Seidler reminds us,

> Feminists have often felt uneasy about notions of 'the good' that have attempted to locate women in positions of subordination within masculine worlds. It was too easy to introduce notions of the good that worked *to silence* women and somehow undermine the diversity of their own notions of ethics, values and their alternative conceptions of the good. Too often, across different cultures, women have been identified with notions of selflessness and putting the needs of others before their own within dominant Christian traditions as they have also been secularized.

That is why, I think, it is helpful to discuss these questions in terms of 'goods' rather than 'values', since there are certainly cruel, degrading and oppressive *values* (though Seidler here seems to lump them together). In discussing this, we have reached the area in which the topic of ethics intersects with power, domination and interests.

One way of marking the distinction between goods and values is by appealing to the commonly used English translation of the Greek *eudaimonia*, namely 'flourishing'. The goods of human beings involve their flourishing. But note that this translation incorporates an analogy that is already misleading, since plants, unlike humans, flourish each in only one unique way. If we consider the most-cited present-day version of this notion, the so-called 'capabilities approach', advanced by Amartya Sen and Martha Nussbaum, this point, and its significance, becomes clearer. For Sen, what counts as human goods is developed through social deliberation that will vary culturally; Nussbaum, by contrast, proposes a list of goods with the goal of their having universal applicability (such as knowledge, play, etc.). But in both cases, the set of developmental capacities need not be co-realizable, and so the failure to fully develop any one of them is only *prima facie* bad – it might be outweighed by the fuller development of another capability (though they each have a minimum threshold). Thus what counts as flourishing is plural and indeterminate, in that there is no perspective-independent way of deciding between these alternatives. But it is not indeterminate in the sense of limitless. If the question 'Where is the good?' is taken to mean Where are those limits?', then *that* is an appropriate task facing the social sciences, notably psychology and cultural anthropology and sociology.

Steven Lukes is Professor of Sociology at New York University. His published work and teaching have focused on sociological theory, the sociology of politics, the philosophy of the social sciences and most recently the sociology and anthropology of morals. His principal books are *Emile Durkheim: His Life and Work* (1972); *Individualism* (1973); *Power: A Radical View* (1974; a third edition was published in 2021); *Marxism and Morality* (1985); and *Moral Relativism* (2008), and two collections of essays. He is also the author of *The Curious Enlightenment of Professor Caritat: A Novel of Ideas* (1995).

Notes

1. Meaning the perspective in which 'I parochialize my own certitude' (xiv). For a deep-reaching discussion of the paradoxes implicit in this perspective, see Keane (2018).
2. This question becomes trickier and more interesting when applied to more distant especially historically distant, contexts, where what Bernard Williams called the 'relativism of distance' (Williams 1985) begins to make sense because the reflective modern person cannot view the alternative of living in the society in question as a 'real option'. Since we live in one interconnected world, I am inclined to say that the relativism of distance applies to temporal not spatial distance.
3. Discussed in Miller and Lukes (2020).
4. See Lukes (2020).
5. It is not clear that Keane entirely fits into this lineage, since his account never leaves the sphere of social interaction, referring rather to the interrelation of first-, second- and third-person stances (Keane 2016).

References

Collins, R. 2004. *Interaction Ritual Chains*. Princeton: Princeton University Press.
Cook, J.W. 1999. *Morality and Cultural Differences*. New York: Oxford University Press.
Darwall, S., A. Gibbard and P. Railton. 1992. 'Toward Fin de siècle Ethics: Some Trends', *The Philosophical Review* 101(1): 115–89.
Das, V. 2012. 'Ordinary Ethics', in D. Fassin (ed.), *A Companion to Moral Anthropology*. Malden, MA: Wiley-Blackwell, pp. 133–49.
Durkheim, E. 2002 [1924]. *Moral Education*. E.K. Wilson and H. Schnurer (trans). Mineola, NY: Dover Publications.
Flanagan, O.J. 2017. *The Geography of Morals: Varieties of Moral Possibility*. New York, NY: Oxford University Press.
Geertz, C. 1988. 'Us/Not-Us: Benedict's Travels', in *Works and Lives: The Anthropologist as Author*. Stanford: Stanford University Press, pp. 102–28.
_____. 2000. 'The Uses of Diversity', in *Available Light: Anthropological Reflections on Philosophical Topics*. Princeton: Princeton University Press, pp. 57–70.
Hirschkind, C. 2001. 'The Ethics of Listening: Cassette-Sermon Audition in Contemporary Egypt', *American Ethnologist* 28(3): 623–49.
_____. 2006. *The Ethical Soundscape: Cassette-Sermons and Islamic Counter-Publics in Egypt*. New York: Columbia University Press.
Keane, W. 2016. *Ethical Life: Its Natural and Social Histories*. Princeton, NJ: Princeton University Press.
_____. 2018. 'Saba Mahmood and the Paradoxes of Self-Parochialization', *Public Books*, 8 March 2018. Retrieved 5 April 2021 from https://www.publicbooks.org/saba-mahmood-and-the-paradoxes-of-self-parochialization/.
Klenk, M. 2019. 'Moral Philosophy and the "Ethical Turn" in Anthropology', *Zeitschrift Für Ethik Und Moralphilosophie* 2: 331–53.
Laidlaw, J. 1995. *Riches and Renunciation: Religion, Economy and Society among the Jains*. New York: Oxford University Press.
_____. 2002. 'For an Anthropology of Ethics and Freedom', *Journal of the Royal Anthropological Institute* 8(2): 311–32.
_____. 2014. *The Subject of Virtue: An Anthropology of Ethics and Freedom*. New York, NY: Cambridge University Press.
Lambek, M. (ed.). 2010. *Ordinary Ethics: Anthropology, Language, and Action*. New York, NY: Fordham University Press.
_____. 2015. *The Ethical Condition: Essays on Action, Person, and Value*. Chicago, IL: University of Chicago Press.
Lévi-Strauss, C. 1963. *Structural Anthropology*. New York: Basic Books.
Lukes, S. 2020. 'Durkheim and the New Sociology of Morality', in H. Joas and A. Pettenkofer (eds), *The Oxford Handbook of Durkheim* forthcoming; Online publication June 2020: DOI: 10.1093/oxfordhb/9780190679354.013.30 [last accessed 5 April 2021].
MacIntyre, A.C. 2013. 'On Having Survived the Academic Moral Philosophy of the Twentieth Century', in F. O'Rourke (ed.), *What Happened to and in Moral Philosophy in the Twentieth Century*. Notre Dame, IN: University of Notre Dame Press, pp. 17–34.
Mahmood, S. 2005. *Politics of Piety: The Islamic Revival and the Feminist Subject*. Princeton, NJ: Princeton University Press.

Mead, M. 1928. *Coming of Age in Samoa: A Psychological Study of Primitive Youth for Western Civilization*. New York: William Morrow.
Miller, K., and S. Lukes. 2020. 'The Other Side of Freedom', *Anthropological Theory* 20(4): 414–37.
Moody-Adams, M.M. 1997. *Fieldwork in Familiar Places: Morality, Culture, and Philosophy*. Cambridge, MA: Harvard University Press.
Nietzsche, F. 2001. *Beyond Good and Evil: Prelude to a Philosophy of the Future*. Part 5. Section 186. Edited by Rolf-Peter Horstmann and Judith Norman. Translated by Judith Norman. Cambridge and New York: Cambridge University Press.
Ortner, S. 2016. 'Dark Anthropology and Its Others: Theory since the Eighties', *HAU: Journal of Ethnographic Theory* 6(1): 47–73.
Robbins, J. 2013. 'Beyond the Suffering Subject: Toward an Anthropology of the Good', *Journal of the Royal Anthropological Institute* 19(3): 447–62.
Shweder, R.A. 1991. *Thinking through Cultures: Expeditions in Cultural Psychology*. Cambridge, MA: Harvard University Press.
Smith, P. 2020. *Durkheim and After: The Durkheimian Tradition 1893–2020*. Cambridge: Polity.
Turnbull, C. 1972. *The Mountain People*. New York: Simon and Schuster.
Williams, B. 1985. *Ethics and the Limits of Philosophy*. Cambridge, MA: Harvard University Press.

Part II

Approaching the Good in Everyday Life

6

'To See a Sinner Repent Is a Joyful Thing'
Moral Cultures and the Sexual Abuse of Children in the Christian Church

Gordon Lynch

[The Church of England's] management of allegations of child sexual abuse reflect not just society's difficulties in coming to terms with it, but also how even institutions dedicated to good can both harbour individuals who are malign and can sometimes be institutionally incapable of effective responses to concerns about the sexual abuse of children.
—Opening Statement of Counsel to the Inquiry, Case Study on the Anglican Church, Independent Inquiry into Child Sexual Abuse, 5 March 2018

One of the defining features of the public standing of Christian organizations in many countries over the past three decades has been a series of cases relating to the sexual abuse of children.[1] Perpetrators of abuse have included clergy, members of religious orders and lay members, and abuse has taken place through social contacts made in churches and schools, as well as through youth-groups and other forms of welfare provision. Although public knowledge of cases of sexual abuse in these contexts was beginning to be well-established by the early 1990s (see, e.g., Bowman 2016; Keenan 2011), this increased significantly in the wake of widely-publicized public scandals that demonstrated both the extent of such abuse and the prior awareness of such abuse by senior church officials.[2] Of particular significance, in this regard, was the extensive reporting given by the *Boston Globe*, during 2002, to the scale and institutional knowledge of child sexual abuse within the Catholic Archdiocese of Boston (Investigative Staff of the Boston Globe 2002). Although these scandals were particularly associated with the Roman Catholic Church, increasing attention has also been paid to the sexual abuse of children in Protestant churches, with the Anglican Church, for example, being a major focus for investigation both for the Royal Commission into Institutional Responses to Child Sexual Abuse in Australia, which concluded its findings in 2017, and for the ongoing Independent Inquiry into Child Sexual Abuse in the UK.[3]

Whilst it has proven difficult to establish whether the prevalence of child sexual abuse is significantly higher in churches and related Christian organizations compared to other social institutions,[4] the scale and recurrence of such cases have undoubtedly had significant institutional implications. In addition to substantial financial costs from the settlement of individual and class actions, funding of support services, and contributions to some wider compensation schemes, there is also evidence of sexual abuse scandals weakening public identification with, participation in, and deference to, the Roman Catholic Church in particular (Bowman 2016; Donnelly 2016; Ganiel 2016).[5] Mass-mediated forms of moral shaming for Christian organizations periodically take place through the presentation of critical findings from public inquiries and reports, as well as documentaries and popularized dramas such as the 2015 Oscar-winning film *Spotlight* and the influential three-part documentary *States of Fear*, which played a key role in the establishment of a national commission of inquiry in Ireland to investigate the abuse of children in residential institutions run by religious orders.[6] They also occur through other public events, such as the widely-publicized response to a report on abuse in the Diocese of Cloyne in a speech to the Dail by the Irish Taoiseach, Enda Kenny, who criticized the attitude of the Vatican as narcissistic, disconnected and dysfunctional and representing 'the polar opposite of the radicalism, humility and compassion upon which the Roman Catholic Church was founded'.[7] In addition to new safeguarding policies and structures, symbolic acts of moral restitution have been made in response by many churches and religious orders through public apologies and expressions of regret, although the value of these remains contested by many survivors of abuse.

Criticisms of Christian organizations in relation to child sexual abuse extend beyond the circumstances in which children were abused to their subsequent institutional responses to disclosures of such abuse. These have included failures to believe accounts of abuse, failures to report knowledge of abuse to statutory authorities, the public undermining of the credibility of complainants by religious leaders, pressures to reach informal 'pastoral' settlements rather than pursue civil or criminal action, responses insensitively shaped by the policies of ecclesiastical insurers, and the circulation of religious staff known to have committed abuse to other placements in which they abused again or were liable to do so (see, e.g., Barth 2010; Gleeson 2016, 2017; Scorer 2014). Such criticisms have repeatedly been made over a number of cases since the publication in 1990 of the 'Winter' report, which concerned cases of abuse by Catholic clergy in Newfoundland (Archdiocese of St John's 1990). This raises the question, noted at the start of this chapter, as to why organizations whose rationale is to be oriented towards the good appear to have such difficulties in making appropriate organizational responses to child sexual abuse.

This chapter will attempt to answer this question, situating its argument in a wider body of recent scholarship that has sought to analyse the nature and significance of moral meanings in social life (see, e.g., Alexander 2003; Lambek 2010; Lynch 2012). It understands moral meanings not simply as 'action-guiding values' but as a form of communication that can enable social actors to legitimize or critique social actions and social authority, construct social bonds based on a sense of moral solidarity, make sense of and shape intersubjective processes, categorize persons and actions within or beyond the acceptable moral boundaries of human society, and shape ethical subjectivities (see Lynch 2014: 171–72).[8] From this theoretical perspective, it will examine whether the cultures of moral communication within Christian churches can operate in ways that hinder effective responses to instances of child sexual abuse. In this sense, it will ask whether problematic institutional responses to such abuse are not so much a conundrum in the face of a claimed orientation to the good but whether the very nature of symbolic communication about the good within Christian churches can itself be a contributory factor to these flawed responses.

In doing so, this chapter seeks to bridge the gap between 'dark anthropology' and the anthropology of morality (Ortner 2016) by encouraging discussion of the ways in which the pursuit of the 'good' in social life does not simply encourage a constructive sense of purpose or place but can also be bound up with causing, or failing to attend to, harm (see also Chong, this volume). Whilst this may take very different forms, given the myriad content, uses and social contexts of concepts of the good, it raises the broader theoretical question about whether systems of moral meaning (and their associated social relationships and practices) inevitably at some point give rise to harm by creating social exclusions, moral blind spots or intolerable forms of internalized moral conflict, or by legitimating harmful practices or structures of power (see, e.g., Alexander 2006; Orsi 2006; Lynch 2015). The intent of such work is not to see the good merely as an epiphenomenon, through which the 'real' underlying social structures of class, capital and power exert damaging effects, but to encourage a critical reflexivity towards the social uses of systems of moral meaning such that it is possible to see both their socially beneficial and harmful effects – including those forms of the good to which we ourselves feel a strong attachment.

In developing this argument, it is important to note from the outset that the system of moral meanings described below does not constitute monolithic cultures which determine social actors in predictable or consistent ways. This is evident, for example, in the different ways in which social actors within Christian organizations respond to cases of sexual abuse whilst participating in shared systems of moral meaning (see, e.g., the varied responses by individuals within the Church of England in response to concerns about abusive behaviour by the Anglican bishop Peter Ball, in Gibb 2017). Other factors, such as fragmented systems of religious governance that make the adoption of consistent child protection standards difficult, can also contribute to poor organizational responses to abuse (see, e.g., Gibb 2017: 7.5.1–7.5.5).[9] Nevertheless, Christian understandings of sin and redemption, like other forms of moral meaning, constitute a recursively reproduced social structure through which social actors interpret events, experience particular forms of sociality and provide legitimation for action. As such, they can contribute to particular kinds of response to child sexual abuse in religious contexts. Whilst the forms of response to child sexual abuse in Christian organizations discussed below do not constitute a comprehensive account of all forms of response that have happened in every case of abuse, they nevertheless represent identifiable patterns that have recurred across a number of cases in different national contexts. As such, they raise the question as to whether the nature and uses of symbolic communication about the good in Christian organizations need to be understood as one factor alongside others that can impede appropriate responses to cases of child sexual abuse.

Abuse and the Moral Transactions of Christianity

It has previously been argued that various forms of sexual abuse within Christian churches are a result of patriarchal theologies in which belief in an all-knowing and all-powerful God reinforces the power and authority of male religious leaders (and of men as sites of this moral authority within the family), who, in some cases, use this power for abusive, sexual ends (Fortune and Poling 1994: 40–41). Such an analysis tends to situate this theological context for abuse in more theologically conservative forms of Christianity. Whilst operations of power are clearly inseparable from both sexually abusive acts towards children, and institutional responses to such acts, it may be more productive to understand these phenomena more broadly in terms of forms of moral communication about the good that take place in a wider range of different Christian traditions.

Whilst taking varying forms across its many histories and traditions, institutional Christianity has been centrally concerned with moral relationships and transactions that situate the individual in relation to sin and redemption. The roots of this concern can be traced in the early transition of Christianity from an intra-Jewish millenarian movement oriented around the belief in the imminent arrival of the Kingdom of God to a movement spreading through the Roman Empire whose theological focus shifted towards the atoning nature of the death and resurrection of Christ. Whilst the earlier millenarian form of Christianity was still concerned with moral transactions – particularly in terms of challenging established moral hierarchies in first-century Jewish society and offering renewed moral standing to those previously considered polluted – the theological shift towards interpreting the significance of the 'Christ-event' exemplified in Pauline literature introduced ways of understanding moral transactions of sin and redemption that have remained foundational to Christian moral cultures since then. Although popular forms of engagement with Christian symbols, spaces and practices have, at times, regarded them more as sources of healing, blessing and luck (see, e.g., Orsi 2010; Williams 1999), and some Christian movements have sought to place a primary emphasis on social justice or environmental concern (Gasaway 2014; McFarland Taylor 2007; Rowland 1988), institutional forms of Christianity have typically placed more primary emphasis on the mediation of moral transactions that enable individuals to be redeemed from sin and bound to the new moral status made possible for them through Christ's atoning sacrifice.[10] These have variously included acts of private and public confession, rituals of baptism and the Mass or Eucharist, and the submission of the self to the moral truths of Christ's redeeming work in response to the preaching of the Gospel or encounter with Scripture.

Such moral transformations from sin to redemption are inescapably intersubjective, as particular individuals both human and divine are experienced as mediators of the good (Orsi 2006). Although institutional forms of Christianity have established moral precepts that have served to define what constitutes 'sin', the moral transactions of redemption are not primarily structured around adherence to a moral code. Instead, they offer various means through which the individual believer is able to lay claim to the moral transformation made possible through the unearned, gracious sacrifice of Christ, in which their redemption is premised on being bound to the continued presence of the resurrected Christ. The transactional nature of this transformation operates on the basis that the individual must accept that they cannot achieve good moral standing before God simply through their own efforts but can receive forgiveness for sin only through submission of their lives to God's redeeming work through the person of Christ. This submission is recursively reproduced through participation in ritual, prayer, worship, confession and other devotional practices, in which the individual believer is reminded to forgive others as they have been forgiven by God. The regular institutional repetition of moral meanings of sin and redemption, and of the moral transactions through which the individual is redeemed, habituates the individual religious subject in its symbolic, emotional and intersubjective regime, potentially making it a significant framework of moral meaning through which they interpret both their own lives and wider society.

The uses, operations and social effects of these moral cultures of Christianity vary in different social, cultural and historical contexts (see, e.g., Robbins 2004; Strhan 2015). However, with regard to cases of child sexual abuse that have come to public attention over the past three decades across a number of different countries, it is possible to identify a number of recurrent patterns in which moral meanings of sin and redemption have intersected both with the perpetration of sexual abuse and institutional responses to such abuse by Christian organizations.

Some of these relate to the ways in which abuse committed by individuals who have roles of particular religious significance is interpreted. As divine presence is made real through material, visual and aesthetic cultures curated by those with particular status and authority within Christian institutions (Meyer 2008), so those mediating figures themselves acquire symbolic significance as part of the network of relationships between heaven and earth through which redemption becomes possible. Shared understandings and practices around the moral transactions of redemption in institutional Christianity can create some sense of moral equality – for all are sinners in need of God's redeeming love. But the status of particular individuals in mediating such redemption through their management of rituals, preaching or role as exemplars of moral transformation can mark them out as having particular significance by virtue of their proximity to the process of redemption made possible through the person of Christ (see, e.g., Guido 2008; Scorer 2014: 28–38). Accepting the special role of these individuals in the wider intersubjective transactions of redemption necessarily involves an investment of trust in them within the wider network of believers for whom they perform this role (even if this trust is maintained alongside an awareness of that individual's personal weaknesses).

Such trust can have a significant bearing on abuse within the Church. In many cases, it has been argued that ordained clergy have been able to establish relationships with children whom they subsequently abused and have been able to continue their abuse without challenge because of the special trust with which they are regarded (see, e.g., 'Father M.' 2007). This trust can also shape responses to suspicions of, or disclosures about, child sexual abuse, with those immersed in these moral meanings of sin and redemption often finding it harder to accept that those with significant religious roles could have committed sexual abuse (Harper and Perkins 2018; Minto et al. 2016). Such moral presumption in favour of the member of the clergy, religious or other respected religious figure against whom allegations of abuse have been made has also, in the past, contributed to public statements by religious authorities, who have called into question the credibility and motivations of those alleging abuse.[11]

The particular moral standing of these figures is also commonly understood with reference to notions of vocation, in which they are believed to have been appointed to these roles (and have themselves understood their progression into such roles) as the result of a calling from God. Such understandings of vocation can frame the ways in which some clergy interpret their own sexual abuse of children, in which moral responsibility for this is handed back to the God who called them to this work. The continuation of their abuse can also be interpreted by them in terms of wider struggles of moral transformation that are taken to be a characteristic of all Christians' lives (see, e.g.,

Celenza 2007). As one participant in a study of priests who had committed sexual abuse put it:

> When I was offending, I couldn't convince myself that God didn't know. I brought it into prayer, treated it as a problem. I handed the problem over to God, treated it as a problem. I handed the problem over to God. It doesn't fit with how I am but this is the way you made me. It's up to you to sort it out. I treated it as God's problem rather than mine. It didn't outweigh the good I was doing. I hoped God would intervene. (Study by the Lucy Faithfull Foundation, cited in Scorer 2014: 32).

The importance given to vocation by others who have themselves been ordained has also, in some cases, led to religious authorities taking a sympathetic view of a perpetrator being allowed to return to some form of ministry on the basis that they should not be wholly cut off from their vocation (see, e.g., Gibb 2017).

The transactional processes of redemption can also provide a framework through which child sexual abuse is interpreted. Such transactions are premised on the beliefs both that all individuals are sinners and that all individuals, regardless of the nature of their sin, are capable of redemption through Christ. In some cases, those who have been sexually abused have interpreted their experiences as sin for which they bear some responsibility, or have been accused of sinful behaviour on disclosure of their abuse to others. Those committing abuse have also been seen as sinners capable of redemption. In many instances, this has led religious authorities to interpret their abusive behaviour as a failing in their spiritual formation requiring some form of intrainstitutional response rather than a criminal act requiring intervention from secular agencies.[12] Due to a belief that the possibility of redemption should always be kept open, there have been cases in which an emphasis on the pastoral care of the person who has committed abuse was given higher priority than taking the strongest possible steps to ensure that other children or vulnerable adults would not be abused by them.[13] The title quotation for this chapter – 'to see a sinner repent is a joyful thing' – is itself taken from oral evidence at a public hearing from a former Abbot of a Benedictine monastery justifying his support for the re-admission of a former monk who had previously committed sexual abuse within another Benedictine community attached to a school in Ireland.[14] Those subjected to abuse have themselves been told that if their abuser has made proper confession, the sin of their abuse has been washed away.[15] As will be discussed in more detail later, the significance accorded to moral transactions of redemption is also evident in attempts by religious authorities to preserve the principle of confidentiality in the rite of confession against calls for the disclosure of any knowledge of sexual abuse of children obtained during that rite.

The centrality of these moral transactions to the practices, emotional regimes and collective memories of institutional Christianity means that

Christian churches, and their related organizations, typically understand themselves as primary sites for human redemption within the wider societies in which they operate. The nature of these transactions does not necessarily imply that members of the Church are morally superior to those who are not, for all are sinners, and redemption is wholly dependent on divine initiative rather than human merit. But they do create an elision between the Church and the Good in which the Church's ability to claim to offer the means for redemption is both predicated on, and reinforces, its ability to project successfully a sense of moral authority.[16] This elision can create a reluctance both amongst some survivors of abuse and those to whom abuse is disclosed to bring this abuse into public knowledge through the criminal justice system because it is believed that this would taint that moral authority. This has previously led to particular protections being made of clergy or religious, who are taken to be representative of that moral authority, with the Ryan Commission in Ireland, for example, finding that lay people were far more likely to be reported to the police for child abuse in residential institutions than members of religious orders (Harper and Perkins 2018: 33).

The ways in which child sexual abuse in Christian organizations is embedded within these moral meanings can present significant, specific challenges to survivors of abuse (see Farrell 2009; Fater and Mullaney 2000; Guido 2008; Orsi 2016; Pargament et al. 2008). In addition to psychologically traumatic effects of sexual abuse, these survivors face the difficulty of interpreting their experience in the context of a rupture within the system of moral meaning they previously inhabited. For a child who is still constructed within Christian organizations as undergoing religious formation in relation to religious adult authority figures, abuse by such a figure can generate doubts for the child as to whether they themselves have committed a sin or whether their abuse may itself form part of a sacred transaction.[17] Such confusion may itself be encouraged by the perpetrator as a way of discouraging disclosure of the abuse (see, e.g., Bohm et al. 2014: 645). The moral meanings of sin and redemption can also create tensions for some survivors between a sense that the sin of the abuse can be addressed through the survivor's own act of forgiveness and the belief that it should be punished through the criminal justice system.[18] The difficulty of understanding these experiences within moral cultures of sin and redemption for those subjected to sexual abuse, both as children and later as adults, is not simply an interpretative one. The intersubjective nature of moral transactions of sin and redemption within Christian organizations means that the disruption of moral meanings is simultaneously interpretative and social. The victim's relationship with a figure through whom redemption has been mediated to them is now fragmented, potentially introducing anxiety about the possibility of being able to access this mediation safely through other relationships. For example, one victim of abuse reported that whilst they felt a strong need to confess their sins, and worried about their moral standing before God, they no longer trusted the safety of the confessional box

(Pargament et al. 2008: 405). This is further exacerbated in the case of individuals who have disclosed having been abused to another religious figure only for that figure to initiate further sexual abuse on them.[19] Alongside this, the victim's relationships with others, including members of their family, who have a strong investment of trust in that religious figure, may also become the site of significant tensions, heightening a victim's sense of isolation or reluctance to make wider disclosures about their abuse.[20]

Sin, Redemption and the Limits of Moral Reflexivity

The argument that moral meanings of sin and redemption shape patterns of responses to child sexual abuse in Christian organizations in unhelpful ways can be seen in the context of a wider critique of the ways in which the content and performance of Christian theology contribute to poor organizational responses to such abuse. Such theological critiques are well-established (see, e.g., Death 2013; Doyle 2017; Fortune and Poling 1994; Gleeson 2017; Gleeson and Zanghellini 2015; Palmer and Feldman 2017; Pattison 1998; Scorer 2014). These have been articulated both in academic contexts, including by professional theologians, as well as in wider public discourse.[21] Such critiques are indicative of the ways in which moral meanings can both operate as structures shaping cultural life as well as being the focus of critical reflexivity, just as can be the case with other social and cultural structures such as class, gender and ethnicity. Moral meanings do not, therefore, generate static moral cultures, but their significance and uses evolve through iterative processes of challenge, defence, reflection and innovation.

Such moral reflexivity is evident in some theological responses to child sexual abuse by Christian organizations. For example, the Faith and Order Commission of the Church of England has published two documents intended to guide theological reflection within the Church in response to cases of child sexual abuse (Faith and Order Commission 2016, 2017).[22] The longer of these, *Forgiveness and Reconciliation in the Aftermath of Abuse* (Faith and Order Commission 2017), explicitly develops the notion that some interpretations of sin, redemption, repentance and forgiveness can lead to harmful pastoral responses to cases of abuse, including child sexual abuse. Examples addressed in the document include simplistic understandings of repentance in which perpetrators fail to take full responsibility for their actions (ibid.: 79–81), failure to recognize that processes of repentance and forgiveness cannot be separated from the need for perpetrators to be punished for their actions through the criminal justice system (ibid.: 63–64), and the implication that survivors of abuse must forgive their abusers in order to fulfil the obligations of God's redeeming love for them (ibid.: 86). The idea that the Church itself may at times be guilty of corporate sin, through failures to prevent or respond appropriately to incidents of abuse, is also recognized, as are the limits such failings place on its ability to perform its pastoral mission of reconciliation (ibid.: 60–61, 110–11).

Despite these recognitions of the ways in which the moral transactions of sin and redemption can intersect in harmful ways with responses to child sexual abuse, the document is nevertheless unable to move beyond these moral meanings in its discussion of the Church's theological response to abuse. The document rehearses the central moral meanings of human sinfulness and the possibility of divine redemption for all, arguing that because abuse is a form of sin it necessarily binds those involved into the redemptive processes of forgiveness (for the victim) and repentance (for the abuser). For bystanders to hate or demonize the abuser, or for survivors of abuse perpetually to remain with feelings of recrimination, constitutes a form of moral failure on their part (ibid.: 42, 89). Whilst forgiveness of the abuser must never be forced on the survivor and may be a long process that can only be embarked upon by the survivor after they have been supported through facing the reality and effects of the abuse on their lives, the process of forgiveness nevertheless remains an aspiration (ibid.: 93, 95–97, 100). Whilst recognizing the psychological trauma of abuse, the call for forgiveness cannot wholly be put aside, because forgiveness remains an inseparable element of the moral transactions of redemption and the meanings of the good life:

> If I am prepared to say those words [regarding forgiveness in the Lord's Prayer], I cannot remain forever fixed in an attitude of retribution, recrimination or revenge. I must be open at some level to the gracious gift of God being extended towards those who sin against me, and to its transforming power for them, as also for me in my relations towards them. Being open to this possibility is part of what it means for us to come to accept unconditional love and forgiveness from God, the maker of heaven and earth and the one in whose image every human being is created. (Ibid.: 89)

Alongside this, the document recognizes that such an emphasis on the moral processes of sin, redemption, repentance and forgiveness is not necessarily a primary concern of survivors of abuse and that some survivors who were consulted during the process of writing it expressed 'real anger that the church seems so preoccupied with forgiveness in the aftermath of abuse, when the focus should be on justice' (ibid.: 10, also 87). Whilst the document makes clear attempts to integrate the expectations of criminal justice into its understandings of the moral transactions of sin and redemption, it is notable that the centrality of these moral meanings within institutional Christianity means that they can only be reinterpreted, and never given up, despite evidence of them being unhelpful to many coming to terms with their experience of sexual abuse within the Church. The centrality of these moral meanings is such that their negative effects can only be understood within this document as the result of 'distortions' of these moral truths, rather than an indication of any fundamental limitations of these meanings when applied to cases of child sexual abuse.

This document might therefore be understood as an example of the limits of moral reflexivity. Those habituated into a system of moral meanings may in some contexts be able to reflect on the harmful consequences of these but struggle to move beyond a sense of the claim of that system on their sense of moral subjectivity. This may be particularly the case in a context such as institutional Christianity, in which the recursive reproduction of these meanings constitutes a fundamental element of both its corporate self-understanding and the role of its leaders and clergy.

The limits of institutional Christianity's capacity to move beyond the demands of the moral meanings of sin and redemption in relation to child sexual abuse are further demonstrated in relation to current debates concerning the rite of confession. These have focused on the issue of whether a priest who has received a disclosure about sexual abuse from an individual in the context of the confessional is under an obligation to pass this information on to child protection agencies, or whether the 'seal' of the confessional – that anything confessed in this ritual remains a confidential matter between confessor and priest – constitutes a more binding moral obligation. Christian churches have demonstrated varying degrees of willingness to adjust their practice of this rite, whilst still maintaining the fundamental moral transaction of repentance and sin that underpins it. The Roman Catholic Church has continued to assert the paramount moral claim of the confidentiality of the confessional, with some senior clergy indicating that they would be willing to go to prison to protect this principle rather than break confidentiality by passing on information relating to child sexual abuse.[23] The recommendation by the Australian Royal Commission into Institutional Responses to Child Sexual Abuse,[24] that the Catholic Church considers withholding absolution from penitents who disclose that they have committed child abuse until they have themselves notified child protection agencies of this, has also not been accepted. The Church of England has adopted a policy in which absolution should be withheld in these circumstances (Faith and Order Commission 2017: 80) whilst continuing to assert the primacy of the principle of the confidentiality of the confessional. This policy was modified further by one Anglican diocese, which issued guidance that those offering the rite of confession should make it clear to a penitent before beginning the rite that any disclosures that raise serious safeguarding concerns may need to be passed on by the priest to other organizations. Whilst this diocesan guidance might appear to place the moral obligation to disclose knowledge of child abuse over that of the seal of the confessional, its meaning is somewhat more ambiguous. As a clarification of that guidance by the diocese has put it:

> This guidance has not – as some have claimed – 'abolished the Seal of the Confessional'. Rather, it is intended to advise the penitent not to divulge in confessing something which would legally compromise the position of the priest – and therefore require that priest to choose between their responsibility to protect someone from harm and the usual requirement of confidentiality. (Davies 2018)

The implication of this policy is therefore that the confessor is being advised not to place the priest in a moral bind by disclosing anything for which the priest might be forced to consider breaking the ritual framework of the moral transaction of confession. However, even the tentative warning in this policy that a priest might conceivably break the seal of the confessional under these circumstances has received strong criticism from theologically conservative commentators, who assert that the moral framework of this rite cannot be compromised in any way.[25]

To conclude, there are reasonable grounds for arguing that flawed responses to child sexual abuse in Christian organizations should not simply be seen as anomalous in the context of their orientation to the good but that the very nature and uses of Christian meanings of sin and redemption have contributed to these. As this chapter has argued, a growing body of material generated through public inquiries, survivor narratives and other public critiques has suggested negative effects of these moral meanings in relation to child sexual abuse in a variety of ways. These include the ways in which understandings of the good underpin forms of trust and vocation that can be exploited or give rise to denial about abuse, lead to concern for the redemption of the abuser being placed before the safety of children or the need for criminal prosecution and give rise to unhelpful attempts to protect the moral authority of the group, which can create difficult internalized conflicts for those who seek to reconcile their experience of having been abused with the moral meanings of sin and forgiveness. In some Christian contexts, this has been a stimulus for moral reflexivity about how such meanings are interpreted and performed. Willingness to engage in such moral reflexivity within the Church remains uneven, however, and even when practised such reflexivity typically seeks to clarify the 'true' meaning of sin, redemption, forgiveness and reconciliation, rather than suspend these notions in contexts where they either hinder child protection responses or cut across the lived experiences of survivors of abuse.

More generally, these examples of the intertwining of the good and harm raise more general questions about the ways in which systems of moral meaning give rise to (or tolerate) unnecessary social pain by creating bonds of trust that discourage moral critique, enabling moral self-justifications for harmful acts, generating collective moral investments in a group's public standing that give rise to denial or defensiveness in the face of claims about its moral failings, or by setting up painful tensions within individuals between the moral meanings they feel they should adhere to and the emotional meanings of their own experience of having been harmed. Whilst these processes take particular form in the context of the relationship between Christian concepts of the good and child sexual abuse, they may equally be observable in different forms through harm caused in relation to other religious or non-religious concepts of the good, including nationalism and humanitarianism.

Over the past three decades, increased public awareness of child sexual abuse within the Church has led both to more sustained scrutiny of the ways in which Christian organizations have responded to such cases and to the development of more formalized child protection procedures within these organizations. The centrality of the moral meanings of sin and redemption within institutional Christianity, however, suggests that these will inevitably continue to shape interpersonal and institutional responses to cases of child sexual abuses in potentially harmful ways. Recognizing this, some professionals and advocacy groups concerned with child protection and organizational responses to abuse have called for the introduction and implementation of statutory requirements that would place clearer legal obligations on the ways in which organizations (including Christian organizations) respond to cases of child sexual abuse. In the UK, for example, it is argued that the mandatory reporting of sexual abuse should be made a legal obligation and that this would, for example, require priests obtaining knowledge of sexual abuse in the context of the confessional to pass this information on to child protection agencies. Such legal expectations about reporting of sexual abuse are already in place in some other countries, with the Catholic Archbishop of Adelaide, Philip Wilson, having recently been found guilty in a criminal court of concealing knowledge of child sexual abuse earlier in his ministry in a landmark case in Australia. If moral cultures of Christianity continue to play some role in flawed responses to child sexual abuse in Christian organizations, it is possible to anticipate more instances of such legal interventions in the future. Such explicit tensions between secular justice and the moral meanings of sin and redemption will doubtless present significant interpretative challenges within institutional Christianity, in which one foreseeable response is that the hostility of secular agencies to the Church merely confirms the status of the latter as the persecuted bearer of the good in a hostile world. At the same time, continued evidence of failings within the Church to adhere to secular standards of child protection and support for survivors of abuse may lead to wider questioning of whether Christian constructions of the good merit legal exemptions (Gleeson 2017), deepening conflicts over moral meaning between some forms of institutional Christianity and increasingly non-religious societies.

Gordon Lynch is Michael Ramsey Professor of Modern Theology at the University of Kent. He was previously Professor in the Sociology of Religion at Birkbeck College, University of London, and is a Faculty Fellow at the Center for Cultural Sociology at Yale University. His public engagement work has included serving as an expert witness for both the Independent Inquiry into Child Sex Abuse and the Scottish Child Abuse Inquiry. He is the author of *The Sacred in the Modern World* (2011), *On the Sacred* (2012) and *Remembering Child Migration: Faith, Nation-Building and the Wounds of Charity* (2015), among other books he has written or edited.

Notes

1. For a summary of a number of relevant commissions and reports in different national contexts, see Terry (2015).
2. See Donnelly (2016) on the changing social conditions in Ireland through which broadcast and print media began to publicize stories of sexual scandal concerning Catholic clergy from the early 1990s; also Parkinson's (2014: 128) observation that whilst such cases of abuse may not have been widespread public knowledge before the 1990s, they were often known within religious organizations themselves.
3. On earlier reports on child sexual abuse in Anglican dioceses in Australia, see Death (2013a: 6). See also Matthews (2012) on sexual abuse in African American churches. Increasing scrutiny has also been placed on organizational responses to child sexual abuse within the Jehovah's Witnesses (see, e.g., Royal Commission into Institutional Responses to Child Sexual Abuse, case study 29).
4. Ref to Australian Royal Commission statistical report. A study of 1,050 individuals who had disclosed experiences of being sexually abused as children in institutional settings in Germany indicated that 49% had reported abuse whilst in secular institutions, 38% in Catholic institutions and 13% in Protestant institutions (Sprober et al. 2014). However, there are considerable difficulties in establishing whether self-reported abuse constitutes a representative sample of the total population of those who have experienced sexual abuse in childhood. Another possible form of comparison is to study conviction rates for sexual offences involving children between those associated with religious organizations and the general population, but neither conviction rates nor rates of disclosure of abuse are necessarily an adequate indicator of actual instances of abuse (see Parkinson 2014: 121, 125).
5. See also Conway (2014) for a comparative study of religious organizational responses to such public scandals in different national contexts, and McPhilips (2017) on public disclosure of cases of child sexual abuse in the Church as an example of cultural trauma.
6. On the significance of both national and international media coverage of cases of child sexual abuse in religious contexts, see also Conway (2014: 331–32).
7. See 'Enda Kenny speech on Cloyne Report', 20 Jul 2011, https://www.rte.ie/news/2011/0720/303965-cloyne1/.
8. This theoretical framework allows for more complex understandings of the role that moral meanings play in shaping subjectivities and social transactions than concepts of 'values' in organizational studies as that which people 'prefer, hold dear or desire' and establishing what is considered desirable or undesirable behaviour (see Palmer and Feldman 2017: 24).
9. See also opening comments by Counsel to the Inquiry in Independent Inquiry into Child Sexual Abuse, Case Study on the Roman Catholic Church, transcript of Day 1, pp. 8–15.
10. The controversy amongst Evangelical Christians surrounding the publication of Steve Chalke's and Alan Mann's (2003) *The Lost Message of Jesus*, which sought to move away from traditional evangelical theologies of atonement, is indicative of the ways in which the understanding of the good associated with such theologies is both the subject of critique by some theologians and pastors and of rigorous defence by many others.
11. See, e.g., final report of the Royal Commission into Institutional Responses to Child Sexual Abuse, case study 26, *St Joseph's Orphanage, Neerkol*, pp. 79–80, https://www.childabuseroyalcommission.gov.au/case-studies/case-study-26-st-josephs-orphanage-neerkol.
12. See, e.g., final report of Royal Commission into Institutional Responses to Child Sexual Abuse, case study 11, *Christian Brothers*, pp. 29–38, https://www.childabuseroyalcommission.gov.au/case-studies/case-study-11-christian-brothers.
13. See, e.g., Independent Inquiry into Child Sexual Abuse, Case Study on the Roman Catholic Church, transcript of Day 9, p. 139.

14. See Independent Inquiry into Child Sexual Abuse, Case Study on the Roman Catholic Church, transcript of Day 10, p. 132.
15. See Independent Inquiry into Child Sexual Abuse, Case Study on the Roman Catholic Church, transcript of Day 1, p. 47.
16. See Alexander et al. (2006) on the social conditions for public audiences to accept performances of cultural meaning as authentic accounts of truth and goodness.
17. See, e.g., Independent Inquiry into Child Sexual Abuse, Case Study on the Roman Catholic Church, transcript of Day 8, p. 21, and Day 9, p. 6.
18. See, e.g., Independent Inquiry into Child Sexual Abuse, Case Study on the Roman Catholic Church, transcript of Day 9, pp. 21–22.
19. See, e.g., final report of Royal Commission into Institutional Responses to Child Sexual Abuse, case study 11, *Christian Brothers*, pp. 24–25.
20. See, e.g., Independent Inquiry into Child Sexual Abuse, Case Study on the Roman Catholic Church, transcript of Day 8, p. 21.
21. See, e.g., questions about the negative role of theology and ritual practice on the Church's response to sexual abuse in opening statements by Counsels for survivors at Independent Inquiry into Child Sexual Abuse, Case Study on the Roman Catholic Church, transcript of Day 1, pp. 31–61.
22. See also the endorsement of these reports as helpful resources for theological reflection in Gibb (2017: 7.1.3).
23. Independent Inquiry into Child Sexual Abuse, Case Study on the Roman Catholic Church, transcript of Day 1, p. 51.
24. See Royal Commission into Institutional Responses to Child Sexual Abuse, *Final Report: Recommendations*, p. 55.
25. See, for example, the comment by the anonymous Anglican blogger, 'Archbishop Cranmer', 'Come and confess your sins but we might have to report you to the police', http://archbishopcranmer.com/canterbury-confess-confession-police/.

References

Alexander, J.C. 2003. *The Meanings of Social Life: A Cultural Sociological Approach*. New York: Oxford University Press.
_____. 2006. *The Civil Sphere*. New York: Oxford University Press.
Alexander, J.C., B. Giesen and J. Mast. 2006. *Social Performance: Symbolic Action, Cultural Pragmatics and Ritual*. Cambridge: Cambridge University Press.
Archdiocese of St John's. 1990. *Report of the Archdiocesan Commission of Enquiry into the Sexual Abuse of Children by Members of the Clergy*. Archdiocese of St John's: St John's, Newfoundland.
Barth, T. 2010. 'Crisis Management in the Catholic Church: Lessons for Public Administrators', *Public Administration Review* 70(5): 780–91.
Bohm, B. et al. 2014. 'Child Sexual Abuse in the Context of the Roman Catholic Church: A Review of the Literature from 1981–2013', *Journal of Child Sexual Abuse* 23(6): 635–56.
Bowman, M. 2016. 'Crisis, Change and the "Continuous Art of Individual Interpretation and Negotiation": The Aftermath of Clerical Sexual Abuse in Newfoundland', *Journal of the Irish Society for the Academic Study of Religions* 3(1): 140–70.
Celenza, A. 2007 'A Love Addiction: Psychoanalytic Psychotherapy with an Offending Priest', in M.G. Frawley-O'Dea and V. Goldner (eds), *Predatory Priests, Silenced*

Victims: *The Sexual Abuse Crisis and the Catholic Church*. Mahwah, NJ: Analytic Press, pp. 59–70.
Chalke, S., and A. Mann. 2003. *The Lost Message of Jesus*. Grand Rapids, MI: Zondervan.
Conway, B. 2014. 'Religious Institutions and Sexual Scandals: A Comparative Study of Catholicism in Ireland, South Africa and the United States', *International Journal of Comparative Sociology* 55(4): 318–41.
Davies, M. 2018. 'Our Confessional Guidance is Not Uncanonical, Says Canterbury Diocese', *Church Times*, 30 May 2018, retrieved from https://www.churchtimes.co.uk/articles/2018/1-june/news/uk/our-confessional-guidance-is-not-uncanonical-canterbury-diocese-says.
Death, J. 2013. 'Identity, Forgiveness and Power in the Management of Child Sexual Abuse by Personnel in Christian Institutions', *International Journal for Crime and Justice* 2(1): 82–97.
Donnelly, S. 2016. 'Sins of the Father: Unravelling Moral Authority in the Irish Catholic Church', *Irish Journal of Sociology* 24(3): 315–39.
Doyle, T. 2017. 'The Australian Royal Commission into Institutional Responses to Child Sexual Abuse and the Roman Catholic Church', *Child Abuse and Neglect* (74): 103–6.
Faith and Order Commission. 2016. *The Gospel, Sexual Abuse and the Church: A Theological Resource for the Local Church*. London: Church House Publishing.
Faith and Order Commission. 2017. *Forgiveness and Reconciliation in the Aftermath of Abuse*. London: Church House Publishing.
Farrell, D. 2009. 'Sexual Abuse Perpetrated by Roman Catholic Priests and Religious', *Mental Health, Religion and Culture* 12(1): 39–53.
Fater, K., and J. Mullaney. 2000. 'The Lived Experience of Adult Male Survivors Who Allege Childhood Sexual Abuse by Clergy', *Issues in Mental Health Nursing* 21(3): 281–95.
'Father M.' 2007. 'Severed Selves and Unbridged Truths', in M.G. Frawley-O'Dea and V. Goldner (eds), *Predatory Priests, Silenced Victims: The Sexual Abuse Crisis and the Catholic Church*. Mahwah, NJ: Analytic Press, pp. 111–20.
Fortune, M., and J. Poling. 1994. *Sexual Abuse by Clergy: A Crisis for the Church*. Eugene, OR: WiPF & Stock.
Ganiel, G. 2016. *Transforming Post-Catholic Ireland: Religious Practice in Late Modernity*. Oxford: Oxford University Press.
Gasaway, B. 2014. *Progressive Evangelicals and the Pursuit of Social Justice*. Chapel Hill, NC: University of North Carolina Press.
Gibb, M. 2017. *An Abuse of Faith: The Independent Peter Ball Review*. Report retrieved 5 June 2017 from https://www.churchofengland.org/sites/default/files/2017-11/report-of-the-peter-ball-review-210617.pdf.
Gleeson, K. 2016. 'Why the Continuous Failures in Justice for Australian Victims and Survivors of Catholic Clerical Child Sexual Abuse?' *Current Issues in Criminal Justice* 28(2): 239–50.
———. 2017. 'Exceptional Sexual Harms: The Catholic Church and Child Sexual Abuse Claims in Australia', *Social and Legal Studies*, published in online addition, 10 November 2017, 1–21.
Gleeson, K., and A. Zanghellini. 2015. 'Graceful Remedies: Understanding Grace in the Catholic Church's Treatment of Clerical Child Sexual Abuse', *Australian Feminist Law Journal* 41(2): 219–35.

Guido, J. 2008. A Unique Betrayal: Clergy Sexual Abuse in the Context of the Catholic Religious Tradition', *Journal of Child Sexual Abuse* 17(3–4): 255–69.
Harper, C., and C. Perkins 2018. 'Reporting Child Sexual Abuse Within Religious Settings: Challenges and Future Directions', *Child Abuse Review* 27: 30–41
Investigative Staff of the Boston Globe. 2002. *Betrayal: The Crisis in the Catholic Church*. Boston, MA: Little, Brown and Co.
Keenan, M. 2011. *Child Sexual Abuse and the Catholic Church: Gender, Power and Organisational Culture*. New York: Oxford University Press.
Lambek, M. 2010. *Ordinary Ethics: Anthropology, Language and Action*. New York: Fordham University Press.
Lynch, G. 2012. *The Sacred in the Modern World: A Cultural Sociological Approach*. Oxford: Oxford University Press.
_____. 2014. 'Saving the Child for the Sake of the Nation: Moral Framing and the Civic, Moral and Religious Redemption of Children', *American Journal of Cultural Sociology* 2: 165–96.
_____. 2015. *Remembering Child Migration: Faith, Nation-Building and the Wounds of Charity*. London: Bloomsbury.
Matthews, D. 2012. *Sexual Abuse of Power in the Black Church: Sexual Misconduct in the African American Churches*. Bloomington, IN: WestBow Press.
McFarland Taylor, S. 2009. *Green Sisters: A Spiritual Ecology*. Cambridge, MA: Harvard University Press.
McPhilips, K. 2017. '"Unbearable Knowledge": Managing Cultural Trauma at the Royal Commission', *Psychoanalytic Dialogues* 27(2): 130–46.
Meyer, B. 2008. 'Religious Sensations: Why Media, Aesthetics and Power Matter in the Study of Contemporary Religion', in H. de Vries (ed.), *Religion: Beyond a Concept*. New York, NY: Fordham University Press, pp. 704–23.
Minto, K. et al. 2016. 'A Social Identity Approach to Understanding Responses to Child Sexual Abuse Allegations', *PLoS ONE* 11(4), online version published April 2016, 1–15.
'Opening Statement of Counsel to the Inquiry, Case Study on the Anglican Church, Independent Inquiry into Child Sexual Abuse', 5 March 2018. https://www.iicsa.org.uk/key-documents/4335/view/5%20March%202018%20Anglican%20Public%20Hearing%20Transcript.pdf (pp. 11–12).
Orsi, R. 2006. *Between Heaven and Earth: The Religious Worlds People Make and the Scholars Who Study Them*. Princeton, NJ: Princeton University Press.
_____. 2010. *The Madonna of 115th Street: Faith and Community in Italian Harlem, 1880–1950*, 3rd edn. New Haven, CT: Yale University Press.
_____. 2016. *History and Presence*. Cambridge, MA: Belknap Press.
Ortner, S. 2016. 'Dark Anthropology and Its Others: Theory since the Eighties', *HAU: Journal of Ethnographic Theory* 6(1): 47–73.
Palmer, D., and V. Feldman. 2017. 'Toward a More Comprehensive Analysis of the Role of Organisational Culture in Child Sexual Abuse in Institutional Contexts', *Child Abuse and Neglect* 74: 23–34.
Pargament, K., N. Murray-Swank and A. Mahoney. 2008. 'Problem and Solution The Spiritual Dimension of Clergy Sexual Abuse and Its Impact on Survivors', *Journal of Child Sexual Abuse* 17(3–4): 397–420.
Parkinson, P. 2014. 'Child Sexual Abuse and the Churches: A Story of Moral Failure', *Current Issues in Criminal Justice* 26(1): 119–38.
Pattison, S. 1998. '"Suffer Little Children": The Challenge of Child Abuse and Neglect to Theology', *Theology and Sexuality* 9: 36–58.

Robbins, J. 2004. *Becoming Sinners: Christianity and Moral Torment in a Papua New Guinea Society.* Berkeley, CA: University of California Press.

Rowland, C. 1988. *Radical Christianity: A Reading of Recovery.* Cambridge: Polity Press.

Scorer, R. 2014. *Betrayed: The English Catholic Church and the Sex Abuse Crisis.* London: Biteback Publishing.

Sprober, N. et al. 2014. 'Child Sexual Abuse in Religiously Affiliated and Secular Institutions: A Retrospective Descriptive Analysis of Data Provided by Victims in a Government-Sponsored Reappraisal Program in Germany', *BMC Public Health* 14: 282.

Strhan, A. 2015. *Aliens and Strangers? The Struggle for Coherence in the Everyday Lives of Evangelicals.* Oxford: Oxford University Press.

Terry, K. 2015. 'Child Sexual Abuse Within the Catholic Church: A Review of Global Perspectives', *International Journal of Comparative and Applied Criminal Justice* 39(2): 139–54.

Williams, S. 1999. *Religious Belief and Popular Culture in Southwark, c. 1880–1939.* Oxford: Oxford University Press.

7
Making the Good Corporate Citizen
Corporate Social Responsibility and the
Ethical Projects of Management Consultancy
in Contemporary China

Kimberly Chong

In the mid-eighteenth century, several thousand Chinese labourers travelled to California with the hope of finding gold. In recent years, we have seen another 'gold rush'. This time it is the Western business elite, who has travelled across the world to make their fortune. Encouraged by a host of government incentives, they have flocked to the metropolises of Shanghai, Beijing and Guangzhou to mine the lucrative 'China market'. Spearheading the nascent operations of large multinationals, Western executives often struggle to cope with the pace of expansion. In particular, they complain that they cannot find the right kind of employees. As Aihwa Ong has pointed out, this is not conceived as a problem of technical expertise. Rather, there exists a widespread perception amongst Western managers that Chinese workers, whilst well educated for their jobs, do not display the requisite social knowledge and dispositions befitting employees of global entities (Ong 2006).[1]

Under Mao Zedong, China ran an autarkic regime, where workers enjoyed lifelong employment in state-run 'work units' (*danwei*), shielded from the pressures of market competition in a socialist command economy. During this time, almost all aspects of public and private life were subject to state control. The Chinese Communist Party even sought to influence people's thoughts (Lynch 1999).[2] In the four decades since Mao's death, China has embraced market capitalism and become firmly integrated into the global economy. It has captured the lion's share of manufacturing work, to become the second largest economy in the world. This dramatic contrast between China's present and recent past is often invoked in narratives that problematize the Chinese corporate subject. For example, Dimitri Kessler (2006) and Andrew Ross

(2006) find that Western managers in China's software industry attribute the 'deficiencies' of Chinese workers to their socialization in a context that is portrayed as the antithesis of global capitalism. Ridding them of their 'socialist' ways or 'irrational' Chinese culture is posed as a managerial conundrum, a hurdle to economic development that must be overcome if China is to move higher up 'the value chain'.

This chapter explores the new forms of subjectivity that are accompanying China's economic modernization, focusing on notions of 'the good' and in particular the good corporate citizen that is desired by Western multinationals and other 'global' corporations. It draws on 16 months' fieldwork inside the China arm of a global management consultancy, where, among other roles, I worked as a contractor in their division of 'corporate social responsibility' or 'CSR'. This consultancy, which I pseudonymously call Systeo, seeks to socialize its employees into a particular vision of the good through its CSR initiatives. Tracking the implementation of these initiatives, and employees' experiences of them, I show how particular understandings of what it means to 'do good' are shaped and contested in the practices of a global management consultancy, thereby opening up insight into how certain kinds of morality are woven into the production of new forms of corporate personhood (Kirsch 2014).

Although there has been a tendency to situate the anthropology of the good in opposition to the 'darker themes' of power, politics and inequality (Ortner 2016), as discussed in the introduction to this volume, in this chapter I show the importance of thinking through both together (see also Lynch, this volume). I take my lead from Dinah Rajak's observation that global corporations seek to create an 'imaginary of a moral self' that intensifies rather than ameliorates the most destructive elements of global capitalism. Writing about the mining company Anglo-American, Rajak argues that 'narratives of philanthropy play a key role neither as the antithesis to the logic of capitalism, nor as the company's conscience, but as the warm-blooded twin to the violence of corporate imperialism' (2014: 266). Whilst in their recent special issue on Energy and Ethics, Mette High and Jessica Smith make the point that studying the ethical logics and deliberations of powerful entities, such as oil companies in their case, is not to endorse their perspectives but rather is an attempt to 'understand [these ethical standpoints] on their own terms in order to respond to them' (High and Smith 2019). Instead of being opposed to the study of power, I suggest that the study of ethics and notions of the good can help us understand how power is produced, co-opted and retained within global capitalism.

For management consultants, the making of moral legitimacy is particularly important – they rely on processes of conspicuous ethicizing to underwrite their otherwise hollow professional standing (Kipping 2011). Invested with extraordinary power to restructure organizations, management consultants are known for failing to deliver. Behind the headlines that highlight the millions (of public money) spent on failed IT management projects is a lingering doubt over consultants' expertise.³ What do consultants actually do, and why do we entrust them to refashion our economy? The scope of their impact cannot be underestimated – almost all large public and private sector organizations will hire a management consultancy at some point. Changes to workplaces such as the growth in outsourcing, the implementation of comprehensive IT systems, and the ubiquitous redefining of the organization as being primarily motivated by performance objectives, can all be traced to management consultants. They do more than advise – consultants produce forms of knowledge: business concepts, ideas and models. These are epistemological tools that create the legitimacy for them to carry out organizational interventions, and which may or may not have their intended effects. Indeed, it is in the event of failure that performing morality – being a good corporate citizen – becomes paramount.

In this chapter, I explore the projects of corporate citizenship through which employees are encouraged to embody a moral ethos, in particular the annual charity bike ride – the most visible of Systeo China's corporate citizenship initiatives. Experiences of suffering, hardship and dislocation are part of an enactment of morality where employees are asked to relate to a 'safe' Other to which they can direct their goodwill. In this way, the production of meaning and affect is carefully managed. However, as we will see, Chinese employees interrogate the morality they are being invited to perform, suggesting that there are limits to which CSR can be depoliticized as a device of 'shared global values' (Rajak 2011). The subjectifying effects of CSR, which Rajak has criticized as a modern reincarnation of Western paternalism and corporate imperialism (ibid.), is challenged by competing visions of the good held by Chinese employees, visions that derive from the post-Mao context, where economic development and morality is mainly controlled by the state (Kipnis 2007).

Fieldwork inside Reflexive Management Production

One of the first questions people ask when I tell them I carried out fieldwork inside a global management consultancy is: 'how did you get access?' Many assume that consultants would be paranoid about having an anthropologist embedded amongst their ranks, not least because what I am interested in – the forms of knowledge and processes of valuation that underpin contemporary managerial techniques – is also what consultants sell. Management consultancies are the central institution in what Nigel Thrift terms the 'cultural circuit of capital' '... [which is] responsible for the production and distribution of managerial knowledge' (Thrift 2005: 61). Consultants trade in reflexive business management – they sell knowledge of the 'practicalities of business', which is, in turn, fed back into business practices. More than once I was accused, only half-jokingly, of being a corporate spy. But the fact that I was interested in the production of managerial knowledge could also be a selling point. According to Greg Downey and Melissa Fischer, business anthropologists have become the exemplary reflexive managerial subject (Downey and Fischer 2006), a depiction that lends itself to corporate collaboration especially in industries built on a foundation of reflexive knowledge, such as advertising (Mazzarella 2003; Moeran 2006) and information technology (Cefkin 2010; Nafus and Anderson 2006). An anthropologist 'for free' could be an attractive proposition if articulated in the right context.

My access was brokered with senior executives convinced of the efficacy of Systeo's corporate culture to produce exemplary corporate subjects. 'Systeo culture' was frequently invoked as a social totality that would swallow anything in its path. Even the *in situ* anthropologist would not be able to escape its effects, a view espoused by one expatriate manager, who told me 'by the time you leave here you will be Systeofied!' Perplexed by Chinese employees who did not display the desired subjectivity, expatriate management was open to the potential of anthropology to shed light on the situation. Many assumed that the problem lay with 'Chinese culture' – the intractability of Chinese employees, because of 'their culture', to yield to Systeo acculturation. But others feared that the ineffective operation of corporate culture, a concept that was originally devised by management consultants, would threaten their status as knowledge experts and thus had potentially negative implications for the project of selling management knowledge externally.

After a stint as an English trainer to Systeo's back-office employees (who carry out the routinized work of processing timesheets and expense claims and arrange business travel for consultants), I was invited to participate in an internal management project concerning Systeo's corporate culture – the 'human capital strategy programme'. The ostensibly overlapping content of anthropological and consulting expertise – that of culture – surely facilitated, if not informed, the invitation. In any case, with this new position came a new means of producing anthropological knowledge – through collaboration with my research subjects (Holmes and Marcus 2006). Effectively I was treated as an external consultant to Systeo's corporate culture – a position that conferred access to Systeo's HR department, internal corporate training, CSR initiatives, and entry to the various consulting offices in its China practice. However, after a year of access, my motivations for carrying out work unpaid started to be questioned. Thus, for the last few months of fieldwork I took on a contractor role in the CSR division, helping to coordinate local CSR initiatives in the China practice.

By participating in initiatives of 'corporate citizenship' – the vehicle through which CSR is implemented – it was hoped that employees would learn to perform the 'core values' that formed the foundation of the firm's 'corporate culture'. Due to my commitment to anonymize Systeo to the best of my abilities, I am unable to disclose the company's core values. However, it should be noted that companies in the professional services industry have strikingly similar core values. This is despite claiming explicitly, or at least implying on their websites, that their core values form the basis of their *distinct* culture or 'way of doing business'. For example, Boston Consulting Group, PricewaterhouseCoopers and KKR – a consultancy, an accounting firm and consultancy, and private equity firm, respectively – all espouse core values of 'integrity', 'diversity/respect for the individual' and 'innovation'. Notably, Boston Consulting Group does not use the term innovation though, preferring instead 'Expanding the Art of the Possible'. Historian Christopher McKenna observes that the two books that are widely cited as initiating the corporate culture movement in the 1980s – *Corporate Culture: Rites and Rituals* and *In Search of Excellence* – have strong links to McKinsey management consultancy's 'brand' of professionalism (2006). The former was based on McKinsey's definition of corporate culture, whilst the latter was written by two McKinsey partners, Tom Peters and Robert Waterman, as part of a strategic decision to commodify the firm's professional practice (ibid.).[4] The now ubiquitous idea that a company's culture is defined by a set of 'core values' derives from the codification of McKinsey's internal notion of what constituted professionalism. Rather than expertise being a source of professional status, for consultants performances of professionalism provide a resource for claiming expertise (Kipping 2011). Moreover, professionalism can be standardized and developed into a full-scale model of organization – McKinsey's famous '7s' model – which places 'shared values' at the centre of organizational coordination. In short, corporate culture hi-jacked cultural analysis for a management product.[5]

It is of relevance to ask why consultants espouse this notion of culture. The idea that organizational culture is a totalizing force that can be engineered at will, whilst clearly rejected by anthropologists (Marcus 1998; Wright 1994) is also a very particular view in organization studies and the field of management. In a paper on risk culture in the finance industry since the 2007–8 financial crisis, Mike Power, Tomasso Palermo and Simon Ashby make the observation that regulators, risk committees and consultants have a tendency to selectively appropriate from the organizational culture literature in their problematization of risk culture (2014). In particular, literature from the 1980s such as the work of organizational theorist Edward Schein is favoured. Schein, who espouses a deterministic notion of culture that can, vitally, be controlled, appeals to experts whose legitimacy rests on assertions of being able to change or at least strongly influence social reality. By contrast, more recent literature that emphasizes a more open, less deterministic conceptualization of culture (e.g. Alvesson 2013) is sidelined. Schein's formulation of organizational culture closely resembles McKinsey's formulation of corporate culture; indeed, Schein was a favourite intellectual source for Systeo consultants in their Powerpoint 'deliverables'. But it was always the spectre of failure – that despite all the exhortations of management consultants such a notion of culture could not produce the desired subjectivities – which animated my investigation. Hence, the aim of this chapter is to draw attention to the various subjectivities inside the consultancy, rather than focusing on subjectivation in the Foucauldian sense, which assumes the smooth production of subjectivities. Furthermore, I suggest that it is by comparing desired subjectivities, as delineated by management practices and discourses, with those that employees actually evidence that we can shed light on the character of knowledge that consultants sell.

According to Nigel Thrift, managerial knowledge, which at its most basic is concerned with the minutiae of interaction and human behaviour, is performative in the sense that embodied performances of this knowledge are required for its authentication (Thrift 2005: 96). In addition, he suggests that the prescriptive character of reflexive managerial knowledge is such that it 'has the power to make its theories and descriptions of the world come alive in new built form, new machines and new bodies' (Thrift 2005: 11). This second notion of performativity bears close resemblance to Michel Callon's thesis of performation. Writing specifically about economic models, Callon argues that economics 'performs, shapes and formats the economy, rather than observing how it functions' (Callon 1998: 2). This thesis has been taken up with gusto in the social studies of finance, where scholars have demonstrated how financial equations and trading algorithms work not to represent but to intervene in the social reality of financial markets (Mackenzie 2006; Mackenzie et al. 2007). Management consultants also produce practical models – those that are actually used in business – that do not necessarily correspond to economic or management theory as taught in universities (Thrift 2005). In so doing, they play an important role in shaping everyday business realities. However, it should be noted that the ways in which these models affect social forms are not necessarily isomorphic with the claims embedded in their theories. Hence, rather than focusing on whether or not models of corporate culture can be considered culture proper, I look at how practices and discourses of acculturation such as corporate citizenship create the legitimacy for managerial interventions in the most basic forms of corporate life.

Corporate Citizenship and the Performance of Morality

Writing about the 'de-radicalization of CSR', sociologist Ronen Shamir observes that 'the community' of CSR discourse can often refer not to local 'stakeholders' but the employees of large corporations. He argues that: '[B]y focusing on employee participation in CSR projects, by enlisting them to contribute time, money and knowledge, and by sharing with them the company's reputation as socially responsible, the normative control is deployed by transforming employees into a "community" and by turning labour relations into a question of employees' satisfaction and loyalty' (Shamir 2004: 683). CSR initiatives provide myriad possibilities for employees to perform the company's core values, and thus constitute an opportunity for subjective transformation (Lambek 2013). Inducting employees into being good 'corporate citizens' constituted a pathway for them to become 'Systeofied'. As Peter Grantham, a consultant from the London office, put it: 'CSR seeks to inspire our employees and reinforce cultural values about "who we are" and "how we operate."' In China, this injunction takes on a rather literal meaning. According to Stephanie Smith, Head of Global Giving, Systeo was only allowed to open offices in China on condition they provided educational and community investment.

In autumn 2008, I participated in Systeo China's 'flagship' corporate citizenship event – a charity bike ride across Sichuan province to raise money for victims of the devastating earthquake that had hit the region on 12 May of that year. To be considered for participation, I had to donate at least one item to an online auction. Other employees would then bid for these gifts, the money going to the Sichuan relief effort. The fifteen employees with the highest bids, and thus who had raised the most money, would be selected automatically. The remaining twenty slots would be decided by putting all the other 'sellers' into a lucky draw.

Just a couple of months after the auction I boarded a flight to Chengdu, the capital of Sichuan province, with all the other Beijing-based employees. Once there we boarded a coach that took us on a tour of the city before arriving at the hotel. Along with our flights and meals, Systeo had paid for us to stay in a 4-star hotel in the downtown area. After 30 minutes to check-in and freshen up, we met outside the hotel for the bike fitting. Gleaming, new mountain bikes were unloaded into the car park. British senior executive Mark McDougall had brought his own, well-used racing bike. The bike mechanics enjoyed teasing him in broken English, saying that it was a great bike maybe ten years ago'. Conversations were stilted but jovial as the participants – consultants drawn from the different China offices – started to get to know each other. We continued chatting over dinner. One consultant, Xing Feng, a native of Chengdu, was in hospital when the earthquake began. 'I was lying in the hospital bed when the walls started to move; I had no idea what was happening,' he recalled. The other participants listened with unwavering attention, some of them visibly moved. 'This is my home and I know people who have lost their homes, friends or family members,' he went on to say. His personal narrative contrasted with that of James Tsang, from Hong Kong but brought up in the US, who spoke in abstract terms that 'in these times, what with the financial crisis, it's good to give something back to society'.

We cycled between fifty and seventy kilometres each day, covering one hundred and fifty kilometres altogether. Mark, the British senior executive, was my 'chaperone'. One of the best riders, he was usually at the front of the pack but periodically he would hang back to check on those behind him. He would often cycle next to me, giving me advice on how to make better use of my gears and encouraging me with comments such as, 'just imagine how amazing you're going to feel when you cross the finishing line – it's gonna be worth all the pain!' Saddle sores were the least of my worries. With a route that included motorways and dirt tracks through industrial processing zones, as well as the expected climbs up Emei Shan and Le Shan, the famous mountains of Sichuan, we found ourselves cycling in harsh conditions. Our clothes were splattered with mud, and a thick layer of dirt covered our faces. The participants – middle-class, white-collar workers – could be forgiven for thinking they had signed up for a survival course not a bike ride. The message that we needed to suffer to do good, that this was an exercise in being 'outside your comfort zone', was deeply apparent.

Blocked roads, collapsed buildings and piles of rubble became familiar sights on our journey. The 'finishing line' was a construction site. A primary school that had been destroyed in the earthquake would be rebuilt, funded by Systeo. Led by the senior executives, we formed a procession of cyclists, greeted by cheers from local government officials, pupils and their parents. The pupils performed a song and dance routine. The consultants presented them with rucksacks stuffed with treats. Then the day's climax – a 'groundbreaking' ceremony in which senior executives were photographed posing with shovels alongside government officials. The next day we visited two more schools. Consultants dished out blankets and laptops. They asked the children if they had heard of Systeo and if they wanted to be management consultants when they grew up. Later we filed into the makeshift canteen and had lunch with the pupils, some of whom were dressed in the traditional costumes of the Yi minority. One little girl notable for her green eyes, so uncommon amongst Han Chinese, drew the most attention. Out came the digital cameras. Groups of consultants and children held their hands up, fingers adopting the 'V' for victory symbol, and smiled to the beat of the flash.

By fetishizing the people they helped, it would appear that Systeo employees considered them to be wholly different. The children were rural citizens, less sophisticated and un-modern in comparison. Deciding who deserves help requires a process of differentiation. Workers considered the children to be of lower *suzhi* (quality) – a concept that has become central to processes of governance in post-Mao China and is typically invoked as a form of social classification that justifies inequalities of power, status and wealth between those with 'high' *suzhi* and those 'lacking quality' (Kipnis 2007). Yet, in some ways, the children were not so different. Only the top fifty students (by test scores) were allowed to attend. Like the consultants, who were typically recruited from elite universities, they were high academic achievers – perhaps one day they would become consultants. The consultants were helping people they could both distance themselves from and identify with. Depicted as less fortunate versions of themselves, the precocious pupils of the destroyed Sichuan schools were the 'safe' Other to which they could direct their good intentions.

Employees sign up to a strange mix of endurance, self-deprivation and indulgence. Given they spend at least five days a week inside an office, cycling one hundred and fifty kilometres across Sichuan was physically as well as mentally challenging. But these were isolated, contained challenges. Unlike the children they visited, the recipients did not stay in makeshift housing but rather a four-star hotel. Similarly eating simple dishes of plain vegetables and rice was a one-off experience of 'the local' not a mundane activity of everyday existence. These were also meticulously planned challenges; by contrast the children were faced with the ongoing instability, uncertainty and precarity of living in the aftermath of the earthquake. I point out these differences because it is precisely by drawing parallels with recipients – the creation of an 'empathic zone' – that employees can be said to be experiencing 'the Other' and thus testing themselves. It is this carefully calibrated testing of the self that is so covetable and definitive of the internal practice of CSR. The bike ride is designed to be experienced as a series of revelatory moments – about their own capabilities, their responses to adversity, their position in social hierarchies, and even the utility of their expertise. These revelatory moments are crucial to transforming the self – that is, to promoting the creation of new subjectivities. One might expect that employees return to work with an improved ethic of graft. Perhaps also they become more content in their everyday work, which might translate into a state of heightened passivity so making them easier to manage. Or most obvious, one might expect that they find meaning, a sense of purpose, in their jobs, which are defined by their inscrutability.

Performing a 'Global' Morality in Post-Mao China

Although long established in Systeo's older geographies (of North America and Western Europe), corporate citizenship was still in its infancy in China. 'It's been hard to get traction – it's been difficult to build corporate citizenship in China,' remarked Stephanie Smith, Head of Global Giving. Tentatively she suggested that that there was 'not a strong heritage of charitable giving due to cultural norms'. Stephanie implied that Chinese employees constrained by 'their culture' did not grasp the idea of charity – giving without the expectation of return – a problem that suggested, in her words, 'a need to increase employee awareness'. This was especially important because 'corporate citizenship is something that develops organically in each region', being comprised of 'employee driven initiatives [and hence] often takes on a "local flavour"'.

As Carolyn Hsu has pointed out, voluntary giving is not a foreign concept to Chinese, who have long seen it as a moral obligation to provide for kin in need (2008: 84). However, giving to strangers – a central principle in Western charitable giving – is not valorised and has only been recently introduced (ibid., also see Rolandsen 2008). Hsu examines the historical development of Project Hope, one of the first, and most successful, charities in the post-Mao era, which was set up to raise funds for rural schools. It elicits donations from individual and corporate donors; the latter includes, notably, Systeo. According to Hsu, the main problem facing charitable organizations in China is that Chinese people find it difficult to trust strangers unless they are engaged in reciprocal relations built up through gift exchanges. As well as noting that charity is a culturally conditioned perception based on a Western conception of universal love, which can thus be applied to those near and distant to us, Hsu observes that such cultural hurdles can be overcome by drawing on existing schemas of moral legitimacy; for example, by recasting hitherto anonymous donations as personalized (and hence trust generative) relations between donor and recipient. Stephanie's assertion, shared by many expatriates, that Chinese employees are held back by a set of norms or cultural values fails to grasp how notions of charity are predicated on configurations of social relations that are not necessarily shared across contexts. As we will see, this failure to consider social relations would not be the only threat to the realization of the desired corporate subjectivity.

During the bike ride, there were nightly team briefings, in which consultants were invited to give their thoughts on the day. One consultant commented that one of the children, of the schools we had visited, had the same mobile phone as him. 'Do they really need our help?' he intoned. A few of us went to a bar afterwards, where the discussion continued. 'It's different for us,' said Chen Jin, a consultant from Beijing, referring to mainland Chinese employees as opposed to expatriates. 'Obviously we have very different lives from these children, but you know thirty, forty years ago ... we weren't so different.' Since market reforms were introduced, income inequality has skyrocketed, and Chinese society has become increasingly stratified. That said, the suggestion that urbanites and rural citizens were equal under Mao is at best nostalgic. Various scholars have pointed out that rural China, although privileged in (Chinese communist) party discourse (Bach 2010), was continuously decimated and devalued for the sake of creating urban China as the vision of socialist modernity (Siu 2007). Nevertheless, Chen Jin's comments do show how memories of China's socialist past continue to inform how people experience and make sense of present-day social differentiation.

Chen Jin had questioned whether these communities were truly deserving of corporate aid on the basis that the recipients appeared to be too similar to them. I should stress that Chen Jin and other Chinese employees were not disengaged from the plight of China's rural poor. They would often forward emails to each other asking for donations to charities dedicated to improving the living standards for rural children. Containing harrowing images of teary-eyed children eating scraps of food, carrying sacks of sticks on their back, hands and faces raw from the cold, these emails stated emphatically who was the deserving subject of charity. Systeo's CSR initiatives had disrupted the overdrawn, if not patronizing, image of the rural child as the uncivilized, inferior Other to the modern, middle-class urbanite that employees propagated.

Yet, this was precisely the opposite of what was intended. CSR initiatives are predicated on, and serve to magnify, the inequality between recipients and donors. Whether represented as integral to their business model, or simply old-fashioned corporate giving, CSR has innovated little on the imperialistic trope of Western folk helping to civilize the developing world. It is by highlighting inequalities that CSR initiatives gain their moral legitimacy – who can truck with measures to help those who are worse off? It is apparent that certain representations of communities are necessary to legitimate CSR as a way of 'giving back' to society. If Chinese employees do not see themselves as superior to the recipients of their goodwill, then the moral imperative that drives the initiative is lost. They might begin to wonder why they have made personal sacrifices – not just the objects they put up for bidding but also four days of annual leave that could have been spent with their family – to cycle across Western China. They have suffered but for what and for whom?

At the end of the event, we were put into groups of three and asked to write an article together based on our experience. The best articles would be published in the company CSR magazine. I was put with Chen Jin and Yu Na, two consultants from Beijing. We sat together on the bus back to Chengdu to discuss what we might write. Yu Na asked a rhetorical question, 'the government would provide help if Systeo didn't, right?' to which Chen Jin agreed. From conversations on the road, I sensed that many employees had chosen to participate in the bike ride in order to see with their own eyes the destruction wrought by the earthquake. A distrust of Chinese media representations, which had saturated primetime TV, night after night, served as one motivation. Buying into the wave of Chinese nationalism that was fuelled by this media explosion was another. As we passed a refuge of temporary shelters, metal cabins with uniform blue roofs, Lisa Teng, a consultant based in Shanghai, pointed out the grand, grey brick government offices in close proximity. 'Buildings for officials get rebuilt before homes for ordinary people – that's China for you,' she lamented. Even though employees thought that the relief effort would be marred by corruption, they took it for granted that the state would be leading the operations.

As Catherine Dolan has argued, the practice of CSR typically claims its legitimacy, or at least rhetorical traction, by claiming to plug gaps in development produced by the absence of the state (Dolan 2010). The lack of formal standards or regulation whether concerning labour practices or factory emissions, for example, is used to justify the growth of CSR practice in these areas. In the United States, where state intervention is often treated with suspicion, the idea that corporations will intervene in everyday life – indeed they should because they provide better, more efficient solutions – is widely accepted. In China, however, the state is seemingly omnipresent. Basic choices concerning human reproduction, media consumption and one's place of residency are all subject to state intervention. This control is enacted through paternalistic ties, not dissimilar to the kind invoked by the practice of CSR. This point is exemplified by the media construction of 'Grandpa Wen', Wen Jia Bao, then Premier of the PRC, the 66-year-old poster 'boy' of the relief effort. TV crews and journalists document him in the trenches, consoling homeless or maybe even orphaned children – the victims of the earthquake. Such media narratives drive home the message that the patron of the relief effort was the Chinese Communist Party, not Systeo or any other Western donor. Stephanie Smith and other employees, expatriate and Chinese, involved in building Systeo China's CSR programme had not thought through how a strong, paternalistic state would impact the effectiveness of CSR to engage employees. I argue that, in this context, the value that Systeo brought to the relief effort was not apparent. And thus the key CSR message, to both external stakeholders and Systeo employees, that Systeo is there to 'make a difference' failed to materialize.

Months after the bike ride, I had lunch with a few consultants. The conversation turned to the topic of corporate citizenship. One consultant, Joanna Li, told me that they do not yet have the culture (*wenhua*) for such initiatives. She said that 'not long ago the government took care of everything – your work, where you lived, people in need'. She was referring to Mao's 'iron bowl' – the set of cradle to grave benefits, including lifelong employment, which prevailed under socialism. 'People don't really consider giving to others, it's just not in the culture right now,' she explained. Joanna's comments seemed to imply that culture, a bit like older ideas of development, was based on a linear teleology. One day Chinese culture would 'catch up' with the West, and then giving to charity would be normalized. Expected even. Until then, Chinese 'culture' would hold back the implementation of CSR. Joanna's thinking seems remarkably close to that of Stephanie Smith, the Head of Global Giving – recall her remark that 'the norms' of giving were not yet established in China. They are both articulating a teleology of values in which culture is understood as central to the production of the good philanthropic citizen.

The idea that there exists a teleology of development that is matched, or evidenced, by a teleology of mentalities may not be anything new. What is interesting is how, in this context, culture is seen as the driver of these teleologies, in contrast to standard modernist notions of development in which culture is posed as a hindrance to producing rational, liberal citizens. It may be the case that this reversal simply reflects the fact that culture is a dominant discourse of management consultancy and is seen as a model for controlling social reality. As I have already pointed out, consultants, despite being hired to create efficiency through the implementation of standardized, rational and technocratic forms of management, in fact base much of their expertise on culture. But the recourse to culture, and in particular the invocation of cultural difference for explaining the failure to conform, could also be read as an unprovocative way of sidestepping managerial control. That is to say, Chinese employees are also adept at apprehending culture for their own self-interest.

Providing a 'High-Level Experience'

The money raised from the bike ride bolstered the already considerable amount raised through a donation drive launched in the immediate aftermath

Making the Good Corporate Citizen 155

of the earthquake, in which the company matched every renminbi donated by an employee. In just one week, Systeo China and its employees had donated over 2 million renminb. (£200,000) to the relief effort. Employees' generosity called into question Stephanie's assertion that 'the norms' of giving were not yet established in China. Given that a sizeable donation had been made, and with ease, why was it necessary to organize a fund-raising bike ride? Some insight can be found by looking at who was eligible to participate. Any employee could donate money, but only permanent employees received the email explaining how they could join in.[6] As we will see, corporate citizenship is seen as form of human investment reserved only for those the company seeks to retain.

Just six months after the bike ride, I was hired as Systeo China's very first 'Corporate Citizenship Coordinator'. In fact, the job was created with me in mind. The experience I had gained working in the Human Capital Strategy Programme was seen as especially relevant, a point I will return to later. Also, having participated in the bike ride, I was well informed to help organize the following year's bike ride, the main task of this position. So I joined a bike ride committee comprised of consultants who had volunteered their project management and logistics skills, and time, to the CSR Programme. Over a series of conference calls, we hammered out a rough sketch of the event; it was my job to translate these ideas into fluent, exciting communications, which would be sent directly to employees and uploaded onto the company intranet.

Very quickly I realized that we were planning a much more ambitious event than the previous year's. There would be more participants – up to sixty employees – and the bike ride would now be open to both employees in the China offices and those outside of China. This was the idea of Emma Jiang, senior executive and bike ride lead. The participation of employees from North America and Europe would, according to her, show that Systeo China was a truly global entity. Another reason for pursuing this arrangement was that it might encourage Chinese employees to take part. Most were in their mid-twenties to mid-thirties and, unlike their parents, had only ever been employed by foreign companies. They saw themselves as part of a generation of Asian cosmopolitans who wanted to work in 'global' environments (Hoffman 2010; Hsu 2005). CSR initiatives such as the bike ride were almost unheard of in Chinese enterprises. Their existence signalled immediately that these were not 'local' entities. Moreover, such events allowed employees to actually meet and interact with Europeans, Americans and Australians.

Emma also expected that foreign employees would jump at the chance of cycling in China. But getting access to them would not be a straightforward matter. We needed to 'reach out' to the CSR leads of the different Systeo geographies. Their Western names indicated what the employee directory confirmed – only Systeo offices in the global North employed specialist CSR professionals. China did not have a CSR lead. A contracted CSR coordinator, I was the next best alternative. Hence, I was asked to present a PowerPoint detailing our plans for the coming bike ride and background information on the previous year's event. David Kraus, the German lead, was the first to comment: 'I know what the [German] senior executives will say: 'that's nice but what does a bike ride have to do with Systeo.' The connection between corporate citizenship activities and Systeo's core business was not apparent. Amelia, the US lead, had different objections. She said she would only want the US geography to be involved if we could 'deliver a high-level experience that rivals the Everest event'. The year before, employees, notably only those from the global North, were invited to 'challenge themselves' by trekking to the Mount Everest base camp, an event of great complexity to organize and one that was collectively judged a 'resounding success'. I was struck immediately by Amelia's emphasis on the individual employee's experience rather than the charities for which the employees would be raising money. Cathleen Doyle, the Ireland CSR lead, seemed to share her concern, interjecting with, 'does anyone on the global corporate citizenship team know you're organizing this?' The tone in which Cathleen asked her question seemed to suggest that we, the Chinese corporate citizenship team, were errant children going behind the backs of our 'Global' parents. The implication was that if Global was not involved then they – the Western CSR leads – could not ascertain the quality of the event, the experience we would deliver, which made them wary of letting 'their' employees participate.

In fact, Global were the ones who suggested we contact the CSR leads. Sitting at my desk, staring at my phone as if it could talk back to me, I felt extremely uneasy. There was something untoward in their questioning, something that suggested we were not just talking about logistics or CSR. Our competency, our skill at performing corporate ethics, was under attack. Amelia stated in no uncertain terms that she would not be sending out our communications to all US employees. In effect, she was refusing access. Only those who had signed up to corporate citizenship interest lists, and Asian American employees, would be made available to us. I was floored. There was a mailing list comprising only Asian American employees? In a 'global' company? And why would only Americans of Asian ethnicity be interested in participating? Amelia's comments seemed to rehearse my own observation that CSR 'works' when employees can identify with the recipients of their goodwill. Except she seemed to suggest that a common ground could only be found on the basis of ethnicity.

There were also controversies over who would be a deserving recipient: 'Where do you draw the line? There are lots of charities which need our support in Ireland so why should we help raise funds in China?' remarked Cathleen. Emma trotted out the global narrative that as a global company Systeo should encourage its employees to participate in charity events in different geographies. Met with awkward silence, Emma added: 'the foreigners, I mean the expatriates who participate in the bike rides ... you should see the children's faces – they have never seen a foreigner before.' I got her point that having expatriates involved gives Chinese recipients a much greater sense of Systeo, that it is a global entity with employees drawn from around the world. At the same time, I could not shake the feeling that we – the China corporate citizenship team – were selling ethnic voyeurism to white employees. The gap between recipient and donor had suddenly been amplified. Such comments did not necessarily suggest a paucity of professionalism or inaccuracy of observation – I had seen for myself the enchanted faces that she spoke of. Rather, it appeared that Emma was unprepared for the CSR leads' spiky questions and negative feedback.

We had not anticipated the CSR leads would act as gatekeepers to employees. If doing good was integral to corporate citizenship activities in all geographies, as is suggested by Stephanie Smith, the Head of Global Giving, Systeo's leadership videos, and the company magazine, then why is employee participation so tightly policed? The finances of corporate citizenship are instructive here. Overall, the bike ride committee hoped to raise at least 250,000 renminbi (£25,000) through the event. However, when going through the project budget, I found out that less than ten per cent of this money would go to charity. Most of it would go into covering the event's costs: the hotels, the flights, the meals, the bike rental, bike mechanics and third parties (e.g. agencies specializing in local logistics). The injunction from Amelia, the US lead, to 'deliver a high-level experience' belies an overarching objective, which is not to raise money for charity but to create what are termed 'engaged employees'.

As I would later find out by reading the business case for my role of China corporate citizenship coordinator, corporate citizenship activities are seen as an input to human capital. Systeo sell and practise internally the idea that CSR is a way of making 'engaged employees', those who actively contribute to the creation of shareholder value. Each CSR lead is under pressure to demonstrate how they have improved employee engagement – this is how their performance is evaluated – which explains why they are wary of letting 'their' employees participate in initiatives organized by other geographies.

As an internal consultant to the 'Human Capital Strategy Programme', I was privy to the range of activities – intra-firm dating events, sports clubs, flexible work arrangements – which were considered deserving of company investment. CSR was yet another example. The naïve theory is that by participating in such activities employees develop a more positive relationship with the company, so enhancing productivity and, in turn, shareholder value. Although I found that the connection with shareholder value was rarely mentioned (it was only made apparent in diagrams that measured the improvement in 'employee engagement' in terms of total shareholder return), on occasion it was explicitly referred to. For example, in an interview with Systeo's Head of Global Giving, Stephanie Smith, she stated baldly that corporate citizenship initiatives 'need to prove return of investment will come' in order to be implemented.

Writing about the partnerships between big business and NGOs, Robert Foster argues that contemporary global capitalism uses consensus as a way of diffusing potentially conflictual relationships and agendas, and in doing so weds ethical praxis with the creation of shareholder value (2014). This kind of bridging between ethics and profit through strategic collaborations is termed 'connected capitalism'. The use of CSR as a tool of acculturation is but another example of how external associations or partnerships, such as investing in local schools destroyed by natural disasters, can be apprehended for the moral aestheticizing of business as usual.

Conclusion

This chapter highlights the importance of studying ethics and notions of the good in what some might refer to as 'non-traditional' field sites, those of powerful elites. Focusing on the implementation of CSR in a global management consultancy that is rapidly expanding its operations in China, I explored how 'the good corporate citizen' is produced and negotiated in the pursuit of profit and global dominance. What is especially interesting is the character of this morality, given that ethics in this context is subordinated to instrumental ends. Employees are invited to perform the company's 'core values', which are more codifications and commodifications of professionalism (McKenna 2006: 193) than ethical coordinates for social action. Indeed, despite the invocation of terms like 'responsibility', in practice there is little recourse to virtue ethics (Laidlaw 2013); rather, morality is defined in negative terms – as what it is not.

Through revelation, corporate citizenship activities are designed to create affective ties that would appear to be defined by the absence of financial concerns. The actual amount raised by the bike ride for the charity is never disclosed, somewhat strange given that this is the explicitly narrated objective of the event. Hence employees, apart from the bike ride committee, are not aware of the slim margins of charitable giving. At the same time, employees do not question the comparative luxury in which they are 'challenged'. It would seem that employees are encouraged to see such changes to the self as not driven by profit. In this way, they can be said to have been 'engaged'. We see that the good in this context is predicated on a sharp distinction between virtue and market value, which chimes with Lambek's conceptualization of the former being defined by the incommensurability of values, and the latter by the commensurability of values (Lambek 2008, 2013). However, it is precisely the commensurability of virtue and market value that produces the ethical effects of CSR.

Recent research on corporate ethicizing (Dolan and Rajak 2011) has highlighted the forms of 'ethical capitalism' that have emerged in recent decades, and that seek to demonstrate that corporations are concerned with more than just profit and that a 'humane capitalism' is possible (De Neve et al. 2008: 17). But the practice of ethics is more than a 'moral bolt on' to business as usual (Rajak 2008); it is integral to capitalism itself. In this chapter, I have shown how the performance of morality is not only a kind of aesthetics designed to improve corporate reputation; it is also practised as a means of bolstering profit. Moral sentiments that derive their meaning from the elision of finance are generated with the view to making subjects who maximize the creation of financial value. Indeed, one of the central contradictions of the CSR initiatives I have examined is that moral legitimacy is drawn through the performance of extra-financial concerns, yet moral authority is generated for the purposes of finance. Contemporary financial capitalism is conceived as, and legitimated by the production of, an ethical project (Chong 2018), of which the making of 'good corporate citizens' is just one part.[7]

However, corporate attempts at producing the idealized moral self are not always successful. The Chinese management consultants with whom I worked held alternate, competing visions of the good that referenced the ongoing influence of state power and the importance of serving national interests. They perform their own 'vernacular ethics' of expertise, in which their work of transforming China's economic landscape is seen as that of 'building a paradise' (Chong 2018). The presence of alternative ethical forms poses a threat to the rhetorical traction of CSR. This would suggest that the efficacy of CSR to produce the 'right' performances of morality is not, as the discourse suggests, universal. Rather, the desired moral self is imagined in continuation with older structures of paternalism and corporate philanthropy. Although there is nothing intrinsically 'Western' about the marriage of ethics to capitalism, the discursive effects of CSR rest upon certain assumptions of how capitalist practices relate to local development, which derive from a long history of Western capitalism. Practices of corporate ethicizing aim to bolster and reassert corporate power in the minds of employees as well as in public perception. The extent to which they achieve this, however, depends on their relationship with other, pre-existing ethical forms that may or may not be commensurate with the forms of corporate morality that are desired.

Acknowledgements

An earlier version of this chapter was published as 'Producing "Global" Corporate Subjects in Post-Mao China: Management Consultancy, Culture and Corporate Social Responsibility' in *Journal of Business Anthropology* 4(2): 320–41.

Kimberly Chong is Associate Professor of Anthropology at University College London. Her research expertise covers financialization and the anthropology of finance, economic and political subjectivities, commensuration and techniques of valuation, economic decision-making and epistemologies of economics. Her first monograph, *Best Practice: Management Consulting and the Ethics of Financialization in China*, which was published by Duke

University Press, won the European Group for Organizational Studies Book Award in 2021. She holds a BA in Economics and Sociology from the University of Cambridge, and both an MSc in Social Anthropology and a PhD in Anthropology from the London School of Economics.

Notes

1. According to Ong, Western managers in Shanghai consider 'the reengineering of Chinese knowledge workers and the production of new business ethics the most challenging part of their work' (Ong 2006: 167).
2. State intervention in private and public life endures in the post-Mao period of market socialism. In some senses, though, it has diminished. For example, people now have far greater choice and control in decisions regarding work and where they live. But in other ways intervention has become more invasive. One obvious example is the imposition of the draconian family planning rules, otherwise known as the 'one-child policy'.
3. For example, 'NHS "has no idea what £300m of management consultancy buys"', *The Guardian*, 4 June 2009. https://www.theguardian.com/society/2009/jun/04/nhs-management-consultancy-costs.
4. McKenna states that 'the managing partners at McKinsey & company created "corporate culture" as a strategic response to the declining demand for the firm's central "product" – the organizational study' (McKenna 2006: 193).
5. http://www.mckinsey.com/insights/strategy/enduring_ideas_the_7-s_framework (accessed 16 April 2015).
6. Because I was not a permanent employee, I should have been disqualified. However, other colleagues lobbied the senior executive who was overseeing the event, telling her about the unpaid work I had done for Systeo's corporate citizenship initiatives. Thus, she decided to make an exception.
7. See also Bear et al. (2015).

References

Alvesson, M. 2013. *Understanding Organizational Culture*. Sage Publications Ltd.
Bach, J. 2010. '"They Come in Peasants and Leave Citizens": Urban Villages and the Making of Shenzhen, China', *Cultural Anthropology* 25(3): 421–58.
Bear, L. et al. 2015. 'Gens: A Feminist Manifesto for the Study of Capitalism'. *Society for Cultural Anthropology*, 30 March 2015. Retrieved 26 August 2020 https://culanth.org/fieldsights/gens-a-feminist-manifesto-for-the-study-of-capitalism last.
Benson, P. 2014. 'Corporate Paternalism and the Problem of Harmful Products', *PoLAR: Political and Legal Anthropology Review* 37(2): 218–30.
Callon, M. 1998. 'Introduction', in M. Callon (ed.), *The Laws of the Markets*. Oxford: Blackwell.
Cefkin, M. 2010. (ed.). *Ethnography and the Corporate Encounter: Reflections on Research in and of Corporations*. New York: Berghahn.
Chong, K. 2018. *Best Practice: Management Consulting and the Ethics of Financialization in China*. Durham, NC: Duke University Press.
De Neve, G et al. 2008. 'Hidden Hands in the Market: Ethnographies of Fair Trade', *Ethical Consumption, and Corporate Social Responsibility (Research in Economic Anthropology, Vol. 28)*. Bingley, UK: Emerald.

Dolan, C.S. 2010. 'Virtual Moralities: The Mainstreaming of Fairtrade in Kenyan Tea Fields', *Geoforum* 41(1): 33–43.
Dolan, C., and D. Rajak. 2011. 'Introduction: Ethnographies of Corporate Ethicizing', *Focaal* 60: 3–8.
Downey, G., and M. Fischer. 2006. 'Introduction', in G. Downey and M. Fischer (eds), *Frontiers of Capital: Ethnographic Reflections on the New Economy*. Durham NC and London: Duke University Press.
Foster, R.J. 2014. 'Corporations as Partners: "Connected Capitalism" and the Coca-Cola Company', *PoLAR: Political and Legal Anthropology Review* 37(2), 246–58.
High, M.M., and J.M. Smith. 2019. 'Introduction: The Ethical Constitution of Energy Dilemmas', *Journal of the Royal Anthropological Institute* 25(S1): 9–28.
Hoffman, L.M. 2010. *Patriotic Professionalism in Urban China: Fostering Talent*. Philadelphia, PA: Temple University Press.
Holmes, D.R., and G.E. Marcus. 2006. 'Fast Capitalism: Para-Ethnography and the Rise of the Symbolic Analyst', in G. Downey and M. Fischer (eds), *Frontiers of Capital: Ethnographic Reflections on the New Economy*. Durham, NC and London: Duke University Press.
Hsu, C. 2005. 'A Taste of "Modernity": Working in a Western Restaurant in Market Socialist China', *Ethnography* 6(4): 543–65.
——. 2008. '"Rehabilitating Charity" in China: The Case of Project Hope and the Rise of Non-profit Organizations', *Journal of Civil Society* 4(2): 81–96.
Kessler, D. 2006. 'Nationalism, Theft and Management Strategies in the Information Industry of Mainland China', in C.K. Lee (ed.), *Working in China: Ethnographies of Labor and Workplace Transformation*. London: Routledge.
Kipnis, A. 2007. 'Neoliberalism Reified: Suzhi Discourse and Tropes of Neoliberalism in the People's Republic of China', *Journal of the Royal Anthropological Institute* 13(2): 383–400.
Kipping, M. 2011. 'Hollow from the Start? Image Professionalism in Management Consulting', *Current Sociology* 59(4): 530–50.
Kirsch, S. 2014. 'Imagining Corporate Personhood', *PoLAR: Political and Legal Anthropology Review* 37(2): 207–17.
Laidlaw, J. 2013. *The Subject of Virtue: An Anthropology of Ethics and Freedom*. Cambridge: University Press.
Lambek, M. 2008. 'Value and Virtue', *Anthropological Theory* 8: 133–57.
——. 2013. 'The Value of (Performative) Acts', *HAU: Journal of Ethnographic Theory* 3(2): 141–60.
Lynch, D.C. 1999. *After the Propaganda State: Media, Politics, and "Thought Work" in Reformed China / Daniel C. Lynch*. Stanford, CA: Stanford University Press.
MacKenzie, D.A. 2006. *An Engine, Not a Camera: How Financial Models Shape Markets*. Cambridge, MA: MIT.
MacKenzie, D.A., F. Muniesa and L. Siu. 2007. *Do Economists Make Markets?: On the Performativity of Economics*. Princeton University Press.
Marcus, G. (ed.). 1998. *Corporate Futures: The Diffusion of the Culturally Sensitive Corporate Form*. Chicago: University of Chicago Press.
Mazzarella, W. 2003. *Shoveling Smoke: Advertising and Globalization in Contemporary India*. Durham, NC: Duke University Press.
McKenna, C.D. 2006. *The World's Newest Profession: Management Consulting in the Twentieth Century*. Cambridge: Cambridge University Press.
Moeran, B. 2006. *Ethnography at Work*. Oxford: Berg.

Nafus, D., and K. Anderson. 2006. *The Real Problem: Rhetorics of Knowing in Corporate Ethnographic Research*. Proceedings from Ethnographic Praxis in Industry Conference.

Ong, A. 2006. 'Corporate Players, New Cosmopolitans, and Guanxi in Shanghai', in M. Fischer and G. Downey (eds), *Frontiers of Capital: Ethnographic Reflections on the New Economy*. Durham, NC: Duke University Press.

Ortner, S.B. 2016. 'Dark Anthropology and Its Others: Theory since the Eighties'. *HAU: Journal of Ethnographic Theory* 6(1), 47–73.

Power, M., T. Palermo and S. Ashby. 2014. 'Searching for Risk Culture in Financial Organizations', paper presented at the Social Anthropology seminar series, Dept. of Anthropology, University College London.

Rajak, D. 2008. '"Uplift and Empower": The Market, Morality and Corporate Responsibility on South Africa's Platinum Belt', *Research in Economic Anthropology* 28: 297–324.

———. 2011. *In Good Company: An Anatomy of Corporate Social Responsibility*. Stanford University Press.

———. 2014. 'Corporate Memory: Historical Revisionism, Legitimation and the Invention of Tradition in a Multinational Mining Company', *PoLAR: Political and Legal Anthropology Review* 37(2): 259–80.

Rolandsen, U. 2008. 'A Collective of Their Own: Young Volunteers at the Fringes of the Party Realm', *European Journal of East Asian Studies* 7(1): 101–29.

Ross, A. 2006. *Fast Boat to China: Corporate Flight and the Consequences of Free Trade – Lessons from Shanghai / Andrew Ross*. New York: Pantheon Books.

Shamir, R. 2004. 'The De-Radicalization of Corporate Social Responsibility', *Critical Sociology* 30(3): 669–89.

Shever, E. 2010. 'Engendering the Company: Corporate Personhood and the "Face" of an Oil Company in Metropolitan Buenos Aires', *PoLAR: Political and Legal Anthropology Review* 33(1): 26–46.

Siu, H. 2007. 'Grounding Displacement: Uncivil Urban Spaces in Postreform South China', *American Ethnologist* 34(2): 329–50.

Thrift, N.J. 2005. *Knowing Capitalism*. London: SAGE Publications.

Welker, M.A. 2009. '"Corporate Security Begins in the Community": Mining, the Corporate Social Responsibility Industry, and Environmental Advocacy in Indonesia', *Cultural Anthropology* 24(1): 142–79.

Wright, S. (ed.). 1994. *Anthropology of Organizations*. London: Routledge.

8
'God Isn't a Communist'
Conservative Evangelicals, Money and Morality in London

Anna Strhan

One Sunday during my fieldwork at St John's, a large conservative evangelical church in London, smiling members of the welcoming team at the doors were handing out copies of a glossy brochure entitled 'Re:Generation Appeal'. This coincided with that Sunday being the church's 'annual giving Sunday', as Pete, one of the ministers, explained at the start of the service. To open the service, Pete read out some verses from 2 Corinthians: 'For you know the grace of our Lord Jesus Christ, that though he was rich, yet for your sake he became poor, so that you through his poverty might become rich.' After the notices, Pete invited Philip, the church treasurer, to speak. Philip, in his early fifties, the global chair of a large financial services corporation, addressed the congregation confidently. He said he wanted to talk about two issues: regular giving, and the Regeneration Appeal. Talking about regular giving, he said that they had expected the next five years to be tough for the church, as giving had fallen in the years following the financial crisis; however, although they had budgeted for a deficit of £250,000 that year, they were somewhat encouraged that it looked more like £100,000 by the time they had closed the books. He said that while they'd had to cut back on certain plans, things seemed ok, but that to keep things running as they were, they would need an increase of 5% in regular giving to the church; for example, if you gave £100 a month it would mean £5 extra. He stated that the average person in the church was giving £30 a week and encouraged people to pray about their giving and then to act on that. He recommended a book called *The Money Mentor*, which he said shows that the core issue here is 'our hearts' and also mentioned 'the stewardship website', to help with budgeting. Philip then talked about the Regeneration Appeal, which was aiming to raise £3 million for building works. Pete said that they had already raised £1.3 million, so they needed another £1.7 million, describing this as a 'once in a decade kind of appeal' to 'help take the work of the church further'.

A member of the congregation then read Philippians 4: 10–23, which the congregation followed in the church Bibles placed on every seat. David, the rector, stood up to preach from the carved wooden pulpit. He began by stating that in the Philippians passage the church in Philippi was 'in partnership with Paul' and that 'partnership' is a favourite word of Paul's in the letter; today he would address what 'true gospel partnership' looks like and 'what financial giving should be like, since it is important to hold these two together'. As was typical of sermons at St John's, David emphasized that being a Christian was countercultural, stating 'true church membership is energetic and corporate, public and unpopular, and selfless and sacrificial'. He then asked the congregation, 'do *you* see yourself as a partner in gospel ministry? Because that is what you are, if you're a Christian, whether you like it or not.' He went on, 'here is the mindset of the true Christian partner, different from the rest of the world, which is self-seeking ... The Christian partner is selfless and sacrificial ... The *true* Christian partner will always be downwardly mobile,[1] seeking to become like Jesus in death.' He then addressed financial giving and said that Paul speaks of giving as an 'investment' that bears fruit that accrues to the Philippians; this might be the fruit of 'others coming to Christ' but is also counted by God in heaven at Judgement Day. He emphasized that this should not lead to the idea of 'good works' or 'purchasing your way to paradise' but was all about 'grace and responding to grace with thankfulness' and quoted St Augustine, saying 'God crowns not your merits as your merits but as his own grace.' He continued:

> perhaps we are too *English* in our attitude to talking about money and whether we are good with our investments ... the issue is not how much money you give, since God values the £3 gift from the student as much as the £3,000 from the recent graduate ... God is pleased with your gift ... like on Mother's Day, when children make a mess while preparing breakfast in bed, but the mother is pleased.

Over coffee after the service, I chatted with Alistair, a corporate lawyer I'd got to know from the Bible study group I'd been attending. He was looking suntanned, having just returned from skiing. I was interested to ask whether he was involved in decisions about church finances; as a member of the Parochial Church Council, it seems he did have responsibility for the church's financial decisions, which here meant deciding whether the Regeneration Appeal would be a good use of money, which he thought it would be. Philip came over to chat with us and mentioned they were happy with the amount of money raised so far, that most of those capable of committing to large financial donations had done so, so it seemed promising the building works would go ahead.

In looking for the good, a congregation like St John's is perhaps not an obvious location – especially in terms of their engagements with money. It's easy to stereotype this type of church, with many affluent members able to gift the church significant sums without forgoing their skiing holidays. These individuals in many ways seem good Weberian Protestants, as the church encourages an ethic of careful household budgeting and avoiding excessive consumption, so individuals can 'invest' more money in church expansion. David articulated an understanding of an idealized evangelical subject who 'partners in the gospel' by financially supporting the church, thus allowing its expansion and reaping future interest in the 'fruit of others coming to Christ', as well as counting towards their own salvation at Judgement Day. It might appear that their actions are thus subsumed under the calculative logic of capital, with the values of faith seemingly monetized and oriented towards self-interest.

And yet, as in the words of Peggy Lee, is that all there is? In what follows, I explore different moral threads interwoven in the thoughts and actions of those at St John's in relation to the place of money in their lives. I argue that as well as a calculative ethic shaped by modes of economic value, we also see a desire for a value beyond value (Skeggs 2014), in which the good is imagined in relation to a transcendent grace that exceeds – and at the same time valorises – capitalist regimes. Approaching conservative evangelicals through the lens of the good moves us, I suggest, beyond the 'othering' of non-liberal religious movements through avoiding dismissing their ideals as 'bad-faith alibis' (Robbins 2013: 457). At the same time, this approach invites attention to the contradictions and eruptions that evade the logic of capital even amongst those who are well rewarded by the current economic order.

The Good, the Bad and the Study of Conservative Evangelicals

In recent decades, scholarship across sociology and other social sciences has examined how capitalism broadly – and specifically the socio-economic-political order termed 'neoliberalism' – perpetuates multiple injustices and suffering, focusing on the operations of power, governmentality and exclusion. As discussed in the introduction to this volume, the anthropology of the good has been seen by some as a reaction against this body of work, underscoring how social life is shaped not only by power and domination but also by questions of the good and ethics.[2] This work has sought to shift our attention to the ways in which people are 'trying to do what they consider right or good, are being evaluated according to criteria of what is right and good, or are in some debate about what constitutes the human good' (Lambek 2010: 1).

Criticisms have been raised that this focus on morality ignores issues of power and inequality or that 'the good' is situated as opposed to injustice, rather than addressing how constructions of ethical life are interwoven with forms of oppression and the violence of inequality and exclusion (Kapferer and Gold 2018; Ortner 2016: 65). In other words, the study of the good should not be separate from the study of 'the bad' or the 'dim side' of morality (Fassin 2015) and should also explore negative moral emotions, and how constructions of the good can contribute to suffering and inequality (see Lynch, Wilkinson, this volume). These debates occur not only in anthropology. Outlining future research avenues in the sociology of morality, Steven Lukes argues that for moral philosophers the Nazis represent radical evil, 'the paradigm of what is beyond the moral domain'. Yet sociologists should, he argues, examine how Nazi leaders secured enthusiasm on a large scale and 'the moral attitudes of the various kinds of Nazi perpetrators' (2010: 559). This might also include 'the limits of their morality', where the humanity of the other human is denied (ibid.).

While not an epitome of evil, by and large, conservative evangelicals – along other socially conservative Christians – represent by virtue of their political and moral views the 'repugnant cultural "other" to anthropologists and sociologists alike', as Susan Harding argued some 30 years ago (1991). The interrelations of conservative Protestantism and capitalism – refracted through the lens of the US Christian Right's support for neoliberal governments from the Regan era onwards – have been a key aspect of this political, cultural and moral othering, as neoliberalism and capitalism tend to be understood as amoral, and their means and ends often as clearly immoral (Lambek 2015b: 13). While Weber's prediction of the disenchantment of the world via the effects of the Protestant stance towards money has not straightforwardly taken place, the Protestant ethic nevertheless continues to provide a sanctification for an impulse to gain, save and give that harmonizes with many aspects of contemporary capitalism – including both its neoliberal and right-wing populist forms.

Much writing about evangelicals and Pentecostals – both academic and popular – portrays these movements as flourishing globally in part due to their close affinities with a spirit of entrepreneurial capitalism. William Connolly has argued, 'The right leg of the evangelical movement today is joined at the hip to the left leg of the capitalist juggernaut' (2008: 44), and Jane Guyer (2007) has traced homologies between neoliberal and evangelical temporalities. At the same time, evangelicalism is often portrayed as offering a sense of certainty that is a soothing balm for the uncertainty and fragmentation accompanying the expanding scale and abstraction of transactions across global capitalist economies, the tensions between the nation state and mobile capital, and growing disparities of wealth and power in the world at large (Comaroff 2010: 32).

In critical dialogue with this literature and drawing attention to its reductionist tendencies, there have been a number of ethnographic accounts of the values and economic practices of charismatic and Pentecostal Christianities (e.g. Bialecki 2008; Coleman 2004, 2011; Daswani 2015; Haynes 2012, 2017), often focusing on prosperity theology. Naomi Haynes argues, for instance, that 'it is a mistake to read the prosperity gospel as simply a spectral parallel of the market, a phantasmagoric shadow of a structural adjusted reality' (2012: 125). Yet there has been comparatively little ethnographic attention given to money's place in conservative evangelicals' lives. Omri Elisha's study (2008, 2011) of socially engaged evangelicals in Tennessee offers insight into how their charitable giving is shaped by incommensurable logics of accountability and compassion. Elisha argues that we need to take seriously 'the ethical dilemmas, existential conflicts, and unintended consequences experienced by socially engaged evangelicals' and move beyond 'the tendency to dismiss them as evidence of hypocrisy or intolerant fanaticism' (2008: 159). By focusing on these issues, we deepen our understanding of how ethical sensibilities are shaped 'in nonliberal religious movements and the extension of those sensibilities beyond ritual confines and into the larger social order' (ibid.).

Following Elisha's humanizing move, my aim in what follows is to explore conservative evangelicals' moral imaginaries through examining how they develop an orientation towards a particular construction of the good in terms of generosity and grace, which shapes their engagements with money. I trace how they experience their ethical stance in relation to wealth as in tension with a wider cultural norm of the 'love of money', shaping their sense of being 'aliens and strangers' within the moral ecology of the city (Strhan 2015). I draw on nineteen months' ethnographic fieldwork carried out with a large, conservative evangelical Anglican church in London, 'St John's'.[3] The congregants are predominantly white, affluent, educated and middle-class, with many members working in corporate law, financial services, medicine and teaching. While not nationally representative of British evangelicalism, St John's is regarded by other evangelical churches as influential in terms of theology and practice (Strhan 2019: 12). As such, it offers insight into how conservative evangelical culture fosters particular ethical sensibilities shaping the relationship between faith and money.

The Celestial City and the Language of Commerce

In the central narratives of Western Christianity, the division of the imagination between the transcendent and immanent and between the Cities of God and of Man, as Augustine put it, is deeply rooted. As Richard Sennett describes, 'when early Christianity took root in the city, ... [it] reconciled itself to the powers of the urban center by dividing its own visual imagination in two, inner and outer, spirit and power' (2002: 373). The early urban Christians used forms of collective practice to sever their attachments to place and keep their focus on the transcendent Word and Light (ibid.). As I have described elsewhere, members of St John's likewise fashion themselves as 'pilgrims through time' (Strhan 2015: 199), shaping themselves and each other as 'exiles', with a strong sense of their cultural and moral distinctiveness from those around them in

London. Through practices such as listening to sermons, prayer, Bible study, singing hymns and relationships with other Christians, they seek to instil a sense of their orientation as journeying towards a transcendent God and a future Celestial City. As one church member expressed it to me, 'since Abraham onwards, we've been looking forwards'.

At the same time, through these practices they seek to understand the city they currently inhabit as transient, and its 'secular' values as lures into idolatry. In this context, the church emphasized that it was the privileged duty of the believer to seek to convert those around them. Members of the congregation were encouraged to experience London as peopled by non-Christians on whom they should show compassion by proselytizing. As a minister put it in a promotional video for the church, 'Do we share the compassion that the Lord God has, that Jesus has for those around us? Are we that passionately concerned for people's eternal destiny?' In reality, church members often struggled with this moral demand to speak, as the church also encouraged them to see themselves as inhabiting an oppressive secular state, within which speaking publicly of their faith would engender 'hostility' and 'hatred' (Strhan 2015: 89). Because of this reserve in speaking about their faith, church members did not necessarily proselytize much themselves. They rather saw the church as carrying out the evangelism they themselves often struggled with, through initiatives such as the church's 'guest events', at which a minister would explain the gospel in a setting designed to be inviting for outsiders, or through the church's other forms of targeted evangelism, such as student 'mission weeks'. Giving money to the church to support its efforts to save souls is therefore a means through which they can understand themselves as showing compassion for those they see as otherwise lost, and it becomes an everyday means through which they see themselves as enacting the good. There was little emphasis at the church on giving to alleviate poverty.[4] Joy, a teacher, told me she had a tense interaction with a liberal Anglican colleague after Joy had suggested inviting some of their 'nominal Christian' colleagues to evangelistic guest events at St John's. She said that her colleague had told her that you didn't need to be a follower of Jesus to be saved and that pleasing God meant 'doing God's will in terms of feeding the hungry, clothing the poor'. Joy said that she found her colleague's position 'really shocking': at stake here was, as she put it, 'an issue of evangelism, about how people are saved'.

This ideal of giving money to the church as a means of showing compassion for others, building up 'wise investments' as a 'true gospel partner', as David expressed it, is constructed in terms of a calculative ethic. This has resonances with Amira Mittermaier's depiction of her Egyptian informants' almsgiving as a form of 'trading with God', articulating a contractual sense of relationship (2014). Their giving, she argues, is simultaneously guided by an alternative Muslim economic theology, 'which highlights abundance and generosity while resisting calculation' (2014: 287). Thus, concepts of trading with God, she argues, 'both mirror and exceed this-worldly economic imaginaries' (2014: 288). The investment language used to describe giving at St John's likewise intersects with neoliberal and capitalist modes of being-in-the-world (Mittermaier 2014). Yet it is also deeply interwoven with the historical languages of Christianity.

As is typical of an evangelical church that locates its identity squarely within the Reformed tradition, St John's places significant focus on the Bible as the Word of God. It is therefore not surprising that biblical economic metaphors percolate the conservative evangelical imaginary. In the Philippians passage that David drew on, discussed at the start of this chapter, St Paul describes desiring that 'more be credited to your [the Philippians'] account'. Peter Brown argues that in late Roman Christianity the language of the Christian gift was a 'daring extension of the earthly language of exchange, commerce, and treasure ... to the unimaginable world of heaven' (2012: 85). Brown notes that there were many reasons for this construction of the good, including how the creation of a vast common market in the Achaemenid Persian empire had influenced Jewish notions of religious giving, which had been appropriated by Christianity. What might seem to us, he writes,

> a crude commercialization of the religious imagination was favoured because at the time, it infused relations with God with a sense of the infinite that echoed the breathtaking expansion of the horizons of the possible that accompanied the rise of a monetarized economy. The volatility, the seemingly limitless opportunities for profit, and the sheer shimmer of such an economy were adopted as apposite ideograms for the incalculable mercy of God. (Brown 2012: 85–86)

In other words, while the language of investment might today seem the opposite of ideas of abundant mercy, in the early Christian imagination, the monetarized economy was the most apt representation of the *in*calculable and transcendent.

At St John's, the language of giving as an investment for the future sounds like a purely self-interested exchange, predicated on the promise of divine reward. Yet we also see a critique of the idea, as David put it, that you could 'purchase your way to paradise', and an emphasis on the importance of God's grace, which we might see as a form of the good. We also see a conscious effort to seek to understand the act of giving to the church as a relational act that is about each individual in their singularity. Brown describes how for the early Christians 'every gift, however small, brought about nothing less than the joining of heaven and earth' (2012: 86), and in the same way, David emphasized that God takes just as much pleasure in the £3 given by the student as the £3,000 given by the recent graduate.

Evangelicalism is often understood as relationally corrosive, fostering an individualistic sensibility. At St John's, we do see emphasis on individuals' singular moral duty to give to the church. Yet the meaning of this practice is also constructed as a communal venture, tinged with expectations of rewards and purpose extending beyond the present. The value of individual gifts is thus amplified in relation to the transcendent and oriented towards the future City of God. At the same time, these acts of giving shape their sense of collective identity as pitted against an unbelieving world, which is constructed as 'self-seeking'. Giving to the church is imagined as breaking down boundaries between heaven and earth as individuals see themselves as agents of the good, partnering with God in the spread of the gospel through their monetary contributions. In this sense, we see how (economic) value is transformed into virtue (Lambek 2015a). As Lambek describes, 'even in a middle-class church service, when the collection plate is passed or when congregants donate to charity, this kind of transformation takes place', which is of 'profound moral significance for participants' (2015a: 235). This is an example of how religion can turn 'the profits and earnings of the everyday world, into such virtues as largesse, generosity, charity, or honor' (ibid.).

'Maximizing Resources' and the Snare of Mammon

As well as biblical languages of investment, the ideal of the good Christian was constructed drawing on expansionist logics drawn from the corporate world within which many members of St John's worked. At the church's annual parochial meeting,[5] the couple of hundred church members present sat at tables laid with meeting agendas, the church's financial reports, glossy annual reports on the church, and minutes of the previous year's meetings. David gave a report on the ministry of St John's that year. His main theme was that the church should not think about 'church planting', which he said was 'unbiblical language', but 'church building' and 'church growing', which he said were biblical. He talked through a slide about how he saw the work of St John's in terms of 'reaching' and 'building', using a flow chart with numerous arrows extending off to various congregations and small groups to show the ambition to 'grow' the church and reach more non-Christians, locally, nationally and globally. This aspiration was also central in a video on the church website. The narrator talked about the numbers of 'younger city workers' and students they were engaged in ministry with, and the numbers who had gone on from the church into preaching, with the head of a theological college saying, 'they've gone out into the city of London, into the UK, and they've gone out into the wider world', illustrated by a shot panning out from the church to an image of the globe. The narrator mentioned the church's 'digital ministry', that 'people near and far listened to 360,000 sermons online in 2013'. The video closed with David saying

> all of this has been achieved by God's grace alone ... There is however so much more work to be done and so much more that could be done, and therefore it's only right that every one of us asks ourselves, 'what part can *we* play in this next phase of God's work here at St John's?' God's given us resources that he wants us to maximize for his honour.

This sense of duty to maximize resources to contribute to the church's ministry was exemplified in the book that Philip recommended to the congregation, *The Money Mentor* by Ash Carter. Each chapter closes with questions for the reader to interrogate their own practices, such as 'How do I actually spend 168 hours per week / my salary? ... How much time do you honestly spend watching TV? ... It would be easy to spend hours every day on those things, precious hours that belong to Jesus' (Carter 2010: 59). This logic of efficiently managing money and time to give as much as possible to the church is emphasized throughout the book, with chapters on tax-efficient giving, including 'making the most of your death'. Carter advises readers to update spreadsheets of all expenditure, weekly, in order to hold themselves accountable. Rather than acknowledging the wider social contexts shaping individuals' economic circumstances, he stresses an ethic of individual responsibility: 'whatever your financial situation, you got there because you wanted to get there' (ibid.: 23). He situates his readers within a wider cultural worship of money, which, he says, is bound up with consumerist desire:

> At every point in history, human beings have looked to their harvests, their families, their trinkets and their toys to fill the deep longing in their hearts that can be filled only by a relationship with God. ... We are sinful, and the advertisers play on our lust for created things, feeding our desire and then feeding *from* it ... That is why we are so complicit in the mess we are in. ... We are sinful. Our hearts are in rebellion against God. Not only mine and yours, but everyone else's too. So we have a whole economy that is built on the universal idolatries of the age. (Carter 2010: 25)

This narrativization of contemporary society as idolatrous in its worship of money was a frequent theme at St John's and was a means through which church leaders sought to establish a relationship between 'the good' and 'the true'. As listening to sermons was presented in the church as the way in which God speaks to individuals, the construction of the good Christian as selfless in their giving – in contrast with the world as self-seeking in its desire for money – can be seen as a form of truth-making (Lambek 2015b: 20), determining what *should* matter for the 'true' Christian. In one sermon, David described 90% of the contemporary Western world 'living as if there is nothing beyond this world and all that matters is cash'. He talked about this in relation to the passage in 1 Timothy, which states 'the love of money is a root of all kinds of evils':

> Paul does not say that *money* is the root of all kinds of evil, does he? It's the *desire* to be rich ... Paul is not against being rich. The Bible is not against money. God made money. God isn't a communist, you might say ... What Paul is speaking against here is the man or woman who desires wealth, who hankers after wealth, for whom making money and advancing in financial terms is an all-absorbing affair.

David talked about the imagery in the 1 Timothy passage, which describes the desire to be rich as 'a snare':

the snare is a noose laid out subtly for an animal into which the animal is designed to put its ... neck. Then once in it [the noose] in such a way that it cannot loosen it, and it involves the animal slowly strangling to death. That is what the desire to be rich exposes you to. The senseless and harmful desires are those desires that rise up within us all the time.

David described these dangers in practical terms that members of the congregation could relate to:

> Allow me to introduce us to Sam. Sam is a fictional person ... recently graduated and moved to London. Sam is a member of a church ... Secretly Sam loves money. Sam has been exposed to a lot of, well, pagan friends, who live around him in the office; who live all out as economic materialists ... Their motto is 'Eat, drink, and be merry, for tomorrow we die.' Most of them plan exotic holidays. Many of them have a season ticket at their local football club, gym membership. They ski, of course, at least once a year, and some of them just pop off for a couple of other weekends where they go to the finest resorts, Verbier and such like. Sam secretly has started to long for all these things too ... [H]e has seen the adverts, he watches the telly, he hears people talk in the office, and he longs to be rich ... Just an extra £2000 a year, or maybe £5,000, so he can live the life, walk the walk, and talk the talk.
>
> How does God see Sam? ... God sees Sam like a person who takes a sword, lays it out at the bottom of the stairs sticking upwards and in the morning walks down the stairs deliberately tripping himself on the second stair from the bottom to see if he might be able to fall on it.

David said, 'the antidote ... is not to become a kind of tapioca-eating-tree-hugging-world-denying hippy ... Money is good. Being poor is not to be preferred ... Rather we should be what you might call spiritual materialists.' He put some figures on this:

> if you are on £55,000 a year and you are a single person, surely you are able to give 20% of that away? ... Maybe you are earning £20,000 a year ... surely you can give away 10% of that? ... Some of us will have savings ... This is a good thing to do ... But I wonder when the last time was you ... [w]ent to your savings and said ... 'I am going to give away 10% of my savings.'

He then warned against pride:

> How often I've heard somebody who works long hours in the city and gets paid extraordinary amounts of money say, 'I deserve it.' Really? Don't be so arrogant. Do you deserve that money more than the woman in Bangladesh sitting with a pile of bricks on her left hammering them on an anvil, breaking them into gravel so that she can make a pile of gravel to be sold for a pittance to the builders so they can build roads in Bangladesh? Do you really think you work harder than her? Of course you don't deserve it. Don't be so proud.

David said those who are rich must be 'generous and ready to share, thus storing up treasure for themselves in heaven', but emphasized 'not that we *earn* our place in heaven, but God has given us things which we are to use for the benefit of others, freely, generously, for the work of Christ and thus to develop our portfolio – you will like that language if you are rich – and to build your portfolio where it actually lasts, in heaven'.

Here we see a construction of the good in terms of generosity contrasted with the contemporary world's idolatrous worship of money. Yet we also see the idea that the love of money is a danger for Christians. Through listening to these teachings and through practices of Bible reading, prayer and participating in church Bible study groups, church members learn to monitor their thoughts and desires according to the ideals of being content with their possessions and generosity towards the church. They are encouraged to narrativize experiences of the contradictions of capitalist desire as an internal struggle between Spirit and Flesh, which also constructs a sense of distinction from the idolatrous city around them. Foucault describes subjectification as taking place through dividing practices: 'the subject is either divided in himself or divided from others' (1982: 208). The naming of the good Christian here, who gives generously, can be seen as a boundary that divides evangelicals from others. But it *also* divides the subject within herself, outlining an *ideal* moral stance that she will fall short of, and therefore encouraging her to work on herself to come closer to this ideal in future (Strhan 2015: 107). In contrast with interventions by Christian leaders such as Pope Francis, there was at St John's no critique of capitalism in terms of the injustices it perpetuates. Rather, the ideal presented is for the evangelical subject to become aware that the possibility of enacting the good is implicated in her every economic transaction. In one sermon, Pete said, 'Every penny of our resources belongs to God himself. We are merely stewards of them. Therefore, it is right to ask of every pound … Will I save it? Will I spend it? Or will I give it? Because the way that I dispose of each pound is a spiritual decision'.

This construction of the good in terms of the virtues of generosity and contentment – and the struggle to maintain these – can be seen in the words of Gemma, a teaching assistant. She told me she felt pressure to 'look nice' at St John's, and 'because everyone looks nice, you end up wanting to buy more things yourself, and you don't see anything wrong with it, because everyone else does that, but it does breed a kind of discontent'. She said that David addressed money in sermons

> because he perceives it as a problem that people in the church are facing … I think that maybe we should be more uncomfortable about the tension between society's expectations and our faith. It is so ingrained into our minds to want that suburban house. It's something that Jeremy [her husband] and I struggle with. Sometimes we wonder if we're being ridiculous giving so much away when we really don't have very much … We couldn't afford to go on our church weekend away. It was £140 a night per person if we wanted en suite.

I asked how she dealt with that sense of struggle. 'Through prayer,' she replied, 'and the wisdom of other Christians. Sometimes seeing the generosity of other Christians is really inspiring.' She said that it was hard not to be judgemental:

> You really need to discipline yourself not to judge others. Like, sometimes I hear people at work saying that they need to do more overtime to have money to go out, and I find myself thinking, 'you're living at home with your parents, when Jeremy and I were both of us living off my salary for three months, what do you *do* with your money?' But that's wrong of me ... If they're not Christians, there's no reason for them to be living otherwise.

In one evening's Bible study group discussion, Hannah, leading the discussion, said that the way we think about money was an area 'that requires real grace from God to change'. She talked about how she thought the notion that what we have earned is *ours* is very deeply ingrained. Emily, another group member, said that the problem was that often we can think 'go on, you deserve it, you're worth it'. A particular issue that Hannah raised was the need to save for our pensions and that worrying about the future can affect giving. Emily replied, 'but we *do* need to get a balance between being generous and being sensible'. Alan, another group member, added, 'and we're always being asked for money, on the TV, by post, there are always so many appeals'.

Challenging the church leaders' binary moral construction of the 'self-serving world' and the other-serving Christian, Janet, another group member, said that non-Christians can offer 'a real example' through their generosity, and she mentioned a colleague who had given very generously to a heart charity. 'Yes, and you wonder,' Emily replied, 'are they saying the same thing about you giving to the church?', showing her awareness that those outside the church would see giving to an already affluent church as a lesser good than other causes. Hannah emphasized the importance of context: 'here [in the Bible passage] it is about supporting and giving to *Christians* in need, not giving to secular charities. It's about that circle of God's grace, that grace abounding to us, that results in our giving, then that results in the thanksgiving and relationship with others.'

In another discussion, the group's sense that their own attitudes towards money should be different from non-Christians was clear. Talking about the 'costs' of being a Christian, Hannah commented that when Philip, her husband, became a partner at his firm, their friends had suggested that they move out of central London to Surrey and buy a bigger house, but they had made a decision to stay in London. 'In your pokey old cottage?' her friend Lucy had said sharply, in reference to Hannah and Philip's large Georgian townhouse. In comparison with many corporate partners of comparable financial services organizations, their lifestyles were relatively unshowy: a rented cottage in Devon being their preferred holiday destination, no second home and no expensive car, and Hannah – a Cambridge graduate – works as a volunteer for an educational charity.

Talking about what their non-Christian friends valued, Philip mentioned that he had said in conversation to a colleague, 'I often wonder why would people want to spend all that money on a Ferrari or whatever?' but then remembered this particular colleague has an Aston Martin. Edward, a banker in his early thirties who was part of the Bible study group, had replied, 'I think people should be able to see the difference in our lives, that we're living differently, that it isn't those things that are making us happy.' Edward's words reflected many church members' sense of duty to embody the good life, although not as an end in itself but rather as a means of 'witnessing' their faith to non-Christians. While being aware that they have material wealth, the source of church members' contentment should *visibly* lie elsewhere, in their relationship with God. As church members discussed their sense that how they spent their money was 'different' from their non-Christian friends and colleagues, they thereby reinforced their sense of moral distinction from non-Christians. Such discussions feed into their perception of a fragmentation between their values and a broader cultural valuing of wealth. Yet in acknowledging the exemplary generosity of non-Christians and wondering about their friends' perceptions of their own giving, they also demonstrate the fragility of these moral boundaries of distinctiveness.

Conclusion

Approaching conservative evangelicals through the lens of the good means taking seriously the ethical sensibilities of a group who seem morally suspect to many and examining how their values are shaped, maintained and challenged in everyday life. Different moral threads are interwoven in their economic imaginaries: we see a broadly 'neoliberal' ethic of individual self-determination to maximize monetary resources in order to give to the church, contributing to a corporate venture that extends globally and draws past and future into the present. There is also a somewhat 'utopian' understanding of money (Dodds 2012; Simmel 2004), in which the £3 gift is equal in value to the £3,000 gift. At the same time, money is a mortal threat: wider society is constructed as in the lure of Mammon, and Christians as also constantly threatened.

Peter Brown describes how in late Roman society the act of giving became a source of competition, with fierce inter-family rivalry goading urban benefactors to compete in giving to their cities. Christian giving, he argues, was a way of escaping this competitiveness. The rich 'valued in the churches a certain lowering of the sense of hierarchy and a slowing down of the pace of competition' (2012: 87). Brown notes that in church they did not have to give large amounts at one time, as long as they gave frequently: 'the sense that the glory of heaven stood behind their every gift enabled the Christian rich to contribute regularly and with that much less strain' (ibid.). Among affluent circles in contemporary London, there is little such competitiveness about charitable giving, but there *is* competitiveness about status. The values cultivated at St John's might be seen likewise as a means of standing apart from this. One trader told me that everyone in his profession was well paid, and 'there's a culture of materialism ... . So it's a question of whether you buy into that as well. So I think it does affect the car I have, I think it affects where I live – all of those things would seem less impressive than they might' to his peers. He said that coming to St John's motivated his work, describing it as 'like a recharge, which is really good, in terms of *perspective* on what I'm doing'.

When I interviewed the minister in charge of city ministry, he likewise talked about the importance of enabling people to see their value as beyond economic value:

> David used to tease me and say, 'it's just idolatry isn't it?' And I'd say, 'no, here's the irony, I think it's slavery,' because ... the junior guys in the city – I mean guys generically – the junior Christians in the city, you're not in control of your circumstances. The boss says jump and you jump. So you're a slave. I look at the managing director of [a large financial services company], the chief executives I know, and I think, it's different for you, you're in control, you control your diary, you can pick and choose. The MDs at [a large financial services company] tell me that the phone rings and it's a client, it could be a chief exec of a FTSE 100 company on the phone, they get an email, and they say, 'why aren't you on the phone? I need to speak to you.' That's the kind of thing you expect a junior grub to get in the food chain, but this is a guy – there's no higher person in the bank – but he's being treated like a junior grub. Because so much of it is professional services. So there is this kind of slavery idolatry battle ...

> Part of the battle for the Christian is to keep reminding them that they are valued not because of the number of noughts on the end of a salary, or the size of their Queen Anne mansion, or the top speed of their Aston Martin ... They are valued because if they're God's children, God has created them in his image; Jesus has died on the cross for them, and God's Spirit dwells within them. It means that we're remarkable ... I just have to keep reminding myself. And so to have the right criteria for their source of value makes a difference.

Church leaders thus sought to develop in church members the 'right criteria' for their source of value in terms of this sense of relationship with God, which will shape their engagements with money, with God experienced as the ultimate 'arbiter, guarantor, and ... redeemer of value' (Lambek 2015a: 228). As well as a means of opting out of the competitiveness of status, giving money to the church and placing limits on spending are also a means for church members to have an increased sense of control over their lives, which many of them do not necessarily feel in relation to working in professional services.

Brown describes the 'glory of heaven' standing behind every Christian gift in the early church. For members of St John's, everyday economic practices become likewise imbued with a transcendent significance and enable them to feel a sense of belonging to something larger than themselves, drawing together the past and the future in the present moment. In her study of international humanitarianism, Lisa Malkki argues that involvement in humanitarian work enables people to feel 'part of something other and bigger than themselves, to *imagine* themselves ... as members of a greater "community of generosity"' and at the same time benefit from the social connections they experience through such work (2015: 12). Members of St John's learn to imagine their giving as contributing to the work of a greater heavenly community while at the same time fostering the church as an earthly community that provides them with a sense of social connectedness. Malkki notes that in humanitarian work the recipient of giving is often presented as the 'passive and pathetic' subject who suffers, in contrast with the active subject, who 'identifies suffering and knows how to act' (ibid.: 7). At St John's, while in practice the church is the direct recipient of congregants' money, church members are encouraged to see the *true* beneficiaries of their giving as the non-Christians around them, who are otherwise headed for eternal damnation and who may yet be saved through the church's proselytizing. It is possible to see this transformation of wealth into sanctity, as Lambek argues, as one reason for the appeal of religion as it 'expands alongside the penetration and expansion of the capitalist economy. Indeed, it may provide the only way not just to siphon off capital, but to transcend capitalist regimes of value' (2015a: 256).

These incommensurable logics at St John's in terms of the calculative, rationalistic ethics entwined in mundane book-keeping, spreadsheets and accountability, and of transcendent grace, gesture towards counteracting moral dynamics deeply rooted within contemporary neoliberal subjectivities. Andrea Muehlebach argues that while much work on neoliberalism places itself in the Weberian and Foucauldian tradition of studying forms of self-formation accruing virtues of work, thrift and productivity, we should also understand neoliberalism as 'a force that can contain its negation – the vision of a decommodified, disinterested life and of a moral community of human relationality and solidarity that stands opposed to alienation' (2012: 25). Yet these differing moral impulses also gesture towards deeper fissures within the human subject in modernity, between dimensions of order, control and rationalization and the vertiginous dimension of ideas of grace, ethics and transcendent possibility that exceed totalizing logics of exchange (Levinas 1969; Strhan 2019: 194). Henig and Makovicky (forthcoming) call for an 'anthropology of gratuitous action', building on Pitt-Rivers' (2017) argument that human sociality is not grounded only in transactional exchange relationships but also on forms of grace and gratuity. Future studies might attend to the significance and articulation of specific ideas of grace and gratuity, and the ways in which these are interwoven within and beyond economic imaginaries.

For conservative evangelicals at St John's, the ideal of giving is anchored through an imaginary focused on ideas of God's transcendent grace and the future promise of the City of God. I have elsewhere argued (2015, 2019), following Stanley Cavell, that transcendental elements and utopian moments may in the end be 'indispensable in the motivation for a moral existence' (Cavell 2004: 18; see also Cooke 2006; Robbins 2016). One of Kant's summary images in the *Groundwork of the Metaphysics of Morals* portrays, as Cavell describes:

> the human being regarding his existence from two standpoints, from one of which he counts himself as belonging to the world of sense ..., and from the other of which he counts himself as belonging to the intelligible world (the province of freedom and of the moral law, presided over by reason, transcending the human powers of knowing). (Cavell 2004: 1)

This image of human nature as divided or double permeates a wide range of philosophical and moral perspectives and, as Cavell describes, offers 'a perspective of judgement upon the world as it is, measured against the world as it may be', and in so doing expresses 'disappointment with the world as it is, as the scene of human activity and prospects', while 'lodg[ing] the demand or desire for a reform or transfiguration of the world' (ibid.: 2). Cavell argues that this interplay of transcendental moments, disappointment and desire is intrinsic to the register of 'moral perfectionism', echoing 'an idea that Socrates ... invokes as listening to one's genius (meaning not our virtuosity but something like our receptiveness), which may require self-disobedience' (2004: 18). Attending to the wider social contexts shaping the formation of these transcendental imaginings and their interrelation with specific conditions of disappointment and desire might deepen our understanding of the location of the good in the world and how this can both anchor and transcend contemporary regimes of value.

Acknowledgements

I wish to thank David Henig, Joel Robbins, Kimberly Chong and Rachael Shillitoe for their helpful comments on earlier drafts of this chapter. This research was funded by the School of European Culture and Languages at the University of Kent and the Leverhulme Trust.

Anna Strhan is Senior Lecturer in Sociology at the University of York. She is the author of *The Figure of the Child in Contemporary Evangelicalism* (2019), *Aliens and Strangers? The Struggle for Coherence in the Everyday Lives of Evangelicals* (2015) and *Levinas, Subjectivity, Education: Towards an Ethics of Radical Responsibility* (2012), and the co-editor of *Religion and the Global City* (2017) and *The Bloomsbury Reader in Religion and Childhood* (2017).

Notes

1. This idea of Christians being 'downwardly mobile' was a self-conscious distancing from prosperity gospel theology, which in other sermons was described as 'blasphemous' in its emphasis on material blessings in the here and now (Strhan 2015: 185).
2. Robbins (2013) does not situate the anthropology of the good in relation to neoliberalism but rather with the loss of the 'Other' in the anthropological imagination through focusing on suffering.
3. Further information about the process of conducting fieldwork with St John's is detailed in *Aliens and Strangers? The Struggle for Coherence in Everyday Evangelicalism* (2015) and *The Figure of the Child in Contemporary Evangelicalism* (2019).
4. This is in contrast with other evangelical churches in the UK, which often place greater emphasis on giving to the poor (see Evangelical Alliance 2012).
5. Every parish in the Church of England is required, under Church Representation Rules, to hold an Annual Parochial Meeting to conduct parish business.

References

Bialecki, J. 2008. 'Between Stewardship and Sacrifice: Agency and Economy in a Southern California Charismatic Church', *Journal of the Royal Anthropological Institute* 14: 372–90.

Brown, P. 2012. *Through the Eye of a Needle: Wealth, the Fall of Rome, and the Making of Christianity in the West, 350–550 AD*. Princeton: Princeton University Press.

Carter, A. 2010. *The Money Mentor: Getting to Grips with Your Finances*. Nottingham: Inter-Varsity Press.

Cavell, S. 2004. *Cities of Words: Pedagogical Letters on a Register of the Moral Life*. Cambridge, MA: Harvard University Press.

Coleman, S. 2004. 'The Charismatic Gift', *Journal of the Royal Anthropological Institute* 10(2): 421–42.

———. 2011. 'Prosperity Unbound? Debating the "Sacrificial Economy"', *Research in Economic Anthropology* 31: 23–46.

Comaroff, J. 2010. 'The Politics of Conviction: Faith on the Neo-Liberal Frontier', in B. Kapferer, K. Telle and A. Eriksen (eds), *Contemporary Religiosities: Emergent Socialities and the Post-Nation-State*. New York: Berghahn, pp. 17–38.

Connolly, W. 2008. *Capitalism and Christianity: American Style*. Durham, NC: Duke University Press.

Cooke, M. 2006. *Re-Presenting the Good Society*. Cambridge, MA: MIT Press.

Daswani, G. 2015. 'A Prophet but Not for Profit: Ethical Value and Character in Ghanaian Pentecostalism', *Journal of the Royal Anthropological Institute* 22: 108–26.

Dodds, N. 2012. 'Simmel's Perfect Money: Fiction, Socialism and Utopia in *The Philosophy of Money*', *Theory, Culture and Society* 29(7/8): 146–76.

Elisha, O. 2008. 'Moral Ambitions of Grace: The Paradox of Compassion and Accountability in Evangelical Faith-Based Activism', *Cultural Anthropology* 23(1): 154–89.

———. 2011. *Moral Ambition: Mobilization and Social Outreach in Evangelical Megachurches*. Berkeley: University of California Press.

Evangelical Alliance. 2012. '21ˢᵗ Century Evangelicals: Does Money Matter?' Retrieved 16 March 2020 from https://www.eauk.org/church/resources/snapshot/upload/does-money-matter-lower.pdf.
Fassin, D. 2015. 'Troubled Waters: At the Confluence of Ethics and Politics', in M. Lambek, V. Das, D. Fassin and W. Keane (eds), *Four Lectures on Ethics: Anthropological Perspectives*. Chicago: Hau Books, pp. 175–210.
Foucault, M. 1982. 'Subject and Power', in H.L. Dreyfus and P. Rabinow (ed.), *Michel Foucault: Beyond Structuralism and Hermeneutics*, 2ⁿᵈ edn. Chicago: University of Chicago Press, pp. 208–26.
Guyer, J. 2007. 'Prophecy and the Near Future: Thoughts on Macroeconomic, Evangelical, and Punctuated Time', *American Ethnologist* 34(3): 409–21.
Harding, S. 1991. 'Representing Fundamentalism: The Problem of the Repugnant Cultural Other', *Social Research* 58(2): 373–93.
Haynes, N. 2012. 'Pentecostalism and the Morality of Money: Prosperity, Inequality, and Religious Sociality on the Zambian Copperbelt', *Journal of the Royal Anthropological Institute* 18: 123–39.
———. 2017. *Moving by the Spirit: Pentecostal Social Life on the Zambian Copperbelt*. Oakland: University of California Press.
Henig, D., and N. Makovicky. forthcoming. 'Favours', in J. Laidlaw (ed.), *Cambridge Handbook of the Anthropology of Ethics and Morality*. Cambridge: Cambridge University Press.
Kapferer, B., and M. Gold. 2018. *Moral Anthropology: A Critique*. New York: Berghahn.
Lambek, M. 2010. 'Introduction', in M. Lambek (ed.), *Ordinary Ethics: Anthropology, Language, and Action*. New York: Fordham University Press, 1–36.
———. 2015a. *The Ethical Condition: Essays on Action, Person and Value*. Chicago: University of Chicago Press.
———. 2015b. 'Living as If It Mattered', in M. Lambek, V. Das, D. Fassin and W. Keane (eds), *Four Lectures on Ethics: Anthropological Perspectives*. Chicago: Hau Books, pp. 5–51.
Levinas, E. 1969. *Totality and Infinity: An Essay on Exteriority*, trans. A. Lingis. Pittsburgh, PA: Duquesne University Press.
Lukes, S. 2010. 'The Social Construction of Morality', in S. Hitlin and S. Vaisey (eds), *Handbook of the Sociology of Morality*. New York: Springer, pp. 549–60.
Malkki, L.H. 2015. *The Need to Help: The Domestic Arts of International Humanitarianism*. Durham, NC: Duke University Press.
Mittermaier, A. 2014. 'Trading with God: Islam, Calculation, Excess', in by M. Lambek and J. Boddy (eds), *Companion to the Anthropology of Religion*. Chichester: Wiley-Blackwell, pp. 274–94.
Muehlebach, A. 2012. *The Moral Neoliberal: Welfare and Citizenship in Italy*. Chicago: University of Chicago Press.
Ortner, S. 2016. 'Dark Anthropology and Its Others: Theory since the Eighties', *HAU: Journal of Ethnographic Theory* 6(1): 47–73.
Pitt-Rivers, J. 2017. 'The Place of Grace in Anthropology', in G. da Col and A. Shyrock (eds), *From Hospitality to Grace: A Julian Pitt-Rivers Omnibus*. Chicago: Hau Books, pp. 211–26.
Robbins, J. 2013. 'Beyond the Suffering Subject: Toward an Anthropology of the Good', *Journal of the Royal Anthropological Institute* 19: 447–62.
———. 2016. 'What is the Matter with Transcendence? On the Place of Religion in the New Anthropology of Ethics', *Journal of the Royal Anthropological Institute* 22(4): 767–81.

Sennett, R. 2002. *Flesh and Stone: The Body and the City in Western Civilization.* London: Penguin.
Simmel, G. 2004. *The Philosophy of Money.* London: Routledge.
Skeggs, B. 2014. 'Values beyond Value? Is Anything beyond the Logic of Capital?' *British Journal of Sociology* 65(1): 1–20.
Strhan, A. 2015. *Aliens and Strangers? The Struggle for Coherence in the Everyday Lives of Evangelicals.* Oxford: Oxford University Press.
_____. 2019. *The Figure of the Child in Contemporary Evangelicalism.* Oxford: Oxford University Press.
Weber, M. 1992. *The Protestant Ethic and the Spirit of Capitalism,* trans. T. Parsons. London: Routledge.

9

Doing Good
Cultivating Children's Ethical Sensibilities in School Assemblies

Rachael Shillitoe

On a bright September morning, I arrived at St Peter's Primary School[1] and made my way up to the school entrance, saying hello to some children as they arrived on their scooters. I had been at the school for two weeks and so was fairly well acquainted with everyday school routines and was building an increasingly good rapport with both children and staff. In the Year Five[2] classroom, I began to help Jane, the class teacher, prepare resources for the morning's maths lesson. We spent forty minutes learning 'place value', where children learnt the value of each digit in a number, and then the children were asked to line up in 'lining up order' to 'get ready for assembly'. As we walked down to the hall, I chatted with Callum, a nine-year-old boy, fond of Minecraft and Pokémon cards. I asked him if he was looking forward to assembly. 'Yeah', he said, 'it just gets a bit boring after a while.' Asking what he meant by this, he responded: 'It just gets a bit samey samey. It's all about being a good person and doing good, and it just sometimes ... yeah ... gets borin".

Drawing on data from a child-centred, ethnographic study of collective worship in English primary schools, this chapter examines 'the good' in everyday school life. In particular, this chapter focuses on assemblies and collective worship as a means through which schools perform, mediate and teach different ideas of the good. Collective worship, or as it was commonly referred to in my field sites, assemblies, is a legal requirement in England and Wales whereby schools have to provide for daily acts of collective worship that are 'wholly or mainly of a broadly Christian character' and reflect 'the broad traditions of Christian belief' (Education Reform Act 1988, Section 7). This piece of legislation is highly contested, with campaigns, court cases[3] and public debates calling for the legislation to be revised or abolished in light of the increasingly diverse and plural population. Although a legal requirement, collective worship is widely unobserved in secondary schools (ages 11–16) and is more commonly found at primary school level (ages 4–11), though the content and regularity of these events varies dramatically across schools (Curtis 2004). One variant is the naming of the event, with schools using both 'collective worship' and 'assemblies' interchangeably. This fluidity between the terms is reflected in this chapter, as I follow the ways in which the terms were used in my field sites. Another variant is the level of explicitly Christian themes and references contained within collective worship, with some involving prayer, hymns and teachings from the Bible, and others having more subtle references or, in many cases, having no direct reference to Christianity.[4] Consequently, assemblies[5] and how the good was understood and discussed during such occasions were often mediated through both religious and non-religious frames of reference, with church schools often drawing on religious teachings to underscore the formation of children's ethical formation. Three schools were used in this study. I spent eight weeks at each school acting as a teaching assistant while conducting interviews with teachers and pupils. St Peter's[6] was a voluntary controlled Church of England Primary; my second school, Sacred Heart, was a Roman Catholic Academy; and my final school, Holly Oak, was a special school. All schools were located in an urban area of the South West of England.

Drawing on this ethnographic data and reflecting on how schools attempt to cultivate children's ethical subjectivities in both religious and non-religious frameworks and, subsequently, how children respond to such strategies, I explore how 'the good' is understood, lived and acted on in daily life. Focusing on the question of 'the good' in relation to childhood – and more specifically schooling – contributes to our understanding of the good by exploring how parents, teachers, children and policymakers construct and enact particular moral ideals and values in everyday life. The ways in which the good is constructed and enacted in relation to childhood exemplifies the dreams, wishes and desires we have for our social worlds, with children standing as the moral visions for the betterment of society (see Strhan 2019: 173). However, examining the good in relation to childhood is also revealing of the anxieties, hopes and aspirations adults have in terms of children's moral formation (Frankel 2012, 2017). When faced with periods of environmental insecurities, political upheaval, increasing populist rhetoric and growing inequality, children represent opportunities to project, plan and realize a different and better reality than the one we currently live in. Consequently, even the seemingly mundane and inconsequential aspects of children's everyday lives are imbued with particular imaginaries and ideas of the good.

Empirically speaking, schools serve as an important site to address and explore the ethical turn within the social sciences and humanities[7] (Boothroyd 2013; Das 2010, 2012; Robbins 2013), as this is not only the space where children are socialized with particular ideas of the good but also a space where children arrive with potentially different and competing understandings of the good due to the various ways in which families may transmit or socialize their children. As Mattingly in her ethnographic research observes: 'each such social and institutional world is characterized by an array of specific norms and practices. Morally speaking, these are not homogenous spaces, and they are often conflicting ones' (2014: 8). Children moving across these spaces and places will encounter and therefore navigate between different visions of the good, and it is this heterogeneity and contestation of the good that we find in everyday school life. Paying close attention to the school as a space in which good is explicitly performed and taught, while also paying attention to how children internalize and negotiate the values embodied in this vision, creates an opportunity to view different visions of what the 'good life' is and the different resources and actions through which this good life is subsequently sought for and achieved.

Studying schools and foregrounding children's understanding of the good can therefore enhance the sociology of morality more broadly in terms of investigating the formation of how individuals conceptualize the good and how this is created and sustained across different spaces and contexts. In this sense, schools and childhood more broadly can contribute to Hitlin and Vaisey's (2013) three core areas of the sociology of morality. Through both looking at the micro level of everyday school life coupled with the meso and macro level of school leadership, educational policy and political rhetoric, we can observe the pressures and pulls on schools to create particular visions of the good and how this is translated and enacted in the classroom. As schools encourage the children to behave and practise particular values in daily school life, we can also examine how morality affects action and how children internalize these values and desired behaviours. This institutional focus also provides a way to explore where these morals are derived from and the variation that might occur across different sites.

To begin with, I sketch out the important contribution that both childhood and education studies have within this field and explore the importance of childhood when considering ideas of morality and the good in social life more broadly. I then move on to data collected from some of my field sites, investigating how children encounter and experience the good in their daily lives and how they negotiate, internalize and reflect on such positions and practices. I begin by exploring the context of morality and values in relation to both childhood and education. I then situate this discussion in conversation with scholarly work on ordinary ethics (Lambek 2010) and suggest that collective worship helps draw attention to these dimensions of ethical life, which consequently shifts and deepens our understanding of the lives of children. I consider understandings of childhood in relation to discourse on ordinary ethics and the anxieties of adults in terms of children's moral formation (Frankel 2012, 2017). Following this, I explore how schools can be seen to be performing their own 'vision of the good' during acts of collective worship (Robbins

2013). I focus on the everyday ethics of collective worship and how schools celebrate the children's ordinary achievements. Finally, I discuss children's desire for authenticity (Taylor 1992) when encountering values and ethical practices in school, reflecting on the cynicism and scepticism that can emerge when such acts are deemed inauthentic. I conclude by arguing that the findings presented in this chapter demonstrate the need to pay closer attention to this ethical dimension of everyday school life – and children's lives more broadly – in order to observe how idealized notions of the good are enacted and performed in everyday life and, in turn, how children accept, contest and negotiate such visions.

Childhood, Education and Morality

Childhood in relation to morality has been an ongoing preoccupation for both sociology and psychology. Jenks (1996) and Mayall (2002) explore how constructions of childhood emerge in relation to children's perceived moral status – or lack of it. According to Mayall (2002), children and young people are found in a paradoxical situation when it comes to matters of morality. On the one hand, children are seen as lacking in the ability to make competent decisions of their own and must therefore defer such decision-making powers to adults, who are considered to be fully complete moral beings. On the other, Mayall (2002) also observes a misfit in this, as children, while being perceived as morally incomplete and immature, are continuously placed in situations where they are expected to take on moral responsibility. This paradoxical situation arises from the various constructions and views of childhood in society. From the 'savage child' to the 'natural child', children's place in society has always been marked by adults and their anxieties over children's biological immaturity (Frankel 2017; Jenks 1996). Writing on morality and society, Durkheim (1978) reflected on his own uncertainty and fear around childhood and the perceived threat children pose to the social structure. On childhood, Durkheim considered that 'one cannot help but tremble with fear' at this 'delightful but fragile mechanism', and that ultimately 'it [the child] is fickle, changeable, capricious, full of disappointment and pleasant surprises' (1978: 148). Speaking directly in relation to childhood and morality, Durkheim in the same essay goes on to state:

> As a rule, neither good nor evil is very deep-rooted in his [the child's] nature; he is incapable of great and sustained effort; good resolutions are no sooner made than forgotten. But at the same time, what eagerness greets novelty! This diminutive conscience is a veritable kaleidoscope. (1978: 148 as cited in Frankel 2017: 22)

There is, then, a view of childhood that is fraught with uncertainty, fragility and risk, and entangled in this is the duty of parents, teachers and society more broadly to ensure children are raised as 'good people', 'good citizens' and that they make the 'right choices'. Durkheim (1978) goes on to suggest how educationalists should support children's moral formation, identifying children as 'organisms' that are 'scarcely formed' and weak in terms of their intellectual ability and capacity. Frankel (2017) draws on Durkheim to explore the relationship between social order and moral action, noting that children were seen as the weak link in society and therefore careful socialization was needed to ensure children's moral inculcation into society. Jenks (1996) observes how the Parsonian paradigm of socialization also reproduces this image of the child as 'potentially dangerous'. Talcott Parsons considered childhood to be the crucial stage for socialization, as the child has 'so far to go' in this respect (1951: 142). Speaking on the internalization of value orientations, Parsons considers these to be, in the main, laid down during childhood and not 'subject to drastic alteration during adult life' (1951: 142). In this way, Parsons' treatment of childhood socialization concerning their ethical formation relies heavily on treating children as merely adults in becoming (James and Prout 1997; Ridgely 2011). Jenks (1996) also observes how Parsons' (1951) treatment of socialization produces an image of the 'profane' child alongside a sense of society's duty to inculcate its own morals and values in order to draw children into the social structure and continue to bolster and reproduce its own norms.

Writing on child migration and morality, Lynch (2014) observes that nation states' cultural imaginaries play a significant role in the socialization of children. In this process, children are formed as part of an 'imagined community of the nation', and such socialization is achieved through various mechanisms within education, fiction, play, music and broader participation in society as a whole (Lynch 2014: 166). The school, as Lynch (2014) argues, is a vehicle within children's socialization, and educational institutions have long been observed as a key space for children's moral formation and a site for civilizing processes (Beck 1990; Elias 2000; Foucault 1977; Watson and Ashton 1995). According to Beck, schools 'reinforce the values learned in the home, and foster new outlooks and behaviour needed in the workplace and other public settings of pluralist societies' (1990: viii). This raises the question: what values (and whose values)? And can we assume a simple correlation between values at home and values at school? A number of scholars (e.g. Rich 1993; Strhan 2017) have found that schools can be places to promote 'middle-class values'. Reay (2006) and Kulz (2017) argue that middle-class children can be viewed as 'valuable commodities' in schools, especially in relation to meeting attainment targets. Dill and Davison Hunter explore 'culture wars' in American schools and the need to attend to how 'schools participate in the legitimation and reproduction of moral order in society', acknowledging that ideas of the good life saturate all areas of school life (2010: 289–90). However, such literature tends to focus on areas of the curriculum and more explicit forms of school life (e.g. sex education) rather than children's everyday lived experience.

Fader, in her work on the moral lives of Hasidic girls in Brooklyn, also calls for more attention to be paid to the 'intimate spaces' of children's lives, including the school, arguing that adults' perceptions about children's moral formation 'may be very different from what adults intend' (2009: 3). Within education studies, there is a significant amount of literature on moral values (e.g. Hemming 2015; McLaughlin and Halstead 2000; Osler and Starkey 2006; Smith and Smith 2013; Wringe 1998, 2006), with schools being a key site of socialization and the inculcation of such values. Schools, as Halstead argues, 'reflect and embody the values of society' (1996: 3). Values are seen in both children and teachers' everyday behaviours and actions, in the aims and ethos of the school, the spatial arrangements of the classrooms, the materials and objects found in the school, the curriculum and the various school-led community projects (Gallagher 2005). However, as I argue in this chapter, my fieldwork demonstrates the significant place assemblies have in the formation of children's ethical subjectivities.

Exploring the Good and the Everyday

Taking Robbins' (2013) work on the good and Lambek's (2010) contribution to ordinary ethics together we can enhance our understanding of the values schools seek to reproduce in assemblies and explore how children enact particular forms of ethics through their everyday actions. Focusing on these micro-practices invites us to observe the often taken for granted aspects of everyday life and reflect on what my participants see as the good in life. At St Peter's, the school had a clear and established 'values framework', which was made up of six core values, with a different value assigned to each term of the school year.[8] These core values permeated throughout all school life, with assemblies focusing on that term's value. During assemblies, the children were encouraged to think about this particular value and were often presented with hypothetical situations, being asked to reflect on how they would act or behave in a given context. Friday assemblies were known as 'celebration assemblies', and a child from each class was awarded a 'super learner' certificate and a 'values champion' certificate. The values champion certificates always referred to the core value of the term, while on occasion touching on others too These certificates were handed out for a variety of reasons, such as the thankful attitude a child had demonstrated during the school week. The values were clearly linked to character and celebrated children who had demonstrated the specific desirable behaviour. The school's values could be seen throughout the school. For example, each classroom had a wall display for the term's value, and there were occasional activities during lesson time that explored the term's value in more depth. Some teachers also integrated this official values discourse into everyday conversations with children, and it was also a footer on every document or letter produced by the school. However, it was only during assemblies where the values were explicitly performed[9] and explored. Each assembly had some sort of teaching that reflected on the value of the term. In addition to this, prayers, greetings, mottos and songs were used, which also helped bolster such values. The school hall, where assemblies took place, also had each value painted in bright colours on every wall.

On the first day of term, Mrs Larson, the headteacher, began the assembly by introducing all the new staff and pupils who had joined that year. After this introduction, Mrs Larson asked the children what they could do to help the new people and make them feel welcome. After a minute or two of thinking time and conferring with their partners, children provided various suggestions, such as helping the new people to find their way around the school, being kind and talking and playing with them at playtime. Mrs Larson thanked the children for their answers and agreed that these were good examples of how they could help. Pointing to the values painted on the walls of the school hall, she said that such actions demonstrate 'our core values such as compassion and how it is important to show compassion and love towards others'. Mrs Larson concluded that 'we need to show respect and compassion to others as these are our school values and we should behave like this in school'.[10] Assemblies at St Peter's Primary were designed to attend to both the virtuous behaviour teachers desired of the children while promoting a wider framework of values under which such virtues could be situated. The framework of values developed by St Peter's and the ethical sensibilities that they attempted to cultivate amongst the children were developed and used to instil their vision of the good within the children and ultimately to create good citizens for the world. However, this may also be interpreted in terms of performing the school's inclusive ethos for particular imagined audiences, such as Ofsted inspectors.

When discussing with me what they thought the aims and purpose of assemblies were, two children, Oliver and Luke, argued that assembly was aimed at making children 'good people' and helping them to think about ways to do good in the world:

> Oliver: They're trying to make us more thankful for the world around us and help other people that are in need.
> Luke: Making us a good person.
> Me: So, they're trying to make you a good person. So, go on, tell me a bit more about this.
> Oliver: Erm, well, they're trying to help us in life to be a good person, be nice to other people and to help and to, I don't know, donate money to charities, help children in need, sponsor ...

Luke and Oliver describe being a good person in terms of being kind to others and showing care and compassion. This idea of 'the good' was intrinsically linked to the school's vision of the good and the types of children it seeks to produce. Lynch (2014), writing on child migration, also observes this process of socialization in terms of children's moral development and how children became symbolic of society in itself. Lynch argues that in modern times the cultural imaginaries of nations play a significant role in the 'public socialization' of children and that such imaginaries consequently inform:

> public understandings of childhood as a period of preparation for citizenship in the nation or empire in which concern for the moral development of the child is seen as a public good and the figure of the child has become a symbol of the 'citizen in embryo'. (2014: 166)

We can observe the practices within assemblies as a particular site of children's moral development where particular visions of the child as a public good are imagined and performed. During assembly, children are encouraged to reflect on hypothetical situations and more often than not are invited to consider how they would feel or react in such circumstances. The school's values and vision of the good were often discussed in relation to non-religious situations or contexts. For example, 'thankfulness' was discussed in relation to Black History Month and being thankful for various individuals and their contributions to arts, science and music. The only explicit references to religion were during songs referencing God or prayer directed to God. The school values were an important feature of everyday life at St Peter's. However, while discussing the school's values, Mrs Larson explained that the values did link in with the school's religious character while still being inclusive and universal.

> Underpinning that [school vision] is our core values. Now, these come out of the Christian faith, but we chose those so that they might be universally accepted, and we focus on one of those every term with other values built on top of that .. we did an Inset day[11] and loads of work on it, and it was quite a democratic process really, and we talked about what the values meant and where they came from out of theology, and we had a lot of talk about what we want for our children at our school and what values underpin our work ... I think we got to about ten, and we all sat down and fought for our values corner, and it was a whole staff agreement ... [the values] are the foundation of everything we do ... what I think is really special about our school is that no one leaves collective worship, it is really inclusive ... and well crikey, if our Muslim families opted out of collective worship, what would I do with ninety kids?

Although Mrs Larson said the values were selected as they were primarily seen as Christian values, she also saw them as universal and therefore appropriate and accessible for the diverse range of pupils at St Peter's. For Mrs Larson, it was simply not feasible to create assemblies that emphasized values as specifically Christian, and doing so would not be inclusive for the diverse range of children that attended the school.[12] As Mattingly observes, it is this 'moral pluralism [that] characterizes ordinary life' (2014: 8), and 'social communities are unlikely to be morally homogenous; there will be multiple and even rival moral schemes and traditions in circulation' (2014: 154–55). It is this morally heterogeneous terrain that schools and teachers have to navigate in daily school life and that is further intensified by a legal requirement for daily worship in all schools, for all pupils, which is to be of a Christian character.

Assemblies at all schools became a type of moral project where the good could not only be performed but also where everyday ethics could be celebrated. At Holly Oak, Joe and Zara described what they did during assemblies and, in particular, in moments of celebration and achievement.

> Me: Can you tell me about assemblies here?
> Zara: They're fun.
> Joe: They're fun, and they're awesome and funny and awesome.
> Me: What do you do in assemblies?
> Joe: You give out certificates.
> Zara: We clap.
> Joe: And we listen to music.
> Me: You listen to music, and you get certificates?
> Zara: We clap for our friends.
> Joe: And we get certificates and then we listen to music.
> Zara: Because people done something really good.
> Me: Really good?
> Zara: Yeah.
> Me: And what sort of good things would someone have done?
> Zara: doing good working ... they can do good thinking.

Zara said that she would 'feel really proud' of her friends who were awarded a certificate. Assemblies at Holly Oak rarely made any reference to any particular religious tradition; however, as with St Peter's and Sacred Heart, the cultivation of children's ethical subjectivities and the celebration of the 'good' was a particularly important part of the act. There were typically reflective and contemplative practices each day, but the time of day for these varied along with the format. However, every week there were both class assemblies and whole school assemblies where good behaviour was celebrated. These were called the 'Star Awards', and every Friday one child from each class was chosen as the 'star' for that week. Before the teacher leading the assembly announced a particular week's stars, children sang and danced to either Heather Small's *Proud* or S Club 7's *Reach for the Stars*. After a few moments, the music was turned down, and the teacher introduced the star awards. One assembly was led by Lisa, who had taught at Holly Oak for several years. 'Right then everyone, now it's time for our special celebration where we get to hear about all the wonderful things some of you have been doing.' Lisa then invited each class teacher to speak for a few moments about which pupil had been chosen as that week's star and why. The child was then invited to the front, and everyone clapped.

In contrast to Holly Oak and St Peter's, at Sacred Heart (a Roman Catholic Academy), the idea of the good was always explicitly referred to in terms of

Christianity and linked to a gospel reading. Assemblies at Sacred Heart were firmly rooted in Catholic teaching, with assemblies designed to resemble Mass in a number of ways. Prayer was a significant feature of assemblies and wider school life, with prayers often selected to reflect both the time of year nationally and in terms of the Roman Catholic tradition. One prayer that regularly featured in assemblies was 'My Friend Jesus'. During one Friday afternoon in late November, children at Sacred Heart made their way from the classrooms towards the hall for their final assembly of the week. Entering to Pharrell's *Happy*, some children sang along or swayed to the music after taking their seats in the hall. While waiting for all the classes to arrive, there was a PowerPoint presentation featuring a slide with the question 'What has made you happy this week?' After welcoming the children, Mrs Allen began by asking the children what they thought had made them particularly happy that week. After hearing from some children, Mrs Allen went on to tell everyone what had made her happy and then began the celebration segment of the assembly. The children's various achievements ranged from showing kindness during lesson time to helping teachers clean up the classroom at the end of art-based activities. At the end of celebrating the various accomplishments in each class, Mrs Allen told the children,

> Well what a wonderful set of achievements everyone. You have all done some really lovely things this week, and you should feel very pleased with yourself. But sometimes we don't always do that, do we, and sometimes we slip up, as we are human. So, let's say a prayer that makes us remember that God will forgive us.

Following this, the prayer 'My Friend Jesus' appeared on the PowerPoint, and all the school began to recite the prayer in unison:

> My friend Jesus, help me to be good,
> To do the things and say the things that all good children should
> And if I sometimes slip a bit and do get out of hand
> Then please my friend Jesus, make the grown-ups understand
> That it isn't always easy to be as good as good can be,
> But I am getting better Lord because you are helping me
> Amen

At Sacred Heart, this idea of children's goodness was celebrated once a week during assembly time. The concept of the good and doing good was framed in terms of forgiveness and specifically God's forgiveness and love, where children are 'always able to be as good as good can be'. The idea of the good at Sacred Heart was also very much linked to the ordinary and the everyday. The achievements by the children were actions they undertook during their normal school day. It was the children's everyday moral actions that were celebrated here. 'My Friend Jesus' was then used to locate this idea of the 'good' in terms of Christian teaching, demonstrating how a relationship with

Jesus can help children to 'be as good as good can be' while also acknowledging the potential for children to 'slip a bit'. Rather than pursuing this idea in terms of sin and Jesus as a heavenly judge, children were encouraged to see Jesus as a friend who will understand and help them when they are not 'being as good as good can be'. Rebecca, a girl from Year Four, told me that:

> We say my friend Jesus prayer to ask for help when we are not in the best of times. When we've been mean to someone and we need to ask for forgiveness. And so, he can guide us through the week. So that we have as good of a week as we can.

Ridgely (2005) also found that religious educators at her Catholic field sites would encourage children to form a friendship with Jesus. By focusing on Jesus as a 'friend or mentor, the catechists moved away from older understandings of Jesus as a judge to whom children must submit without question' (Ridgley 2005: 227). The adults in Ridgely's (2005) research wanted to encourage this image of Jesus to make the children feel comfortable – and experience the church as a safe and judgement-free space. Outside the school hall at Sacred Heart was a reflection area where children could write down suggestions as to how they could 'make Jesus welcome in their everyday lives'. In a basket below was a range of suggestions from children, including the following: 'I could care for my friends and family helping them by doing my best. Also, I could work hard for my parents and do what I was told to do. That is how I will welcome Jesus in Advent'.[13]

As Hemming (2015) also found at the Catholic field site for his research, an ethic of love for God strongly underpinned the school's ethos and values. This focus on Catholic values at Hemming's (2015) school was seen in relation to a strong collective identity rather than in terms of diversity or individual rights. Ideas of love for God and seeing Jesus as a friend were also clearly expressed throughout life at Sacred Heart. Building on Hemming (2015), I observed how this love for God and Jesus and children's moral formation were expressed and enacted in everyday interactions at home and at school. In this way, we can draw some similarities between all three field sites, as although Sacred Heart has an explicit Christian ethic, St Peter's an implicit Christian ethic and Holly Oak was not linked to any religious tradition, all three field sites privileged and celebrated the everyday as a site of children's ethical formation.

Ordinary Ethics

Although children's good behaviours were acknowledged at other moments in everyday school life at all three schools, it was assembly time that formally reflected on how children can be good at school and at home. Das (2010) attends to the intricacies of these kinds of interlinked social contracts in her work on ordinary ethics. Das (2010) discusses the nature and limits of ordinary ethics, how we are to understand quotidian ethical acts and how we are to distinguish between that which is ordinary and that which is ethical. Veena Das's (2010) argument is that we can recast many of our ordinary habits as forms of moral action and that our public rituals, and the rules that surround them, are grounded in everyday life. In her work on life after experiencing trauma and violence, Das (2007) argues that it is through descending into the everyday rather than ascending into the transcendent that individuals can recover, and that as a result we can observe that the everyday in itself is an achievement. Drawing on the work of Das (2007, 2010, 2012) helps us to situate the assembly as a site of moral action and a daily ritual that seeks to ground, legitimize and reproduce particular framings of what it means to be good and do good. Children at all three schools articulated an understanding of being good in relation to demonstrating the school's values through their everyday activities. Showing kindness, respect and care for the other was especially important. Within this was a particular framework of morality that focused on individual responsibility.[14] Amy, a Year Four pupil from Sacred Heart, commented on this during an interview when she reflected on the purpose of assemblies:

> Me: What do you think the point of assembly is?
> Amy: I think it's to like improve yourself and be like and it's also mostly about behaviour and being good.

The point of assembly, as Amy observes, is about 'improving yourself', both in terms of behaviour and being good. Children's ethical self-formation here can also be thought of in light of Foucault's (1988) work. Foucault observed the relations between things, the other and oneself, while questioning 'how we are constituted as moral subjects of our own actions?' (1984: 49). Foucault (1988) defines technologies of the self as follows:

> [Technologies of the self] permit individuals to effect by their own means or *with the help of others* a certain number of operations on their own bodies and souls, thoughts, conduct, and way of being, so as to *transform themselves* in order to attain a certain state of happiness, purity, wisdom, perfection, or immortality. (1988: 18 italics my emphasis)

Both Amy and Callum (at the beginning of the chapter) reflect on assembly as being a transformative opportunity, a time to think about how to be a better friend, sister, brother, student and pupil. During one assembly at St Peter's, Mrs Larson announced that the school's Parent Teacher Association had purchased three new benches for the school playground. The pupils were told that they would arrive the following week, and pictures of the benches were then displayed on the overhead projector for the children to see. They were painted in bright colours, and carved into the centre of the bench were the words 'Buddy Bench'. The 'Buddy Benches', as Mrs Larson explained, were not only to be used as benches but also as way to know if someone felt lonely and needed a friend. She told the children that, during playtime, if 'you're feeling lonely or sad, or maybe you have no one to play with or you just need someone to talk to, go and sit on this bench. Now everyone sitting here knows this and so if you see someone alone, sitting on this bench, what do you think you should do?' Hands shot up around the room. A child from Year Four said, 'go and be their friend. Ask them if they're ok and if they want to play with you'. Mrs Larson agreed and said these benches were an opportunity for everyone at St Peter's to be a better friend and to show kindness to everyone. In this way, we can think of assemblies as supporting the development of the children's 'technologies of the self' as they encourage children to take individual responsibility for their own actions in order to effect change and improve their own capacity for moral perfectionism. However, Foucault (1988) acknowledges that an individual's practices are not created by the individual themselves. They are achieved in relation to others and through 'patterns that the individual finds in his culture and which are proposed, suggested and imposed on him by his culture, his society and his social group' (Foucault 1997: 122).[15]

We can see this awareness of how self-fashioning practices and care for the self are supported or imposed by others in Luke and Oliver's reflections earlier, when they observed that the school was 'trying to make us a good person'. Mattingly's (2014) elaboration of Cavell's (2004) work on moral perfectionism also provides a lens through which to understand these practices. Mattingly (2014) discusses how Cavell's ethics has an explicitly social dimension whereby your ethical actions are not judged by some impartial transcendent judge; rather, they are questioned and examined by those around us in our daily acts and everyday conversations. Mattingly's (2014) account of Cavell goes on to explain that in such conversations we are in dialogue with someone personally significant and that this is 'essential for reflective self-consideration' (2014: 90) as we are asked to reveal ourselves and, in the words of Cavell, this becomes 'one soul's examination of another' (Cavell 2004: 49 as cited in Mattingly 2014: 90). It is this collective self-examination of each other's moral capacity and actions that is discussed and reflected on during assemblies in schools. Children are not only told how and why to become a better person but that we all can help each other to do good. In slight contrast, at Sacred Heart, through the prayer 'My Friend Jesus', children are encouraged to also think about this moral questioning in relation to a friendship with Jesus. Although a transcendent other, the prayer encourages children to focus on Jesus as being a friend and as someone children can turn to and rely on for moral guidance and as a being that can help children to reflect on their own moral standing. The school community, in this way, encapsulates the Cavellian friend through which children are encouraged on a daily basis to reflect on the moral standing of themselves and others with the aim of becoming better people and having a better school community.

Valuing Authenticity

However, some children did comment on the repetitive nature of values in school and, at times, how this led to a certain scepticism regarding their meaningfulness.

> Toby: But the thing is ... the values, the values, they're so ... like I've gone for every year I've had to go through all the values, can we just stop already man! ... I was in nursery ok. I came in on the first day of nursery ... and basically every year, we have the same values just so –
> Doug: And again, and again and again and again! ... It's kind of like they're forcing it into our brain because they do it over and over again
> Toby: It's mushing our brain ... I don't want to become an adult!

Although children at St Peter's commented on the importance of the school values, many spoke of the repetitiveness in the way the values were sometimes applied to or featured in everyday school life. Lambek (2015) argues that it is ritual and the performance of ritual that helps to produce the criteria by which we make ethical judgements. Drawing on Rappaport (1999), Lambek suggests that ritual acts are 'embodied, highly formalized, and embedded within what [Rappaport] called liturgical orders' (2015: 22). However, one weakness of ritual is that if it becomes static and fixed it may lead to the over-sanctification of the liturgical order (Lambek 2015). Values are grounded in sanctification and ritual order, but if such performances are unable to adapt to the changing needs of the community, they can lose their significance and meaning. Observing such assemblies over the course of a term, I noticed how, if time was lacking, the process of awarding certificates to the values champion was rushed. The children also reflected on this, describing assemblies as sometimes boring. Abi from Year Five in St Peter's talked about how values could sometimes be indiscriminately applied and that anyone could get a values champion certificate.

> Sometimes it's all really boring because sometimes it's the same old, same old. It's just like um ... [puts on a different voice, with an element of sarcasm] 'because he was very thankful to his friends this week' [pulls face].
> Two other children at St Peter's spoke of how children would make jokes about the school's values and mock them in given situations.
> Bella: It's just like, sometimes, not needed.
> Me: What do you mean?
> Bella: Like, I know being thankful is important, but sometimes, it just sounds silly.
> Sandy: Yeah! Like when we're in the dinner queue and like, you know when someone passes you a spoon and you're like [Sandy changes her voice and adds sarcasm] 'oh thank-you!'
> Bella and Sandy both laugh.
> Bella: It's just not needed sometimes.

In this sense, assemblies and the celebration of the school's values were a way to reaffirm the 'moral parameters' of the children's social worlds (Abbott 2019: 68). However, due to the focus and attention the school gave to continually performing and displaying their core values, children felt they were exaggerated and, at times, inappropriate. Researchers within the Jubilee Centre warn 'that such interventions may fail to give young people the opportunity to reflect on when and where gratitude is appropriate, thus promoting an indiscriminate and uncritical "attitude for gratitude"' (Arthur et al. 2015: 8). The children's reflections show their desire for authenticity (Taylor 1992, 2007) and valuing this in relation to values, commenting on how a lack of authenticity can question the credibility and legitimacy of the school's established set of values.

Conclusion

The good and the cultivation of the ethical subject was at the heart of assemblies at all three schools. The assembly is used by the schools as a 'part of ethical self-improvement' to create and shape 'good' citizens for the world (Hirschkind 2006). Although the schools differed in how this was imagined and the ways in which both religion and non-religion were mediated during these occasions, there were similarities throughout the field sites. The prominence afforded to celebrating children's ordinary achievements, viewing the everyday as a site of children's ethical formation and a means to achieve a particular form of moral perfectionism, was found at all schools. With all this said, there are challenges when investigating the good ethnographically. There are both theoretical and methodological difficulties and perhaps tensions when exploring the good, especially in childhood. On the one hand, we need to attend to the individual experience and the agency[16] of those we are studying. On the other, we also need to balance this with an examination of those structures, institutions and more formalized instances of the good that permeate and shape our social lives. Children's agency and meaning-making could be observed at all schools, with self-care, self-reliance and individual reflection seen as means for children to cultivate their own ethical subjectivities. However, as the good in children's lives is so obviously and explicitly guided by the structures, institutions and adults around, it is imperative to focus on this too. Assemblies and the emphasis on self-care contained within them became a central part of the schools' moral project. Foucault's earlier work on disciplinary regimes and institutions offers us a way to consider the formation of children's moral selves and the power and roles of the broader social structures under which they are placed.

Ultimately, the value of these empirical examples of the good at play in our social worlds illustrates the messy, imbalanced and heterogeneous ways in which individuals live, perform and struggle with the good. Using childhood as a frame through which we can observe how moral thriving and ethical discernment are socialized and how schools deal with the multiplicities of social norms and moral repertoires provides for a unique and critical way to understand both the transmission of the good but also the negotiation of the good in everyday life.

Rachael Shillitoe is a Research Fellow at the University of Birmingham, working on a project exploring public perceptions of the relationship between science and religion. Her research is primarily in the sociologies of religion and childhood and education studies. She is currently completing a monograph examining children's experiences of collective worship in schools, *Negotiating Religion and Non-religion in Childhood: Experiences of Worship in Schools* (under contract with Palgrave Macmillan, in their Childhood and Youth Series).

Notes

1. St Peter's primary school is located in an urban area of the South West of England with children aged between 4–11 years old in attendance.
2. Children aged 9–10 years old.
3. The most recent public contestation involved two parents who challenged the legal requirement of collective worship by launching a high court case against their child's school (McDonald 2019). The National Governance Association has called to abolish collective worship in schools without a religious character. See https://www.nga.org.uk/News/NGA-News/Pre-2016/May-Sept-14/NGA-responds-to-Telegraph-article-on-Collective-Wo.aspx (accessed 14 September 2016). The National Secular Society calls for the complete abolishment of worship in schools, and this is one of their campaigns. See http://www.secularism.org.uk/end-compulsory-worship/ (accessed 8 August 2016). Humanists UK also seek for the abolishment of collective worship and provide advice for parents. See https://humanism.org.uk/campaigns/schools-and-education/collective-worship/ (accessed 11 October 2016).
4. Space does not permit here a full examination of collective worship/assemblies in schools. For further literature and discussion, please see: Hull (1975); Cheetham (2000, 2001 and 2004); Gill (2000, 2004); Smith and Smith (2013); Clarke and Woodhead (2015, 2018); Crumper and Mawhinney (2018); Shillitoe (forthcoming).
5. For the purposes of consistency, assemblies will be the term used in this chapter; however, informants often used both.
6. All schools' and participants' names have been replaced with pseudonyms. Ethical approval was granted by the University of Worcester's ethical review board, and voluntary informed signed consent was provided by all participants.
7. For a useful summary of the cross-disciplinary 'ethical turn', see Boothroyd (2013: 1–27) and Sheldon (2013: 15–19).
8. The school's full list of values was as follows:
Thankfulness
Compassion
Unity
Respect
Hope
Trust

9. Although values were lived and seen throughout wider school life, I use the word performed here to denote the performance of values in line with Goffman's (1959) work.
10. Although on this occasion Mrs Larson referred to behaving well in school, there were many times during my fieldwork that good behaviour was spoken of in relation to outside of school (e.g. playing nicely in the park) and embodying the school values at home and in the wider community.
11. Inset days are in-service training days for teachers, whereby teachers attend school without pupils present in order to undertake specific training to develop their teaching practices.
12. See Shillitoe and Strhan (2020) for non-religious children's experiences of prayer in assemblies
13. This resonates with Orsi's (2005) work on material childhood in relation to advent. Orsi (2005) notes how the perception of children's 'cognitive limitation' presents particular issues when it comes to Advent. As such, Orsi's participant, Sister Mary, has to materialize time in the form of a calendar and in doing so 'invisible minutes and hours acquire a solidity borrowed from the corporeal experience of children' (Orsi 2005: 76).
14. See Laidlaw (2010) and (2014) for a discussion on agency in relation to responsibility and how ethical judgements often involve the 'attribution of responsibility' (2014: 185).
15. This approach also speaks to Carrither's (1990) use of pedagogy and how human beings hold each other to particular standards. Carrither reflects on the relational process this can take, observing how teachers 'must frame the moral rules imaginatively to conform with fluid, changing circumstances; and in so framing the rules, teachers change them' (1990: 200).
16. Laidlaw (2010: 152) critiques agency as used in practice theory and actor network theory due to the way agency often misses the 'intermediating agencies'– those agencies outside the individual. Laidlaw (2014) also critiques how agency can be reduced to 'actions only conducive to certain outcomes, those that are structurally significant' and as a result how agency 'becomes identified with the efficacious pursuit of one's own power and position' (2014: 5–6). However, in this work, I am using agency in the way Mahmood (2005) and Strhan (2019) do, and I speak to the various modalities agency can take, acknowledging that it does not always have to speak to resistance but also compliance and docility. See Shillitoe and Strhan (2020) for further discussion.

References

Abbott, O. 2019. *The Self, Relational Sociology, and Morality in Practice*. London: Palgrave Macmillan.

Arthurs, J., et al. 2015. *An Attitude for Gratitude: How Gratitude is Understood, Experienced and Valued by the British Public. Research Report*. The Jubilee Centre for Character and Values: University of Birmingham.

Beck, C. 1990. *Better Schools: A Values Perspective*. London: Falmer.

Boothroyd, D. 2013. *Ethical Subjects in Contemporary Culture*. Edinburgh: Edinburgh University Press.

Carrithers, M. 1990. 'Why Humans Have Cultures', *Royal Anthropological Institute of Great Britain and Ireland* 25(2): 189–206.

Cavell, S. 2004. *Cities of Words: Pedagogical Letters on a Register of the Moral Life*. Cambridge, MA: Harvard University Press.

Cheetham, R. 2000. 'Collective Worship: A Window into Contemporary Understandings of the Nature of Religious Belief?', *British Journal of Religious Education* 22(2): 71–81.

———. 2001. 'How on Earth Do We Find Out What Is Going On in Collective Worship? An Account of a Grounded Theory Approach', *British Journal of Religious Education* 23(3): 165–76.

———. 2004. *Collective Worship: Issues and Opportunities*. London: SPCK.

Clarke, C., and L. Woodhead. 2015. A New Settlement: Religion and Belief in Schools, The Westminster Faith Debates.

———. 2018. A New Settlement Revised: Religion and Belief in Schools, The Westminster Faith Debates.

Crumper, P., and A. Mawhinney. 2018. *Collective Worship and Religious Observance in Schools*. Oxford: Peter Lang.

Curtis, P. 2004. 'End Daily Worship in Schools, Says Ofsted Head', *The Guardian*, 11 June 2004. Retrieved 23 January 2020 from https://www.theguardian.com/education/2004/jun/11/schools.uk.

Das, V. 2007. *Life and Words: Violence and the Descent into the Ordinary*. Berkeley: University of California Press.

———. 2010. 'Engaging the Life of the Other: Love and Everyday Life', in M. Lambek (ed.), *Ordinary Ethics: Anthropology, Language, and Action*. New York: Fordham University Press, pp. 376–99.

———. 2012. 'Ordinary Ethics', in D. Fassin (ed.), *A Companion to Moral Anthropology*. Malden, MA: Wiley-Blackwell, pp. 133–49.

Dill, J., and J. Davison Hunter. 2010. 'Education and the Culture Wars: Morality and Conflict in American Schools', in S. Hitlin and S. Vaisey (eds), *Handbook of the Sociology of Morality*. Switzerland: Springer, pp. 275–92.

Durkheim, E. 1978. *On Institutional Analysis*. London: University of Chicago Press.

Elias, N. 2000. *The Civilizing Process: Sociogenetic and Psychogenetic Investigations*, trans. E. Jephcott. Oxford: Blackwell.

Fader, A. 2009. *Mitzvah Girls: Bringing up the Next Generation of Hasidic Jews in Brooklyn*. Princeton, NJ: Princeton University Press.

Foucault, M. 1977. *Discipline and Punish: The Birth of the Prison*. London: Penguin.

———. 1984. *The Care of The Self: The History of Sexuality Volume*, trans R. Hurley. London: Penguin.

———. 1988. 'Technologies of the Self', in L. Martin, H. Gutman and P. Hutton (eds), *Technologies of the Self: A Seminar with Michel Foucault*. Amherst: University of Massachusetts Press, pp. 16–49.

———. 1997. *Ethics: Essential Works of Foucault 1954–1984*, Vol.1, in P. Rabinow. London: Penguin.

Frankel, S. 2012. *Children, Morality and Society. Studies in Childhood and Youth*. London: Palgrave Macmillan.

———. 2017. *Negotiating Childhoods: Applying a Moral Filter to Children's Everyday Lives*. London: Palgrave Macmillan.

Gallagher, M. 2005. 'Producing the Schooled Subject: Techniques of Power in a Primary School'. Unpublished PhD Thesis: University of Edinburgh.

Gill, J. 2000. 'The Nature and Justifiability of the Act of Collective Worship in Schools'. Unpublished PhD Thesis: University of Plymouth.

———. 2004. 'The Act of Collective Worship: Pupils' Perspectives', *British Journal of Religious Education* 26(2): 185–96.

Goffman, E. 1959. *The Presentation of the Self in Everyday Life*. London: Penguin.

Halstead, J.M. 1996. 'Values and Values Education in Schools', in J.M. Halstead and M. Taylor (eds), *Values in Education and Education in Values*. Abingdon: Routledge, pp. 3–14.
Hemming, P.J. 2015. *Religion in the Primary School: Ethos, Diversity, Citizenship*. Abingdon: Routledge.
Hirschkind, C. 2006. *The Ethical Soundscape: Cassette Sermons and Islamic Counterpublics*. New York: Columbia University Press.
Hitlin, S., and S. Vaisey. 2013. 'The New Sociology of Morality', *Annual Review of Sociology* 39: 51–68.
Hull, J. 1975. *School Worship: An Obituary*. London: SMC Press.
James, A., and A. Prout. 1997. *Constructing and Reconstructing Childhood*, 2nd edn. London: Falmer.
Jenks, C. 1996. *Childhood*. London: Routledge.
Kulz, C. 2017. *Factories for Learning: Making Race, Class and Inequality in the Neoliberal Academy*. Manchester: Manchester University Press.
Laidlaw, J. 2010. 'Agency and Responsibility: Perhaps You Can Have Too Much of a Good Thing', in M. Lambek (ed.), *Ordinary Ethics: Anthropology, Language, and Action*. New York: Fordham University Press, pp. 143–64.
_____. 2014. *The Subject of Virtue: An Anthropology of Ethics and Freedom*. Cambridge: Cambridge University Press.
Lambek, M. 2010. *Ordinary Ethics: Anthropology, Language, and Action*. New York: Fordham Press.
_____. 2015. *The Ethical Condition: Essays on Action, Person and Value*. London: The University of Chicago Press.
Long, R., and S. Danechi. 2019. 'Faith Schools in England: FAQs'. Retrieved 9 January 2019 from https://researchbriefings.parliament.uk/ResearchBriefing/Summary/SN06972.
Lynch, G. 2014. 'Saving the Child for the Sake of the Nation: Moral Framing and the Civic, Moral and Religious Redemption of Children', *American Journal of Cultural Sociology* 2: 165–96.
Mahmood, S. 2005. *Politics of Piety: The Islamic Revival and the Feminist Subject*. Princeton, NJ: Princeton University Press.
Mattingly, C. 2014. *Moral Laboratories: Family Peril and the Struggle for a Good Life*. Berkeley: University of California Press.
Mayall, B. 2002. *Towards a Sociology for Childhood: Thinking from Children's Lives*. Buckingham: Open University Press.
McDonald, H. 2019. 'Parents Win Right to Prayer-Free Alternative to Religious Assemblies', *The Guardian*, 20 November 2019. Retrieved 8 January 2020 from https://www.theguardian.com/education/2019/nov/20/oxfordshire-parents-win-right-to-prayer-free-school-assembly.
McLaughlin, T., and J.M. Halstead. 2000. 'John Wilson on Moral Education', *Journal of Moral Education* 29(3): 248–68.
Orsi, R. 2005. *Between Heaven and Earth: The Religious Worlds People Make and the Scholars Who Study Them*. Princeton, NJ: Princeton University Press.
Osler, A., and H. Starkey. 2006. 'Education for Democratic Citizenship: A Review of Research, Policy and Practice 1995–2005', *Research Papers in Education* 21(4): 433–66.
Parsons, T. 1951. *The Social System*. London: Routledge and Kegan Paul.
Rappaport, R. 1999. *Ritual and Religion in the Making of Humanity*. Cambridge: Cambridge University Press.

Reay, D. 2006. 'The Zombie Stalking English Schools: Social Class and Educational Inequality', *British Journal of Educational Studies* 54(3): 288–307.
Rich, J.M. 1993. 'Education and Family Values', *The Educational Forum* 57(2): 162–67.
Ridgely, S. 2005. *When I was a Child: Children's Interpretations of First Communion.* Chapel Hill: The University of North Carolina Press.
_____. 2011. 'Introduction', in S. Ridgely (ed.), *A Methods Handbook: The Study of Children in Religions.* London: New York University Press, pp. 1–18.
Robbins, J. 2013. 'Beyond the Suffering Subject: Toward an Anthropology of the Good', *Journal of the Royal Anthropological Institute* 19: 447–62.
Sheldon, R. 2013. 'Ordinary Ethics and Democratic Life: Palestine-Israel in British Universities'. Unpublished PhD Thesis: University of Kent.
Smith, G., and S. Smith. 2013. 'From Values to Virtues: An Investigation into the Ethical Content of English Primary School Assemblies', *British Journal of Religious Education* 35(1): 5–19.
Shillitoe, R. (Forthcoming). *Negotiating Religion and Non-religion in Childhood: Experiences of Worship in Schools.* Switzerland: Palgrave Macmillan.
Shillitoe, R., and A. Strhan. 2020. '"Just Leave It Blank" Non-religious Children and their Negotiation of Prayer in School', *Religion.* DOI: https://doi.org/10.1080/0048 721X.2020.1758230.
Strhan, A. 2017. 'I Want There to Be No Glass Ceiling: Evangelicals': Engagements with Class, Education, and Urban Childhoods', *Sociological Research Online* 22(1): 1–15. DOI: 10.5153/src.4259.
_____. 2019. *The Figure of the Child in Contemporary Evangelicalism.* Oxford: Oxford University Press.
Taylor, C. 1992. *The Ethics of Authenticity.* Cambridge, MA: Harvard University Press.
_____. 2007. *A Secular Age.* Cambridge MA: Harvard University Press.
Watson, B., and E. Ashton 1995. *Education, Assumptions and Values.* London: David Fulton.
Wringe, C. 1998. 'Reasons Rules and Virtues in Moral Education', *Journal of Philosophy of Education* 32(2): 225–37.
_____. 2006. *Moral Education: Beyond the Teaching of Right and Wrong.* Dordrecht: Springer.

10

Locating an Elusive Ethics
Surface and Depth in a Jewish Ethnography

Ruth Sheldon

Turn it over and over, for all is in it.
—Pirkei Avot (Ethics of the Fathers): 5:22

Searching for the Good: Dressing up Orthodox

On a cold January morning, wearing a borrowed long skirt, high-neck woollen jumper and dark grey hat, I walked from my home in a gentrified, multicultural area of Hackney, North London to a strictly orthodox Jewish (Haredi) children's centre in the nearby Jewish neighbourhood of Stamford Hill. I had been invited there by Gila,[1] an Israeli Haredi woman involved with an orthodox Jewish maternity network, in order to attend a mother and baby drop-in session with my son. Proud of her professional standing, Gila was surprisingly keen to act as my 'gatekeeper'. It was following her detailed instructions that I dressed in a long skirt and covered my frizzy hair, which contrasts so obviously with the sleek sheitels (wigs) worn by married Haredi women in accordance with the laws and customs of tzniuth.[2] In these early days of fieldwork, the seemingly mundane question of what to wear had been an intense source of anxiety for me. My reluctant participation in what I took to be a patriarchal dress code felt like a necessary though uncomfortable pretence, an instrumental means of gaining entry to insular orthodox settings. There, I hoped to access my 'real' object of study of the Jewish ethics of neighbouring, 'Jewish ethical teachings', which I took to be grounded in religious texts.[3] As I pushed my son in his buggy along the familiar streets, sensing my uncanny similarity to the, in my eyes, passive and oppressed Haredi mothers that I passed, I found myself strangely dissociated from my orthodox feminine body. This unease intensified when, upon meeting Gila at the reception, she looked me over and commented approvingly, 'oh I didn't recognize you; you did it [the Haredi look] so well.'

Whilst Gila had helped me to make inroads into Haredi settings, our encounters thus far had felt both uncomfortable and, somehow, superficial. At our first meeting, I had barely sat down at her dining room table when she asked 'Are you Jewish?' I nodded. 'Both your mother and your father?' I nodded again. 'You look Jewish.' I shifted uncomfortably, aware that some part of me was pleased to belong in her terms. It seemed my Jewish parentage was, for now, sufficient for Gila within what felt like her racialized conception of Jewish identity.[4] Settling back in her seat at the head of the table, she described her professional relations, as a Jewish-Israeli 'foreigner' in Stamford Hill, with the threatening non-Jewish others she encountered: 'coloured people', 'women who prefer women'. I flinched at her language, bringing to mind my friends from a nearby Liberal synagogue who continually experienced the violence of such racialized and homophobic terms. Then, after talking at length about 'our community's' need to police its social and psychic boundaries, she began to angrily recount the story of an ongoing war between herself and her Muslim next-door neighbours. For twenty-seven years they had maintained a tense relationship, which fluctuated with events in the Middle East. One year ago, Gila's family had decided to rebuild a garage in their garden; suddenly the neighbours had turned 'nasty', harassing Gila's family, sending the police to her house and making antisemitic comments to her children. She continued, 'so how do I know that the people I'm working with – you understand? [How can I trust that they won't also 'turn'?] This is about *the* Muslims – it's not about – as I say I'm not worried about the English neighbours or anybody. You understand I know that they are not going to do these type of things.'

I listened quietly as Gila wielded the trope of the psychologically volatile, vengeful Muslim, 'too close for comfort', alongside her totalizing rendering of Jewish community. Then, when with relief I finally turned the recorder off, I found myself once again subject to her categorical judgement as if my ambiguous position must be resolved before we parted. 'Is your husband Jewish?' she asked looking at me directly. I shook my head, avoiding eye contact, aware that, from her perspective, out-marriage transgressed Jewish law and also threatened Jewish continuity within an already hostile secular world. Without pausing, she countered, 'And what do your parents think of that?' Weakly, I answered 'They don't mind.' 'I see. Good for them.'

Writing my fieldnotes on the bus carrying me back from Stamford Hill to more comfortable terrain, I found myself strangely detached from the material that I had gathered, aware that such a 'relevant' story about feuding Jewish and Muslim neighbours met the remit of my project but putting off indefinitely the task of transcribing this interview. To what extent should I take Gila's enactment of particularist and patriarchal Jewish laws, and her hostile representations of her Muslim neighbours, as a case of (a culturally relative) 'Jewish ethics' in my study? What would be the consequences of treating this material at surface value?

The Violence of the Good: The Law of the Skirt

This question, arising in my early fieldwork encounters with Gila, of how to locate the ethical and moral as an empirical object, has in recent years become a topical issue in sociology as well as anthropology (Introduction, this volume; Alexander 2003; Lynch 2012). Within this burgeoning interdisciplinary field, debates have crystallized, broadly speaking, between scholars of 'the good', 'values' and 'the sacred', and proponents of 'ordinary ethics'. While these approaches encompass a range of philosophical influences, one significant theoretical move traversing the 'anthropology of the good' (Robbins 2013) and the cultural sociology of the sacred (Alexander 2003; Lynch 2012) has drawn on a Durkheimian framework in order to study what people think of, and symbolically represent as 'the good' in their social relations (Seidler, this volume). Such framings share a picture of moral life as ultimately shaped by a domain of coherent sacred values that are set apart from, and structure or regulate everyday life. They also converge in claiming to renew the critical and comparative leverage of social scientific accounts of morality, by offering a neutral account of how the good, and the bad, are culturally mediated (Alexander 2003; Robbins 2016). At the same time, ethnographers influenced by ordinary language philosophy have offered a different vision of what it means to study the ethical. Here, ethics has been located in the entailments of the relation to the other in everyday life, particularly under precarious conditions, and so as inherently connected to contingencies of desire, violence and vulnerability (Das 2007, 2010). While it has been noted that orientations to the Good and ordinary ethics are not mutually exclusive, it has become apparent that these debates do not only pivot around different conceptions of the ethical/moral but are implicated with questions around the Christian, colonial and masculine genealogies of related categories, including the sacred, religion, ritual and law.[5] Furthermore, while epistemological and methodological tensions have remained relatively implicit in these conversations, it is clear that these genealogical critiques cannot be divorced from contested visions of what it means to enquire into the ethical. Thus, for Veena Das, questioning the seemingly neutral framing of 'the Good' as a realm of 'higher ideals' is also bound up with her sense of ethnography as an ethical mode of enquiry that dwells with marginalized others and attends to their struggles to secure, maintain and endure a precarious everyday (Das 2015).[6] Contrary to claims that such approaches appeal to universalistic notions of humanistic empathy (Robbins 2013), Das suggests that ethnographers may enact a form of indifference, even violence, by claiming an abstracted view from a distance, and frames the act of empathizing with the other's experience as an achievement rather than a given.⁷ From this perspective, rather than operationalizing a given theoretical framework, the ethnographer should undertake the risky and demanding work of placing herself within an immanent, emerging story and descend into relationships with her fieldwork interlocutors. This requires that she, 'perform considerable work on herself to acknowledge both her separateness from her respondents and her sense of "being-with" or in the midst of a world, which, if not entirely new, has now been disclosed as having aspects that she did not anticipate' (2015: 373).⁸

In this chapter, I begin from the seemingly superficial act of putting on a skirt in order to contribute to this framing of ordinary ethics from the perspective of my Jewish ethnography. Specifically, I refigure Das' ethical gesture of descent and dwelling in the ordinary as a iterative movement between surface and depth, which I claim has 'indigenous' Jewish resonance. Learning from the Jewish women who guided my fieldwork, I will explore how this embodied method of enquiry can reveal unexpected meanings and transcendent relations to others within the everyday instantiation of Jewish laws governing feminine clothing. Drawing implicitly on psychoanalytic and Hasidic understandings, I will develop the claim that this oscillating movement can bring ethnographers into contact with enigmatic depths of ourselves and others that exceed symbolic representations (Frosh 2008; Zornberg 2016).⁹ This will ground my engagement with a key question underpinning the debate around *where* the good is in the world. *How* can I, as a Jewish ethnographer – myself shaped by dominant Christian, colonial and masculine grammars – risk thinking anew in developing knowledge of ethical life? (Puett 2014).

Now viewed from a Durkheimian perspective, Gila's emphasis on what Robbins terms 'corporate unity' (2016: 776), the symbolic value of the integrity and survival of Jewish community, would be a straightforward example of the ultimate good. Following this theoretical logic, Gila's Muslim neighbours clearly functioned as a profane or impure other, the object of feelings of hatred and disgust that are the necessary corollary of symbolic solidarity (Lynch 2012). In addition, Gila's demand for my conformity to laws around modest dress showed how 'the good', in this case a moral ideal of Jewish femininity, differentiated between 'authentic' and 'inauthentic' Jews and so defended the moral community against ambiguity. Talking, for example, with Rachel, a member of the observant Adeni (Yemeni) Jewish community in Stamford Hill, she had highlighted how clothing marked out ambiguous Jewish others, including non-European Mizrahi Jews such as herself, or assimilated Jews such as myself. Angrily she told me how her Haredi neighbours had stopped speaking to her after they had seen her wearing trousers, explaining, 'I'm not Jewish to them, they just look down on me.' Rachel's response reveals how, as Ayala Fader (2009) has argued, material signs of modesty constituted a semiotic language, marking difference and religious authenticity.¹⁰ For scholars of the good, such an approach has a powerful appeal, showing the higher values 'really' at stake in relation to a seemingly mundane action of wearing a skirt. In particular, it seems to address the charge of banality levelled against ordinary ethicists, who, it is claimed, merely reproduce the 'truism' that ethics is located in the everyday (Zigon 2014). Focusing on what Gila explicitly represented as the good, however troubling, would, in this framing, provide a tangible focus for my study of neighbourly ethics.

In the course of our initial exchanges, Gila certainly seemed to embody a familiar image of a law-bound, defended Jewish orthodoxy. Talking with Rachel, I had become intensely aware that Gila's exclusive claim for Jewish identity was an act of annihilation against those who resisted her gender norms and so were constituted as not really Jewish. These tensions were somehow at stake in my emerging relationship with Gila. They were carried in my conflicting desires to conform to and to resist her values as I dressed in the skirt that elicited her approval. I imagined somehow that in drawing closer to this other 'Haredi woman' I was at risk of being either incorporated into this totalizing community or expelled from it. This raised complex ethical questions about 'the good' that were somehow un-nameable within a neutral framework that treats violence as a culturally relative category. In other words, while within the terms of a neutral theory of sacred values I could reproduce what Gila represented as 'good', it was not possible to name or to understand the splitting of 'the good' and 'the bad', belonging and exclusion, as an ethically violent relation.

But there was also a second sense in which it seemed to me that limiting my focus to studying sacred values would be troublingly superficial. In recent years, the rapidly growing Haredi community in Stamford Hill have been the focus of both sociological and media attention. For example, in her widely cited study of attitudes towards 'the ethos of mixing' within the London borough of Hackney, Susanne Wessendorf (2014) portrayed the Haredi community in Stamford Hill as (alongside 'Hipsters') uniquely problematic, identifying their refusal to participate in exchanges beyond their own social milieu as evidence of their (pathological) insularity. Furthermore, the figure of the oppressed orthodox woman has been mobilized to support public denunciations of the Haredi community for contravening universal 'modern' British values of gender equality.[11] Within this political context, imposing a Durkheimian analysis of the Haredi community would therefore confirm everything that is already known about Jewish particularism. Here, it would be no surprise that orthodox Jews shape a moral community constituted around the friend-enemy matrix, prioritizing patriarchal law over ethics, in which love takes the form of loyalty to 'their (or our) own'. To put this in the vocabulary of political theology, this is the Judaism oriented by the symbolic law that keeps the ethical/monstrous Other at bay and denies the possibility of a human connection that is made possible by universal secular-Christian modernity (Frosh 2008).[12] Now, as Ayala Fader (2009) has explored, there is clearly some truth in the claim that Haredi Jews mobilize countercultural forms of religious femininity in order to 'hyperbolize' Jewish difference.[13] Nonetheless, wider public discourses of orthodox Jewish distinctiveness also function as powerful modes of othering, which keep 'the Haredim' at a comfortable distance. And so I felt that following the path laid out by scholars of the good would be superficial in ways that have ethical implications. For in a sense, Gila *had* allowed me to sustain an ambiguous position thus far in our encounters. It was I who was left somehow resistant to deepening our relationship, not seeking, for example, to learn more about the meaning of what I experienced as an oppressive patriarchal law of the skirt. And yet without allowing myself to move deeper into the community, surely I could only perpetuate the prejudice of what was already known?

Threats to the Ordinary: Ambiguous Others

A few weeks later, Gila and I were standing once again on the street outside her office. I was still searching for that elusive object named 'ethics', and so, with an air of desperation, I asked Gila directly: how would she advise me to learn about this? Gila smiled,

> Well that isn't something you can learn 'in one go'; we learn it all through our lives, from a very young age. A young child eating meals learns that these are the blessings [to say over particular foods], these are the things that you should and shouldn't do.

I replied, exposing my vulnerability, confessing my own deracinated relation to what Fader (2009) describes as the embodied language of orthodox Judaism. 'What about for people like me who did not grow up learning this?' As usual, Gila's answer was unequivocal,

> Well the Lubavitch will do something, or you can try the shul [synagogue] in Wenton Row. But you must be careful: don't go to any of this 'new' – what do they call themselves – 'reform' Judaism. You know a lot of them aren't really Jewish and it isn't really Judaism.

I kept quiet, struck again by the violence of Gila's distinctions and now holding a shameful secret: my weekly visits, in my jeans and trainers, to the study group of a local liberal synagogue. In that self-proclaimed feminist space, I had learnt that there was a tradition within Liberal Judaism – which emerged out of a historical engagement with Christianity and Enlightenment rationalism – of articulating an ethical 'core' of values that could be differentiated from law. This apparent disregard for law was one source of the orthodox perception that liberal and reform Judaism had somehow been Christianized and was as such a deep fault-line between these communities. Apparently oblivious to my shifty expression, Gila leaned in and began to probe my identity again: 'what is your maiden name – is it Sheldon?' I nodded silently, withholding the narrative that this family name Sheldon had been anglicized by my Czech and Austrian grandparents, part of a history of racialization, and assimilation, that contributed to my own rupture from Jewish tradition. Gila continued: 'And what was your mother's name?' I replied, 'Katz'. Gila's eyes lit up. 'Oh Katz! That's the name of the highest priests you know ...'.[14] Again I stayed quiet, concealing how this hidden name carried another aspect of my family's break with Judaism: my mother's visceral rejection of the culture of gender inequality that she had experienced in the orthodox synagogue that she attended as a girl.

It was in March, shortly before the festival Purim, when I took Gila's advice, put my borrowed skirt back on and paid my first visit to Wenton Row. A local independent modern orthodox synagogue, I had been told that it attracted European, Iranian and Indian Jews of widely varying levels of observance and that the rabbi held classes on Shabbos (Saturdays) that included studying a text known as 'Ethics of the Fathers'. And so it was that I found myself sitting quietly on a bench with a friendly member of the shul, Sonia, in the upstairs women's gallery of this atmospheric former chapel.[15] We had arrived early, and the chazzan (prayer leader) was leading the prayers while the few other men present joined in, in stops and starts. Listening to the quiet murmur as Sonia leaned over the balcony to check if there was a minyan (the ten men needed for the service to proceed), I was struck by the precarious situation of this small community and moved by the attempt to sustain practices that were unfamiliar to me, and yet somehow resonant. More people had arrived by the time the rabbi moved to the front of the shul and began to speak about the special meaning of this day, 'Shabbat Zachor', which is dedicated to remembering: 'at this time we remember the story of Amalek, the nation who attacked the Israelites for no reason'. Drawing an analogy with the Nazis and ISIS, he continued,

> And while our instinct might be to seek an explanation for *why* they are attacking us, we should not be tempted down this path. For if we try to find solutions, we might think that maybe, if we are less different, we won't be attacked. But the truth is that there is no explanation, and so our response should be to become more connected to our Judaism and to Hashem [our God].

Earlier, I described how, for Veena Das, ordinary ethics is framed around relations to the other under conditions shadowed by violence and is attentive to those for whom securing the everyday is an achievement. Participating in the precarious life of Wenton Row, a community for whom the survival of tradition is continually at stake, I began to sense how this notion of maintaining the everyday as an achievement has distinctive Jewish resonance. For the struggles of Wenton Road to achieve a minyan reflect a wider decline in modern orthodox Jewish observance in Britain (Staetsky 2015), and this sense of impending loss is shadowed by histories of the devastation of Jewish life, on a scale that is hard to articulate. This, I suggest, provides a frame for understanding the defensiveness of the rabbi's invocation of Amalek, the enemy, against the background of Jewish destruction, deracination and assimilation. At stake were ambiguous histories of Jewish patriarchy and racialization, carried communally and in my own family, shaping law-governed forms of life in the present. This meant that for orthodox Jews inhabiting the multicultural, secular landscape of contemporary Hackney, in addition to the named 'enemy', the non-Jewish other, there was a deeper threat that was not explicitly named. That was the ambiguous Jew: the one who had drawn dangerously close to the hegemonic Christian-secular society, a culture that demands assimilation under the sign of the universal.

Towards the end of the Shabbat Zachor service, the rabbi raised his eyes to the women's gallery, and Sonia muttered in my ear 'prayers for healing'. As the women around me fed him the Hebrew names of sick acquaintances, she leaned in to ask me 'what's your Hebrew name?'[16] Her question caught me off-guard; I hesitated for a moment and then confessed, 'I don't know. I don't think I have one.' She shrugged, and I looked back down at my prayer book, and the impenetrable Hebrew text swam before my eyes. As I sat, tracing the odd Hebrew letter in the prayer book, unable to contribute prayers for healing, I began to realize how I might be an ambiguous semi-assimilated figure for the women I was meeting, unable to contribute to healing even as I apparently yearned to do so. In this way, I was gradually appreciating the risk that *I* posed, for example, to Gila, even as she, perhaps, sought to 'redeem' me (Fader 2009): the trust required on her part in engaging an ambiguous, secularized and assimilated Jew, whose investments in this research were highly enigmatic. And this raised a question of my ethical responsibility, to resist the temptation to distance myself from her 'culturally relative' commitments to the 'good' in order to deepen my attentiveness to what was at stake in our tense relationship. To consider, in other words, how such violent assertions of exclusive moral community might be shaped by horizons of precarity and vulnerability, with which I was implicated.

The Transcendent in the Ordinary: Shira's Dress Sense

When the service had ended, Sonia led me downstairs, where the softly spoken matriarch of the synagogue had, as usual, prepared what was perhaps the major draw for many shul attendees: her renowned kiddush buffet meal of European and Indian Jewish dishes. There Sonia introduced me to Miriam, a local artist, who, I would learn, practised an esoteric form of orthodox Jewish observance. Miriam looked me in the eye and with disconcerting directness asked, 'What are you doing here?' I explained that I was working on a research project on the theme of Ethical Monotheism. 'Oh it's good to have a project', she asserted with more than a hint of sarcasm and then continued, 'well of course for us Jews, Christians aren't monotheists because they have the trinity – you know the idea that God can be split into the spiritual and material – it's ridiculous.' She began to talk about an art class she teaches with three strictly orthodox women in Stamford Hill who she said 'are really rather wonderful in the way they think and talk'. Then, as the beginning of the Rabbi's study session was announced, Miriam downed her whisky and made a dash for the exit, while I reluctantly turned away from this scene of 'ethical teaching' to politely assist the women washing up in the kitchen. Sometime later, I met up with Miriam again when she offered to show me around Stamford Hill and introduce me to some people. She looked down at my legs. It was a boiling hot day, and I had rushed to our meeting point, my bare ankles just visible beneath a long skirt. She stubbed out her roll-up cigarette and smiled: 'you might feel more comfortable if you put some tights on, eh?' I hesitated, ashamed of my 'mistake', which exposed my orthodox illiteracy, yet also recalling my mother's anger as I flinched at this repressive demand. Then, somehow trusting in Miriam's somehow – paradoxically – feminist ethos, I allowed her to guide me home to retrieve some tights, staying with the mundane tensions of this dress-code to see where this might lead.

In September, as Jewish New Year approached, I was still searching for that elusive ethical object. Encouraged by Miriam, I finally put my long skirt back on and followed up on a suggested fieldwork contact with a Satmar woman called Shira. The Satmar, I had been told, are amongst the strictest and most observant of Haredi Jewish groups, and so it was with a sense of trepidation that I made the initial phone call, introducing myself as a 'Jewish woman wanting to learn'. 'What do you mean you would like to learn about ethical teachings?' Shira asked, posing a question I had come to dread. But something in her tone made me drop my defences, 'to be honest, I'm not really sure', to which she replied that she would be happy to meet. And so a few days later I arrived on her doorstep. I was surprised to meet a woman just a few years older than me, wearing glasses, a shpitzel head covering[17] and an understated smile. Early in our conversation she told me that she was training as a therapeutic counsellor, and then towards the end of our conversation she said, 'I have the sense that you would like me to teach you?' I replied that I would like that. 'Let me think about it, I am not sure I would know how to do it.'

In the subsequent weeks, we began to meet regularly, and Shira encouraged me to take things slowly. Somehow in our emerging friendship it seemed possible to take risks. She had asked me directly if my husband was Jewish, and when I nervously told her 'no', she asked 'how does that work?' in a tone less of judgement than of curiosity. Now we were sitting together on the first day of Succos, a festival that evokes the precarious, exilic quality of Jewish existence. I asked Shira if she would mind my recording the conversation, given that it was a holiday when her own use of electrical equipment was prohibited. She left the decision up to me, and despite my desire to 'capture' this 'data', I intuitively chose to keep the recorder switched off. In the hours that followed, as a deeper intimacy developed between us, it somehow seemed to me that keeping this law had opened up an adjacent ethical possibility, a way of being together made possible through conforming to this apparent prohibition.

As we sat together, Shira talked of her family's experience of the violence of the Shoah and of her own ambiguous belonging to the Satmar community. She told me how her mother, a Hungarian Jew, had been very detached from her emotions, how her parents like many in Stamford Hill were traumatized and somehow fearful people. She had not, it turned out, always been Satmar, rather her parents had been drawn to the Satmar rebbe (leader) when she was young, so in a sense she was still an outsider. We talked about my family and of how Jewish traditions were not passed down, of assimilation, anger and shame. She asked me, 'how do you find it when you are learning?' and I told her that there were aspects that were somehow familiar to me. She smiled and said something that in one sense troubled me, invoking the belief in naturalized gender differences that had contributed to my own rupture from Judaism, and yet simultaneously touched me, in somehow acknowledging my desire to repair this loss of meaning: 'you know that the Hassidic teaching is that a woman has an internal Torah, she is born with the Torah inside of her. So when you are learning Torah now, it resonates with the Torah that is already inside of you.'

A few months later, we were sitting at Shira's table again, talking about her therapeutic work. I was surprised to learn that she had been working with a teenage boy who was Muslim. She told me that the work had been difficult; he had been aggressive at school, and she was nervous, 'what if he would attack me?' She added, 'because he was a Muslim as well that raised issues for me that I needed to think about'. A short time later, she was elaborating on the detail of Jewish laws – for example, of cooking, eating, dressing and talking – that organize her everyday life, when a surprising connection began to emerge. There are laws about everything, she explained, written in the bible, but there is also a further dimension of these actions, an inner dimension of connecting, of drawing connections deeply, 'so we could do an ordinary thing and just be dry, and the same thing and do it with a quality, a richness, relating to the soul. It's a kind of passionate experience of being Jewish and how to relate that in our everyday life.' She continued,

> A lot of the laws don't make sense, but we still do them, and that's really the, the power of a Jew. I'll give you an example: we have a law that we mustn't wear wool and linen [shatnez] together in clothing. Now to the mind it does not make sense, what's wrong with wool and linen, I mean? But there are certain laws that we don't know why and we're asked to keep them ... but it does something to a person to keep the law without knowing why.

She added that this was a distinctively gendered aspect of Judaism, for while men learn to study the reasons for laws, it is women who focus on how to embody the practice. I registered my discomfort and anger as she justified Haredi women's exclusion from textual study in terms of an essential, naturalized difference between the genders. I paused and then asked if she could put into words what it 'does to her' when she keeps the law of wool / linen without asking why. She explained

> it makes me have a connection way deeper than intellect or understanding, of listening to some power ... telling me what to do, and I trust him so I'm going to listen whatever the case. And it helps me in life and in my counselling. It is a way of learning to be uncomfortable, learning to own feelings and staying with what I'm feeling.

Later, I pressed her further on this question of dress, still preoccupied with the discomfort I felt in my modest skirt. She explained that, for her, modesty is about how she clothes herself, but again this surface act opens up an internal quality. Modesty is, she explained, about the capacity to hold things, anxieties, inside you without immediately externalizing them. It is about not pretending to know things you don't know; it is about the capacity to hold and listen. And as *I* listened intently to Shira's account of how she keeps laws of dress, something shifted in my relationship with her. The opposition of symbolic law and ethics that had felt so visceral in my encounters with Gila was in this context being transfigured. In evocatively articulating this relationship of 'doing before hearing' (Levinas 1990), Shira had somehow inverted my assumed relationship between 'values', knowledge and action, transfiguring my relation to laws that, from another perspective, were patriarchal and exclusive. She thus opened up a sense of an adjacent possibility: that keeping such laws could *also* be about allowing oneself to sustain discomfort and trust in the unknown quality of a relationship with an enigmatic other, an act of simultaneously connecting with one's own ambiguity that, in this important way, makes intimacy possible.

Conclusion

In this chapter, I have claimed that in order to engage with the question, 'where is the good in the world?' we must first address prior epistemological and methodological concerns, which are also ethical. Challenging the hierarchy that sees philosophy as providing concepts and ethnography as a source of evidence (Das 2015), I have traced how my inherited theoretical schema for locating ethics, specifically the opposition of a transcendent, sacred realm to the immanent, mundane everyday, has been transfigured in the course of my fieldwork. In contrast to an approach that objectifies ethics as higher 'values' that then compel (via codified laws or emotive force) everyday social relations, I have framed ethics as a difficult process of, as Stephen Frosh (2008) puts it, 'making contact' under precarious conditions permeated by racialized and patriarchal representations of the other. My approach has turned around what initially seemed to be a purely superficial question: what should I wear for my fieldwork? Now, thinking of the debate between Robbins and Das, this question can be considered superficial in two distinct senses: my putting on a skirt might be a banal pretence, a means to an end in my study of ethical teachings or it might in Robbins' framing have an *obvious* meaning, as a symbolic instantiation of both a higher particularist value and a patriarchal law.

However, the narrative I have developed through turning over this question has, I hope, challenged such a theoretically secured approach to the ethnographic study of ethics. In contrast, I have sought to exemplify how an embodied method of reluctantly putting on a skirt and then staying with the discomfort of this superficial action has brought me into a deeper relationship with those I seek to know.[18] My claim is that the women who taught me to repeat what felt like an alienating symbolic gesture of feminine conformity enabled me to engage in, as Das (2015) puts it, 'ethnographic work on the self'. This iterative act brought to the surface histories of rupture, exclusion and assimilation, histories that were carried in distinctive ways by myself and my fieldwork interlocuters, and which shaped our relationships. By allowing these hidden depths to surface, it became possible to make contact with aspects of myself and of others that otherwise blocked the development of more intimate relationships, and this opened up a connection with Shira through which aspects of Jewish ethics emerged that I had not anticipated. Guided by Shira, I began to learn how, within a potentially violent religious tradition, apparently wedded to an absolute truth, we can locate an ordinary ethics that is radically open to the unknown. She showed me how the uncomfortable gesture of conforming to a seemingly patriarchal and exclusive law can allow for a deeper connection with the transcendence of the other, the possibility of transfigurative contact across symbolic difference, even under precarious, potentially hateful conditions.

Against representations of the good in terms of a Christian and masculine realm of higher symbolic values, a Jewish and feminist practice of oscillating between surface and depth has emerged in this chapter. And this locates ethics in a deepening relationship to the fragile potentiality of the ordinary.[19] It is also, significantly, a creative movement for uncovering unanticipated meaning that, as I learned in this fieldwork, traverses Jewish textual, domestic and ethnographic practices. Thus, in the *Ethics of the Fathers*, the text that I skipped at shul as I helped the women with the mundane task of washing up after the meal that brought this community together, there is a classic midrash on the study of the Torah:[20] 'Turn it over and over, for all is in it' (Pirkei Avot: 5:22, cited in Zornberg 2009: 238). Avivah Zornberg elaborates: 'precisely because it contains all, the Torah requires this kind of transfigurative study: the plough exposes new surfaces of earth to the light and the student reveals unexpected or long-buried facets of meaning.' In this chapter, I have narrated my search for transcendent 'ethical teachings' that seemed always beyond reach. Yet, in taking up a Hebraic method of turning over the surface, an ethical possibility for intimate contact with the other has emerged within Jewish everyday life.

Acknowledgements

I would like to thank Dangoor Education for a grant for the project *Ethical Monotheism*, out of which this work comes. Thanks also to the research participants for their trust and guidance, and to the other members of the wider research team, Stephen Frosh, Ben Gidley and Lenita Törning.

Ruth Sheldon is a Lecturer in Religion and Social Science in the Department of Theology and Religious Studies at King's College London. She is the author of *Tragic Encounters and Ordinary Ethics: Palestine-Israel in British Universities* (Manchester University Press, 2016) and is currently working on a monograph exploring the ethics of neighbouring in contemporary London.

Notes

1. Throughout this chapter, pseudonyms have been used for individuals and institutions to protect the identities of research participants.
2. Tzniuth, or modesty, has various meanings that are broadly focused on constraining the body. While tzniuth applies both to women and men, the differential ways in which it is encoded and practised relate, as Fader (2009) describes, to beliefs about gendered difference and appropriate relations, including, most notoriously, the responsibility for women to protect men from the potential for arousal. Insofar as tznuith is encoded in laws of feminine clothing, it encompasses detailed specifications and customs regarding the length of skirts, sleeves, high necklines and the covering of hair after marriage.
3. This study of Jewish ethical relations to the neighbour is part of a larger project on 'Ethical Monotheism'. This was initially framed as an investigation into monotheistic value systems, including with regard to major textual sources that influence the religions' approach to social and ethical concerns, as taught in the UK. I would like to thank Dangoor Education for the grant that funded this project.
4. Within orthodox Judaism, Jewish descent is matrilineal. The question of Jewish identity is thus answered, with reference to Jewish law (Halacha), in absolute terms. During my fieldwork, I encountered a number of people who were the children of Jewish fathers and had suffered the painful exclusion of being told that they were not 'halachically' (i.e. authentically) Jewish (see Kasstan 2016 for one such narrative).
5. See, for example, the comment pieces by Clarke, Das and Lambek in response to Robbins (2016).
6. Alongside well-established critical engagement with the Protestant genealogies of post-Enlightenment social theory from scholars of Islam, I draw in this chapter on a parallel set of interventions emerging from the field of Jewish ethnography (Boyarin 1996; Fader 2009). My approach takes up Boyarin's (1991) framing of Jewish ethnography as both redressing the relative marginalization of Jews as historically ambiguous subjects of ethnographic study and as bringing Jewish thought and traditions into critical dialogue with social theories and epistemologies that have been within a dominant Christian culture (see also Seidler, this volume).
7. See Puett (2014) for a related discussion of how such universalistic, 'neutral' theoretical models can work at a metalevel to distance the anthropologist from disturbing and tragic registers of lived ethical experience.

8. While Das' claim here resonates with James Laidlaw's (2014) account of the exercise of the ethnographic imagination as an ethical mode of reflective self-formation, my approach is more attuned with her keen emphasis on the relational ground, the mutual vulnerability of both teacher and student, within such scenes of ethnographic learning. There are important connections here with Vic Seidler's framing of the emotional work of ethnography in this volume.
9. Here I am taking up Stephen Frosh's (2008) question regarding the potential of forms of communication that 'exceed' the symbolic to facilitate meaningful, non-violent contact between neighbours. My approach diverges, however, from the more hyperbolic emphasis on encountering 'the real' within life and death events, by attending instead to the texture of words and gestures within everyday contexts.
10. Fader frames her convincing account of Hasidic feminine modesty in Foucauldian terms, as a technology of the self oriented towards teleological norms. While attending to modesty as a moral discipline is clearly pertinent, my approach contributes to emerging enquiries into the relationship of law and ethics (see also Clarke 2015) by suggesting what may be missed by a totalizing rendering: in this instance, the presence of that aspect of Hasidic philosophy, which is oriented to the unknown.
11. Examples include conflicts over posters calling for gender segregation on the street during a Torah procession; an alleged ban on Belz (Haredi) women driving; tensions between Christian and Jewish members of a newly established interfaith council over the issue of men shaking women's hands.
12. As Boyarin and Boyarin (1993) argue, the notion of the overcoming of Jewish law is integral to secular Christianity's teleological narrative of the emergence of a universal ethics that transcends difference.
13. Though Fader's analysis also complicates a simplistic account of Haredi insularity, as she highlights how this religious stringency coexists with participation and fluency in secular modern culture.
14. The Kohenim, or priestly caste, are considered to be descendants of Moses' brother Aaron and continue to have special obligations within orthodox synagogues.
15. Within orthodox Jewish synagogues, women and men sit separately. Communal prayers are led by men, and the halachic obligation to participate in these is binding on men only.
16. Her question referred to the name that is given to a Jewish child (traditionally boys) at birth for use in the synagogue.
17. A shpitzel is a partial wig with hair at the front and the rest covered by a small hat or headscarf, which is worn by particularly observant Hasidic women.
18. The anthropologist Clara Han (2014) has made a different but related case for a relationship between ethics and modes of pretending. Researching neighbourly relations within a context of urban poverty, Han reveals the kindness entailed in acts of pretending *not* to recognize the shameful critical moments of neighbours while engaging in subtly supportive actions. This she suggests opens up the possibility for 'inexhaustible relational and temporal capacity within human beings ..."inexhaustible depth" that makes it possible to be open to visions other than our own' (2014: 88).
19. This is also an insight figured in different ways in the writings of Emmanuel Levinas (see Aronowicz 1994) and Walter Benjamin's observation that 'we penetrate the mystery only insofar as we rediscover it in everyday life' (cited in Scholem 2012).
20. Within Judaism, a delimited concept of Torah refers to the written scriptures, but Torah is also much broader than this, evoking *all* Jewish learning, and in this sense a form of life.

References

Alexander, J.C. 2003. *The Meanings of Social Life: A Cultural Sociology.* New York: Oxford University Press.
Aronowicz, A. 1994. Translator's Introduction, in *Nine Talmudic Readings by Emmanuel Levinas.* Bloomington, IN: Indiana University Press.
Boyarin, D., and J. Boyarin. 1993. 'Diaspora: Generation and the Ground of Jewish Identity', *Critical Inquiry* 19(4): 693–725.
Boyarin, J. 1991. 'Jewish Ethnography and the Question of the Book'. *Anthropological Quarterly* 64(1): 14–29.
_____. 1996. *Thinking in Jewish.* Chicago: University of Chicago Press.
Clarke, M. 2015. 'Legalism and the Care of the Self: Shari'ah Discourse in Contemporary Lebanon', in P. Dresch and J. Scheele (eds), *Legalism: Rules and Categories.* Oxford: Oxford University Press.
Das, V. 2007. *Life and Words: Violence and the Descent into the Ordinary; Foreword by Stanley Cavell.* Berkeley: University of California Press.
_____. 2010. 'Engaging the Life of the Other: Love and Everyday Life', in M. Lambek (ed.), *Ordinary Ethics: Anthropology, Language and Action.* Ashland, OH: Fordham University Press, pp. 376–99.
_____. 2015. 'Adjacent Thinking: A Postscript', in R. Chatterji (ed.), *Wording the World: Veena Das and Scenes of Inheritance.* Ashland, OH: Fordham University Press, pp. 372–99.
Das, V. et al. 2015. 'There is No Such Thing as The Good: The 2013 Meeting of the Group for Debates in Anthropological Theory', *Critique of Anthropology* 35(4): 430–80.
Fader, A. 2009. *Mitzvah Girls: Bringing Up The Next Generation of Hasidic Jews in Brooklyn.* Princeton, NJ: Princeton University Press.
Frosh, S. 2008. Elementals and Affects, or On Making Contact With Others', *Subjectivity* 24(1): 314–24.
Han, C. 2014. 'The Difficulty of Kindness: Boundaries, Time and the Ordinary', in V. Das et al. (eds), *The Ground Between: Anthropologists Engage Philosophy.* Durham: Duke University Press, pp. 71–93.
Kasstan, B. 2016. 'Positioning Oneself and Being Positioned in the "Community": An Essay on Jewish Ethnography as a "Jew-ish" Ethnographer', *Scripta Instituti Donneriani Aboensis* 27: 264–83.
Laidlaw, J. 2014. *The Subject of Virtue: An Anthropology of Ethics and Freedom.* Cambridge: Cambridge University Press.
Levinas, E. 1990. *Nine Talmudic Readings.* Trans. Annette Aronowicz. Bloomington, IN: Indiana University Press.
Lynch, G. 2012. *The Sacred in the Modern World: A Cultural Sociological Approach.* Oxford: Oxford University Press.
'Pirkei Avot (Ethics of the Fathers): 5:22'. 2009. *The Murmuring Deep: Reflections on the Biblical Unconscious,* A.G. Zornberg. New York: Schocken Books Incorporated, pp. 238.
Puett, M. 2014. 'Ritual Disjunctions: Ghosts, Anthropology, and Philosophy', in V. Das et al. (eds), *The Ground Between: Anthropologists Engage Philosophy.* Durham, NC: Duke University Press, pp. 218–33.
Robbins, J. 2013. 'Beyond the Suffering Subject: Toward an Anthropology of The Good', *Journal of the Royal Anthropological Institute* 19(3): 447–62.

_____. 2016. 'What is the Matter with Transcendence? On the Place of Religion in the New Anthropology of Ethics', *Journal of the Royal Anthropological Institute* 22(4): 767–81.
Scholem, G. 2012. *On Jews and Judaism in Crisis: Selected Essays*. Philadelphia: Paul Dry Books.
Staetsky, D. 2015. *Strictly Orthodox Rising: What the Demography of British Jews Tells Us about the Future of the Community*. London: JPR.
Wessendorf, S. 2014. *Commonplace Diversity: Social Relations in a Super-Diverse Context*. Basingstoke: Palgrave Macmillan.
Zigon, J. 2014. 'An Ethics of Dwelling and a Politics of World-Building: A Critical Response to Ordinary Ethics', *Journal of the Royal Anthropological Institute* 20(4): 746–64.
Zornberg, A.G. 2009. *The Murmuring Deep: Reflections on the Biblical Unconscious*. New York: Schocken Books Incorporated.

11

Radical Hope as a Practice of Possibilities
On the Fragility of Goodness and Struggles for Justice in Postwar Bosnia and Herzegovina

David Henig

On an afternoon in July 2017, I arranged a meeting with Remzija, who I have known for more than a decade, and one of her daughters in Sarajevo, Bosnia and Herzegovina (BiH). It was the first time I was meeting Remzija since her husband, Tarik, passed away in June 2016. Tarik was one of my closest friends and interlocutors for many years; our friendship dated back to the early days of my fieldwork in 2008. It was therefore a highly emotional moment, charged with deep sorrow but also with anticipation and hope.

When Remzija and her daughter emerged at the corner of the shopping centre where we had agreed to meet, she was wearing a veil. In the past, she would wear her veil only on specific occasions of public piety such as visiting the mosque during Ramadan, or when attending collective prayers for the dead. Now, however, the veil was indexing a rupture in her life and her ongoing mourning and love for her late husband. Yet it also expressed her new ethical striving to create a life worth living even in the midst of her struggles and suffering.

As we sat in one of the buzzing cafés that encircle the shopping centre and ordered our drinks, we talked about Tarik's death and how it took everyone by surprise as he was only 49 years old. Remzija recounted the wave of solidarity Tarik's untimely death engendered among his colleagues at work, in the neighbourhood where they lived, and in his village, where he is now buried. She was deeply moved by the numerous expressions of kind-heartedness towards her and their daughters. In recent months, Remzija continued, it had mainly been the women's mosque association, composed largely of the widows whose husbands, fathers and brothers died during the Bosnian War (1992–1995), many of them during the Srebrenica genocide, that had embraced her and offered unconditional solace. Yet our conversation soon changed direction. It happened at the very moment when Remzija finished drinking her coffee and pushed the cup away to the corner of the table. There was determination and resoluteness in the gesture as she prepared herself to talk about something else. Until his death, Tarik was the chief breadwinner in the family. His sudden death had left the family vulnerable. Not only did Remzija and her children have to find a new source of income to sustain themselves; as she was soon to find out, Remzija would also have to fight for her right to access Tarik's pension. Although she knew that securing the pension would be an uphill struggle at best, and many people discouraged her from pursuing it, Remzija did not give up. What kept her going in such difficult circumstances?

In the course of our encounter in 2017, and during our subsequent conversations over the following two years, it became clear that no matter how heartbreaking the loss of Tarik had been, Remzija refused to reduce her current situation to pain, despair and suffering. From the moment of Tarik's sudden death, she and her children adamantly hoped that despite their current predicaments something good would emerge out of the tragic loss that had turned their lives upside down. Her courageous adamancy to fight, and the practices of hope she had developed over time in this struggle, allowed her to cultivate an ethical stance from which she was able to strive for a good beyond the void that was presently overwhelming her life. In this chapter, my primary concern is with the question of what made Remzija's ethical stance possible, in a situation 'when the conditions to despair are all but overwhelming' (Lear 2006: 146). Taking Remzija's practices of hope as a point of departure, my broader aim here is to contribute to the anthropology of the good by ethnographically elucidating how 'people organize their personal and collective lives in order to foster what they think of as good, and to study what it is like to live at least some of the time in light of such a project' (Robbins 2013: 457).

Radical Hope as a Practice of Possibilities

The concepts with which Remzija and her daughters expressed and acted upon their striving for a good were articulated in the language of hope (*nada*). In what follows, I trace 'a complex patchwork of different kinds of hope' (Schielke 2015: 11) that Remzija *cultivated* and *practised* against the odds that she faced. Her response – hoping that something good will emerge from her present circumstances – was not an expression of idle passivity, nor was it naive escapism of any kind. On the contrary, it was an expression – in thought and action – of what the philosopher Jonathan Lear describes as *radical hope* (2006). For Lear, radical hope is an ethical stance that emerges in the face of dramatic ruptures and 'the destruction of the *telos*' of one's way of life (2006:

57). The idea of *radical hope* is radical because it recognizes the importance of having the courage to pursue new horizons of anticipation, conviction and striving amidst such circumstance (see also Wilkinson, this volume). These horizons provide individuals and communities with a new context of significance and meaning to their actions in the moments of dramatic ruptures, and thereby open new pathways for imagining new possibilities as to how one could pursue a life worth living (Lear 2006: 57). Lear explores radical hope in his philosophical meditation on the words of the last great chief of the Crow nation, Plenty Coups (1848–1932), and how the Crow culture as a way of life ended as the Crow nation was defeated and confined to a reservation. What does it mean to find a new way to be a Crow and live a Crow way of life in a situation of cultural, material and physical decimation? For Plenty Coups, as Lear suggests, it meant cultivating the moral courage to imagine new opportunities for the Crow way of life to flourish amidst the dire circumstances of the present. And this moral courage to engage in imagining what is *possible* rather than *actual* in the maelstrom of calamitous events is what Lear describes as *radical hope*.[1] In his tour de force argument, Lear uses the Plenty Coups and the Crow nation story as a way to understand human vulnerability and resilience amidst cultural-cum-societal breakdowns and the loss of an entire way of life. As Lear puts it, he is concerned with 'the field of possibilities in which all human endeavors gain meaning' amidst actual circumstances (2006: 7). Radical hope is thus for Lear a practice of possibilities.

In this chapter, I follow Lear's inquiry into how radical hope can become a practice of possibilities in situations of suffering and dramatic ruptures. My specific concern here is with how radical hope emerges from individual dramas of everyday life. In turn, I ask what makes radical hope possible in such circumstances. These individual dramas, I argue, are equally generative for our understanding of how people realize the good in their everyday lives through practices of hope. This echoes Cheryl Mattingly's call for anthropologists to work not only on the problem of 'actualities but also of possibilities and their ethical implications' (2014: 28). Situating her own inquiry into the struggles for a good life in the context of what she calls 'a perilous moral ordinary' among African American families caring for children with chronic medical conditions, Mattingly asks how these possibilities are 'bound up with suffering, even moral tragedy' (2014: 29). As in the case of Remzija, for the families studied by Mattingly it was again a practice of hope that kept the families going as they were striving to obtain 'some version of a good life' (2014: 5). But what does it mean to hope in such dire circumstances?

Joel Robbins (2013: 458), in his programmatic essay on an anthropology of the good, identified studies of hope as one of the burgeoning areas of social science inquiry into the ways in which individuals and communities create something good in their lives. In recent years, anthropologists as well as sociologists have attended to hope primarily as a temporal practice (Bryant and Knight 2019; Janeja and Bandak 2018), and as a practice of progressive politics

(Back 2020; Hage 2012). However, there is more at stake. As Zigon observed, such a narrow focus on hope 'might be called the Augustinian folk-model of hope as pointing down the linear path of time toward the better future' (2009: 257). For both Zigon and Mattingly, hope is as much a moral project as it is a temporal practice. For the families Mattingly writes about, to hope is a moral call that is 'bound up in views of what it means to live a good life, to be a good person' (2010: 3). But 'to hope' is something that needs to be cultivated and *practised*, not as a form of denial, or simply an emotion, but as 'a stance toward reality' (2010: 4), even if the reality is dire and hopeless at present. As Mattingly adds, hope is a practice 'of creating, or trying to create, lives worth living even in the midst of suffering, even with no happy ending in sight' (2010: 6).[2] In other words, hope is a practice of imagining possibilities and acting on them.

Building on this body of scholarship that explores the entanglements between the human condition and suffering, and what practices of hope such an entanglement engenders to forge new horizons of possibilities in small moments of everyday life, I follow the life story of Remzija's family and their refusal to give up despite the trying circumstances. As Piers Vitebsky (2008) remarked, anthropologists take a story, or a singular moment from their fieldwork, on which they hang their analysis. Such moments, Vitebsky suggests, work 'as the foundation of a social analysis because we can take the event as typical – so long as we are not too concerned with change. But the untypical moment can also be revealing, and point to a tectonic shift in the relationship between a person's past and his or her future' (2008: 243). I take the life story of Remzija's family and the dramas they have endured as intertwined with 'the tectonic shifts' caused by the vicissitudes of different political-cum-societal magnitudes unfolding at different scales over the past three decades as a way to open up the question of how people realize something good in their lives amidst suffering and despair. These tectonic shifts include the violent disintegration of socialist Yugoslavia, the Bosnian War (1992–1995) and ensuing postsocialist and postwar dispossession and precarity, culminating in Tarik's death. Grounding my analysis in the experiences of particular individuals living in particular socio-historical junctures – and tracing their struggles to realize a fragile good in their lives – is, I contend, a productive way to explore 'a number of ethical and existential issues' in 'a variety of actual social situations before hazarding generalisations' (Jackson 2013: 11). Further to asking *what* is the good, or *where* the good can be located and realized, this chapter also probes *when* and *how* people realize the good in their lives. I therefore follow Remzija's family life story to reflect on how, in the situations of family tragedies and ruptures (the *when*), the practices of hope (the *how*) allow individuals to imagine and realize a good 'beyond what is presently given in their lives' (Robbins 2013: 458).

Before Radical Hope

I have known Tarik's and Remzija's family for over a decade. They lived in the village where I originally started my fieldwork back in 2008 (Henig 2020). At the time of my fieldwork, the family used to live squeezed inside an old wooden house that was built in the 1950s. They inherited it from Tarik's parents. Tarik was grateful to his late parents for the house, but there was no way he could install running water or a bathroom there. The family of five found living in the old house increasingly constraining and uncomfortable. Building a more spacious brick house became for the family a source of aspiration and hope, and a dream of a normal life worth living. Yet, at the same time, it embodied frustration and increasing hopelessness, as this dream seemed to be beyond the family's reach due to the protracted precarity in which villagers like Tarik and Remzija found themselves stuck in the postsocialist, postwar years. The story of Tarik's family is common in postwar Bosnia and Herzegovina, one that Stef Jansen aptly described as filled with yearnings for 'normal lives' (Jansen 2015). A 'normal life' is a widely shared object of yearning in BiH and across all ex-Yugoslav countries (Greenberg 2011). The notion of normal lives emerged from the experiences of fragility as a result of a life trajectory that has been radically altered by the violent disintegration of the socialist Yugoslavia. It functions as a horizon of both temporal orientation and moral striving. In BiH, it captures the experiences and predicaments of Bosnians of all walks of life in the postsocialist, postwar present that engenders the sense of an absent 'normality' in people's lives. As Stef Jansen and other authors aptly document, the concept of 'normality' operates as hope and aspiration regarding how one's life *ought* to unfold as opposed to what it *is* in the present and when the present is experienced as lacking any normality. However, in the BiH context, the aspirations for 'normality' are not oriented solely towards the future (the *ought*) but also towards the socialist Yugoslav past (the *was*), as a source of normality and positive value (Jansen 2015: 38).

Like other Bosnians of their generation who were born and grew up in the heyday of socialist Yugoslavia, Tarik's and Remzija's families enjoyed relative prosperity and stability in the early decades of post-Second World War Yugoslav socialism. Tarik's father joined other male villagers who were flocking as *gastarbeiters* (guest workers) to the Federal Republic of Germany in the 1960s and early 1970s. The wave of guest workers brought German Marks back to their villages. Later, when they retired and came home, the stream of foreign currency continued through their 'German pension'. Tarik's generation found relatively prosperous jobs closer to home in the Yugoslav factories. Although the Yugoslav economy was drowning in debts in the 1980s, Tarik could still rely on his father's 'German pension' to pursue his aspirations. Tarik started planning to get married and build his own house in the village. He married Remzija in 1990 as the Yugoslav federation was crumbling. Soon afterwards, the Bosnian War broke out. Rather than building a new house,

Tarik decided to send his wife and his ageing parents to a safer place away from the frontline, which soon engulfed the village. He joined the Bosnian Army and remained with other villagers in the nearby hills, defending their houses. In 1994 Tarik was injured by grenade shrapnel. The doctors saved his life, but they did not manage to remove all the shrapnel from his body, which continued to cause debilitating pain until his death. When Tarik recovered, he returned to the frontline, where he remained until the end of the war. He stayed in the army for some time after the war. Remzija and her husband, now with their first child and his parents, returned to the village, where his parents both died in 1996. In 1997 Tarik left the army and planned to return to work so he could finally build a family house where he, Remzija and their child could live. Upon his departure from the army, he received a flock of sheep as compensation for his work and war sacrifices. The animals were, however, in bad shape, and soon afterwards he contracted brucellosis from one of the sheep and fell ill for a year. As with his shrapnel injury, Tarik suffered from the aftereffects of brucellosis until his death. It was Remzija who held the family and their smallholding together while Tarik remained bedridden, and the family was without any income apart from the limited social benefits Tarik was receiving for his war injuries.

After his recovery, in around 2000, Tarik had a string of temporary, poorly paid jobs in the timber and construction industry, as the factory where he used to work before the war was plundered, privatized, plundered again and eventually closed for good. Remzija continued working hard on their smallholding and occasionally sold dairy products while taking care of three children. This was the time when the first effects of laws recently imposed by the international community on benefit payments and privatization of state assets hit the places where Tarik was working; he also lost the benefit payments to which he was entitled because of his war injuries (Jansen 2006: 188; Klepal 2018). Although he fought over many years with the state bureaucracy to get his benefits back, Tarik was never successful. However, it was also a time when various forms of microloans mushroomed across the country, on which people like Tarik and Remzija relied to 'live decently' (Jašarević 2017: 93) in a situation of protracted precarity and despair. The family saw microloans as an opportunity to fulfil their dream and finally build a new house. With a series of microloans, combined with help from neighbours, by 2004 Tarik and Remzija managed to build a basic roofed structure on the outskirts of the village. At the time, neither Tarik and Remzija nor other people in Bosnia fully understood, as Larisa Jašarević documented, that the microloans that were often presented in 'the language of assistance and service' (ibid.) in fact entailed a high interest that kept people constantly in a spiral of indebtedness.

Until this point in narrating their lives, both Tarik and Remzija perceived the vicissitudes in their life stories as somewhat manageable. As Tarik put it to me in 2012, 'no matter how bad things were, I hoped that the war would end one day, and I hoped that I would recover from the sickness.' These were the kinds of vicissitudes that Michael Carrithers (2009: 3) characterizes as *expectable*. This does not mean, Carrithers writes, 'that they are necessarily *expected* especially in the sense of being prepared for and under control'. However, as Carrithers adds, 'Some eventualities may fall relatively easily under a more or less automated response, but others, those we experience as vicissitudes, may leave us speechless and confused, without a ready interpretation of what has happened' (Carrithers 2009: 3; italics in original).

The vicissitudes that left the family disoriented and increasingly hopeless were caused by the fact that since the early 2000s Tarik had not been able to find a stable job. Indeed, the conjuncture of the two processes – privatization that exacerbated unemployment, and indebtedness driven by the microloans schemes – resulted in Tarik's prolonged unemployment and the family's struggle to pay the debts off. This meant that any further construction work on the house had to be put on hold indefinitely. It also halted their aspirations and aggravated the feeling that their lives were stuck and moving nowhere (Hage 2009). As we will see later, this situation had also significantly affected Tarik's health. This was the period when the narrative of their life shifted from having aspirations for a better (normal) life towards perceiving their lives in terms of misery and suffering (*patnja*).

When I met the family in 2008 for the first time, Tarik was still unemployed. The family struggled to get by while the pressure from creditors was increasingly looming over Tarik. It was 'more painful than the shrapnel left from the war injury in my neck', as he put it on many occasions. He was not alone in the villages where I was conducting fieldwork at the time – in fact, this was rather a common story (Henig 2020). The situation eventually became unbearable. Tarik felt that his family's life was stuck in limbo. In 2009, after nearly a decade of struggling, Tarik decided along with a few other male villagers to go and work abroad. He stayed in Azerbaijan for six months, earning enough money to pay off some of the family's debts but not enough to finish the new house as he recounted to me in 2012 when we met again.

In 2014, I returned to Bosnia and found myself sitting in the living room of a flat in a Sarajevo suburb. Tarik was sitting next to me on the sofa. There were a few familiar objects in the room: a TV set, a couple of framed family photographs, a familiar green string of praying beads hanging next to the door frame and Remzija's hand-made knitted decorative cloths carefully arranged on the few pieces of furniture and providing the sense of homely warmth that I remembered so well from their old house in the village. Six years after our first encounter, and having joined other villagers on the run from desperation to find a job for both of them, Remzija and Tarik now resided on the outskirts of Sarajevo. 'We're like refugees again', was Remzija's first sentence when she welcomed me in the living room, comparing her current situation with her experiences of displacement during the war. 'What can I do?', sighed Tarik, looking at me while trying to roll a cigarette. Like many other Bosnians, he couldn't afford to buy cigarettes any more and had started rolling his own using tobacco of variable quality obtained through friends or on local markets and which was causing him respiratory problems that he hadn't had before. When he had finally rolled three cigarettes, he sat more comfortably. We had not seen each other for two years −24 months that had yet again been vicissitudinous and that had profoundly transformed their lives.

The years of failed attempts to secure a job in the Zvijezda highlands had led Tarik to try to seek a better fortune abroad again. The decision had been made with much hesitation but also with the hope of finally having a chance to save enough money to move to the new house and live a decent life. So Tarik tried his luck and went to Kazakhstan as a construction worker. There, no one from the Bosnian building brigade received a single salary. The agent from Bosnia who got Tarik the job went completely silent. All the Bosnians who arrived with Tarik were stuck in Astana without any means of living or returning home. Tarik and the others had to ask their families to buy them tickets to get home. 'Most of us', he bitterly recounted, 'had to take another *kredit* [loan] although the reason we went to Kazakhstan was to earn enough money to pay our existing loans back'. When Tarik returned, his struggle to find a job continued, and all the family's savings had gone into getting him back. In the end, it just became too much to bear. 'Let me show you something', Tarik said, pulling out from under the coffee table a plastic box full of various pills that he had started taking in the last few years. The diagnosis he had received as a result of accumulated stress, while being in his mid-forties, was far too common a story in Bosnia: high cholesterol, high blood pressure and diabetes while still suffering from the after-effects of his war injury and the brucellosis that he had contracted in the late 1990s.

A few months before our reunion in 2014, Tarik's brother had found a job for him in a factory in Sarajevo. Although the job was rather unstable, and the contracts available in the factory ranged from a month to three months, it was Tarik's first regular and decent income earned in Bosnia in more than a decade. Now living in the village became an obstacle, as commuting was too expensive, and it turned out to be cheaper if the family moved to the suburbs of Sarajevo. No one seemed to mind the move. The daughters were excited, and there were good prospects for Remzija finding a job as well. In 2014, Tarik and Remzija finally felt that they had overcome their misery and suffering and that their lives had gained some prospective hopeful orientation once more.

Had they left the village and the plans and hopes to finish their dream house for good, I wondered? Having known Tarik and Remzija for many years, I knew how strongly attached they were to the village. I also knew how much the family dreamt about moving to their new, bigger and more comfortable house. What will happen to the house now, I asked? 'We go back regularly, to do some work around the new house', both Tarik and Remzija replied, 'cutting the grass, watering the apple trees, sweeping the floor' − referring to small, quotidian practices that kept the flame of hope alive. Then he added, 'inshallah [God willing], I will build a bench and a table underneath an apple tree so we can sit in the shade and drink coffee next summer.' Both were convinced – in their hopes and in their humble actions and practices of hope such as watering the apple trees, cutting the grass, sweeping the yard – that one day the family would complete the house and return to the village.

One June morning in 2016, I received a message that Tarik had passed away in Sarajevo. Aged 49, he had suffered a heart attack. His heart exploded from the pressure, as his daughter told me, and she added, 'here, in Bosnia debts kill people, it was too much for him.' The family did not return, and the unfinished house remained abandoned.

Radical Hope

Vicissitudes, small and large, predictable and unexpected, are inherent to the human condition. Although the death of loved ones is one of the vicissitudes that is expectable, this does not mean, as Michael Carrithers (2009) reminds us, that it does not create a dramatic rupture, leading to vulnerability and disorientation. Indeed, in 2017, a year after Tarik's death, Remzija was still not able to find words to talk about what had happened on the early morning in June 2016 when she received the phone call from the factory informing her about the tragedy. She only had memories of absence. 'I don't remember anything,' she told me, when she tried to recall the first few minutes, hours and days without Tarik. All she could remember was how on that morning she had prepared as usual a pot of Bosnian coffee for the two of them. But Tarik did not return. The memory of two empty cups and an untouched pot of cooling coffee haunted her so much that she had had to hide the red coffee pot in the cupboard and buy a new one. 'I didn't know what to do and where to turn,' she continued. Remzija's life was in ruins and without any sense of telos. Moreover, as I recounted earlier, the family relied primarily on Tarik's income. Tarik left behind debts, which had to be repaid, and no savings, while the family was still living in a rented flat. This became an immediate challenge for Remzija and her two younger daughters. While Remzija was still mourning, disoriented and paralysed – physically as well as emotionally – her daughters took the situation into their own hands. They found jobs in Sarajevo restaurants and started earning enough to cover the rent and other basic bills. Participating in the activities of the local mosque was the only thing Remzija could manage at the time.

It would be tempting to reduce the tragic life story of Tarik and Remzija I have described so far into a story of suffering. Remzija undoubtedly suffered. The family was undergoing an extremely painful period of grieving while also facing economic hardship. The daughters regularly share old images of Tarik on social media with comments like 'Dad, why did you leave us?' even years after the tragic event. But the moments of rupture and breakdown were in other ways generative for the family, imbued with potentiality and moral courage to strive for something new that might be lacking in their life, as the anthropologists of the good have pointed out (Mattingly 2014; Robbins 2013: 458). What gave Remzija and her daughters courage to strive for something good amidst the tragic loss and economic struggles was a practice of hope. In what follows, I track a patchwork of different kinds of hope whereby the family navigated a way out of the abyss of suffering and uncertainty. In doing so, I reflect on three particular moments of 'narrative re-envisioning'[3] (Mattingly 2014): the *whens* and the practices of hope (the *hows*) whereby Remzija was able to imagine possibilities of, and cultivate a stance oriented towards a good beyond what was given in her life at the time.

Fight for Tarik

Navigating bureaucracy was perhaps the most trying task Remzija faced immediately after Tarik's death. The postwar politico-bureaucratic arrangement in Bosnia and Herzegovina is notorious for its complexity and opacity (Jansen 2015). Until his death, it was always Tarik who dealt with these matters, and yet only with limited success. Being aware of Tarik's previous failed attempts in getting the benefit payments for his war-related injuries, Remzija anticipated problems. This only exacerbated her despair and disorientation in the early days of her life without Tarik. With the help of Tarik's brother, she started putting together all the documents about Tarik's previous jobs and his service in the army in order to apply for the state pension she was entitled to as his widow. It was a tedious and endless task.[4] At times, Remzija felt that she would never be able to complete it. But a network of relatives eventually succeeded in collecting all the documents but one. The only missing piece in putting together this paperwork jigsaw was a financial statement from the employer about the pension insurance it was obliged to pay on behalf of Tarik for the last two years of his employment. The company was in no hurry issuing the documents and delayed for more than two months, leaving Remzija and her daughters in limbo. Yet Remzija persevered. When I asked Remzija what drove her persistence in her fight with the company while also struggling to get by in her day-to-day life, her immediate answer was one word – hope (*nada*). Then she further clarified, 'I hoped that I would be successful,' and added, 'I hoped that I would achieve at least something [*barem nešto*],' thus leaving space for doubt and potential failure as well.

As Remzija and I met several times for interviews and discussed this period of her life, I realized that the fight with the company, however tiring and frustrating, also gave Remzija courage to *actively* hope for something again.[5] Yet she was painfully aware that she was walking a tightrope, and the danger of slipping into the abyss of despair and hopelessness was constantly imminent. So how exactly does one practise hope in such circumstances? As Cheryl Mattingly (2010) and Jonathan Lear (2006) suggest, to hope is not only an existential and temporal stance towards one's situatedness in the trying present. It is also an ethical stance – having courage to hope – that requires cultivation, in thought and action, over time. When reflecting on the struggles with the company, Remzija openly said that the family needed the pension to ensure some long-term, albeit limited, financial stability.[6] But she also pointed out that the family had managed to get by thus far even without it. Indeed, the daughters started working immediately, and Remzija eventually found a cleaning job about a year later as well. In other words, one of the drivers of her motivation in this situation, to follow Jarrett Zigon's argument on the ethics of hope, was to 'get out of the breakdown' she was facing (2007: 139). As Zigon writes, the response to the moments of moral breakdowns is thus not motivated by acting 'to be good' but rather persevering in order to get out of the breakdown. In turn, it is one's way out of the breakdown that 'is considered good, not the act itself' (2007: 140). Although I largely agree with Zigon about the centrality of hope in situations of moral breakdown (Zigon 2009), unlike Zigon, I wouldn't separate the motivation for a good from one's action in such situations completely. As we shall see later, this is particularly the case in a situation where the motivation to act is other-person oriented towards 'doing something good' (doing it *for* someone), rather than simply virtue-oriented 'to be good' (in a given situation), which might be the consequence of the former action.

Indeed, the financial security that would bring more stability, however important, wasn't the only motivation of Remzija's actions. There was something else at stake than simply that. 'At first', she explained, 'I called the company every day. I went to talk to Tarik's boss several times a week. They probably got tired of my insistence, but I couldn't help it.' These repetitive activities – calling, visiting, asking – to borrow from Cheryl Mattingly's analytical toolkit, became in the early days of her life without Tarik Remzija's *practices of hope*. Indeed, as she further explained, 'It kept me busy, and it gave me strength to keep going.'[7] Doing so day-by-day became for Remzija a practice of creating a life 'worth living even in the midst of suffering, even with no happy ending in sight' (Mattingly 2010: 6). And indeed, there were many days of despair during this period, when she felt hopeless, as the doors of the offices remained locked, phone calls went unanswered, and she was denied entrance to the factory by the gate guards.

At this point in her narrative, the moral engine[8] driving her actions was grounded in her conviction that she was doing it *for* Tarik. She would never forgive herself if she did not try to fight for what Tarik in her view deserved, and for all the suffering he had endured during his short yet vicissitudinous life. 'Doing it for Tarik' punctuated her narrative and drove her courage and motivation to hope that she would eventually be successful. After two months of daily pressure, but also of frustration and despair, the company eventually released the documents. Focusing on getting the missing papers became an object of good and helped Remzija not to give up. Furthermore, she was able to slowly *re*orient her thoughts and actions towards something that was beyond her immediate reach. Put differently, these early practices of hope allowed Remzija to cultivate a new temporal-cum-moral horizon oriented towards a good – that is, 'doing it for Tarik'.

Envisioning Possibilities: Fighting for Justice

After Remzija finally received the missing paperwork, it immediately transpired why the company was delaying its release. For the two years of Tarik's employment, the company did not pay his pension insurance even though it was obliged to do so.[9] Without these missing payments, Remzija was facing uncertainty as to whether she would be granted the pension. This was yet another moment of despair in the unfolding struggle. 'It felt like starting all over again,' she said. At this point, her narrative had changed, and a new engine of hope emerged. Remzija decided to *fight* with the company over the missing payments. How did she arrive at this decision? How did she envision a possibility that such a fight could achieve anything? I queried.

Her decision to fight was not motivated simply by her precarious situation and the need to ensure at least some small but stable pension. It also, and more importantly, was propelled by her outrage about the immoral and predatory practices of the company. 'I wanted to get justice,' she said resolutely. But, she added, 'I wanted to get truth and justice, not only for Tarik but for everyone working there.' This seems to me a crucial moment in her narrative, as it points to her courageous ethical stance and her capacity to envision something good (i.e. 'getting justice for everyone'), which is 'historical and social before it is individual', transcendental or normative (Mattingly 2014: 22). Put differently, Remzija's decision to 'start all over again' needs to be situated within broader 'social and historical horizons that are crucial in shaping personal commitments' (Mattingly 2014: 21). Indeed, over the postwar years, Remzija has experienced time and again how her late husband, her siblings but also close neighbours in the village and many other Bosnians of all walks of life were treated by their employers in a similar way and the struggles and despair they had to endure (Kurtović 2015). Furthermore, she experienced how this treatment leads ordinary Bosnians like Tarik to live lives that are entangled in the spiral of indebtedness and precarity, which, in turn, as one of his daughters said, regularly 'kill people in Bosnia'. In Remzija's own words, 'I had had enough of it.'

Through a network of friends from the mosque, as well as through Tarik's brother, she alerted and mobilized a handful of Tarik's former colleagues who were still working in the factory at the time. Remzija and Tarik's brother persuaded them to follow up with the company about whether their pension insurance had been paid or not over the duration of their contracts. In the weeks that followed, they met regularly. They plotted and discussed tactics on how to increase pressure on the company, coordinating who would make the phone calls, or who would knock on the doors of the bosses and on which days. Tarik's case created a precedent, and the company couldn't obstruct the release of the documents any longer. There was a growing discontent among the workers. It soon transpired that this was indeed the case for many other workers, and in particular for those who were employed on similar precarious contracts to Tarik's. Tarik's untimely death thus exposed the wider financial machinations of the company with the pension payments.

This was a transformative moment for Remzija when it came to understanding her own situation and actions, which were up to that point oscillating between despair and suffering, between new beginnings and sudden dead ends, with glimpses of hope in between. These new small achievements in the struggle against the company gave Remzija a new telos. The struggle for justice created a new context for the significance of her actions and further cemented her conviction that something good would emerge out of Tarik's death: namely, getting justice, not only for Tarik but for other workers and their families who struggle to get by in their day-to-day lives too. Yet she was painfully aware that the struggle was far from over.

The next step in their fight was to make the company repay its debts. This proved to be an uphill struggle. Everyone knew it, but no one gave up. And again, they all got together regularly in a local café or sat on the benches outside the neighbourhood mosque after the evening prayers, or in Remzija's living room, turning these places into unlikely grounds for experiments in hope and possibility – that is, into 'moral laboratories' (Mattingly 2014: 14–15). There, they again discussed tactics on how to make the company repay its debts, and thus get justice. In the following weeks, Remzija along with the other workers threatened to shame the company publicly, in the media. With the help of a lawyer, who was Tarik's brother's friend from the local mosque, they were also able to put together a letter in which they threatened the company with legal action. This collaborative struggle, which originated in Remzija's living room out of despair, put the management on the back foot. After several weeks of silence, Remzija received a letter in which the company announced that it would transfer the missing payments it owed to Tarik. Not all workers, however, have been successful as yet, and the fight for their payments continues as I write these lines. Remzija and those lucky ones who obtained a similar letter continue to support the remaining (ex-)workers in their struggle against the company.

Giving One's Life

Even today, when Remzija reflects on this time, she shakes her head in surprise at how they (she, her family and the other workers) were able to experiment in hope and envision the possibilities of actions. She secured Tarik's pension.

Although this gave her life a sense of stability, she and her daughters continue to struggle to get by in their day-to-day lives like their fellow Bosnians. But her hope, her decisions and her actions, motivated initially by doing something 'for Tarik', and later by 'getting justice for Tarik *and* also other workers', became a horizon of a good that she was striving towards in the years without Tarik. This shifting horizon and narrative also shows that one's notions of the good, and striving for it, are not fixed but change over time (Mattingly 2014).

Three years later, looking back at the struggle for the pension – justice – and the collaboration with other workers and their families has also transformed how Remzija reflects on Tarik's life and death and the pain she and her daughters had to endure. Retrospectively, his sudden death and the struggles, despair and suffering it engendered slowly became for Remzija a narrative of sacrifice (*žrtva*). What we can see here is again Remzija's narrative envisioning in action. Although the language of sacrifice in her narrative draws on Islamic vocabulary (Henig 2020: 72–77), Remzija came to understand Tarik's death as sacrifice in terms of achieving a greater good. As Maya Mayblin and Magnus Course remind us, sacrifice both as a trope and a practice exists also outside of strictly religious and ritual contexts. It refers to a range of situations and practices that have in common a conviction that 'something (or someone) new can be created through the irreversible giving up something else, most prominently, a life' (2014: 309). As Michael Lambek further adds, attribution of sacrifice to divergent acts and practices 'can change over time, being prospective or retrospective as well as immediate' (2014: 432–33). To acknowledge Tarik's death as sacrifice beyond the ritual context would be, as Lambek further suggests, 'to say it takes place in the interests of some larger good' (2014: 433). Indeed, the Bosnian word *žrtva* means both a victim and a sacrifice. In many respects, Tarik was a 'victim of the system', but he also sacrificed his life for others. The story of Tarik thus encompasses both meanings and shows the radical possibilities entailed in such narrative envisionings.[10] And indeed, this is also how Remzija started engaging with her own situation while she was still mourning her beloved husband. In narrating her struggles, despair and suffering, Tarik's death-as-sacrifice became narratively re-envisioned as a good that was not at the time given in the life of Remzija and her family, as well as in the lives of Tarik's former colleagues – it was a good-as-getting-justice. What carried her through the vicissitudinous years after Tarik's death was her courage to hope and to imagine that the outcomes of her actions might bring about some possible good. I saw Remzija for the last time in 2019. She had just received a text message on her mobile phone, informing her that yet another worker was successful in forcing the company to repay his missing pension insurance. I saw the spark of a smile in her face for the first time in many years. She then read the text message aloud and contemplated, 'you see how many lives his sacrifice saved.'

Conclusion

In this chapter, I traced the moments of everyday life punctuated by tragedies and suffering (the *whens*) and the practices of hope (the *hows*) emerging from these situations. I have tried to show how the entanglement of suffering and hope became generative rather than disempowering for Remzija's response to her trying circumstances. As Remzija's vicissitudinous life story illustrates, it was a transformative journey in striving for and realizing something good, which transformed along the way as well. Her striving was not oriented towards a good that would be a fixed object. Hers was good as a shifting possibility to strive for things to be otherwise. In her hopes and struggles, Remzija gathered and cultivated a patchwork of moral resources and practices that propelled her to act in relation to what she imagined and hoped for as possible. By developing and pursuing practices of hope, Remzija cultivated an ethical stance from which she was able to imagine possibilities of life beyond what she had in her current situation, and in turn she acted to realize these possibilities. In recent years, anthropological debates on the good have evolved into rather polarized and incommensurable binaries, critically portraying the focus on the good either as disentangled from the underlying 'dark' conditions, which produce inequalities, suffering and despair in the contemporary world (Kapferer and Gold 2018; Ortner 2016); or as a normative position detached from ordinary ethics of the everyday (Venkatesan et al. 2015). Yet this has never been the agenda of the original proposal for an anthropology of the good in the first place (Robbins 2013). Furthermore, as Mattingly (2010, 2014) and others showed (Knauf 2018; Rogers 2009), individual as well as collective striving for the good, and for a life worth living, is a fragile endeavour, always entangled in suffering, despair and doubt, and in which the outcomes of one's striving are uncertain. But this does not mean that we ought to dismiss these imaginings as naive, unimportant or some kind of 'false beliefs', detached from 'the rough ground of the everyday' (Al-Mohammad and Peluso 2012). On the contrary, an ethnographic inquiry into the good takes these entanglements on the rough grounds of the everyday life seriously as a point of departure for exploring what imaginings and practices of possibilities they generate at a given socio-historical juncture.

Acknowledgements

This work was supported by the Czech Science Foundation (under grant number 19-11397S).

David Henig is Associate Professor of Cultural Anthropology at Utrecht University. He is the author of *Remaking Muslim Lives: Everyday Islam in Postwar Bosnia and Herzegovina* (2020) and the co-editor of *Economies of Favour After Socialism* (2017).

Notes

1. Drawing on Aristotle, who understood courage as a moral virtue (Ethics, Book III, 127–35), Lear understands radical hope as 'an important ingredient of such courage' (2006: 107).
2. This resonates with Alain Badiou's anti-utopian writing on hope. In his book on St Paul, Badiou describes hope as a 'a simple imperative of continuation, a principle of tenacity, of obstinacy' (2003: 93) in the situations of struggle and suffering (see also Stef Jansen's work on Badiou in Jansen 2019).
3. In her wider project of narrative phenomenology, Mattingly defines narrative re-envisioning as 'the activity of coming to see oneself in a new way, coming to reform one's sense of possibility and reframe one's commitments. But it also includes the task of becoming a kind of person capable of formulating and acting upon commitments that one deems ethical' (2014: 20).
4. On the difficulties of getting the 'right' documents and 'document*ality*' of citizenship in postsocialist, postwar Bosnia and Herzegovina, see Jansen (2015); Klepal (2018); Vasilijević (2018).
5. Active hope, Jarrett Zigon writes, 'is the temporal orientation of intentional and ethical action, and is that which allows for acting in those moments of breakdown' (2009: 266).
6. The pension is about €75/month.
7. In the conversation, Remzija used *snaga* (strength) and *nada* (hope) respectively.
8. I borrow this phrase from Dyring, Mattingly and Louw (2017), who coined the term as an 'analytical lodestar' to attend to 'the fundamental question of the ethical drives in human life' (2017: 9).
9. This is unfortunately not an unusual practice for many employers in postwar BiH.
10. I am grateful to Jaroslav Klepal for this point.

References

Al-Mohammad, H., and D. Feluso. 2012. 'Ethics and the "Rough Ground" of the Everyday: The Overlappings of Life in Postinvasion Iraq', *HAU: Journal of Ethnographic Theory* 2(2): 42–58.
Back, L. 2020. 'Hope's Work' *Antipode*. Early view. Retrieved 1 April 2021 from https://doi.org/10.1111/anti.12644.
Badiou, A. 2003. *Saint Paul: The Foundation of Universalism*. Stanford: Stanford University Press.
Bryant, R., and D.M. Knight. 2019. *The Anthropology of the Future*. Cambridge: Cambridge University Press.
Carrithers, M. 2009. 'Introduction', in M. Carrithers (ed.), *Culture, Rhetoric and the Vicissitudes of Life*. Oxford: Berghahn, pp. 1–17.
Dyring, R., C. Mattingly and M. Louw. 2017. 'The Question of "Moral Engines": Introducing a Philosophical Anthropological Dialogue', in C. Mattingly, R. Dyring, M. Louw and T. Schwarz Wentzer (eds), *Moral Engines: Exploring the Ethical Drives in Human Life*. Oxford: Berghahn, pp. 9–36.
Greenberg, J. 2011. 'On the Road to Normal: Negotiating Agency and State Sovereignty in Postsocialist Serbia', *American Anthropologist* 113(1): 88–100.
Hage, G. 2009. 'Waiting Out the Crisis: On Stuckedness and Governmentality', in G. Hage (ed.), *Waiting*. Melbourne: Melbourne University Press, pp. 97–106.

———. 2012. 'Critical Anthropological Thought and the Radical Political Imaginary Today', *Critique of Anthropology* 32: 285–308.
Henig, D. 2020. *Remaking Muslim Lives: Everyday Islam in Postwar Bosnia and Herzegovina*. Urbana, Chicago: University of Illinois Press.
Jackson, M. 2013. *The Wherewithal of Life: Ethics, Migration, and the Question of Wellbeing*. Berkeley: University of California Press.
Janeja, M.K., and A. Bandak (eds). 2018. *Ethnographies of Waiting: Doubt, Hope and Uncertainty*. London: Bloomsbury.
Jansen, S. 2006. 'The Privatisation of Home and Hope: Return, Reforms and the Foreign Intervention in Bosnia-Herzegovina', *Dialectical Anthropology* 30(3): 177–99.
———. 2015. *Yearnings in the Meantime: 'Normal Lives' and the State in a Sarajevo Apartment Complex*. Oxford: Berghahn.
———. 2019. 'Anthropological (in)Fidelities to Alain Badiou', *Anthropological Theory* 19(2): 238–58.
Jašarević, L. 2017. *Health and Wealth on the Bosnian Market: Intimate Debt*. Bloomington: Indiana University Press.
Kapferer, B., and M. Gold (eds). 2018. *Moral Anthropology: A Critique*. New York and Oxford: Berghahn.
Klepal, J. 2018. '"The Only Thing I 'Earned' in the Damned War Was PTSD." Reconsidering Veteran Sociality and Politics in Bosnia and Herzegovina', *Southeast European and Black Sea Studies* 18(4): 489–507.
Knauft, B. 2018. 'Good Anthropology in Dark Times: Critical Appraisal and Ethnographic Application', *The Australian Journal of Anthropology* 30(1): 3–17.
Kurtović, L. 2015. '"Who Sows Hunger, Reaps Rage": On Protest, Indignation and Redistributive Justice in Post-Dayton Bosnia-Herzegovina', *Southeast European and Black Sea Studies* 15(4): 639–59.
Lambek, M. 2014. 'Afterthoughts on Sacrifice', *Ethnos* 79(3): 430–37.
Lear, J. 2006. *Radical Hope: Ethics in the Face of Cultural Devastation*. Cambridge, MA: Harvard University Press.
Mattingly, C. 2010. *The Paradox of Hope: Journeys through a Clinical Borderland*. Berkeley: University of California Press.
———. 2014. *Moral Laboratories: Family Peril and the Struggle for a Good Life*. Berkeley: University of California Press.
Mayblin, M., and M. Course. 2014. 'The Other Side of Sacrifice: Introduction', *Ethnos* 79(3): 307–19.
Ortner, S.B. 2016. 'Dark Anthropology and Its Others: Theory Since the Eighties', *HAU: Journal of Ethnographic Theory* 6(1): 47–73.
Robbins, J. 2013. 'Beyond the Suffering Subject: Toward an Anthropology of the Good', *Journal of the Royal Anthropological Institute* 19(3): 447–62.
Rogers, D. 2009. *The Old Faith and the Russian Land: A Historical Ethnography of Ethics in the Urals*. Ithaca: Cornell University Press.
Schielke, S. 2015. *Egypt in the Future Tense: Hope, Frustration and Ambivalence Before and After 2011*. Bloomington: Indiana University Press.
Vasiljević, J. 2018. 'Citizenship as Social Object in the Aftermath of the Yugoslav Break-Up', *Nations and Nationalism* 24(4): 1142–61.
Venkatesan, S. et al. 2015. 'There is No Such Thing as the Good: The 2013 Meeting of the Group for Debates in Anthropological Theory', *Critique of Anthropology* 35(4): 430–80.

Vitebsky, P. 2008. 'Loving and Forgetting: Moments of Inarticulacy in Tribal India', *Journal of the Royal Anthropological Institute* 14(2): 243–61.

Zigon, J. 2007. 'Moral Breakdown and the Ethical Demand: A Theoretical Framework for an Anthropology of Moralities', *Anthropological Theory* 7(2): 131–50.

———. 2009. 'Hope Dies Last: Two Aspects of Hope in Contemporary Moscow', *Anthropological Theory* 9(3): 253–71.

Part II Commentary

Maeve Cooke

Where is the good in the world? This volume invites us to consider its place in human lives, drawing our attention to the variety of ways in which a concern for the good structures, shapes and orients human agents and is embedded in everyday habits, practices, cultural and religious traditions, as well as in the various social institutions that stabilize social meanings. On a theoretical level, the volume endorses the recent ethical turn in anthropology and sociology, emphasizing the need for theorizing about the good that is at once creative and critical. Such ethically attuned theoretical approaches would open new imaginative spaces, disclosing possibilities for human lives to be other than they are, while at the same time alert to the multiple ways in which constructions of the good are interwoven with subjugating power, repression, inequality, exclusion and violence. Furthermore, they would be attentive to the plurality of conceptions of the good while addressing the question of how to discriminate evaluatively between them.

The call for such theorizing reaches beyond the disciplines of anthropology and sociology to philosophy, political science, religious studies, history, psychology, literary studies and other areas of investigation and reflection. Indeed, it speaks to everyone concerned with empirical exploration and critical thinking in relation to social change for the better.

My own philosophical approach to thinking about the good in the world has been profoundly shaped by the tradition of critical social theorizing that has come to be known as Frankfurt School critical theory – a line of theorizing that builds on the materialist twist the early Marx gave to Hegelian idealism. However, in the following I use the terms 'critical social theory' or 'critically engaged theorizing' in a broad sense to describe the kind of creative and critical theorizing about the good, based on wide-ranging, carefully conducted ethnographic and sociological studies, evidenced by the chapters in this volume.

If theorizing about the good is to remain a creative and not just reactive endeavour, its practitioners must move beyond their usual disciplinary horizons and engage in conversation with one another. Within my own theoretical horizon, the six ethnographic studies in Part Two of the volume not only confirm the salience of central motifs in Frankfurt School critical theorizing; they encourage me to move beyond existing versions of it.

To begin with, the six studies support Frankfurt School advocacy of a theoretical approach that is at once immanent and transcendent (Cooke 2006a: 37–45). Immanence refers to the anchoring of the theory's critical perspective in ethically significant, subjective experiences within actual social reality that feed into the ethical conduct of everyday life. Transcendence refers to the theory's position that projections of an alternative, better society cannot rest content with actually existing ideas of what constitutes a good life and the kind of society necessary for this; rather, they must reckon with the possibility that the actually existing ideas are ethically objectionable (ideological, partial, authoritarian, etc.). It also refers to the theory's universal reach: its claim to a validity that extends beyond a given context of inquiry to all humans, irrespective of sociocultural and historical considerations.

In the iterations of Frankfurt School critical theory by its second- and third-generation proponents, the immanence of their approach is the basis for claims to be 'postmetaphysical'. I do not fully embrace the postmetaphysical stance taken by thinkers such as Jürgen Habermas, Axel Honneth and Rainer Forst (Habermas 1992; Honneth 1995, Forst 2012; for a critique of Habermas' interpretation of 'postmetaphysical', see Cooke 2019: 75–78; Cooke 2021). Nonetheless, I endorse what I call their non-authoritarian impulse, a rejection of the imposition of a particular view of the ethically good life on individual agents in a way that prevents any questioning of its validity (Cooke 2006a: 16–17). Ethical authoritarianism is closely connected with epistemological authoritarianism, an exercise of authority that asserts the indisputable truth of assertions, again denying those subjected to it the freedom to interrogate their validity.

Alongside its assertion of an immanent perspective, Frankfurt School critical theory claims a context-transcending power, which is the basis for its claim to rationality and corresponding universal reach (Cooke 1994). For Habermas and many of his successors, the theory's claim to rationality is based on a reconstruction of general features of human practices. In Habermas' case, a reconstruction of the communicative use of language (Habermas 1984, 1987), and in Honneth's case, a reconstruction of the general human expectation of, and need for, intersubjective recognition (Honneth 1995). In the critical theories of Habermas and Honneth, these reconstructions provide the basis for purely *formal* conceptions of the good life and good society that are agnostic as to the merits of specific conceptions. Their formalist approach to the good is continued today by other theorists in the tradition, such as Martin Seel (1995), Rainer Forst (2012) and Rahel Jaeggi (2018). (I say more about this below.)

The six case studies provide strong ethnographic support for the Frankfurt School motif of immanent transcendence, showing in various ways how a concern for the good is entailed in the self-other relations of ordinary life – a concern that extends beyond personal interest and the interests of a particular community. It also extends beyond the present towards future rewards and possibilities. This is evident especially in Strhan's and Sheldon's chapters, based respectively on field work in London at a conservative evangelical church and an ultra-orthodox Jewish children's centre. It is also a theme that emerges in Shillitoe's study of collective worship in English primary schools. It is apparent, too, in Henig's chapter based on fieldwork in postwar Bosnia and Herzegovina, which shows how traumatic experiences of destruction, loss and injustice led Remzija and her daughters to conduct their lives within a horizon of hope, making them receptive to future new possibilities radically transcending those available to them at the time.

However, the case studies also challenge contemporary Frankfurt School theories in two connected respects. They call into question the resolutely *formal* approach to the good adopted today by its leading exponents and, closely connected with this, the *negative* perspective on society that continues to be a striking feature of theories in this tradition.

In a variety of ways, contemporary theorists such as Habermas, Honneth, Seel, Forst and Jaeggi maintain that theorizing should be confined to identifying the formal characteristics of possible good lives and good societies. Speaking generally, by 'formal' they mean features of human experiences or practices that are not coloured by specific values. Thus, for example, Habermas' theory of moral validity is concerned only to identify the formal properties of morally valid principles: it holds that such principles must be universalizable and arrived at by way of an argumentative procedure that is oriented towards truth and satisfies demanding conditions of equality and inclusivity. It holds back from evaluating the moral validity of all concrete articulations of the principles in question by individuals or groups. In consequence, it is not concerned with 'thick issues' of identity and self-realization. This abstinence in ethical matters extends to his theory as a whole, which he insists must remain agnostic regarding the validity of the substantive content of specific ideas of the good life or good society (Habermas 1992: 14–15).

I see this formalist self-understanding as part of the negativist stance that, with rare exceptions, Frankfurt School theories have always adopted in their critiques of the social conditions of their times (Honneth 2008: 785). Rather than directing attention towards positive elements in existing social reality that are conducive to progressive social change, theories in this tradition seek to highlight how social structures, institutions and relations *violate* the social conditions for actualizing the good – for living a good life in society. Admittedly, such negativism could be viewed merely as a matter of emphasis. In *Re-Presenting the Good Society* (Cooke 2006a), I advise interpreting it in this way, pointing out that critique of the prevailing social conditions is inescapably bound to ideas of the good society, both on the side of the theory and on the side of those to whom the theory speaks, although these ideas are often implicit. For, lacking any utopian projection of what a good society would look like, the theorist's critique would lack motivating power. I contend that a critical social theory's motivating power depends in significant measure on its ability to engage the imagination of its addressees through evoking representations of a good society, whether these take the form of vivid examples or remain indeterminate and inchoate. However, this is not as a rule acknowledged by contemporary Frankfurt School theorists.

Their negativist approach can be explained in part by a suspicion of utopian thinking and consequent reluctance to evoke determinate pictures of an alternative society. For some contemporary theorists, positive projections of what it would mean to lead a good life or live in a good society run the risk of a kind of moralism that reflects the smug self-satisfaction and complacency of Western liberal-democratic societies. In such cases, the negative orientation is driven by a commendable concern to respect the diverging and possibly conflicting ideas of the good held by individuals and groups. The cost, however, is the diminished motivating power of their theories. In my book I argue that such theories are wrong to attribute the problems besetting utopian thinking to the pictures of the good it evokes (Cooke 2006a: 161–88). I claim that critical theories can avoid moralism and other unwelcome consequences, and take account of value pluralism, even if they project substantive ideas of better lives and better societies (on value pluralism, see Cooke 2020; cf. Robbins 2013). In support of this argument, I show that ethical authoritarianism is not an inevitable consequence of evoking pictures of a good life in a good society. If critically engaged social theories self-reflexively acknowledge the imaginary – fictive – status of their projections of a determinate good, and open them to contestation and revision, they can avoid this danger (Cooke 2006a).

In sum, a formalist, negativist stance is not necessary to avoid bad utopianism and moralism and to acknowledge and respect the diversity in human societies of ideas of the good. In any case, as indicated above, pure formalism is not possible. Formalism is merely a matter of degree: there is no sharp dividing line between formal and substantive conceptions of the good for human beings, since even highly formal conceptions of the good life and good society must have some determinate content; otherwise they would be unable to arouse the ethical imagination and lack motivating power.

Since a formalist approach to the good is neither necessary, possible or desirable, I urge contemporary critical social theories to explicitly acknowledge their substantive ethical commitments. For, when critical social theories suppress or obscure their own ethical concerns, they hinder robust interrogation of the validity of these concerns and are vulnerable to the accusation of ethical authoritarianism. Thus, my call is issued in the name of the same non-authoritarian impulse that leads Habermas in the opposite direction, prompting him towards formalism and advocacy of ethical abstinence as regards the validity of the substance of specific ideas of the good. Ironically, he thereby falls prey to the very danger his formalist approach seeks to avoid.

In the context of critically engaged social theorizing, advocacy of ethical abstinence is troubling for a further reason. This relates to the question of societal change for the better and the practices of self-cultivation and self-transformations of self that may be required to achieve it. Such practices are oriented by a concern for the good in a substantial sense – with the specific content of ideas of the good as they are incorporated in the everyday lives of concrete human beings. If, as I have proposed elsewhere, there is an intimate relationship between self-transformation and societal transformation (Cooke 2020), critically engaged theorists must explore the complexities of this relationship and pay attention to its implications for the question of *praxis*. Ethically abstinent approaches, which disregard the substantiality of the good, do not do this.

In light of this position of ethical abstinence, it is noteworthy that transformation through *praxis* has always been a central component of the Frankfurt School approach (Cooke 2006a: 9–24). Its critical diagnoses of existing social reality are coupled with emancipatory projections of a transformed society – of alternative, better, social conditions in which the theory's normative aim, typically freedom or happiness for all individuals, could be actualized. A distinctive feature of Frankfurt School theories is that they call for transformation through intentional human action. Indebted to Marx rather than Hegel in this respect, they posit a close connection between theory and human activity aimed at changing social conditions for the better in an ethical sense – between theory and *praxis*. By way of concrete struggles and interventions, human agents must endeavour fundamentally to change the social conditions that impede their development as free or happy human beings. A further distinguishing feature is that they call for fundamental transformation of consciousness as part of the emancipatory struggle: transformation of the prevailing social arrangements is held to demand transformation of perceptions of what constitutes truly valid needs and interests. The classic formulation of this position is the Marxist thesis of ideology as systemically induced false consciousness. Its proponents hold that humans who suffer from the effect of certain social conditions may be unaware either of the *causes* of their suffering or *that* they are suffering; moreover, they are likely to be oblivious to the *systemic* or *structural* obstacles blocking this awareness. This view is prominent in first-generation Frankfurt School theory: Adorno and Horkheimer's *Dialectic of Enlightenment* expresses it emphatically (Horkheimer and Adorno 2002). In the meantime, however, this conception of ideology has fallen into disrepute (Cooke 2006b), and most contemporary theorists in the Frankfurt School tradition do not subscribe to it. Indeed, from Habermas' *Theory of Communicative Action* onwards, which disputes the relevance of *any* idea of ideology as false consciousness for analysis of advanced capitalism (Habermas 1984, 1987), few theorists have seriously engaged with the relationship between transformation of consciousness and emancipatory transformation of society.

I see a close connection between lack of attention to the importance of transformation of perceptions in the effort to achieve a better society and advocacy of ethical formalism. Theories concerned with the *substance* of the good, with the specific content that the idea of the good has for particular individual humans, consider the ways in which the good impacts on the consciousness, affects, behaviour and life-conduct of these individuals in their everyday lives. Theories concerned with evaluating the substance of the good must, in addition, take a position on the validity of these ways of relating cognitively, affectively and behaviourally to self and others, and to the world in general. By contrast, theories that adopt a *formalist* approach to questions of the good remain normatively indifferent to the substantiality of the good – to concern for the good as it plays out concretely in human lives in the real world. Correlatively, they pay no attention to the question of the kinds of fundamental cognitive, affective and behavioural changes required for the purposes of the fundamental transformation of social conditions that they envisage. Similar tendencies are evident in disciplines such as sociology and anthropology, where a reluctance to take a position in matters of ethical validity has contributed to neglect of the question of self-transformation (Cooke 2020). Moving away from a position of ethical abstinence enables attentiveness not only to the ways in which a concern for the good structures, shapes and orients human agents but also to the question of how societal transformation is connected with self-transformation, and the self-cultivation that contributes to this. It is important to notice that the movement is never straightforwardly in one direction only. Changes in social conditions may lead to self-transformation, and self-transformation may lead to changes in social conditions. However, from the point of view of Frankfurt School critical theory, which emphasizes the *struggle* for emancipation, one would expect the movement from self-transformation to societal transformation to be of special importance. But – due to its disregard for the substantiality of the good – it tends to overlook the importance of fundamental self-transformation, paying little attention to the ways in which practices of self-formation and self-cultivation may be required in order to achieve a better society. Nor is it attentive to the ways in which such practices are used to reproduce troubling power hierarchies, to deepen social inequalities and to increase social exclusions. The ethnographic case studies in this volume, through their attentiveness to the substantiality of the good, help to make good these deficiencies. They draw attention to a variety of contexts in which a concern to realize the good is explicitly connected with practices of self-cultivation and self-transformation; in addition, some of the studies show how such practices can be exploited for purposes that run contrary to the normative aims of critically engaged social theorizing.

All six studies show how concern for the good in a substantive sense is bound up with practices of self-cultivation and self-transformation. The goods in question are what Charles Taylor calls 'hypergoods', which are a source of general orientation and concrete guidance for specific human subjects in their endeavours to lead ethically good lives (Taylor 1989: 63–67; see also Cooke 2018). Hypergoods are held to be incomparably more important than other goods, providing a standard from which these must be evaluated (examples are 'beauty', 'divine love' or 'justice'). Thus, Shillitoe's study of collective worship in school assemblies places it in the context of moral visions for the betterment of society, showing how it cultivates children's subjectivities in accordance with the dreams, wishes and desires the educators (and parents) have for the social world. In Strhan's study, members of the evangelical church community are required to work on their selves in order to overcome divisions within themselves between materialist capitalist desire and spiritual desire for salvation through grace and divine love. In Sheldon's study, it is the ethnographer who works on herself, overcoming her deeply-rooted prejudices against the rigidity and closure of ultra-orthodox Jewish conceptions of the good, leading to a transformation of her moral vision that enables her to recognize in these conceptions an ethics that is radically open to the unknown.

The studies also contribute in a second respect to theoretical reflection on the question of formation, cultivation and transformation of selves from the point of view of societal transformation. They do so negatively, by showing how practices of self-cultivation and self-transformation serve the reproduction of subjugating and repressive power hierarches and are manipulated by corporate interests that promote the inequalities, exclusions and forms of violence generated by contemporary global capitalism. Lynch's study of the response of institutionalized Christianity to child sexual abuse by the clergy and religious shows how vocabularies of sin and redemption are used to interpret abusive behaviour as a failing in spiritual formation that requires an intra-institutional response in terms of forgiveness through divine love rather than criminal persecution. Through prayer, worship, confession and other devotional practices, abusers are enjoined to engage in a process of moral transformation that will lead them to accept the need for submission to God's will if they are to achieve divine forgiveness. Just as God will forgive the abusers' sins if they embark on the requisite journey of moral transformation, their victims, too, are urged to act in the spirit of divine love and to forgive those who abuse them. Lynch points out that this prevents the victims from developing moral vocabularies that would permit them to interpret their experiences as moral violations and discourages them from seeking legal reparations.

The pernicious side of an emphasis on self-cultivation and self-transformation is also prominent in Chong's account of the construction of new forms of corporate personhood, based on her fieldwork inside the China arm of a global management consultancy. Here an ethos of corporate social responsibility is used to socialize employees into a particular vision of the good that intensifies rather than ameliorates social inequalities and exclusions. Company initiatives such as a three-day bike ride across Sichuan province are presented to employees as a means of helping to alleviate local suffering but are in fact designed to bring about a kind of self-knowledge that takes the corporation's values as its normative framework. Chong recounts how the bike ride in which she participated was planned as a series of revelatory moments, disclosing to employees the limits of their capabilities, their position in social hierarchies and in general their strengths and weaknesses as employees. Furthermore, although sold to employees as an opportunity to 'experience the other' through empathetic encounters with locals, and as a means for altruistic charitable giving that would alleviate the effects of a devastating earthquake in the province, the careful staging of the bike ride served to reinforce the employees' prejudices about the backwardness of the local communities, fostering an ethics of inequality and exclusion, and did not in fact benefit these communities materially.

Lynch's and Chong's studies show that the call for self-cultivation and self-transformation can be exploited in ways that reproduce and strengthen pernicious power hierarchies. If, as I claim, societal transformation may require such 'work on the self', this creates a dilemma for critically engaged social theorizing. Lynch stresses the importance of relentless and thorough-going self-reflexivity, in which the members of specificommunities would engage in constant questioning and reinterpretation of the moral meanings of the key concepts at play in their pursuit of the good. To this we may add the need for explicit acknowledgement by the communities involved of the ways in which interpretations of meanings are mediated by authority figures, together with an openness to questioning the rational justification for claims to authority, both on the side of the authority figures and those over whom they exercise their authoritative power.

Certainly, critically engaged social theorizing should encourage self-reflexivity and the rational contestation of claims to authority. On occasion, however, this may not be enough. Sometimes, fundamental societal transformation calls for a fundamental *reimagining* of what it means to lead an ethically good life, and for corresponding new moral meanings. Henig's study of Remzija's self-transformation in postwar Bosnia and Herzegovina is helpful here. It focuses on her cultivation and practice of an attitude of 'radical hope'. The hope is radical in the sense that it constitutes a moral project of creating a new field of possibilities amidst the dire circumstances of the present moment, in which it is impossible even to imagine what these might be (Lear 2006). It seems to me that at certain times in history – and perhaps we are living through one of these times – critically engaged social theorists, too, must endeavour to become creative makers of meaningful space. In other words, they must strive to combine empirical investigations and rigorous intellectual analysis with poetic imagination.

Maeve Cooke is Full Professor of Philosophy at University College Dublin, Ireland and a member of the Royal Irish Academy. She has published two monographs in critical social theory: *Language and Reason: A Study of Habermas's Pragmatics* (MIT Press, 1994) and *Re-Presenting the Good Society* (MIT Press, 2006) and is the author of many articles in the areas of social and political philosophy. She is on the editorial board of several scholarly journals and has held visiting appointments at leading universities in the USA and Europe.

References

Cooke, M. 1994. *Language and Reason: A Study of Habermas's Pragmatics*. Cambridge, MA: MIT Press.
———. 2006a. *Re-Presenting the Good Society*. Cambridge, MA: MIT Press.
———. 2006b. 'Resurrecting the Rationality of Ideology Critique: Reflections on Laclau on Ideology', *Constellations* 13(1): 4–19.
———. 2018. 'Higher Goods and Common Goods: Strong Evaluation in Social Life', *Philosophy and Social Criticism* 44(7): 767–70.
———. 2019. 'Discourse Ethics', in P.E. Gordon, E. Hammer and A. Honneth (eds), *The Routledge Companion to the Frankfurt School*. New York: Routledge, pp. 65–81.
———. 2020. 'Disobedience in Civil Regeneration: Radical Transformations in The Civil Sphere', in J. C. Alexander, T. Stack and F. Khosrokhavar (eds.), *Breaching the Civil Order*. Cambridge: Cambridge University Press, pp. 235–60.
———. 2021. 'Existentially Lived Truth or Communicative Reason? Habermas' Critique of Kierkegaard', *Constellations* 28(1): 51–59.
Forst, R. 2012. *The Right to Justification: Elements of a Constructivist Theory of Justice*, trans. J. Flynn. New York: Columbia University Press.
Habermas, J. 1984 and 1987. *The Theory of Communicative Action*, trans. T. McCarthy. Cambridge, MA: MIT Press.
———. 1992. *Postmetaphysical Thinking*, trans. W.M. Hohengarten. Cambridge, MA: MIT Press.
Honneth, A. 1995. *The Struggle for Recognition: The Moral Grammar of Social Conflicts*, trans. J. Anderson. Cambridge: Polity Press.
———. 2008. 'Critical Theory', in D. Moran (ed.), *The Routledge Companion to Twentieth Century Philosophy*. London and New York: Routledge, pp. 784–813.
Horkheimer, M., and T.W. Adorno. 2002. *Dialectic of Enlightenment: Philosophical Fragments*, trans. E. Jephcott. Stanford, CA: Stanford University Press.
Jaeggi, R. 2018. *Critique of Forms of Life*, trans. C. Cronin. Cambridge, MA: Harvard University Press.
Lear, J. 2006. *Radical Hope: Ethics in the Face of Cultural Devastation*. Cambridge, MA: Harvard University Press.
Marcuse, H. 1970. *Five Lectures: Psychoanalysis, Politics, and Utopia*, trans. J. Shapiro and S. Weber. Boston: Beacon Press.
Marx. K., and F. Engels. 1967. *The Communist Manifesto*. Harmondsworth: Penguin Books.

Robbins, J. 2013. 'Monism, Pluralism, and the Structure of Value Relation: A Dumontian Contribution to the Contemporary Study of Value', *HAU: Journal of Ethnographic Theory* 3(1): 99–115.

Seel, M. 1995. *Versuch über die Form des Glücks: Studien zur Ethik*. Frankfurt am Main: Suhrkamp.

Taylor, C. 1989. *Sources of the Self*. Cambridge, MA: Harvard University Press.

Wellmer, A. 1985. 'Reason, Utopia, and the *Dialectic of Enlightenment*', in R. Bernstein (ed.), *Habermas and Modernity*. Cambridge: Polity Press, pp. 35–66.

Index

Abbott, O. 13–14, 19, 20, 194
   commentary on 114
Abend, G. 10–11, 14, 15
acceptance and belonging, moral decision making and 71–2
activism, 1960s Europe 92, 95, 96–7
'activist anthropologist' role 9
adaptiveness/flexibility 50–1
Addams, J. 11–12, 85, 88
aesthetic and ethical judgment 53
aesthetic/ideational approaches vs scientific facts/truths 4–5
African Americans 12, 218, 219
Agamben, G. 80
agony of 'the good'. *See* social suffering
ambiguous others 205–7
American Sociological Association 14
Anscombe, E. 94
anthropologies of the good 3–10, 16–19, 110–12
   theoretical perspectives 35–44, 79–83
Aristotle 17, 47, 48, 49
Austin, J. 55
Australia: child sexual abuse in Christian Church 123–4, 133, 135
authenticity, valuing 193–4
auto-ethnography 91–3
   Durkheim, morality and social theory 96–9
   everyday ethics: cross-generational and gendered perspective 99–102
   gender, difference and the Good 102–5
   memories and genealogies 93–6

Back, L. 16
Bargheer, S. 20
Barnes, B. 62
Bauman, Z. 13, 65–7, 72
Beck, C. 184
'being for the other' 65–6
Bellah, R. et al. 14
belonging and acceptance, moral decision making and 71–2
Benhabib, S. 19–20, 64, 67
Bible 162, 167, 169–70
bike rides. *See* corporate social responsibility (CSR) and management consultancy projects, China
Blum, L. 95
Bosnia and Herzegovina, post-war struggles 216–17
   pre-war life and post-war changes 220–4
   radical hope 224–9
   radical hope as practice of possibilities 217–19
   summary and conclusion 230
Boston, Catholic Church 123
Boston Consulting Group 145
Bourdieu, P. 41–2, 83–5, 88
Brown, P. 167, 173, 174–5

Cabot, H. 6–7
Calhoun, C. 12
Callon, M. 146
Campbell, D. 81
'capabilities approach' 117
capitalism
   global and 'connected capitalism' 155–6
   and Protestantism 163, 164

See also Evangelicals, London; neoliberalism
care, gendered relations of 20
care/techniques of self 17
and others 19–20, 81, 191–2
caregiving/care in practice 77–8, 85, 86–7
Carrithers, M. 222, 224
Carter, A. 169
Cassaniti, J. and Hickman, J. 82
Cavell, S. 18, 49–50, 175–6, 192
Chakrabarty, D. 2
charitable giving
China 149–50, 156
See also Evangelicals, London
child protection procedures 135
child sexual abuse in Christian church 123–6
moral transactions of sin and redemption 126–31
theological responses and limits of moral reflexivity 131–5
children
corporate social responsibility (CSR) project, China 148–9, 150
See also school assemblies
Christianity 105
See also child sexual abuse in Christian Church; Evangelicals, London; school assemblies
citizenship. *See* corporate social responsibility (CSR) and management consultancy projects, China
collective effervescence 39–41
colonization of life worlds 53–4
complicity in violence 54–5
confession and disclosure: child sexual abuse in Christian Church 133–4
conflict and compromise
humanitarian ideals in practice 82
value experience as 42–3
Connolly, W. 164
consciousness-raising 99, 100, 103
contentment and generosity: Evangelicalism 171–3
contextualization 52–3
conversion and proselytizing: Evangelicalism 166, 168
Cooke, M. 20
corporate social responsibility (CSR) and management consultancy projects, China 141–3
corporate citizenship and performance of morality 146–9
fieldwork inside reflexive management production 143–6
management production 143–6
performing 'global' morality 149–52
providing 'high-level experience' 152–6
summary and conclusion 156–7
critical (social) theory 20–1
Frankfurt School 139, 234–8
immanent and transcendent 235–6
cross-disciplinary interventions/ interdisciplinary approach 2, 93–5, 101
Crossley, N. 61, 62, 66–7
Crow nation and Plenty Coups, US 218
cultural difference 5, 7
cultural and historical perspectives 54
culture
corporate/organizational 143, 144–6
and language 95
and nature 96, 104

dark anthropology 6–7, 8–9, 110, 125, 142, 230
Darwall, S. 116
Das, V. 18, 52, 54–5, 92, 112, 190–1, 202–3, 210–11
demarcation problem 111–12
desires and values 36–7. *See also* subjective and objective values
Diamond, C. 52, 53, 112
Dill, J. and Davison Hunter, J. 184
diversity
of individual/within person values 41–3
vs suffering 110–11
'doing good' 80
'double hermeneutics' 1
double-consciousness 12
'Dreyfus affair', France 97
Du Bois, W.E.B. 12, 22
dualistic moral theorizing, critique of 63–7
Dumont, L. 4–5, 7, 42, 105
Durkheim, E. 10, 12, 39–41, 63–5, 67–8, 71, 72, 96–8, 105, 183–4
commentary on 114–15

Education Reform Act (1988), UK 180–1
Elisha, O. 165
embodied experience 70, 77, 87
embodied method of enquiry. *See* Jewish ethnography and feminine dress code
embodied practices 17, 54, 193
emotional distress/personal issues of researchers 85–6, 100–2, 105
epistemological shifts 4–5, 6–8
error theory 37
ethical abstinence 238, 239
ethical action, judgment and knowledge 47–8
ethical authoritarianism 235, 237
ethical life, perspectives on 46–56, 111–14
'ethical turn' in anthropology 8–10, 111–12
European 'refugee crisis' 6
evaluative and final goods 49
Evangelicals, London 161–3
   celestial city and language of commerce 165–8
   good, bad and study of 163–5
   'maximizing resources' and snare of Mammon 168–73
   summary and conclusion 173–4
Evans-Pritchard, E.E. 94–5
everyday ethics
   consciousness-raising and 103
   cross-generational and gendered perspective 99–102
   school assemblies 185–90
   See also ordinary ethics
exemplary persons, encounters with 42–3
experience and language 94, 103

Faith and Order Commission of the Church of England: *Faith and Reconciliation in the Aftermath of Abuse* 131–3
false consciousness 238
family obligations 64–5, 67, 71–2
family secrets 70
family suffering. *See* Bosnia and Herzegovina, post-war struggles
Farmer, P. 85–6
Fassin, D. 80, 82, 164

Faubion, J. 49
'fax' model of socialization 41–2
feminine dress. *See* Jewish ethnography and feminine dress code
feminism 20, 98, 99, 102–4
fictionalism 37
final goods 49
financial hardship. *See* Bosnia and Herzegovina, post-war struggles
Finch, J. 64, 71
   and Mason, J. 71
flexibility/adaptiveness 50–1
flourishing 21, 116–17
forgiveness and repentance: child sexual abuse in Christian Church 131–2
formalism 237, 239
'forms of life' 95–6
Foucault, M. 17, 80, 81, 82, 91, 92, 94, 99, 171, 191
fragility and notion of 'normal life' 220
France
   anti-Semitism 97–8
   May '68 protest, Paris 98
Frankfurt School 139, 234–8
friendship and kindness 191–2
functional and final goods 49
functionalism 12–13, 63–4, 96, 98

Gadamer, H.-G. 47–8, 48
Geertz, C. 95, 110–11
gender
   and cross-generational everyday ethics 99–102
   difference and the Good 102–5
   relations of care 20
   See also Jewish ethnography and feminine dress code
generosity and contentment: Evangelicalism 171–3
Giddens, A. 1, 13
global and 'connected capitalism' 155–6
'global' morality, performing 149–52
Goffman, E. 69–70, 115
The Golden House (Rushdie) 1
Golder, B. 81
Graeber, D. 4, 7, 8, 38

Habermas, J. 53–4, 235, 236, 237, 238
habitus 41–2
happiness and suffering 46–7, 110

Haynes, N. 164–5
health interventions and issues 77–8, 80, 86–7
  war injuries and related problems 221, 223, 224
Herman, B. 68
Hermann, J. 68–9
Hitlin, S. and Vaisey, S. 12–13, 15–16, 60, 64, 68, 182
Hohenlohe, A. 100–2
Holdsworth, C. and Morgan, D. 71–2
Holocaust/Shoah 65, 100–2, 104–5, 209
Honneth, A. 235, 236
hope 2, 3, 8, 16. *See also* Bosnia and Herzegovina, post-war struggles; practices of hope; radical hope
Hsu, C. 149–50
human flourishing 21, 116–17
humanitarianism 80–1, 82, 83, 175
hypergoods 239–40

ideational/aesthetic approach vs scientific facts/truths 4–5
ideology as false consciousness 238
idolatry 51
immanent and transcendent critical theory 235–6
incommensurability 25, 51, 53 55, 156, 175, 230
individualism and collectivism
  Evangelicalism 167–8
  See also relational sociology
individuals, diversity of values within 41–3
intellectual vs metaphysical perspectives on ethical life 47–8, 51–3
interdisciplinary approach/cross-disciplinary interventions 2, 93–5, 101
intersubjectivity
  child sexual abuse in Christian Church 130–1
  See also entries beginning relational
ISIS and Nazis analogy 206

Jackson, M. 18, 19, 219
Jansen, S. 220
Jenks, C. 183, 184
Jewish ethnography and feminine dress code 200–2, 210–11

ambiguous others as threats to the ordinary 205–7
the transcendent in the ordinary 207–10
violence of the Good 202–5
Jewish identity/race
  early Christianity 126–7
  France 97–8
  Holocaust/Shoah 65, 100–2, 104–5, 209
Joas, H. 65, 72
judgment
  aesthetic and ethical 53
  ethical 17, 23, 47–8, 111–12; moral 12, 13, 19
  practical 17, 48, 53, 56
  psychoanalytic insight and 48

Kant, I. 96, 104, 105, 176
Keane, W. 10, 26n7, 112, 113, 115
kindness and friendship 191–2
Kleinman, A. 82, 85
  Wilkinson, I. and 77, 86
Klenk, M. 112
Knauft, B. 9
knowledge
  epistemological shifts 4–5, 6–8
  ethical action, judgement and 47–8
  managerial 143–4, 146
Korsgaard, C. 49

Laidlaw, J. 16–17, 54–5, 81, 82, 99, 111–12, 114
Lambek, M. 10, 17, 99, 111, 163, 164, 168, 174, 175, 185, 193, 229
language
  and cultures 95
  Evangelicals and commerce 165–8
  and experience 94, 103
  and ordinary ethics 17–18, 49–50
  ordinary language philosophy 17–18, 92, 95–6, 202
Laugier, S. 49
Lear, J. 217–18, 225–6
legal obligations and Christianity 135, 180–1
liturgical order 50–1
Lorde, A. 104
Lucy Faithfull Foundation 129
Lukes, S. 12, 95, 164
Lynch, G. 184, 186–7

MacIntyre, A. 115
McKenna, C. 145
Mackie, J. 37
McKinsey 145
Mair, J. 91, 99, 100, 102
Malkki, L. 175
management consultancy. *See* corporate social responsibility (CSR) and management consultancy projects, China
Mandelbaum, M.H. 70
Mannheim, K. 38
Martineau, H. 10–11
Marx, K. 97, 238
Marxist/neo-Marxist approaches 5, 13, 98
masculinity 96, 99, 103–4
Mattingly, C. 17, 18–19, 182, 187, 192, 218, 219, 225–6, 227, 228, 229
  and Throop, J. 17, 18–19, 21
Mayall, B. 183
Mayblin, M. and Course, M. 229
Mead, G.H. 20, 62
metaethical philosophy 37
metaphysical vs intellectual perspectives on ethical life 47–8, 51–3
migration 6
Mittermaier.A. 166–7
Moody-Adams, M. 116
moral decision making 71–2
moral facts 63, 114, 115
morality
  childhood, education and 183–5
  Durkheim and social theory 96–9
  and ethics 113
  performance of (*see* corporate social responsibility (CSR) and management consultancy projects, China)
  in practice 67–72
  science of 10–12
Morgan, M. 66, 67
Muehlebach, A. 175
Muslim(s)
  –Jewish relations 201–2, 209
  family suffering (*see* Bosnia and Herzegovina, post-war struggles)

naturalist argument for goodness 48–50, 56

nature
  and culture 96, 104
  and sacred 50–1
Nazism 164
  Holocaust/Shoah 65, 100–2, 104–5, 209
  and ISIS analogy 206
negativism 237
neoliberalism 5, 6, 8, 9, 80, 110, 163–4, 173
Nietzsche, F. 19, 115
N'kang's girls' puberty ritual 40
non-governmental transnational organizations 80
nowhere and everywhere 46–56, 111–14
Nussbaum, M. 117

objective and subjective values 37–44
obligations
  family 64–5, 67, 71–2
  legal 135, 180–1
ordinary, threats to and transcendent in 205–10
ordinary ethics 17–18, 49–50, 92, 202, 203–4. *See also* everyday ethics
ordinary language philosophy 17–18, 92, 95–6, 202
ordinary moral competence and expectations of others 68–72
organizational culture 145
Ortner, S. 6, 8–9, 22, 110
'other worlds' 5
other(s) 6
  ambiguous 205–7
  'being for the other' 65–6
  care of self and 19–20, 81, 191–2
  expectations of 68–72
  oriented motivation to act 226–7

Parsons, T. 12–13, 184
paternalism/patriarchy
  child sexual abuse in Christian Church 126
  corporate social responsibility (CSR), China 151–2
personal is political idea 102, 103
personal issues/emotional distress of researchers 85–6, 100–2, 105
phenomenological approaches 18–19
philosophy
  and anthropology 9–10, 16–19

and social theory 16–22
See also specific philosophies and philosophers
Plato 4, 47
Plummer, K. 2
post-structuralism 94, 104
  feminist 103
postulates 50–51
practical judgment 48, 53, 55
practices of hope 226–7
pragmatist philosophy 20
pre-social morality 65–7
processual/relational approaches 62–3
proselytizing and conversion: Evangelicalism 166, 168
Protestant/Anglican Church
  child sexual abuse and report 123–4, 131–3
  St Peter's primary school 180, 181, 186–8, 190, 191–2, 193–4
psychoanalytic insight and judgement 48

queer ontology/values 37, 38–9, 40
queer theory 104

race and racism
  African Americans 12, 213, 219
  feminism 103
  See also entries beginning Jewish
radical hope. *See* Bosnia and Herzegovina, post-war struggles
Radical Philosophy group 93, 95–6
Rappaport, R. 39, 50–1, 193
'real world' and dark anthropology 6–7
reality of the good, critique of 35–6
reflexivity
  management production 143–6
  moral, limits of 131–5
  self-critical 82, 83–6
relational perspective 19–20. *See also* other(s)
relational sociology 60–3
  critique of dualistic moral theorizing 63–7
  and morality in practice 67–72
  summary and conclusion 72–3
relativism 8, 52–53, 111
repentance and forgiveness: child sexual abuse in Christian Church 131–2

researchers
  caregiving/care in practice 77–8, 85, 86–7
  emotional distress/personal issues of 85–6, 100–2, 105
  resistance and activism 9
rituals
  Christian 127
  confession 133–4
  sacred/liturgical order 50–1
  school assemblies 191, 193
  and values 39–41, 42–3
Robbins, J. 2–3, 6, 7–8, 9, 18, 46, 79–80, 105, 163, 185, 210–11, 218–19
  commentary on 110, 111, 113
Roman Catholic Church
  child sexual abuse in 123, 124, 133, 135
  Sacred Heart Academy 181, 188–90, 191, 192
Rouse, J. 69
Rushdie, S. 1, 2
Rylko-Bauer, B. et al. 86–7

sacrifice 229
sanctification 50–1
'savage slot' and 'suffering slot' 6
Sayer, A. 12, 19, 21
Schein, E. 145
Schinkel, W. 84
school assemblies 180–3
  authenticity, valuing 193–4
  childhood, education and morality 183–5
  exploring the good and the everyday 185–90
  ordinary ethics 190–2
  summary and conclusion 194–5
science of morality 10–12
scientific facts/truths vs ideational/ aesthetic approach 4–5
scientific rationalism 97
scientific and technical knowledge 48
scientific worldview vs values 37–8
self-transformation and societal transformation 238–41
Sen, A. 117
Sennett, R. 165
sexual abuse. *See* child sexual abuse in Christian Church

Shamir, R. 146
Shoah/Holocaust 65, 100–2, 104–5, 209
sin and redemption. *See* child sexual abuse in Christian Church
Singer, M. 86–7
Skultans, V. 87
Smart, C. 70
 and Neale, B. 71
Smith, P. 115
'social fact', morality as 63
social narratives and values 42–3
social phenomena 61–2, 63, 68
social suffering 77–9
 critique of social science approach 83–6
 'the good' debate 79–83
 See also suffering/'suffering subject'
social theory and philosophy 16–22
socialization, childhood 184, 186–7
societal transformation, self-transformation and 238–41
sociology of moral life: 'old' and 'new' 10–16, 19–22
special school: Holly Oak 181, 188, 190
Stivers, R. 13
students
 activism, 1960s Europe 92, 95, 96–7
 corporate social responsibility (CSR), China 148
subjective and objective values 37–44
suffering/'suffering subject' 6, 7–8, 35, 79–80
 vs diversity 110–11
 and happiness/well-being 46–7
 and radical hope (*see* Bosnia and Herzegovina, post-war struggles)
 See also social suffering
survivors/victims of child sexual abuse in Christian Church 130–1
Switzerland: happiness study 46–7
synagogue attendance 201, 205, 206–7

tact 69, 70
Taylor, C. 95, 113, 239–40
technical and scientific knowledge 48
techniques of self. *See* care/techniques of self
theoretical perspectives 35–44, 79–83
Thrift, N. 143, 146
Tolstoy, L. 110

Torah 209, 211
transcendent and immanent critical theory 235–6
transcendent in the ordinary 207–10
transcendental vs 'ordinary ethics' 17–18
Trouillot, M.-R. 6
trust: child sexual abuse in Christian Church 128, 134
truth(s)
 and falsity 51
 scientific facts vs ideational/aesthetic approach 4–5
Turner, V. 40

undecidability 56
unity, value of 40
universality/universalism
 goodness 1
 moral theory, critiques of 10–11, 19–20
 suffering 7–8
 values 5
unselfconsciousness of ethical life 53
US
 Crow nation and Plenty Coups 218
 schools 184–5
 sociology 12–13, 14
utopianism 18, 237

value(s) 3–5, 10–11, 12–13, 14, 19, 47–50, 62, 64–66, 70, 78–80, 85–86, 112, 173–4, 185–7, 193, 202–4, 236–7
 anthropological concept of 5
 Christian 173–4, 187–8
 vs goods 115–17
 meta-values 49, 55, 56
 schools 184, 185–6, 187–8, 191, 193–4
 theoretical approaches 36–44
 and virtue 47, 168
Venkatesan, S. et al. 91
vicissitudes 221–2, 224
victims/survivors of child sexual abuse in Christian Church 130–1
virtue ethics 17, 19–20, 112
Vitebsky, P. 219
vocation: child sexual abuse in Christian Church 128–9, 134

Warde, A. 69
Weber, M. 10, 12, 19, 38, 42–3, 86, 100, 164
Weil, S. 93, 94
Williams, B. 52–3, 112, 113

Winch, P. 93–4, 95
Wittgenstein, L. 53, 55, 93–6, 97, 100, 103
women's movement. *See* feminism

Zigon, J. 82, 219, 226

www.ingramcontent.com/pod-product-compliance
Lightning Source LLC
Chambersburg PA
CBHW051535020426
42333CB00016B/1935